RIOTOUS
PERFORMANCES

RIOTOUS

PERFORMANCES

The Struggle for
Hegemony in
the Irish Theater,
1712–1784

HELEN M. BURKE

UNIVERSITY OF NOTRE DAME PRESS
Notre Dame, Indiana

Designed by Wendy McMillen
Set in 11.2/13 Fournier by Four Star Books
Printed in the U. S. A. by The Maple Press Company

Library of Congress Cataloging-in-Publication Data

Burke, Helen M., 1950–
Riotous performances : the struggle for hegemony in the Irish theater,
1712–1784 / Helen M. Burke
p.   cm.
Includes bibliographical references (p.   ) and index.
ISBN 0-268-04015-X (alk. paper)—ISBN 0-268-04016-8 (pbk. : alk. paper)
1. Theater—Ireland—History—18th century.   I. Title.
PN2601 .B87   2003
792' .09415'09033—dc21

2002013896

As to his remark about the Theatre, it has ever been the very Place where the People have distinguished their Patriot Spirit; and when their Remonstrances have been, by ministerial Influence, obstructed to the *Powers that be,* this has always the *Succedaneum* they have made Use of, to shew their Sense of whatever Grievance or Oppression they have laboured under.

Libertus, *Remarks on Two Letters,*
Dublin, 1754

Contents

Acknowledgments

Many people and institutions have helped to make this book possible, and it is my pleasure to acknowledge and thank at least some of them here. The research for this book was accomplished with the help of a National Endowment for the Humanities Fellowship, an American Society for Eighteenth-Century Studies Irish-American Travel Fellowship, and a grant from the Council on Research and Creativity at Florida State University. The dean and chair at my own institution also generously granted me a sabbatical to complete the writing of this book.

As I pieced this research together over the past eight years, I sought input or advice from a number of people in the field of eighteenth-century Irish studies, including Simon Davies, Andrew Carpenter, Arch Elias, Christopher Fox, David Hayton, and Neil York. Each of them willingly shared their expertise with me, and I am very grateful to them for this generosity. To my fellow laborers in the field of eighteenth-century Irish theater studies, John Greene and Christopher Wheatley, I owe a special intellectual and personal debt; their unflagging interest in Irish theater and their camaraderie at conventions over the years were invaluable.

I am grateful, too, to Carol Colatrella, Doug Canfield, Bob Markley, Jean Marsden, Jessica Munns, Charlie and Lezlie Stivale, James Thompson, and David Wheeler. These friends from across the country have provided me with advice and support since my earliest days in the profession. Closer to home, I have been fortunate to have in my own department such intellectually challenging and supportive colleagues as Ralph Berry, Mark Cooper, Karen Cunningham, Barry Faulk, Karen Laughlin, Rip Lhamon, Linda Saladin, and Laura Rosenthal. Scott Kopel has also lent invaluable technical support as I wrote the manuscript.

Special thanks are due to Maire Kennedy at the Gilbert Library, Joanna Finegan at the National Library of Ireland, and Bernadette Cunningham at the Royal Irish Academy, who assisted me in locating or identifying material. Thanks also to the staff at the British Library, Cambridge University Library, the Folger Library, the Massachusetts Historical Society, and the Florida State Library for their assistance. A portion of chapter 2 has appeared in *The Clothes That Wear Us: Essays on Dressing and Transgressing in Eighteenth-Century Culture*, edited by Jessica Munns and Penny Richards (Delaware University Press), and a portion of chapter 8 has appeared in *Eighteenth-Century Life* (Johns Hopkins University Press). I thank both those presses for allowing republication. I am also very grateful to Barbara Hanrahan, my editor at the University of Notre Dame Press, and Sheila Berg, my copyeditor, for helping to prepare this book for publication.

Finally, my warmest thanks to my family in Cork and my friends in Dublin, Peter and Siobháin Denman, Vera and Lee Komito, and Hilary Tovey, who are unfailingly welcoming and hospitable when I turn up on their doorsteps each summer; and most of all, my thanks to Jim O'Rourke who manages to make life one continual riotous performance.

Introduction

The "critical and dangerous State of the Stage in Ireland"

In his ninety-two-page pamphlet, *An Humble Appeal to the Publick, Together with some Considerations on the Present critical and dangerous State of the Stage in Ireland* (1758), Thomas Sheridan looks back on his career as manager of Dublin's Theatre Royal and details his long struggle to bring the theater into conformity with its London counterpart. The rhetoric of the British civilizing mission is also central to this account. Sheridan casts himself in the heroic role of the planter-settler who risks life and property to bring order, rationality, and law to a space that is barbaric. When he took over the management of the Theatre Royal (Smock Alley) in 1745, the manager claims, "the Play-House was looked upon as a Common," and in this lawless space neither private property nor human rights were respected. "To such an absurd height had Popular Prejudice risen, that the Owners were considered as having no Property there, but what might be destroyed at the Will and Pleasure of the People; that the Actors had not the common Privileges of British Subjects, but were actual Slaves; and that neither the one nor the other, were under the Protection of the Laws."[1] Like the prospective settler, however, Sheridan saw the potential in this wild theatrical field, understanding that it might yield a dramatic crop comparable or even superior to that of the theaters in the British metropolitan center if it was subjected to British laws and regulations: "he clearly saw, that if there were a new Constitution established under new Regulations; if Order succeeded to Anarchy, and Decorum to Brutality; if it should be proved that the Theatre was under the Sanction of the Law, and the Performers enjoyed the common Privileges of *British* Subjects . . . the *Dublin* Stage under good Management might soon vie with those of *London,* and, upon some farther Advantages annexed to it, might in time far exceed them" (19). For a time, too, he writes, he succeeded in his civilizing task. In less than two years after he took over the management of Smock Alley, he had quieted the noisy upper gallery and cleared the stage of intruders, thus ridding the stage of the "two great Nuisances universally complain'd of" (11), and by daring economic speculation — he refers to himself as "one of the most romantic Adventurers that the World has produced" (20) — he was able to lure over some of the best players from the London stage. Then followed five years of polite and peaceful audiences, a golden era, Sheridan predicts, that will live long in memory; those who frequented the theater during that time, he imagines, "will often give Accounts of it to their Children and Grand-children, when the Stage shall probably be relapsed into it's [*sic*] former Barbarism" (21).

This prediction about a likely relapse into "Barbarism," however, brings us to the other side of Sheridan's narrative — to that history of continued resistance that leads the manager to describe the state of the stage in Ireland as "critical and dangerous." In 1747 when he first tried to clear the stage of intruders, Sheridan writes, he encountered "an Opposition, which, whether it be considered with respect to the badness of its Foundation, the Virulence with which it was carried on, the vast Numbers engaged in it, and the length of Time taken up (for it lasted many Weeks) exceeded any thing of that Kind ever known in a civilized Country" (10). He carried the day on that occasion but not without making "numberless Enemies" (22), and, unbeknown to him, these enemies grew as he continued his reform campaign. The size and force of this second opposition, however, finally became apparent to him on the "memorable Night of the Subversion of the Theatre" when an "enraged Multitude" (34) wrecked the playhouse and sent the manager himself running for his life. Describing that 1754 attack, Sheridan writes: "Long had they [his enemies] been working under Ground, whilst the Governor of the Citadel remained in a perfect State of Security, till the very instant that the Mine was sprung, the Breach made, and Ruin entered. Astounded at first with the suddenness of the Blow, he knew not what to think, or which way to turn him; but it was not long before the whole dark Plot was revealed to him, and the black Scenes, with all their Actors disclosed" (24). In a pamphlet written some fourteen years later, Sheridan also ventured the generalization that the theater in Ireland had always existed under a state of siege, and he argued that under the culminative effects of such attacks, it had once again reverted to its former state of barbarism. The specific opposition Sheridan had in mind on this occasion came not from a riotous "Multitude" in the playhouse but from theatrical competitors—he was pressing the Irish Parliament in 1772 to pass legislation that would limit the number of playhouses in Dublin and create a monopoly for the Theatre Royal—but it is clear from the similarity of the imagery that Sheridan sees the net effect as being the same: oppositions of all sorts, he implies, re-create the theatrical common or "waste."

> Would any one in his senses think of inclosing a common at great ex-
> pence, of manuring and tilling the ground, when it is in the power of
> any one that pleases to break down the inclosure, and claim an equal
> right to the produce of the soil? This has been always the actual state
> of the theatre in Ireland. While it was inclosed, it produced good
> crops to the possessors. When the fences were broke down, it of
> course became a waste; and it is now rendered so entirely a waste, that
> it probably never will be inclosed again, unless a law be made to se-
> cure the property to the undertaker.[2]

In chapters 4 through 8 in this book I provide a detailed analysis of these various "fence breakings" and suggest that Sheridan's narrative is not always reliable when it comes to describing the manager's own role in relation to these oppositions. I cite these pamphlets, nevertheless, because they highlight the contested nature of the eighteenth-century Irish the-ater and because they serve to introduce my broader thesis about the politi-cally generative nature of this conflict. Before as well as during the period of Sheridan's tenure as manager (1745–58), unauthorized "Actors" from different positions in the social, political, and cultural spectrum of Irish life challenged hegemonic structures with their riotous performances and the-atrical oppositions, and by the 1770s, I argue, this overdetermined counter-theater had effectively transformed the Irish theater into a space where (as Sheridan puts it) anyone could "claim an equal right to the [theatrical] pro-duce." If such a claim has to be argued, it must also be stated, it is because this "critical and dangerous" Irish theater has disappeared from the lens of theatrical historiography, and it is therefore this historiography, with its implicit assumptions about social identity and theater, that must be first in-terrogated if we are to recover this more dynamic stage.

Sheridan's theatrical history, as evidenced in the above account, accepts British law and culture as normative, and it equates any resistance to these norms with a condition of backwardness, irrationality, and senseless destruction (the "Opposition" that he encountered in 1747 "exceeded any thing of that Kind ever known in a civilized Country"; the multitude who attacked his theater in 1754 were "enraged"; and the competitors who threatened him in 1772 laid "waste" the theatrical enclosure). Such ideological assumptions are also built into the Irish theatrical histories that were produced during the eighteenth century, two of the most important of which—Benjamin Victor's *History of the Theatres of London and Dublin from 1730 to the Present Time* (1761–71) and Robert Hitchcock's *Historical View of the Irish Stage* (1788–94)—were written by Englishmen who were outspoken supporters of government. In the introduction to *An Historical View*, for example, Hitchcock cites approvingly those Greek and Roman lawgivers who understood "the mutual connection . . . between the success of the stage, and the welfare of the state," and throughout his work he repeatedly reminds the Dublin Castle administration of the potential usefulness of the theater as a site for reinventing power. "I cannot help remarking, that to those chief governors who court popularity, no place presents a better opportunity of attaining it, than the theatre," he writes at one point, and he adds, "Through the course of this work, I have had occasion to observe, that the more popular the Lord Lieutenant was, the oftener he frequented the theatre."[3] Hitchcock also unproblematically assumes, as Sheridan does, that the theater became more orderly, rational, and successful to the extent that it catered to the ruling elite,[4] and he equates any challenge to this order with an attack on decency and civility. The faction that opposed Sheridan's theater in 1747, for instance, is represented as a "set of wanton, dissolute gentlemen . . . (the greatest nuisance than any city ever groaned under)" (1:191), and those who attacked it in 1754 are accused of spreading chaos and ruin throughout the stage and the state in the name of that "daemon of discord," political party (1:227). Referring to the condition of the Theatre Royal in the aftermath of the 1754 "riot," Hitchcock writes: "A theater which a few hours before, might have reflected honour on the most civilized nation, was in a few moments left an unexampled monument of barbarity" (1:248).

As postcolonial theorists have argued, however, such designations of irrationality are produced in colonialist histories specifically to eviscerate the radical potential of modes of sociality that are incommensurate with the colonial state, and it is the triumph of this colonialist mode of representation, at one level, that we can read in the near-universal insistence in Irish scholarly circles today that there was no political or cultural challenge to British norms in the Irish playhouse—in effect, no Irish theater—before the founding of the Irish Literary Theater at the end of the nineteenth century. The legacy of this colonialist way of thinking, for instance, can be seen in Esther K. Sheldon's *Thomas Sheridan of Smock-Alley* (1967), one of the most frequently cited and influential twentieth-century works on the eighteenth-century Irish stage. Because it is such a detailed, carefully researched work, Sheldon's study seems, at first view, to be very different from the factually sloppy and clearly partisan work of Hitchcock. But in arguing that David Garrick's presence in 1745 gave the season "an unprecedented brilliance" that was "not to be surpassed in Dublin until the twentieth century,"[5] or that the duke of Dorset's frequent presence at the playhouse during the 1751–52 season made it one of Smock Alley's "most brilliant" seasons to date (170), Sheldon reproduces the eighteenth-century historians' view that British metropolitan culture and politics are the measures by which the progress of the Irish theater is to be evaluated. And like them also, she regards any opposition to this progress as instances of cultural regression or barbarity. She uses the term "the Kelly riot," for example, for what Sheridan calls the "Opposition" of 1747 or what other contemporaries simply called the "Gentlemen's (or "Gentlemans") Quarrel" (82),[6] a renaming that already relegates this resistance to the status of the illicit and the irrational. And her summary judgment on this event effectively reproduces the judgment of the Dublin court of (British) law that found against these "rioters" when they were brought to trial; commenting on the court's judgment against Kelly and for Sheridan in this trial, Sheldon writes, "So Kelly's drunken behavior and his friends' destructive violence secured Sheridan the reform which gained him a place in stage history" (103). The Gentlemen's Quarrel is thus consigned to the dustbin of history, where it exists not as a "critical" alternative to past or present kinds of theater or politics but as an example of meaningless, irrational violence that disrupts the march of progress.

This is not to suggest that colonialism is solely to blame for these kinds of occlusions and dismissals. As David Lloyd is careful to show in *Ireland after History*, nation-states adhere to notions of progress and backwardness almost as much as colonial states,[7] and it is thus the legacy of Irish nationalist forms of theater historiography, with its implicit acceptance of modernist notions of social identity and theater, that must also be considered to understand the disappearance of the eighteenth-century "critical and dangerous" Irish theater. The Gentlemen's Quarrel again usefully illustrates the erasures that were produced by this mode of historiography. In their own day, Kelly and his faction were identified by hostile Sheridan supporters in terms that suggested they occupied an ambiguous religious and social terrain: they were "either professed *Papists*, or worse, *mercenary Converts*," and they were both "the Offspring of Savages and Tyrants" and "Connaught Counts."[8] In chapter 4 I suggest that such ambivalent religious and social identifications point to "the Gentlemen's" status as members of the dispossessed native Irish or old English Catholic gentry, and I argue that it is in the context of the broader resistance of this class—a resistance that often entailed straddling religious, cultural, and social worlds—that we must read the Gentlemen's Quarrel. Early Irish nationalist historiography, however, did not recognize the existence of such ambivalently positioned social subjects, nor did it admit the possibility that such a resistance by the dispossessed could occur in the heart of eighteenth-century Dublin. The prevailing paradigm, rather, was that offered by Daniel Corkery in his influential study of eighteenth-century Irish culture and poetry, *The Hidden Ireland* (1924), and in Corkery's conceptualization, "Ascendancy" Irish and "Gaelic Irish" were categories that fixed a subject firmly at one side or another of a vast cultural, religious, and economic divide. The former, according to Corkery, were property-owning Protestants, living in prosperity on big estates or in fine houses in the towns and cities; the latter were peasants, barely eking out a wretched living in remote bogs, hills, and mountains.[9] The effect of this paradigm of static social relations and clearly articulated cultural, religious, and economic differences can also be seen in the other major twentieth-century study of the pre-nineteenth-century Irish theater, La Tourette Stockwell's *Dublin Theatres and Theatre Customs, 1637–1820* (1938). To explain what she takes to be the uniformly English orientation of the early Irish theater, Stockwell explicitly invokes Corkery and his vision of the radical depletion of native energy and leadership. "The Irish gentry, the people to whom the tradition of Gaelic leadership belonged, had been driven out of Ireland because conditions there were made intolerable for Catholics of an aristocratic temper," she writes. "Because of their poverty and exile the Dublin theatre was deprived of the support of the people who might have made of it a national theatre."[10] The sutured notion of colonial identity that is implicit in Corkery's work and other nationalist studies is also invoked when Stockwell describes the Dublin audience as a "psychological unit, composed of landlord classes and urban tradesmen," a group whose "country was England," whose "civilization was English," and who "looked toward London as Mohammedans look to Mecca" (174).

Twentieth-century Irish theater studies have also compounded the problem caused by this nationalist insistence on stable and coherent subject positions by its acceptance of a notion of "theater" that has been similarly shaped by a dichotomous logic. For the genealogy of this way of thinking about theater, it is again useful to return to Sheridan. Central to Sheridan's reform project, as evidenced by his attempt to silence the upper gallery and to remove intruders from the stage, was the disciplining of theatrical space and of theatrical audiences. This kind of disciplining, it is generally recognized, also gave rise to the European bourgeois theater, an institution that increasingly divorced audiences from the actors and fictional world on the stage and increasingly divorced the study of the theater from the study of the drama. As Joseph Roach writes, the nineteenth-century projectors of the field of *Theaterwissenchaft*, or theater science, focused on such supposedly objective and nonliterary facts as the conditions of historic performances, theater architecture, staging, and acting style while allocating the dramatic text—the supposed domain of the imagination and of subjective judgment—to literary critics.[11] By the end of the nineteenth century, too, there was an unprecedented privileging of drama over theater in European culture. Commenting on the unusual nature of this privileging in world cultures, for example, Richard Schechner writes, "[O]nly 'modern [i.e., European] drama' since the late nineteenth century has so privileged the written text as to almost exclude theater-performance altogether."[12] It would seem that the rise of cultural nationalism was at least partly responsible for this elevation of the status of the dramatic text. W. B. Yeats, Augusta Lady Gregory, and Edward Martyn, for instance, consciously put the "literary" at the foreground of their Irish nationalist theatrical project (their aim in founding the Irish Literary Theatre was "to build up a Celtic and Irish school of dramatic literature"). And, as Loren Kruger has shown in *The National Stage*, other European countries, including England, France, and America, were equally interested in using the drama to invent a coherent national tradition.[13]

The effect of this privileging of the dramatic text in Irish theatrical historiography, however, has been to create yet another measure by which there can be said to be no politically "dangerous" or "critical" theater before the nineteenth century. Christopher Murray's recent introduction to Irish drama between 1690 and 1800 in *The Field Day Anthology of Irish Writing* is a case in point. In support of the claim that the seventeenth- and eighteenth-century Theatres Royal were "manifestations of colonial rule" that had very little connection with the people of Ireland, Murray points to the prevalence of "Ascendancy ideology"—the point of view that "refinement, reason and good taste were the hallmarks of the ruling aristocracy, striving under the guidance of the lord lieutenant to bring peace and prosperity to a troubled land"—in the serious drama and prologues that were written for these theaters. This slippage from "theater" to drama, coupled with a functionalist view of drama itself, then allows him to conclude that there was no political resistance before the arrival of cultural nationalism; "it was not until the nineteenth century," Murray writes, "that this [Ascendancy] ideology was questioned and opposed, when the Irish Literary Theatre was established by Yeats, Lady Gregory and Edward Martyn."[14] In *A New History of Ireland*, J. C. Beckett also uses the sole measure of the drama—in this case the fact of the Dublin stage's heavy reliance on English dramatic mainpieces—to reach a similar conclusion about the politically conservative nature of the Irish theater. In this theater, as in other areas of eighteenth-century cultural life, Beckett writes, "the influence of London was predominant."[15]

To recover the "critical and dangerous" dimension of the eighteenth-century Irish theater, then, it is necessary to turn to a mode of historiography that follows neither the standard colonial nor the standard national model and to a conceptualization of theater that refuses the bourgeois disciplinary division between dramatic text and theater, stage and audience. In the case of historiography, such alternate models have already been mapped out by postcolonial and Gramscian theorists. In *Ireland after History,* for example, Lloyd argues that the force of what has been labeled "the irrational" can only be recovered by a materialist form of history that calls into question not only the findings of traditional histories but also the temporal axis of progress and regress that structures such histories:

> The historicist view of the irrational is, as we have seen, mapped onto a temporal schema: forms marginalized with regard to the state are attached to the prehistory of the nation and become sites only attainable through regression. And it is the temporal axis itself structured along movements of progress and regress, that materialist history calls into question. In its place is posed a topological model of relations, which

is not so much the core/periphery model . . . as a map of movements and contiguities, conjunctions and incommensurabilities, wherein the irrational is located in/as spaces of radical discontinuity with the rationale of developmental history.[16]

This notion of the social as a "map of movements and contiguities, conjunctions and incommensurabilities," rather than as forms projected on to a linear schema, is also central to Ernesto Laclau and Chantal Mouffe's thinking in *Hegemony and Socialist Strategy*. Retaining from Gramsci the concept of hegemony, with its assumption about the unsutured nature of the social, Laclau and Mouffe create an image of a social terrain that is always crisscrossed by antagonisms, but they also go beyond Gramsci in suggesting that *any* site of difference, not class alone, can be a locus of social conflict. "Any position in a system of differences," they write, "insofar as it is negated, can become the locus of an antagonism."[17] Social change, moreover, is made possible by this multiplication of sites of difference and conflict. Because the field of antagonism is so overdetermined, they write, it is always open to the possibility of articulating new kinds of collective subjects and ultimately new kinds of hegemonic blocs.

Such a dynamic and fluid image of the social is also implicit in many of the histories that have come out of Irish studies in the past ten years. At every level of eighteenth-century Irish society, these newer Irish histories suggest, there were fractures and instabilities in subject positions, and at many different moments throughout the century, there were cross-religious, cross-ethnic, and cross-class conjunctions and alliances that opened the possibility of new kinds of social and political formations. The political formation that has been variously described as "colonial nationalism," "Irish Protestant nationalism," or "patriotism" provided one such line of fracture and movement, as Thomas Bartlett has demonstrated in *The Fall and Rise of the Irish Nation* (1992). Motivated by resentment of England's subordination of the Irish Parliament and by the growing belief that they themselves were best equipped to govern Ireland, a small but vocal subset of Irish Protestants began to agitate for greater constitutional and economic liberties at the end of the seventeenth century, and over the course of the eighteenth century, as Bartlett has shown, the patriot reformers who followed in their footsteps gradually began to appropriate an Irish identity. This Irish identification did not necessarily make them any more tolerant of Irish Catholics (many Irish Protestant nationalists, indeed, remained deeply concerned about the possibility of a Catholic resurgence). But, as Bartlett notes, "it drove a wedge between English and Irish Protestants . . . that helped dissolve that Protestant union on an Anglo-Irish basis . . . and it helped blur the distinction between Irish Protestants and Irish Catholics." By the 1790s "Irish Protestants were being described as merely 'another description of Irishmen.'"[18]

A Catholic population that refused to stay in its assigned position of abjection created another kind of fault line, as well as the potential for other kinds of movements and conjunctions. The poverty and deprivation of the Catholic population was very real throughout the century, and, as traditional nationalist historians have argued, the penal laws undoubtedly caused much of this deprivation. Catholic outright ownership of land, for example, went from 14 percent in 1703 down to a mere 5 percent in 1776.[19] However, as the political, economic, and social studies of Bartlett, Kevin Whelan, T. P. Power, and others have shown, Catholics never passively accepted this downturn in their economic and social status. Through a variety of practices, including strategic conversions (selected family members would conform to the established church), collusive "discoveries" in land titles, and the use of trustees, many Catholic families managed to retain an interest in land. And even when the old Catholic landowning families were reduced to the status of "middlemen" or head tenants on their former estates, they retained much of their power and influence in their local communities; as Whelan's studies have shown, these middlemen constituted an "underground gentry" who served as the locus of an alternate native Irish lifestyle and value system and as a point of politicization for the Catholic rural masses.[20] The effect of this kind of indirect Catholic challenge is also registered in an interesting passage in the anonymous pamphlet *The True Life of Betty IRELAND* (1753). Betty Ireland, as her name suggests, is an allegorical figure for Ireland, and this figure complains bitterly that she is unable to get her "Business" done because of the "strange Mixture of People on her Estate, who are always at Daggers drawing with one another." Nor can she resolve this problem, because she is unable to tell the law-abiding "Whites" from the rebellious "Blacks": "They are *Whites, Blacks,* and *Black* and *White.* The *Whites* only are allowed to be *Land-holders;* but the *last,* by hiding half the Face when they converse with her, pass for *Whites,* and make good their *Titles.* The first are dreadfully maligned by the *Blacks,* who are unhappily the more numerous, *lay old Claims* to her *Lands,* and are ever watching for an Opportunity to make a *Riot,* and take forcible Possession."[21]

This surreptitious Catholic challenge to the status quo, moreover, was not confined to the country. When opportunities to invest in land were unavailable, as Maureen Wall's groundbreaking research first showed, Catholics went in considerable numbers to the cities where they quietly amassed fortunes by engaging in trade and commerce (as early as 1718, for example, we find Archbishop William King complaining that "the papists . . . have already engrossed almost all the trade of the kingdom").[22] This emerging urban Catholic middle class was also instrumental in bringing the question of Catholic equality to the forefront of the political debate in the latter half of the century. Adopting an accommodationist, loyalist rhetoric to ensure that their voices would be heard, urban Catholics began agitating for Catholic rights in their political pamphlets and revisionist histories at midcentury, and they played a leadership role in the Catholic Committee (1760) and later in the United Irishman.[23] The existence of a Catholic "convert" interest in parliament and in other professions also served as a further point of Catholic infiltration into the established order. As Louis Cullen points out, "[W]hether nominal converts or convinced ones, converts retained links with catholic relatives and other catholic families, and their outlook almost invariably remained sympathetic to their former co-religionists."[24] "Blacks," as well as "Black and White" to use *Betty IRELAND*'s metaphor, were everywhere.

In the capital city of Dublin, a politicized crowd served as another source of political disruption and also as another locus of ethnic, religious, and class exchange. Bourgeois writers in Dublin, like their counterparts in London, liked to represent the Dublin crowd as an unruly "mob" that acted purely out of instinct and irrational impulses. In *The Men of No Property* (1992), however, Jim Smyth persuasively argues that the Dublin crowd is better conceived as a structured, informed, and purposeful entity that acted to express the political ambitions and desires of a largely artisan, preindustrial workforce. The Dublin street "riots" of 1759, 1779, and 1784, Smyth's analysis shows, took their meaning from the greater political and economic conflicts of the day, and in the last two of these events, middle-class patriots joined with the lower-class crowd in asserting their opposition to repressive economic and political legislation. As Catholics continued to flow into the capital throughout the century, too, this urban crowd became increasingly representative of the Irish people as a whole. When the century opened, Dublin was largely a Protestant city, but by 1798 it was about 70 percent Catholic and, by this time, too, as Smyth points out, contemporaries generally assumed that the Dublin crowd was predominantly Catholic.[25]

The Irish theater in the eighteenth century, I argue in this book, was another site where this struggle for hegemony took place; though to bring this struggle into focus, it is necessary to move beyond the dichotomy drama-theater and its implicit privileging of the dramatic text and its historic links to positivist and progressive modes of thinking. The term "performance" as it has been defined in contemporary Performance Studies also maps out this alternate conceptual and material space. As Richard Schechner has argued in *Between Theater and Anthropology*, the term "performance" can be taken to encompass any kind of "restored behavior" or "twice-behaved behavior" that a culture uses to explain itself to itself and others, and as such the concept of performance opens up the seams between drama, theater, and everyday life.[26] Commenting on Schechner's definition, Roach notes that "theatre, as a high-culture form, remains important in this formulation as a genre with a rich theoretical lexicon, in light of which the cultural significance of other performance modes may be interpreted," but, he adds, "the concept of restoration [also] extends performance to include what Brooks McNamara terms 'invisible theater' and Michel de Certeau calls the 'practice of everyday life.'"[27] In relation to the Irish theater, this formulation means, for example, that those rituals attendant on the "government play" and the viceregal "command performance"—occasions when the viceroy and ruling elite came together at the playhouse in a glittering show of power and unity—can be studied alongside those dramatic texts that expressed Ascendancy ideology. And it means that those playhouse rituals and dramas, in turn, can be inserted into that larger matrix of elite-sponsored public festivities and celebrations that were designed to reinvent power in the larger world outside the playhouse. As Sean Connolly notes in *Religion, Law and Power,* the government, civic authorities, and individual members of the landlord class habitually marked public holidays and other special anniversaries and occasions with festivities in which "paternalist benevolence was combined with the ritualized depiction of social gradation." In Dublin, for example, official holidays were marked by the firing of volleys, the ringing of bells, and solemn processions of civil and ecclesiastical dignitaries through the streets, and these displays of authority and hierarchy were generally followed by lavish dispensations of food and drink to the populace at large.[28]

This widening of the field of performance similarly allows us to see the complementary relation between this official theater and those dramatic reiterations of native Irish stupidity or brutishness that are encapsulated under the rubric "the stage Irishman," and it brings this latter kind of "restored behavior" into an ideological conjunction with those extra-theatrical Protestant practices and behaviors that served to produce the Irish

Catholic as an improper political subject. The rites and practices associated with the commemoration of 1641, for example, were one important set of performances of the latter kind. October 23 was the anniversary of the outbreak of the 1641 uprising, and on that day every year, the Protestant people of Ireland drew back from their daily activities (the government stopped work, businesses closed down) and attended church, ostensibly to offer thanks for the victory of Protestants over Irish Catholics during that mid-seventeenth-century rebellion. But as T. C. Barnard demonstrates in his extensive study of the sermons that were preached at these commemorative services, they also served to rehearse in lurid, mind-searing detail the supposed atrocities committed by the native Irish against the settlers during the 1641 rebellion, and everything from the Gaelic Catholic people's "wild savage way of living in single cottages and dismal unhabitable places" (a phrase from John Ramsay's 1714 sermon) to their attachment to their Gaelic language, with its oral and scribal culture, was cited as proof of this persistent lack of civility.[29] At other times of the year, Protestants could also have these images of native Irish and Catholic incivility restored by reading Sir John Temple's *The Irish Rebellion* (1646), the historical work that served as the source of many of these sermons; or by perusing Archbishop King's *The State of the Protestants of Ireland Under the Late King James's Government* (1691). The latter focused on the Jacobite wars of 1688–91, but as Bartlett notes, there was such an obvious ideological connection between these two historical works that enterprising publishers soon began issuing them in a single joint edition. Both works were also readily available to Protestant readers; they went through at least ten editions in the eighteenth century.[30]

There are obvious continuities between the Irish Protestant sermons and histories described above and a play like *The Beaux Stratagem* (1707), to draw from the repertory of a playwright, George Farquhar, who has been described as first embodying the "Ascendancy treatment of the Stage Irishman."[31] The Irish Catholic who gains admission into the home of a landed English family by false pretenses and then plans a violent assault on that family under the cover of darkness—Foigard/Mack-shane is involved in a "horrid Plot"[32] to hide Count Bellair in Mrs. Sullen's closet with the ultimate aim of ravishing her—is a figure of the 1641 Irish rebel who, according to Protestant tradition, lulled settler families into a false sense of security by pretended friendship. And he is also a type of the Irish Jacobite who, in the Protestant imaginary, was always conspiring with the French—the count is an officer in the French army—to undo Protestant domestic security. It was not unusual for Irish Protestant texts to draw on sexual imagery to represent this Jacobite threat as Farquhar's play does. *The Farmer's Letters to the Protestants of Ireland,* which the Irish Protestant playwright and novelist Henry Brooke published in Dublin in 1745, for example, reminds readers of the sexual assaults supposedly committed by Irish Jacobites during the 1688–91 wars when it wants to stir up Protestant animosity against the current Jacobite invader: "Those Wretches seized our Properties as of Right, and entered our Houses by Violence; they insulted our Misery, and perpetrated all Kinds of Villainy; they invaded the Marriage Bed, they compelled the Parents to behold the Rape of their Daughters; our Submission encouraged them to proceed to new Injuries, and if we resisted, we were dragged to Execution for Rebellion."[33] Like the sermons, *The Beaux Stratagem* effects the criminalization of the Irish Catholic on cultural as well as political grounds. As Aimwell suggests in the following exchange, the native Irishman's low origin and incompetence in the English language is itself the necessary "evidence" that he is a deviant who needs the correction of British law.

AIMWELL: The Son of a Bogtrotter in *Ireland;* Sir your Tongue will condemn you before any Bench in the Kingdom.
FOIGARD: And is my Tongue all your Evidensh, Joy?
AIMWELL: That's enough.
FOIGARD: No, no, Joy, for I vill never spake *English* no more. (4.2.60–64)

If there was a constant demand for such "evidence" of Irish cultural and political inferiority—*The Beaux Stratagem* was performed regularly on the Irish stage until the end of the eighteenth century[34]—as well as for the opposite evidence of ruling-class superiority, it was due, at one level, to the manifestly sectarian nature of eighteenth-century Irish society. The act of reiterating and repeating central fictions, of course, is basic to the maintenance of all societies, as cultural anthropologists have pointed out, but such acts or performances, it is also recognized, are needed with an additional urgency in societies where social inequities are most pronounced. In the words of Paul Abbott, "[D]iscrimination must constantly invite its representations into consciousness, reinforcing the crucial recognition of differences which they embody and revitalising them for the perception on which its effectivity depends. . . . It must sustain itself on the presence of the very difference which is also its object."[35] The reiterations of native

Irish stupidity and duplicity, as well as the public displays of elite power and benevolence, were such an embodying of difference for the purpose of revitalizing the unequal dispensation of power, property, and social status in eighteenth-century Irish society. As Frantz Fanon points out, the colonizer must endlessly construe himself in heroic, idealized terms—"[T]he settler makes history; his life is an epoch, an Odyssey. He is the absolute beginning: 'This land was created by us'; he is the unceasing cause"— while, as Homi K. Bhabha notes, "the *same old* stories of the Negro's animality, the Coolie's inscrutability or the stupidity of the Irish *must* be told (compulsively) again and afresh, and are differently gratifying and terrifying each time."[36]

It would also be a mistake, however, to take a *deterministic* view of such restored behaviors, as Connolly does, for instance, when he infers from the field of official public performance that Ireland by midcentury was "a stable political order with a supine Catholic population."[37] As Elin Diamond notes, the very notion of reiteration carries with it not only the possibility of continuity and sameness but also the possibility of improvisation, disruption, and change:

> While a performance embeds traces of other performances, it also produces experiences whose interpretation only partially depends on previous experience. This creates the terminology of "re" in discussions of performances, as in *re*embody, *re*inscribe, *re*configure, *re*signify. "Re" acknowledges the pre-existing discursive field, the repetition— and the desire to repeat within the performative present, while "embody," "configure," "inscribe," "signify," assert the possibility of materializing something that exceeds our knowledge, that alters the shape of sites and imagines other as yet unsuspected modes of being.[38]

A closer look at the eighteenth-century Irish theater reveals that it was such an unstable and dynamic performative field; we could say of the colonial reiteration in this site what Bhabha says about colonial subjectivity itself: namely, that it was "played out—like all fantasies of originality and origination—in the face and space of the disruption and threat from the heterogeneity of other positions."[39] The "other positions" that disrupted the colonial theater, moreover, can be mapped onto the oppositions described in the recent Irish histories, as Christopher Wheatley has demonstrated with his groundbreaking study, "*Beneath Ierne's Banners*" (1999). From the 1660s to the end of the eighteenth century, as Wheatley's nuanced study has

shown, Protestant writers who were themselves descendants of English settlers used the drama to challenge English political and cultural hegemony
and to articulate and define their own evolving sense of Irishness. It must
also be said, however, that these Irish Protestant patriots were not acting
alone when they issued these challenges, and it must be noted that there
were sites of disruption other than the scripted drama. Between 1712 and
1784, as I demonstrate in this study, an emerging Catholic middle class, a
dispossessed native gentry, and an increasingly politicized Dublin "mob"
also used the playhouse to challenge dominant political and cultural values
and attitudes. And these other unauthorized actors, in common with Irish
Protestant patriots, articulated their antihegemonic desires through explosive acts like theater "riots," as well as through more processual countercultural behaviors such as staging Irish plays, wearing Irish manufacture,
singing Irish songs, or mounting oppositions against the Theatre Royal.
This book does not purport to give an exhaustive history of this countertheater; my aim rather is to focus on selective "riotous performances," as
I call these disruptive acts, and show that they are intelligible within non-
hegemonic political, social, and cultural frameworks. The countertheater
that occurred within the theater, I demonstrate, takes its meaning from a
matrix of other symbolic acts that contested the colonial power structure
outside the playhouse, including, for example, Williamite street theater,
Irish Protestant patriot plays and pamphlets, tavern performances of Irish
music, Catholic political tracts, rural folk dramas, Gaelic poems, weavers'
riots, "aggregate" meetings, and Volunteer parades.

 At one level, then, *Riotous Performances* is a work of political and cultural excavation, an attempt to uncover the embedded significance of behaviors and practices that have been dismissed as irrational, meaningless,
or folkloric in standard theatrical histories. As in Diamond's formulation,
however, these riotous performances also altered the nature of the sites in
which they occurred, so that this work of recovery has to operate at a dia-
chronic as well as a synchronic level. The Irish Protestant patriots who
began acting up in the playhouse in the first quarter of the century had no
conscious intention of including Catholics or the "mob" in their imagined
community. But as I show through an analysis of the *Tamerlane* "riot" of
1712 and the practice of wearing Irish wool "stuff" (chapters 1 and 2), the
unauthorized stagings of these patriots blurred the boundaries between
Irish Protestant and Irish Catholic and opened up a space for the latter subject to speak (chapter 3). By midcentury, too, these overdetermined oppositions in the playhouse had created the conditions that Laclau and Mouffe

(elaborating on Gramsci) associate with "organic crisis": "a conjuncture where there is a generalized weakening of the relational system defining the identities of a given social or political space, and where, as a result there is a proliferation of floating elements."[40] And if this state of fluidity resulted initially in bitter internal Irish conflicts—the Irish theater at mid-century, I argue, was the site of an intense struggle between Catholic-identified gentry reformers and Protestant-identified populist reformers (chapters 4, 5, and 6)—it also created the conditions for the emergence of a new national hegemonic bloc. The contours of this bloc are already discernible in the so-called *Mahomet* riot of 1754 (chapter 7), and it came fully into focus in the Smock Alley "riot" of 1784 when an audience, united across religious, class, and ethnic lines, acted to dislodge the imperial subject (in the person of the viceroy) from the theater (chapter 8).

It was in order to contain the theatrics of this heterogeneously constituted Irish people, I argue in the epilogue, that the Irish Parliament passed the first Irish Stage Act in 1786. This act was the final outcome of a push to regulate the theatrical institution that had begun in the late 1750s, but it also stands, I suggest, as a monument to the "critical and dangerous" state of the theater in eighteenth-century Ireland. More broadly, it serves as a reminder that "Protestant" and "Catholic," "Anglo-Irish" and "native Irish," "gentry" and "mob" were themselves performative enunciations that were always provisional, always capable of being reconfigured into new oppositions and new kinds of political and cultural alignments.

CHAPTER 1

"A mind to turn Play'r"

Irish Protestant Patriotism and the Tamerlane "Riot" of 1712

We think it were fit,
You should stay in the Pit,
Unless each has a mind to turn Play'r.
Think not to invade
Our Privilege and Trade,
As you would the Prerogative Royal.

*A New Song on the Whiggs Behaviour
at the Play House . . . (1712)* [1]

On November 4, 1712, before a performance of Nicholas Rowe's *Tamerlane*, a band of Irish Protestants jumped onto the stage at Smock Alley and their leader Dudley Moore recited Samuel Garth's prologue, a text that had been forbidden by the government for two years in succession. Some members of the audience applauded this unorthodox performance while others hissed it, and the disturbance died down only when six armed soldiers appeared on the scene. A few days after this event, Moore and several of his supporters were charged with "Riotous and Seditious Practices" at the playhouse, and shortly before they were due to appear in court, the lord chancellor himself made a public pronouncement on the gravity of their offense. At a specially convened meeting in Dublin Castle, Sir Constantine Phipps informed the lord mayor, aldermen, and magistrates that the recital of the prologue was both a "Defiance of Authority" and an attempt to "rob her Majesty of that Part of her Prerogative[,] . . . The Power of Making Peace and War," and he urged the city officials to "single out the most flagrant Offender" and "prosecute him with the utmost severity of the Law."[2]

What happened in the next two years, however, was that Irish Protestants put the government itself on trial. When the case came to trial on February 5, 1713, the court quashed the indictment against the "rioters," and when the attorney general filed a new information against Moore alone and ordered the jury to be struck according to an English precedent, Moore's lawyers turned the hearing into a constitutional debate, arguing, among other things, that the legal proceedings constituted an infringement on the liberties of the subject.[3] Later the same year, the Irish House of Commons also took this matter up as part of a general inquiry into what it felt was Phipps's mishandling of a number of political matters during his years in office. The Irish Commons agreed by a substantial majority that Phipps had tried to "pre-judge the Merits of the Cause then depending between her Majesty and *Dudley Moore, Esq*," and this finding became part of a petition, made to Queen Anne in December 1713, asking for the removal of the lord chancellor from office.[4]

Some members of the Irish House of Lords also weighed in against the government in this theatrical matter. The lords conducted their own investigation into Phipps's alleged misbehavior in office, and the majority voted to exonerate him. But seven lords, including the archbishop of Dublin, William King, and the head of Ireland's most prominent family, Lord Kildare, issued a protest, arguing, among other things, that the lord chancellor had prejudged the theatrical case "by declaring what passed in the Play-House, on his late Majesty's Birth-Day, to be a great Riot, the Issue then to be tried in Court being, as we conceive, whether it was a Riot or no." They also disputed Phipps's claim in his speech to the city officials that the prologue had been legally prohibited for two years or that it sought to "impeach" the queen's right to wage war or make peace. Speaking of the alleged prohibition, the protesters wrote: "[I]t is put in the Speech, as an Aggravation, that the Prologue spoken in the Play-Houses had been forbid by the Government two Years successively; whereas we know of no such Prohibition, nor do we conceive that the Subjects are generally obliged to take Notice of any Prohibition as from the Government, or to be construed to act in Defiance of Authority, where the said Prohibition is not made public by Proclamation or Declaration, and we know of none issued in this Case."[5] Informal government prohibitions, this argument suggested, carried no weight in the playhouse or elsewhere.

Twentieth-century commentators have tended to view these acts of defiance in the playhouse, courthouse, and Parliament as expressions of Irish Protestant hostility toward a Jacobite-leaning, Tory ministry in the uncertain closing years of Queen Anne's reign,[6] and in these accounts the *Tamerlane* riot emerges as a reactionary, anti-Catholic, and anti-Irish act. Irish Protestants themselves also explicitly portrayed the event in this light in the self-exculpatory pamphlets they prepared for their somewhat alarmed English contemporaries. The writer of *The Conduct of the Purse of Ireland in a Letter to a Member of the Late Oxford Convocation, Occasioned By their having conferr'd the Degree of Doctor upon Sir C——— P———* (1714), for example, goes to great pains to represent Phipps's opponents as "English and *North British* Protestants" who "look upon this Kingdom [England] as their Mother and Protectress" and who have no "Interests separate from it,"[7] and he emphasizes that the Williamite rituals of these Protestants were entirely loyalist and conservative. If this "Protestant Nobility and Gentry used to celebrate the Days of King *Williams'* Birth, and of the Battel at the *Boyne*," it was entirely out of gratitude to William for having "redeem'd them from Imprisonment, from Poverty, from Persecution . . . and from certain Death" and for having "restored to them their Estates, their Laws and Liberties, their *Churches* and their *Colleges*" (19–20). And similar sentiments, this writer suggests, motivated this nobility and gentry to request the *Tamerlane* performance and the Garth prologue at the playhouse:

> Such hath been their Sense of that great Deliverance, and Gratitude towards their Deliverer, that they delighted in the Representations and Repetitions of whatsoever hath been written, or designed to do Honour to his Memory. For this Reason such of them as met, upon that Occasion in *Dublin,* constantly bespoke the Play called *Tamerlane,* and the Prologue to it, written by Dr. *Garth.* These they thought to be innocent and grateful Expressions of that Sense which they ought to have of so great a Deliverance; as such they took great Delight in them; and in so doing they had before this Person's [Phipps's] Government, being encourag'd and countenanc'd by the Presence or Approbation of their former Governors. (20)

The criminalization of these "innocent and grateful Expressions" by Phipps's regime, this writer then argues, was part of a larger attempt to displace loyal Protestants from power and to replace them at every level with Jacobites, Catholics, and new converts of native Irish extraction (15), and he cites the involvement of Sir Toby Butler, Mr. Cornelius O'Callagan, Mr. Garratt Burker, and Mr. Swiny in the prosecution of Moore as evidence of this plan. The first of these men was the "Sollicitor-General to the late King *James*" and "a known and profess'd Papist," the second was "a new Convert Lawyer, bred at St. Omers," and the last two had Irish-sounding names that sufficed to prove their disloyalty. "I shall content my self," this writer states, "with the mention of their Names only" (30).

The author of *The Resolutions of the House of Commons in Ireland, Relating to the Lord-Chancellor Phips* [sic], *Examined; With Remarks on the Chancellor's Speech* (1714), who identifies himself as "a Member of the House of Commons in Ireland," gives an almost identical explanation as he works to justify the Irish Commons' resolutions censoring Phipps. Again it is argued that the Whigs are "Honest, Loyal, Protestants, firm Sticklers for the present Establishment both in Church and State," and that Phipps's administration worked to displace these loyalist Protestant subjects with disloyal Irish Catholics: "The Race of men whom he [Phipps] discourages, are all of English Extraction; while the O[h]s, the M[ac]ks, and the Descendants from the Murderers of Forty One meet with his Encouragement and Favour; and from thence take all Opportunities to insult the English Protestants." And again there is an insistence that the Protestant custom of honoring the memory of King William takes its meaning exclusively from the Protestant people's past struggle with their internal Catholic enemy; if Protestants were "Lovers of the Memory of *King William*," it was because that king had delivered them from a Jacobite era when "their Lives, their Estates were in the hands of the Destroyers, their Persons imprisoned, and their Estates seiz'd by the old Popish Proprietors." Responding to the opinion in some quarters in England that it was the Protestants, not the Catholics, who were being disloyal, this writer also states emphatically: "I would lay my Life that there is not a Protestant in that Kingdom [Ireland], that . . . would not readily spend the Last Drop of his Blood in the Defence of her present Majesty, whilst the favour'd new Coverts and Papists, with their boasted *Loyalty*, would to a Man turn Recreants to the Government, and join with the Pretender."[8]

What is repressed in these accounts is the Irish Protestant history of conflict with Her Majesty's government that produced this productive confusion between Irish Protestants and Irish Catholics and that necessitated these protests of Protestant loyalty, and when that other history is reinstated, as I demonstrate in this chapter, the 1712 *Tamerlane* "riot" and Irish Williamite performances in general take on a more complex, proto-nationalist meaning. As the author of the *Conduct of the Purse* pamphlet implicitly acknowledged when he wrote that the Protestants "look upon this Kingdom as their Mother and Protectress," the orthodox view of the English-Irish relationship was that it was a parent-child relationship. This view assigned agency exclusively to the English partner in the governing Anglo-Irish Protestant alliance; as the "Mother" kingdom, it was England's role to decide policy and to provide protection for Ireland, and it was Protestant Ireland's duty to gratefully accept these rulings and this protection. Since the end of the seventeenth century, however, members of the Protestant community in Ireland had represented themselves as brother-sharers in the legacy of the 1688 "Glorious Revolution," and through various acts of self-assertion, they had indicated they were trying to shake off this dependent "child" role with all its decidedly colonialist connotations. Like other political struggles, too, Irish Protestants carried on their struggle within a network of symbolic practices and material spaces, and Williamite performances and the playhouse, I argue, were at the heart of this mesh. If Williamite performances served to reinscribe Catholic exclusion from the body politic (and there is no doubt they did), they also served to map a new subversive kind of Irish Protestant imagined community onto the Irish landscape.

The first Williamite celebration took place on College Green on November 4, 1690, and its intent was clearly anti-Jacobite and anti-Catholic. It was, in effect, the Protestant community's response to the triumphalist, native Irish Catholic street theater that had greeted James II the previous year. In March 1689 James II had landed in Kinsale, and as he made his way along the road from County Cork to Dublin, he was hailed by enthusiastic native Irish crowds. The lanes and hedges were lined with "the Half-pike and Bayonet Rabble, called Raparees," a hostile Protestant witness stated, and in Carlow, the same writer notes, the king had to beg to be protected from the kisses of "rude Country Irish Gentlewomen."[9] When James reached the outskirts of Dublin, there were more elaborate celebratory displays, some of which had distinctively Catholic elements. As he made his "first entrance into the Liberty of the City," the same source reported, "there was a Stage built covered with Tapestry, and thereon two playing on Welch-Harps; and below a great number of Friars, with a large Cross, singing; and about 40 Oyster-wenches, Poultry and Herb-women, in White[,] . . . dancing, who thence ran along to the Castle by his side, here and there strewing Flowers; some hung out of their Balconies Tapestry, and Cloath of Arras; and others imitating them, sewed together the Coverings of Turkey-work Chairs, and Bandle-Cloth Blankets, and hung them likewise on each side of the Street" (26–27). These populist demonstrations of support were complemented by the more scripted pageantry of Dublin Castle and Dublin Corporation officials. At the city limits the king was met by the lord mayor, aldermen, and other dignitaries, and after receiving the sword and the keys of the city and hearing welcoming speeches, he and the viceroy, Tyrconnell, processed to the castle, accompanied by troops of dragoons, coaches, gentlemen on horseback, heralds, and servants of the castle household (27). "As he marched thus along," a contemporary writer noted, "the Pipers of the several Companies played the tune of *The King enjoys his own again,* and the People shouting and crying, *God Save the King:* And if any Protestants were observed not to shew their Zeal that way, they were immediately revil'd and abus'd by the rude Papists" (28).

When King William III marched into Dublin on July 5, 1690 (O. S.), four days after the victory at the Boyne, the scene was reversed. As another observer remarked, the Protestants now "ran about shouting and embracing one another and blessing God for his wonderful deliverance as if they had been alive from the dead; the streets were filled with crowds and shouting and the poor Roman Catholics now lay in the same terrors as we [Protestants] had done some few days before."[10] A Protestant king now rode through the city "in great splendour" to St. Patrick's Cathedral to hear a Te Deum, and an alternate Protestant group of castle and city officials accompanied him.[11] The street theater that occurred on William's birthday on November 4 of the same year, then, was a kind of replaying of this July victory celebration. During the day, J. T. Gilbert reports in his *History of the City of Dublin,* the militia consisting of "2500 foot, troops of horse, and two troops of dragoons, all well clothed and armed were drawn out and gave several vollies," and in the evening the new Williamite elite as well as Dublin's humbler Protestant citizens gathered to celebrate on College Green. The "Nobility and Gentry," Gilbert writes, were invited by the lord justices "to a splendid entertainment and banquet" in Clancarty House, while in front of the house, the "people drunk in their Majesties' health" from a hogshead of claret and watched "a very fine firework" on the Green.[12] In locating their celebration in and around this house on the

Green, the Protestant community was also setting the stage for the larger remapping and recoding of native Irish places and estates that would occur in the aftermath of the Williamite victory. Clancarty House was the home of the sister of the earl of Clancarty, a Jacobite leader and a member of one of Ireland's most distinguished and ancient Gaelic families. When the Williamite forces took over Dublin, they took possession of this Gaelic family's house on College Green and made it the headquarters of the new government, and a year later the earl of Clancarty himself was sent to the Tower and his vast Cork estates seized.[13]

The parliamentary drama that was enacted at Chichester House (also located on College Green) two years later, however, revealed that the Protestants of Ireland also equated the Williamite victory with the right to share equally in the legacy of the Glorious Revolution, and Williamite celebrations were also soon invested with this more subversive political meaning and desire. Chichester House was the home of the Irish Parliament, a legislative body that, on the surface, looked like its counterpart in England. In effect, though, it was a far less independent entity. Poynings' Law, which was passed in 1494–95, ensured that no bills could be introduced in the Irish Commons without the prior approval of the Irish and English councils, and it mandated that for a bill to be enacted, it had to be in the same form in which it had passed the great seal of England.[14] In the first contentious parliament after the victory at the Boyne, Irish House of Commons members made it clear that they had every intention of challenging this law and any other English law that interfered with their interests. They launched a bitter attack on royal officials who had appropriated forfeited lands or returned these lands to Catholics; they threw out a mutiny act; they rejected a revenue bill; and they passed a daring resolution saying that they had the sole right to prepare heads of bills for raising money.[15] This last act caused the viceroy, Viscount Sydney, to describe the Irish Commons, privately, as "a company of madmen" who "talk of freeing themselves from the yoke of England, of taking away Poynings' law,"[16] and he publicly showed his displeasure for this behavior by proroguing parliament and delivering a formal protest to its members. He was "troubled," he told the Irish Commons, "that you who have so many and so great obligations . . . should so far mistake yourselves, as to intrench upon their Majesties' prerogative and the Rights of the Crown as you did on 27 October last, when by a declaratory vote you affirmed that it is the sole and undoubted right of the Commons of Ireland to prepare heads of bills for raising money."[17]

William Molyneux's *The Case of Ireland's being Bound by Acts of Parliament in England, Stated* (1698) also explicitly articulated the Protestant aspiration for political equality and domestic self-governance, and in this seminal work of Irish Protestant nationalism, William III is also explicitly reconfigured as an Irish Protestant patriot. Molyneux dedicates his controversial *Case* to William III, a gesture that is itself appropriative, and he continues his transvaluation of the Williamite sign on the first page of this dedication. True, he first praises William for rescuing "these Nations from Arbitrary Power, and those Unjust Invasions that were made on our Religion, Laws, Rights and Liberties"—thus for his role in delivering England and Ireland from the encroachments of the native Irish and French enemy in 1688–91.[18] But when he implores William to defend "those *Rights* and *Liberties* which we have Enjoy'd under the Crown of *England* For above Five Hundred Years, and which some of late do Endeavour to Violate" (17), he is referring to the contemporary struggle between the English and Irish Parliaments, and in this reconceptualization William is cast as the hero of the "Poor Subjects of Ireland" (18) against the encroachments of a specifically *English* enemy. By representing the Irish subject as a younger brother who is entitled to the same Williamite heritage as his older English brother—"Your most Excellent Majesty is the *Common Indulgent Father* of all your Countries; and have an *Equal* Regard to the *Birth-Rights* of all your *Children;* and will not permit the *Eldest* because the *Strongest* to Encroach of the Possessions of the *Younger*" (17–18)—the *Case* also implicitly rejects the mother-child colonial paradigm and ascribes the same political and economic rights to the "Subjects of Ireland" as to the subjects of England.

The case for Irish constitutional equality that Molyneux goes on to construct under the aegis of William III—the dedication ends with the phrase "At your Majesty's Feet . . . I throw it" (19)—further complicates the Williamite signifier. Molyneux's refusal of the colonial paradigm is built, in the first place, on the notion of inherited rights based on a common English ancestry, an argument that if exclusively pursued would have made the *Case* a defense solely of the liberty of the Irish Protestant community. It is this limited kind of nationalism, for example, that Molyneux advocates in the following passage, in which he refutes the notion that England assumed the right to govern Ireland through conquest: "Now 'tis manifest that the great Body of the present People of *Ireland*, are the Progeny of the *English* and *Britains,* that from time to time have come over into this Kingdom; and there remains but a meer handful of the Antient *Irish* at this day; I may not say one in a thousand: So that if I, or any body else, claim the like Freedoms with the Natural Born *Subjects* of *England,* as being Descended from them, it will be impossible to prove the contrary" (35). Once again, it appears, a colonial English subject is asserting his rights and privileges by erasing the native Irish other from the landscape, even if this time the ethnic cleansing is done by the stroke of the pen rather than the sword. However, Molyneux also makes the claim that Ireland should not be bound by the English Parliament on the very different grounds of natural rights and contractual agreement, and this argument works to blur the boundary between native and settler, thus giving a wider nationalist import to this text. In keeping with his Lockean argument that the consent of the people is the only basis for legitimate government—"All Men are by Nature in a state of Equality" until "by their own *Consent* they give up their Freedom, by entring into Civil Societies for the Common Benefit of all the Members thereof" (116–17)—Molyneux has recourse to the myth of an ancient contract between the native Irish people and an English king, a myth that implicitly suggests that the native Irish population are part of the five-hundred-year-old "Nation" (88) he is defending. Of the "Original Compact" that the "People of Ireland" received after Irish kings, princes, bishops, and abbots all voluntarily submitted to Henry II in the twelfth century, Molyneux writes: "I am sure 'tis not possible to shew a more fair Original Compact between a King and *People,* than this between *Henry* the Second and the *People of Ireland, That they should enjoy the like Liberties and Immunities, and be Govern'd by the same Mild Laws, both Civil and Ecclesiastical, as the People of England*" (46). "The People of Ireland" here are not "the Progeny of the *English* and *Britains,*" as implied earlier, but the native Irish or Gaelic inhabitants of Ireland, and, in this conceptualization, the nation of Ireland originated at the moment when native Irish and English subjects entered into a social contract. A contractual, ethnically diverse model of the Irish nation, in other words, substitutes for the earlier kin- or blood-based model that worked to erase the native Irish people from the national scene. This other, more inclusive form of nationalism, too, is suggested by the nature of the sexual relationship between Richard Strongbow, a leader of the "First Expedition of the *English* into *Ireland,*" and the daughter of Dermot, King of Leinster (26–27). In noting that this marriage occurred through "Compact" (27) and not through conquest or rape, Molyneux underlines his claim that from the beginning Ireland existed on terms of equality with England. But in recalling this marriage, he also implicitly suggests that the five-hundred-year-old "Nation" he is defending is a hybrid nation, the product of an interracial union.

The cult of William in eighteenth-century Ireland, then, took shape in the context of the Irish Protestant community's continued effort to realize Molyneux's goals as well as in the more obvious context of its continued attempt to assert dominance over the internal Irish Catholic enemy, and if this other patriotic meaning of the Williamite ritual was repressed, it was undoubtedly because of the overwhelmingly negative English response to this first political overture. Molyneux's work was denounced by the English Commons as being "of dangerous consequence to the crown and people of England by denying the authority of the king and parliament of England to bind the kingdom and people of Ireland, and by denying the subordination and dependence that Ireland hath, and ought to have, upon England as united and annexed to the imperial crown of this realm."[19] And as if to remove any further doubt about what they thought of this Irish bid for constitutional equality and liberty, the English Commons passed the Woolen Act the following year (1699), a bill that restricted one of Ireland's most important industries. John Cary, a Bristol merchant who took a prominent part in the campaign to restrict the Irish wool trade, articulated the imperial attitude behind the Woolen Act when he stated, "[U]nless Ireland was bound up more strictly by laws made in England it would soon destroy our woollen manufactures here; wherefore I proposed to reduce it (with respect to its trade) to the state of our other plantations and settlements abroad."[20] The merchant class that was the main beneficiary of the Glorious Revolution in England thus made it very clear to Irish Protestants that it was not prepared to share the spoils of this Williamite victory. To the merchants, Ireland was not, as Molyneux had argued, a sibling nation with equal political and economic rights but a bastard colony that had to be "bound up more strictly by laws" in the interest of the mother country.

That Irish Protestant patriots refused to give up their struggle is clear from the ceremony that marked the unveiling of the statue of William III on College Green on July 1, 1701. This large equestrian statue, which was erected at the expense of the Dublin Corporation, served, at one level, as an expression of the city fathers' fierce anti-Catholicism. When Protestants resumed control of city hall in 1690, one of their first acts was to pass a municipal bylaw disenfranchising Catholic freemen, and during the 1690s, as Jacqueline Hill notes, they passed other measures to ensure that only Protestants held civic posts.[21] The statue of William, sitting high on his prancing horse, embodied this Protestant will to dominance. Dressed as a victorious Roman general, with a truncheon in his hand, the monument configured the Williamites as masters and the Jacobites and the Irish Catholics as a beaten and defeated people. The inauguration rituals on July 1, the anniversary (O. S.) of the Battle of the Boyne, would also have worked to further underscore the monument's militaristic and anti-Catholic overtones. When local Irish Protestant leaders joined with the English Dublin Castle officials in a parade around the statue on this occasion, they symbolically re-created the victorious Anglo-Irish Protestant alliance that had won the 1688–91 war, and as Gilbert's account reveals, the presence of the militia and the noise of the gunfire would have provided additional visual and aural reminders of the victory:

> The Lord Mayor, aldermen, sheriffs, masters, wardens, and common councilmen of the city, having assembled at the Tholsel at 4 p.m., walked thence in formal procession to College-green, preceded by the city musicians and by the grenadier companies of the Dublin Militia. Some time after the city officials had reached College-green, the Lord Justices arrived, and were conducted through a line, formed by the grenadiers, to the statue, round which the entire assembly, uncovered, marched three times; the kettle-drums, trumpets, and other music playing on a stage erected near the front of the monument. After the second circuit, the Recorder delivered an eulogy on King William, expressing the attachment of the people of Dublin to his person and government, and at the conclusion of this oration a volley was fired by the grenadiers, succeeded by a discharge of ordnance. At the termination of the third circuit round the statue, the Lord Justices, the Provost and Fellows of the University, with numbers of Williamite noblemen and gentry, were conducted by the Lord Mayor, through a file of soldiers, to a large new house on College-green for their reception, where they were entertained.[22]

A closer look at the precise syntax of the 1701 inaugural ceremony and at the statue itself suggests that there was also another kind of power play going on at the interior of this Williamite street drama. From the account above, it is clear that it was city officials, not government officials, who were the producers and lead players in this performance. It was they who "conducted" the lord justices around the monument; it was they who provided the script for the Williamite eulogy; and it was they who provided all the entertainment (the College Green reception mentioned above was only the first of the day; at the end of the evening, the lord mayor and city officials prepared another entertainment for the lord justices in the lord mayor's house). This appropriation of the role of principal player took its meaning, I suggest, from the other ongoing struggle of the city fathers: namely, their struggle to protect the city's charters and municipal rights and privileges against Dublin Castle encroachment. Even though the Dublin Corporation had set aside the Jacobite charter in 1690 and even though city officials could speak of the city reverting to its "auncient Protestant government," the viceroy and privy council still exercised considerable control over this body as they had to approve all the chief civic officials. Thus, as Hill notes, "regardless of which monarch or dynasty was on the throne, the danger of royal encroachments on local liberties had not vanished."[23] The Williamite ritual described above was also structured, I suggest, in the consciousness of this kind of threat. Behind the public show of hospitality and solidarity, the city fathers were tacitly signaling that they, not the London-appointed officials, ruled Dublin. The Williamite monument itself also articulated this other kind of political message through the engraved and gilt inscription on the white marble tablet on the statue's pedestal:

> Gulielmo Tertio;
> Magnae Britanniae, Franciae et Hiberniae
> Regi,
> Ob Religionem Conservatam;
> Restitutas Leges,
> Libertatem Assertam,
> Cives Dublinienses Hanc Statuam
> Posuere.

If William was the preserver of religion, he was also the restorer of laws and liberty, this inscription implied, and it was this constitutional heritage of laws and liberty, too, that the Protestant citizens of Dublin were claiming or "possessing" when they erected the statue in the middle of their city, just outside the doors of their parliament.

If there was a need for repeated rituals around this statue in the decades that followed, it could be argued, it was also because Irish Protestant overtures for equal rights and liberties in parliament were repeatedly rebuffed. Every November 4 after 1701, the viceroy (or in his absence, the lord justices) held a levee in the castle for the lord mayor, city officials, nobility, and gentry. This whole group then paraded as far as St. Stephen's Green and back, stopping on the way to pay respect to the monument on College Green; as in the 1701 ceremony, the parade circled the statue of William three times, and again the troops discharged their volleys of musketry.[24] In the first decade of the century, these parades would have included participants such as the Speaker of the Irish House, Alan Brodrick, and the faction in parliament and city hall who supported his ongoing struggle for constitutional equality. Brodrick had been one of the most outspoken advocates of a strong anti-Catholic policy in the 1690s but he had been also one of the leaders of the "madmen" who had opposed Viscount Sydney in the 1692 Parliament, and in the 1703–4 parliamentary session, for example, he went on the offensive again. He and Robert Molesworth, another Irish Protestant who was a known defender of commonwealth principles, led the House of Commons to draft a resolution that expressed concern over Ireland's economic hardships and the recent attacks on her constitution, and this petition called on the queen either to permit "a full enjoyment of our constitution" or provide a union between the two countries.[25] As Hill notes, there were signs that the Dublin Corporation shared these sentiments; the same month that the 1703 Commons resolution was passed, the Corporation granted honorary freedom to Molesworth.[26] The queen's reply to the Commons resolution in 1704, was not encouraging, however, and in the spring Brodrick was dismissed from office for no other reason but, as a colleague wrote, "your hearty espousing your country's interest and appearing as became a true patriot."[27]

For such "true patriot[s]," then, the circling of the Williamite monument on November 4 would have functioned as a compensatory ritual, providing a symbolic way to reiterate claims to Irish liberty and equality that they were repeatedly failing to actualize in Parliament. In *Cities of the Dead*, Roach discusses the *effigy* as something that, like performance itself, "fills by means of surrogation a vacancy created by the absence of the original," and he notes the special importance of the effigy of the dead king in providing a sense of continuity and affiliation to a community that has suffered loss.[28] The annual November 4 parade around the Williamite effigy was such a ritual of surrogation, driven by the Irish Protestants' need not only to reinscribe the defeat of the Jacobite enemy but also to restore their failed dream of sharing in the legacy of the Glorious Revolution.

◆◆◆

The Theatre Royal at Smock Alley, located just outside the gates of Dublin Castle and about a half mile from the House of Parliament and the monument on College Green, was another site where these patriots performed Williamite rituals of surrogation, though the Williamite performances in that location, I suggest, also took their meaning from an internal struggle for hegemony that had been going on in that institution (Ireland's only professional theater) since the 1689–91 war. As William Chetwood relates, the first performance at Smock Alley after the war was made possible only by the assistance of Dublin Castle; when the playhouse opened in winter 1691, Chetwood notes, the first play (Shakespeare's *Othello*) "was acted by Officers mostly about the Castle" as the regular company had been dispersed during the "Troubles."[29] In the two decades that followed, successive viceroys also continued to treat Smock Alley as if it were a court institution, as indeed it had been in the period before the war. During the stormy parliamentary season of 1692, for example, Viscount Sydney reportedly tried to deploy the playhouse to distract his political opponents; after he prorogued the rebellious Irish Parliament, it was later said, he "promoted Plays, Sports, and Interludes for the Amusement of the Plundered People."[30] In summer 1698 the second duke of Ormond also took the Smock Alley troop with him to Ormond Castle in Kilkenny to entertain his guests, just as his grandfather, the first Duke of Ormond, had taken "his players" from Dublin to entertain the university at Oxford some twenty years earlier.[31] And in 1709 the earl of Wharton himself recruited players in London to ensure that he and his entourage were well entertained while in Ireland. A friend of Wharton's in London wrote at this time, "I dined with him [Wharton] the other day, and he told me he had got a set of Players to go over into Ireland in May next, so what with Parliament at Chichester House, Balls in the Castle and Comedies at the Theatre, I hope we shall pass our time well this summer in Dublin."[32] As in the prewar period, too, the viceroy and his circle continued to act as important patrons of the stage, supplying many of the material needs of the company. From the documents relating to a dispute between the English player John Thurmond and the Smock Alley patentee and sharers in 1713, we learn that the viceroy and high-ranking military officers (Lord Cutts and General Ingoldsby) donated their "birthday suits" to the players and that officers of two regiments subscribed a day's pay to permit the indigent Thurmond to remain in the country.[33] More important, successive viceroys and their administrations continued to appear at the theater and, in so doing, attracted crowded houses. When the duke of Ormond honored the performance of George Farquhar with his presence in 1704 (Farquhar was appearing in his own play *The Constant Couple*), for example, the actor-playwright netted one hundred pounds instead of the usual fifty.[34]

In the decade after the war, however, a more socially diverse crowd also began to compete with the court for control over this symbolically significant institution, and this crowd was "Irish" in the sense that it was made up of men and women who were born in Ireland or who thought of Ireland as their permanent home. The signs of this shift occurred during the Restoration when Dublin's wealthy citizens began to express an interest in the theater for the first time. In 1678 a prominent Dublin citizen, Robert Ware, urged the mayor and aldermen to attend the "*Kings Theatre* in their own Persons" on holidays and festivals as a means of encouraging the "Freemen" of the city to attend, and he suggested that these freemen also provide an allowance of twelve pence to apprentices "to recreate themselves at these times at the *Theatre*, in lieu of these sportes this Cittie was bound to entertain them with."[35] By the 1690s, too, it is clear that such nonelite Dubliners were turning up at the Theatre Royal. When John Dunton, a London bookseller, visited Dublin in 1698, he noted that the Dublin Theatre Royal "is free for all Comers and gives entertainment as well to the broom man as the greatest Peer," and he also remarked that the "Spectators" were not "one degree less in *Variety* and Foppery, than those in another Place [London]."[36] The archbishop of Dublin also tacitly revealed this "Variety" when he wrote in 1694 complaining that "the young men of the metropolis . . . attended more to the Play-house than to their studies" (39).[37] These "young men" were Trinity College students, and most of them would have come from an Irish Protestant professional or country gentry background.

Changes in the management of the Irish theater also meant that, for the first time, Ireland's professional, commercial, and landed classes could become patrons of the Theatre Royal. During the 1690s, the practices of offering "benefit nights" for specific actor or playwrights and raising subscriptions for the support of the players were introduced in the Irish theater.[38] These innovations, potentially at least, allowed anyone with money to patronize and thus exercise some influence over the theater. When the playhouse was dark for the death of William III in 1702, for example, "Ladys of Quality" raised a subscription to support the company,[39] and although these "Ladys" could have been part of the castle coterie, they could also have been "Ladys" from an Irish Protestant or (though this is less likely) from an Irish Catholic or "convert" background. The shift to a shareholding model in the management of the theater similarly opened up an opportunity for more local control. The theater continued to be managed, as it had been before the war, by Joseph Ashbury, an Englishman who had close ties with the castle (he had served as a member of the King's Guard of Horse, for example, while the duke of Ormond was viceroy).[40] But in the 1690s, following the practice of the London theaters, Ashbury permitted some of the leading actors at Smock Alley to become "sharers" in the annual profits in the company, and as Irish-born players were beginning to assume leading roles in the company at about this time, this innovation also served to localize the theater. Thomas Griffith, for example, is listed as one of the first shareholders, and he was a native Dubliner.[41]

By the turn of the century, too, Irish Protestant patriots had begun to use performance to remap this location as their own, as is evident from *St. Stephen's Green, or, The Generous Lovers*, a comedy produced on the Smock Alley stage in 1699. Captain William Philips, the play's author, was a descendant of Elizabethan planters in Ulster, and his father had earned a place of honor in Irish Protestant history as the governor who urged the Apprentice Boys to shut the gates of Derry against Jacobite forces in 1688.[42] In dedicating his play to William O'Brien, third earl of Inchiquin, however, Philips signaled that he was part of that small group of Irish Protestants who were now identifying with an Irish rather than an English interest. O'Brien was a Protestant who had served with distinction in King William's army, but he was also a descendant of one of the most famous Gaelic kings (Brian Boru) and a member of a prestigious Irish family that continued to patronize native Irish arts and culture throughout the eighteenth century. As Eileen MacCarvill notes, the Gaelic poet and historian Aodh Buí Mac Cruitín dedicated his *Brief Discourse in Vindication of the Antiquity of Ireland* (1717) — the first work in English to attempt to refute anti-Irish histories — to William O'Brien, and fourteen other members of this Thomond family also subscribed to this work.[43] By dedicating his work to an O'Brien, then, Philips imaginatively aligned himself with this circle of Irish poets and historians; as he explicitly states in the first line of his dedication, it was a shared nationalist as well as theatrical interest that attracted him to this patron: "This Play had a double Reason for seeking Shelter under your Lordship; I Writ it, and for our *Irish* Stage, and You are the chief Friend which either has."[44]

The first Smock Alley spectators who saw *St. Stephen's Green* would also have had the experience of looking at a specifically "*Irish* Stage," and by creating this sense of shared space, this play was already engaged in the process of nation making. In *Imagined Communities* Benedict Anderson argues that the newspaper played a central role in the evolving nationalism of the eighteenth-century Americas because of its ability to refract daily comings and goings, marriages, and economic news into "a specific imagined world of vernacular readers"; the newspaper, he states, created "an imagined community among a specific assemblage of fellow-readers, to whom *these* ships, brides, bishops and prices belonged."[45] But the theater, as the case of *St. Stephen's Green* illustrates, has an even more powerful capacity to refract worlds for a specific assemblage of fellow observers because it can work simultaneously in many different semiotic systems. From the opening scene of this play, for example, Smock Alley spectators would have found themselves gazing on a world that was recognizably their own; the setting for many of the scenes is St. Stephen's Green, a fashionable park that had been developed in the early Restoration period, and a new piece of scenery—the first ever of an Irish landscape—had been painted to depict this setting.[46] This sense of being in an Irish landscape also would have been reinforced by the dialogue. Characters talk of taking "the Air on the *Strand*" (1.1.55) or of meeting at "Chappellizard" (Epilogue, 17) (two fashionable meeting places on the outskirts of Dublin); of not giving someone "the value of a Rapparee Fathing" (5.1.86) (worthless Jacobite currency); of begging "an Estate of Forfeited Lands" (5.2.177) (an allusion to the recent Williamite confiscations). As an orderly, pleasant, and artfully designed public space, St. Stephen's Green is also a synecdoche for an Irish society that is culturally sophisticated and rational, and by recoding Irish space in this positive way, this play continued the struggle that Molyneux had begun in his *Case*. In the opening pages of his work, Molyneux had implicitly invited others to imitate his "Performance" (24) in arguing against English encroachment on Irish rights and liberties. England, he disingenuously argued, would never think "of making the least Breach in the *Rights* and *Liberties* of their *Neighbours*, unless they thought they had *Right* so to do; and this they might well surmise, if their Neighbours quietly see their Inclosures Invaded, without *Expostulating* the Matter . . . and shewing Reasons, why they may think that Hardships are put upon them therein" (23–24). *St. Stephen's Green*, I suggest, was the first dramatic work to respond to this call, though it makes its case against English encroachment not by expostulating on the hardships caused by such an invasion but by emphasizing the already existing order and civility of the Irish "Inclosure." There is only one direct reference to recent political events in this play, and that occurs when the Irishman, Bellmine, tells the English-man, Freelove, that he dreads marriage "as much as our Farmers do the Wool-Bill" (1.1.126–27). But by establishing the civility and refinement of Irish life, the play consistently undermines the ideological premise that was behind this "Wool-Bill" and behind all English legislation relat-ing to Ireland: namely, that Ireland was a wild and savage land that needed (and deserved) to be bound and restrained by laws made in the metropoli-tan center.

The play begins its attack on hegemonic English attitudes with the following exchange between Freelove, who has just arrived in Ireland for the first time, and his friend, Bellmine:

FREELOVE: (*Looking about*) A pleasant place this! The Name of it?
BELLMINE: *St. Stephen's Green.*
FREELOVE: I like the Air.—I am glad your House has the benefit of it. (1.1.98–102)

The unspoken countertext here is the English traveler's account of Ireland—an account that, from the time of Giraldus Cambrensis on, had empha-sized the barbarity and wildness of Ireland and (implicitly) the superiority of English civilization and culture.[47] In the exchange between Freelove and the fop, Vainly, the play also continues this transvaluation of Irish space, this time attacking the Irish elite themselves for their unpatriotic attitudes. Vainly, an Irishman, displays his anti-Irish bias when he states that he is "forced to go to *England* once a year, to refine [his] understanding" and to enjoy "pleasures" and "Conveniences" that are not to be had in Ireland (3.1.236–38, 3.1.248–50). But in the following exchange, these assump-tions about England's superiority and Ireland's inferiority are interrogated and revealed to be intellectually bankrupt:

FREELOVE: I have been told you have all those [conveniences] here.
VAINLY: Oh not one, Sir, not one.
FREELOVE: You have good Wine?
VAINLY: Yes, yes, that's true, I had forgot that.
FREELOVE: Plenty of all sorts of Fish and Flesh.
VAINLY: Phoo, they are perfect Drugs. Plenty of Meat and Drink: but nothing else.
FREELOVE: The People are Civil and Obliging.
VAINLY: Especially to Strangers.

FREELOVE:	And Hospitable.
VAINLY:	To a fault, Sir.
FREELOVE:	The Air is good, a temperate Climate.
VAINLY:	Much the same as in *England*.
FREELOVE:	The Soil is Rich.
VAINLY:	Oh, 'tis too Rank.
FREELOVE:	What necessaries then, or what pleasures do you want? You have fine Women.
VAINLY:	They are kind I suppose. (3.1.251–68)

Unable to restrain himself, another Irishman, Sir Francis Feignyouth, interrupts at this point and condemns Vainly as a "Worthless Contemptible Wretch" for "entertain[ing] Strangers with your aversion to your Country, without being able to give one Reason for it" (3.1.273–76), a statement that sums up the play's attitude to those who remain prejudiced against the country of their birth.

In identifying English metropolitan culture as the greatest source of danger and disruption to the Irish world, *St. Stephen's Green* also displays its Irish patriot sympathies and its ideological alignment with Molyneux's *Case*. Lady Volant, the play's chief villain, is an Englishwoman who has settled in Ireland (she says at one point that she had done "tolerably well, since my being *Naturaliz'd*" [3.1.139–40]). But far from exercising a beneficial effect on her adopted country, as the standard myth of English imperialism claimed, this newcomer from London threatens to undo the whole fabric of society by her fraudulent marriage to Sir Francis Feignyouth. Timothy, the steward who assists Lady Volant in her scheme to cheat Sir Francis out of his estate, adds another layer of anti-English satire to the plot as he is, in many ways, a parody of Teague in Sir Richard Howard's *The Committee; or the Faithful Irishman*, a play that had been staged at Smock Alley two years before.[48] The relationship between the two characters is suggested by their common name—Timothy is the English equivalent of the Gaelic name "Teague"—and by the similarity of their histories; when Lady Volant first met Timothy in London, we are told, this servant, like his Teague counterpart, was also "half Starv'd, and in Rags" (3.1.14). In a direct inversion of *The Committee* plot, however, this Timothy finds prosperity and an improved standard of living in Ireland rather than England. As he tells his old friend and fellow servant, Trickwell, he "thrive[s] very well in this Country"; if he is fat, it is because "Ease and Plenty have made this Alteration, Eating well, and Lying soft" (4.1.12–14). Even the Timothys or

"Teagues," this play suggests, are thriving in present-day Ireland. By re-
solving the conflict of the play with the marriage of Freelove and Amelia,
too, *St. Stephen's Green* implicitly dramatizes Molyneux's notion that Ireland and England are equal partners in a "Compact." Over the course of the
play, the principal lovers, Freelove, an Englishman, and Amelia, an Irishwoman, test each other's sincerity and virtue by each pretending to be pen-
niless, seeking through this subterfuge to determine if there is a moral defi-
ciency in the other. The resolution of this tension, then, comes with the
discovery of economic and moral equality, and it is on this basis that the
Anglo-Irish marriage finally takes place. Remarking on the similarity of
the lovers, Bellmine states, "Fate design'd you for each other. . . . [Y]ou are
not more alike in Tempers than in Fortune" (5.2.275–77). This discovery of
moral and economic parity also resonates on the political plane. If Irish and
English subjects are social, moral, and economic equals, then they are also
political equals and consequently should not exist in a relation of "subordination and dependence," as the English Parliament had suggested in its
defense of the Woolen Act.

By 1699, then, Irish Protestant patriots like Philips were using the
drama to remap the Irish playhouse as an Irish institution, and through the
drama they were expressing their desire for greater political equality for
themselves if not their native Irish counterparts (Timothy or Teague, the
representative of the native Irish in this play, as we have seen, is still consigned to the servant's role). If Nicholas Rowe's Williamite drama *Tamerlane* became an instant favorite with this group in the opening years of the
new century, I suggest, it was because it was available for similar ideological investment, despite its distinctly English political origin. *Tamerlane*
was first performed in London in 1701, and it was immediately recognized
in its own day as a piece of political propaganda. The eponymous hero was
an idealized figure for the reigning English monarch, William III, and in
showing the righteousness and success of Tamerlane's war against the
tyrannical Bajazet, Rowe and his Whig friends hoped to move the English
Parliament to unite behind the war effort against Louis XIV. Victory "is
yet to come," Rowe wrote in the dedication to the play, "but I hope we
may reasonably expect it from the Unanimity of the present Parliament,
and so formidable a Force as that Unanimity will give Life and Vigor to."[49]
The play's longevity on the London stage, however —between 1716 and
1776, for instance, *Tamerlane* was performed at least once every year[50] —
can best be explained by its apparent ability to reconcile the expansionist
aims of the post-1688 fiscal-military state with an older English tradition of

personal and constitutional liberties.[51] I suggest it was the play's ability to work simultaneously on both these ideological fronts—to glorify conquest *and* constitutional liberties—that also made it particularly ripe for Irish Protestant appropriation.

Tamerlane was first performed in Dublin soon after it appeared in London and quickly became the standard entertainment for the evening of November 4.[52] After the parade around the statue on College Green, the Irish Protestant community would gather at Smock Alley for a performance of this play and, as the writer of the *Conduct of the Purse* pamphlet pointed out, until the coming of Phipps, these performances were generally "encourag'd and countenanc'd by the Presence or Approbation of their . . . Governors" (20). One reason for *Tamerlane*'s popularity with this audience undoubtedly was its apparent ability to legitimate Protestant conquest and Catholic subjection by providing antithetically evaluated representations of the Williamite hero and the Williamite foe. In Rowe's play Tamerlane's attack on his enemy is justified by repeatedly demonstrating Bajazet's extreme violence. Not content with piling up anecdotal evidence of Bajazet's past savagery—he is a destroyer of land and crops (1.1.84–88), a "League-Breaker" (2.1.150), a rapist (2.2.337–41)—the play continually puts Bajazet's "native Fury" (1.1.55) on display for the audience. On one occasion, for example, Bajazet orders his men to strangle the Greek prince, Moneses, in his presence (5.1.185–86) and on another occasion he tries to murder his daughter, Selima, with his own hands (5.1.273). When Tamerlane and his forces finally draw their swords to prevent this last murder, then, their intervention appears entirely defensible; as Tamerlane himself comments, the "rank World," as represented by Bajazet, "asks" to be disciplined: "'Tis a rank World, and asks her keenest Sword, / To cut up Villainy of monstrous growth" (5.1.335–36). For a London audience, such evidence of the world's "Villainy" could serve as a rationale for the creation of Britannia, the nation that felt it was providentially ordained to rule the world, and in this context Bajazet would configure not only the Catholic French enemy but also the colonial populations that Britain came to see as its hostile other. As Linda Colley points out, Britons increasingly defined themselves not only against the Catholic French but also against "the colonial peoples they conquered, peoples who were manifestly alien in terms of culture, religion and colour."[53] For a Dublin audience, however, these scenes would also have served to legitimate the creation of the sectarian Irish Protestant state, much like the sermons that were preached in Protestant churches every October 23, the anniversary of the 1641 uprising.

As noted, October 23 commemorative services generally rehearsed the reputed atrocities committed by the native Irish against the settler community during the 1641 uprising, and in these sermons and in the Irish Protestant histories that supplied their material, the image of the "savage Turk" was often used to convey the inhumanity of a people under the sway of Catholicism. In an October 23 commemorative sermon in 1690, for example, one preacher argued that "[t]he plotting, contriving and mischievous spirit is the very spirit that rules and influences popery at this day which religion (if it deserves so good a name) exceeds all other (the Turkish not excepted) in barbarous bloodshed and cruelty. "[54] And in arguing for the legitimacy of the Protestant acceptance of the government of William and Mary in his highly influential and frequently reprinted *The State of the Protestants of Ireland under the late King James's Government* (1691), Archbishop King wrote: "If a Christian Army should go at this time into *Greece* to redeem the Christians there from the slavery of the *Turks*, I would enquire of any indifferent Casuist, whether it were lawful for the oppressed *Grecians* to accept of that deliverance, and to join heartily with and recognize their Redeemers."[55]

The rationale that *Tamerlane* offers for the final "caging" of Bajazet would also have been familiar and comforting to an audience who knew the arguments of King's *State of the Protestants of Ireland*. That Tamerlane should decide to cage his enemy at the end of this play is itself not surprising as this caging was part of the general lore about the Tamerlane-Bajazet conflict (Marlowe, for example, also uses it). In this play, however, Rowe also builds in an additional justification for his hero by showing that the idea for this cruel punishment originated first with the Turkish king, and this kind of preemptive strike logic would have resonated in a particularly meaningful way with Irish Protestants. Though there were no massacres during the Jacobite period, King justified subsequent Protestant oppression of Catholics on the grounds of what *might* have happened had James and the Catholics won the war. Like a "hungry Wolf," "they had devour'd us in their Imaginations," King states, and he suggests that Catholics admit as much: "Many of them make no scruple to confess, That there was no medium, but that either we or they must be undone, and when that was the unavoidable choice, that they, according to their own confession, had put on us, I assure my self the World will not only excuse us, but will think it was our Duty to have done what we did, since they had left us no other visible way but this, to avoid certain and apparent Destruction."[56] In justifying Bajazet's caging, this play uses a similar logic. At an early point, Tamerlane asks Bajazet, "What had I to expect, if thou had'st conquer'd?" (2.2.133), to which Bajazet responds, "I would have cag'd thee, for the Scorn of Slaves" (2.2.144). When Tamerlane then decides to inflict this brutal humiliation on his enemy—Bajazet is "Clos'd in a Cage, like some destructive Beast," and "born about, in publick View" (5.1.347–48)—he appears to be reacting defensively rather than aggressively. The Protestant subject's violence in the aftermath of conquest, *Tamerlane* would have suggested, is the product of the Catholic subject's own evil and destructive character.

If this play served to justify the Protestant state's penal laws—its way of "caging" the enemy—it also served to articulate the frustrated Irish Protestant desire for constitutional and economic parity with their English neighbors, their desire to become brother-sharers in the Williamite heritage of the Glorious Revolution. As John Loftis notes, Rowe's *Tamerlane* is not only "a call to arms" but also a dramatization of "the Whig constitutional position"; in two key scenes—the first between Tamerlane and Bajazet and the second between Tamerlane and the Turkish holy man—Lockean principles of constitutional government and religious liberty are explicitly expounded and defended.[57] As a counter, for example, to Bajazet's political absolutism, his defense of the rights of kings to satisfy their "Ambition" and "Noble Appetite" (2.2.82, 84), Tamerlane advocates a politics governed by "Leagues," "cool Debates," and a regard for "the People" (2.2.66, 64, 105). And in opposition to the Turkish dervish's religious absolutism—the demand that the emperor "Drive out all other Faiths" but Islam—Tamerlane defends the rights of individuals to worship as they please:

> . . . to subdue th' unconquerable Mind,
> To make one Reason have the same Effect
> Upon all Apprehensions; to force this,
> Or this Man, just to think, as thou and I do;
> Impossible! Unless Souls were alike
> In all, which differ now like Human Faces. (3.2.77–82)

Such speeches were included in this text, I suggest, to reassure audiences in the London metropolitan center that their own hard-fought political and religious liberties would not be jeopardized by the kind of buildup of military powers that was happening in the post-1688 state. But in the process of legitimating its own imperialism, this text also supplied arguments for less advantaged subaltern subjects like the Irish Protestants. Tamerlane's statement to Axalla, for example, that nature owns "An Equal Right in Kings and common Men" (2.2.33) would have served to confirm the Irish Protestant patriot's belief in the righteousness of his struggle for parliamentary equality, and Tamerlane's reminder to Bajazet that he should remember "The Common Tye, and Brotherhood of Kind" (2.2.171) would have served as a reminder of the broader political "Brotherhood" that this Protestant patriot sought to build.

At a deeper structural level, too, through the mechanism of the Tamerlane-Axalla plot, the play effectively tropes the triumph of an imagined community of brothers over an imperial monarchy, thus dramatizing the kind of shift in political paradigms that Irish Protestant patriots desired. As Anderson argues, the nation, "regardless of actual inequality and exploitation," is always conceived as a "deep, horizontal comradeship" and as a "fraternity."[58] In the first act, the play establishes that the relationship between Tamerlane and Axalla is this kind of horizontal, fraternal one. Even though Tamerlane is king, he greets Axalla as a partner and with the name of chosen brother and friend:

> Welcome! thou worthy Partner of my Laurels,
> Thou Brother of my Choice, a Band more Sacred
> Than Nature's brittle Tye. By Holy Friendship!
> Glory and Fame stood still for thy Arrival,
> My Soul seem'd wanting in its better half. (1.1.121–25)

We are also given a verbal image of this sacred "Band" that is based on "Choice," not blood ties, when the Turkish dervish describes the fighting men—"Bright Troops" who "from thence/ On either Hand stretch far into the Night" (5.1.224–25)—who accompany Tamerlane and Axalla to Bajazet's tent to rescue Selima. And this militant brotherhood is fully realized dramatically on the stage at that climactic moment in the last act when Tamerlane and his troops burst in and "drive Bajazet and the Mutes off the Stage" (5.1.321–24). For an Irish audience, this climactic moment when a vertical, authoritarian form of government is displaced by a horizontal, egalitarian form of power could function as a dramatization of their wished-for desire to substitute the status of nation for the status of colony.

The very quality, then, that made *Tamerlane* politically useful in England—its apparent ability to reconcile an older English discourse of liberty with a new discourse of empire—made it potentially dysfunctional from the point of view of English power in Ireland, because the Irish Protestant audience who viewed it did not stand in the same relation to liberty as their counterparts on the mainland, and this dysfunctionality, I suggest, became apparent in the playhouse in 1712. In *Imagined Communities* Anderson also argues that European imperial powers became unwitting disseminators of nationalism in their colonies in the nineteenth century when they tried to frame their political ambitions in a national rhetoric borrowed from America and France. To make empire appear more attractive, Anderson suggests, these powers (including Britain) appeared in "national drag" on the world stage, but in so doing they inadvertently supplied modular forms of the nation to their own colonial subjects who then formed breakaway nations of their own.[59] The case of the Smock Alley riot suggests, however, that this ironic drama of national dissemination occurred at a much earlier stage in the history of empire. At a time when the Dublin Castle administration proved particularly autocratic, as it did between 1710 and 1714, Irish Protestant patriots could find a script for rebellion in English Williamite texts such as *Tamerlane* and the Garth prologue, and these scripts brought the hitherto concealed image of the Irish Protestant nation on to the stage of the Theatre Royal.

◆◆◆

As we have already seen, two pamphlets written after the theatrical disturbance located this event in the framework of renewed Protestant-Catholic, Williamite-Jacobite tensions, and there is no doubt that these tensions were very real during the last years of Anne's reign because of uncertainty about the succession. There is also no doubt that the English Tory ministry's choice of ministers for Ireland did little to alleviate Irish Protestant anxiety on this score. The viceroy, the duke of Ormond, was a member of a distinguished Irish Protestant family (the Butlers) and a man who had the admiration and respect of many Irish Protestants, but Sir Constantine Phipps, who served as Ormond's lord chancellor and later as a lord justice, was an Englishman and a "highflying" Tory, who had made his reputation by defending Dr. Sacheverell during his famous trial.[60] The lord chancellor's appointment of "converts" to political office and positions of power also did little to calm Irish Protestants' fears; as we have seen, Protestants would also later accuse Phipps of surrounding himself with "the O[h]s, the M[ac]ks, and the Descendants from the Murderers of [Sixteen] Forty One."

The disturbance in the playhouse, however, can also be read against the background of renewed English-Irish tensions created by the government's attempt to reassert its control over political institutions and significant sites of assembly that Irish Protestants were beginning to think of as their own. Sir John Brodrick, the son of the M. P. Alan Brodrick, was arrested in a Dublin coffeehouse, for example, for having criticized the administration, and another Irish Protestant was prosecuted for having "treated her majesty in a public company with great disrespect."[61] To cite the author of *The Conduct of the Purse*, "Gentlemen were informed against for Words of little or no Signification. . . . [T]he whole seem'd as it were design'd to convince Protestant Gentlemen, that the Government had no Mind to let them meet together at all" (24–25). More seriously, the Dublin Castle administration, led by Phipps, made a serious attempt to assert control over the Tholsel, the city hall. Between 1711 and 1713, Dublin city election results were repeatedly disapproved by the privy council in an effort to impose a Tory mayor on the Whig-dominated Dublin Corporation, and Robert Molesworth spoke for many when he complained that "that devil the chancellor" was being given the freedom "to run about like a roaring lion . . . devouring the liberties and privileges of the City."[62] Attempts to question this exertion of executive power also brought accusations of disloyalty and, indeed, of collusion with the Irish Catholic enemy. A pamphlet entitled *Her Majesty's Prerogative in Ireland; The Authority of the government and Privy-Council There: and the Rights, Laws, and Liberties of the City of Dublin Asserted and Maintain'd* (1712) argued that "Factious Protestants" as well as Catholics were to blame for the 1641 rebellion and went on to suggest that a similar unholy alliance was behind the city controversy and behind Williamite commemorations: "[S]ome of their [Factious Protestants] Posterity at this Day drink to the *pious Memory of Oliver Cromwell;* and have the Impudence to join it with the *glorious Memory of King William.* The Principles of the Ancestors are rooted in the Progeny; and the Occasion of this very Controversy, which we are now upon, is one blessed Effect of so hopeful a Plantation. Nor is it at all strange that Papists and *such* Protestants should unite in this cause."[63] These antagonisms also soon spread to Parliament. Early in the 1711 parliamentary session, Archbishop King wrote to Jonathan Swift that he feared that "the business of the city of Dublin" would "beget ill blood, and come into Parliament,"[64] and his fears proved well founded. The 1711 parliamentary session was again a highly contentious one, marked by controversies over the powers of the lord lieutenant and privy council, and it ended, significantly, with the Irish Commons proclaiming, in an address to the lord lieutenant, "their steady adherence to the principles of the late Revolution."[65]

The stage of the Theatre Royal, a half-mile walk from College Green, then, was another platform on which Irish Protestants could proclaim this commitment to Revolution principles. This platform became particularly significant in the light of the government's refusal to celebrate King William's birthday in 1711 and 1712. In 1711 the viceroy refused to lay on the customary banquet on November 4, and that year also the government forbade the speaking of Garth's prologue for the first time.[66] The following year, Phipps, acting as lord justice in place of the absent viceroy, again forbade the prologue, discouraged the annual custom of dressing William's statue for the November 4 birthday celebration, and, more important, refused to join in the procession around the statue on College Green.[67] In thus neglecting to honor the birthday, Phipps effectively cast himself as the enemy of William and the Irish Protestant nation that had established itself under the aegis of the Williamite sign, and it was to play Tamerlane to this English Bajazet, I suggest, that Dudley Moore (himself the younger brother of an Irish M. P.) turned up at the Theatre Royal on the evening of November 4, 1712.

Moore's unorthodox performance also had a populist dimension, if we are to credit the account of the "riot" that appeared in the progovernment newspaper, *Lloyd's News-letter*. The opposition originated at a midday dinner in honor of King William at the Tholsel, this newspaper sarcastically reported, when those who preferred "the memory of a dead Prince before the Duty they owe to their living Sovereign" drank Williamite healths and "Fired . . . Liberty and Property Guns," and it gained strength after these Williamite supporters spent the afternoon in Lucas's, Eustace's, and other coffeehouses and gaming rooms in the city.[68] *Lloyd's News-letter* described the "Box Ladies" who applauded Moore and his supporters in the playhouse (see below) as "s[luts]" who later met to "play a Game at Putt" according to an "Original Contract" with the protesters after the performance,[69] thus implying that these women supporters were whores whom these men had linked with during their afternoon's carousing. But such a contemptuous characterization can also be read as an indication that the Moore faction had a populist component; it drew its support from below as well as from above. When Moore and his supporters burst on the stage, then, they brought this new kind of imagined community into view, much as Tamerlane does when he and his "Troops" burst in and displace Bajazet and his mutes in Rowe's play, and the incendiary nature of the prologue that Moore spoke on this occasion would have added a further subversive edge to the staging. Garth's prologue begins with a call to arms and invokes the memory of William in the interest of renewing the war against France and her Jacobite allies:

> Today, a mighty Hero comes to warm
> Your curdl'd blood and bids you Britons arm.
> To Valour much he owes, to Virtue more;
> He fights to save and conquers to restore.[70]

But the prologue also reminds audiences of the Williamite legacy of "Freedom," and when delivered by the brother of an Irish member of Parliament, this reminder could also be interpreted as a call to "pull down Tyrants" like Phipps who were undermining Irish Protestant authority:

> His generous Soul for *Freedom* was Design'd,
> To pull down Tyrants, and unslave mankind;
> He broke the Chains of Europe; and when we
> Were doom'd *for Slaves*, he came and *set us free*.[71]

The other, anti-English connotation of this disruptive performance was also apparent to government supporters. *A New Song on the Whiggs Behaviour at the Play House on the 4th of this Instant, November 12, at a Play call'd TAMERLAIN*, which appeared in *Lloyd's News-Letter* a few days after the playhouse disturbance, purports to express the dissatisfaction of the Smock Alley players who were displaced when Moore and his supporters invaded the stage. But it is clear that this song also expresses the dissatisfaction of the metropolitan English power, threatened by the political and economic ambitions of its Irish Protestant subalterns:

> You Whiggs of Renown
> Both of Country & Town,
> Who of late in our Play-House were seen;
> And mounted the Stage
> With Fury and Rage,
> As if a Great Hero had been:
> How comes it about,

You now grow so stout!
Thus quite to run out of your sphere:
We think it were fit,
You should stay in the Pit,
Unless each has a mind to turn Play'r.
Think not to invade
Our Privilege and Trade,
As you would the Prerogative Royal;
At this rate to be sure,
We must soon shut our door,
If we strive to be Honest or Loyal.[72]

The stage and the pit correspond, respectively, to the space of a "Privilege[d]" English "we" and an economically and politically subordinate Irish "you," this song suggests, and in mounting the stage, Moore and his supporters had run "out of [their] sphere," signaling their ambition or "mind" to be central players in the Irish political and economic drama. *Lloyd's News-letter* also implied that the "riot" that followed Moore's staging had this protonationalist significance, even as it gives the following derogatory account:

[T]he Show began, and 6 Grenadeers [*sic*] appearing with Guns and broad Swords, our Worthies were very quiet, only by the by, cast some Reflections on Sacheverell, struck a Fellow of the College for hissing at their indecent Behaviour, as did the Ladies in the Galleries, who these valiant, sensible Gentlemen abused with their Tongues, in a bitter manner, because as 'tis said, the Gallery Ladies chose to wear red Roses, in Honour to the English Nation, as the Box Ladies did Oranges, who clapped their Friends again and again, which so animated the P[uppies] that it is thought they will scarce be able to open their Eyes in 9 Days, the usual time allowed to W[helps] to see.[73]

The puppy imagery here was clearly meant to insult and belittle Moore and his supporters by portraying them as arrogant upstarts. Indirectly, however, it also admits a kind of birthing had taken place at the Theatre Royal that evening, and the allusion to the ladies' symbolic decorations gave this birthing an implicitly nationalist significance. If "the Gallery Ladies chose to wear red Roses, in Honour to the English Nation," then it is clear

that "the Box Ladies" who wore "Oranges" and who applauded "the P[up-
pies]" did so in honor of an Irish Protestant nation that, though still unnamed, was already challenging English hegemony.

When the conflict shifted from the theatrical to the legal and parliamentary domains in the next two years, Irish Protestants themselves also
framed it as a conflict about Irish rights and liberties, though this nationalist discourse tends to surface only in texts that were prepared for internal Irish consumption. *A Defence of the Constitution: or, An Answer to an
Argument in the Case of Mr. Moor; Lately publish'd by One of her Majesty's
Council* (1714), an anonymous pamphlet that was published only in Dublin, is a case in point. This pamphlet is a response to a 1713 pamphlet that
defended the government's use of English legal precedent to strike the
jury in the Moore trial, and it begins in a seemingly conciliatory way by
acknowledging that Ireland received her laws and constitution from
England: "those Securities for our Lives, Persons, and Estates . . . are
warranted to us by the *Constitution* or Original Compact, of which the
Commons in Parliament Assembled, are Guardians or Conservators."
In language that leaves little doubt about his anti-English sentiment,
however, this writer then goes on to add that "[t]his *Constitution* is the
only thing that *Ireland* is beholding to *England* for, as *England* and many
other Nations have been to their Conquerors, for their Laws and Civilities, " and he suggests, further, that the unconstitutional behavior in relation to Moore's trial has struck at the very heart of Ireland's newfound
national liberty:

> *Ireland* has had of late as great an Eclaircissement as any Nation
> ever had before. From the utmost Barbarity and Obscurity, it has
> become considerable, both for Arts and Arms; and has adorn'd the
> Age with some of the most celebrated Wits, as well as the most re-
> nowned Heroes.
>
> But the thing wherein it shines most, is that Spirit of *Liberty,*
> which is inherent in great Minds and illuminated Understandings.
>
> *Liberty,* which has deserted most parts of *Europe,* seems to have
> chose *Ireland* for its Seat at last, which always has been attended with
> Credit, Riches and Glory.[74]

The patriot fervor that animates this text is like that which animates Molyneux's *Case* and Philips's *St. Stephen's Green,* and it seems to be born not
just from abstract political principle but from a love of place as well.

A similar pride in Irish places and institutions marks *The Speaker. A Poem inscribed to Alan Brodrick, Esq. Speaker to the Honourable House of Commons Met at Dublin, November 25, 1713. Before his Grace the Duke of Shrewbury,* another text that was printed only in Dublin. This poem uses the conceit of a walk on College Green to celebrate the reelection of Alan Brodrick as Speaker of the Irish House of Commons in 1713, an event that marked the beginning of the final act in the showdown between Phipps and the patriot faction in Parliament. The duke of Shrewsbury, the new viceroy, was sent to Ireland in 1713 to resolve this conflict between Phipps and the Irish Protestants, but he met his first defeat on November 25, 1713, when the Commons elected Brodrick Speaker over the court nominee. Brodrick had been a key player in opposition politics since the 1690s, and, significantly, he was also the attorney general who had led Moore's defense in 1713. Under Brodrick's leadership, too, the Commons began its investigation into Phipps's behavior, and when the viceroy failed to follow its recommendation to remove the lord chancellor, the Speaker and his supporters forced the shutdown of Parliament in spring 1714. By turning "Play'r," Irish Protestants, no less than Moore, made a shocking spectacle of their contempt for Her Majesty's government in Ireland, an analogy that the new viceroy himself gestured at when he wrote, "I have made the figure rather of a viceroy in a play than of one who had the honour of her majesty's patent."[75]

The writer of *The Speaker* suggests that, like Moore, Brodrick and his supporters were acting out a specifically Williamite script when they made a farce of Her Majesty's government, and as this poem makes clear, this script was as much about Irish Protestant patriotism as it was about anti-Catholicism. In his imaginary walk "towards the *Colledge-Green*" [*sic*], the poet's attention is caught first by the statue of William, and in describing this "Effigy," the poet initially portrays the Williamite subject as the hero of a conquest narrative:

> Father we went, and saw an Effigy,
> On Marble Pedestal, 'twas mounted High.
> 'Twas Great *Nassau*, bridling his Prancer strong,
> As He's described in *Garth's* Immortal Song.
> 'Twas he I saw that Truncheon in his Hand
> Fierce Armies, and great Nations could Command.
> 'Twas He—The Verdant Laurel wreath'd around,
> The mighty Conqueror's Sacred Temples bound:

Laurels at *Boyne* and at *Namure* he won;
And ne're before the Victory put on.[76]

When the poet turns from contemplating "Great *Nassau*" mounted high on his equestrian pedestal to "Great *Brodrick*" mounted high in the Speaker's chair, however, the emphasis shifts and the tone becomes more rhapsodic, and it is clear that in this context the Williamite hero is also a figure for the Irish patriot, the one who speaks and acts on behalf of "*Ireland's* Sons and Patriots":

We walkt, the Crowd grew thick, we saw the Dome
Where *Ireland's* Sons and Patriots wont to come . . . ;
Three Hundred Men from all the parts Select,
To make good Laws, and Villanies detect. . . .

High o're the rest Great *Brodrick* mounts the Chair,
Mysterious was his Countenance and Air:
He Spake, the listen'ing and admiring Throng
Hung on the Charming Musick of this Tongue.
Great Storm of Wit! Full Tide of Eloquence!
Bold and Clear Spirit! Bright Fire! And finisht Sense![77]

Dudley Moore was another such patriot figure, I have been arguing, and by mounting the stage of the Theatre Royal on November 4, 1712, he, like Brodrick, served to define a new imagined community of "*Ireland's* Sons and Patriots."

In *The Early Irish Stage*, William Smith Clark states that the Irish stage's first recorded "riot" had no long-term consequence; after the indictment against the "rioters" was quashed, he suggests, the whole affair soon blew over and "the commotion which might have involved the Dublin Theatre Royal in a *cause celebre* was quickly forgotten."[78] The 1712 theatrical event, however, was not quickly forgotten. Some sixty years later, as I show in chapter eight, other patriots who wanted to use the Irish stage as a site of protest would recirculate the arguments of the Irish lords who had supported Dudley Moore in 1712, and more immediately in the 1720s and 1730s, other Protestant "Sons and Patriots" of Ireland would continue this patriot counterdrama through such transgressive practices as wearing Irish "stuff" and singing "native tunes." Because the significance of this kind of Irish Protestant counterdrama was not limited to the conscious intentions of its authors and actors, this "riot" can also be regarded as a defining moment in the struggle to create a stage for *all* the people of Ireland. In *Nation and Narration* Bhabha points out that the nation as a discursive construct is always struck in its interior by a productive ambivalence: it "reveals, in its ambivalent and vacillating representation, the ethnography of its own historicity and opens up the possibility of other narratives of the people and their difference."[79] The "riotous performances" of Ireland's Protestant "Sons and Patriots," like Molyneux's seminal *Case*, were similarly ambivalent productions, and as I demonstrate in the next two chapters, they opened up a space for the return of other kinds of Irish Catholic "players" and another kind of Irish Catholic nationalism.

CHAPTER 2

Disrupting the "Government Play"

Swift and the "Home-spun Witlings" of the 1720s and 1730s

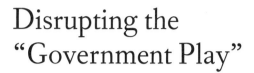

I confess, that from a Boy I always pitied poor *Arachne*, and could
never heartily love the Goddess, on Account of so *cruel and unjust a
Sentence*, which however, is fully executed upon *Us* by *England*.
                    Jonathan Swift, *A Proposal for the Universal
                    Use of Irish Manufacture* (1720)

At a theatrical benefit for Dublin's weavers at Smock Alley on April 1, 1721,
the manager and leading actor, Thomas Elrington, opened the evening's
entertainment with a poignant appeal to the audience and particularly the
"Ladies" to give up their imported fabrics and begin wearing Irish wool
"stuff."[1] In a prologue written specially for this occasion by the Dublin
schoolteacher and poet Dr. Thomas Sheridan, Elrington began:

> Great Cry and Little Wool — is now become
> The *Plague* and *Proverb* of the *Weavers-Loom.*
> No *Wooll* to work on, neither *Weft* nor *Warp*;
> Their Pockets empty, and their Stomachs sharp.
> Provok'd, in loud Complaints, to you they cry,

Ladies relieve the *Weavers,* or they dye.
Forsake your *Silks* for *Stuffs,* nor think it strange
To shift your Cloths, since you delight in Change.

Elrington, who was about to play Hamlet, was wearing "stuff "himself on this occasion, and he drew attention to this fact as he attempted to persuade the audience to follow his lead: "See, I am dress'd from Top to Toe in *Stuff,* / And by my *Troth* I think I'm fine enough." At the close of the evening's performance, the Dublin-born actor Thomas Griffith also announced that this event marked the beginning of a new theatrical "Project." In an epilogue written by Sheridan's friend, Jonathan Swift, he stated that from now on, *all* the noble heroes and heroines of the drama would be dressed in fabrics purchased in Meath Street and the Combe, streets at the heart of the Liberties, Dublin's weaving district. And he asked the audience to follow the stage court's "Fashion" whenever they came to the playhouse:

> We'll dress in *Manufactures* made at home;
> Equip our *Kings* and *Generals* at the Coomb.
> We'll Rigg from *Meath-Street, Egypt*'s haughty Queen,
> And *Anthony* shall Court her, in *Ratteen.*
> In *Blew Shalloon,* shall Hannibal be clad,
> And *Scipio* trail an *Irish Purple Plad.*
> In *Drugget* Dress, of thirty Pence a Yard,
> See *Philip*'s Son amidst his *Persian* Guard;
> And proud *Roxana,* fir'd with jealous Rage,
> With fifty Yards of *Crape,* shall sweep the Stage.
> In short, our Kings and Princesses within
> Are all resolv'd the Project to begin;
> And you, our Subjects, when you here resort,
> Must imitate the Fashion of the Court.[2]

A letter Archbishop King wrote on April 8, 1721, also suggests that these playhouse "Subjects" answered this plea. After noting the unimaginable "poverty of the kingdom" and the "intolerable" cries of the starving linen, woolen, and silk weavers, King writes: "It is true everybody bestirred themselves to get them a supply, the Dissenters, the Roman Catholics, the Deans and Chapters, the College, nay the Play-house gave a play to this purpose which raised seventy-three pounds. . . . The gentlemen and ladies did their part by clothing themselves in the manufactures of the country, I mean many of them, which has been a great help, but still short of the necessity."[3]

This kind of dress performance was repeated many times during the century. The players did not fulfill their promise of dressing all their "Kings and Princesses" in materials purchased in the Combe and Meath Street, but on many occasions they dressed casts in "Irish manufacture" and advocated the use of native-made materials in prologues and epilogues (see fig. 1). And on many occasions, too, the "gentlemen and ladies" showed up at important sites of assembly—the playhouse, Dublin Castle, church, concert and assembly halls—dressed in native fabrics. It is clear from a newspaper account that appeared in July 1784 that the practice of wearing Irish "stuff" retained its association with Swift and the theater throughout the century. After publishing a ballad satirizing the viceroy's behavior during what was arguably the most serious theatrical disturbance of the century (see chapter 8), the *Hibernian Journal* moved on to the topic of supporting the local weaving industry, which it introduced with the following anecdote:

In the year 1730, the same species of distress as that our manufactures lately complained of, predominated in the city of Dublin, but particularly in the Earl of Meath's Liberty, which if not the seat of industry must always be the mansion of wretchedness and despair. The patriot Dean Swift, who was ever the declared and faithful friend of the Weavers, while they conducted themselves with honesty and sobriety, being applied to on so melancholy an occasion, prevailed on the Managers of both Theatres, to advertise a benefit play; he writ the Prologues, and Doctor Sheridan the Epilogues, for these performances, which were attended by an infinite concourse of the country Gentlemen and Ladies, as well as of the Citizens of Dublin. The Dean himself, with the Clergy of his chapter, appeared in the pit, and were received with peculiar applause by the rest of the audience. The money collected at the exhibitions, and from many private donations sent in afterwards, amounted to a great sum, which was faithfully and judiciously distributed. The Dean mentions this relief in his usual facetious manner, in a letter to the late Lord Bolingbroke and concludes thus:— "I have done something for our poor Weavers; but till the fools of

Figure 1. "A Lady in a Fashionable Full Dress of Irish Manufacture."
The Hibernian Magazine, June 1779. By permission of the British Library. PP.6154k.

Ireland resolve to wear none but the manufactures of their own country, occasional benefactions are but a sop in the pan, and will never produce more than a hasty snack to a few, while multitudes, whom no relief can reach, are perished with their wives and children." How applicable is this truth to our present times? *Let us go and do so likewise.*[4]

The writer here, it seems, has conflated the 1721 performance with a later performance in the 1730s. On May 14, 1735, the group of breakaway performers who played at the new Rainsford Street theater in the Earl of Meath's "Liberty" revived the 1721 prologue and epilogue for a performance of *Othello*, attributing both, as this newspaper writer does, to "Dr. Swift."[5] This very inaccuracy, though, testifies to the strength of association in the popular mind between Swift and the practice of wearing Irish "manufacture." Whenever this issue was raised, either in discourse or in practice after 1721, the Dean, as it were, "appeared in the pit."

In this chapter I argue that this kind of Irish "stuff" trope takes its meaning from the discourse and practice of Irish Protestant nationalism, and I suggest, moreover, that this figure, as it was reiterated in performance and discourse, represented a widening of the Irish imagined community that had sprung into existence in reaction to English oppression in the first decades of the century. In her recent study of Irish dress, Mairead Dunlevy argues that "the promotion by the society based around Dublin Castle of 'Irish costumes' in native fabrics had no real 'national' significance as the aristocracy was principally interested in it as fancy dress," and she goes on to argue that for a distinctly Irish national dress we have to wait until the cultural revival at the end of the nineteenth century when organizations like the Gaelic Athletic Association (1884) and the Gaelic League (1893) began to devise a national costume based on such traditional Celtic garments as the *brat* and *léine*.[6] This, however, is to ignore the productive political effect of Irish Protestant alienation in the face of England's continued refusal to meet their demands for political and economic equality. In another letter written around this time, Archbishop King wrote: "If the English in Ireland be treated as Englishmen, they will be Englishmen still in their hearts and inclinations, but if they be oppressed, they will turn Irish, for fellowship in suffering begets love and unites interest."[7] The cross-dressed figure that began to appear in the playhouse and other venues in the 1720s and 1730 testified to this Irish "turn" among Protestant patriots; by its appearance, I argue, it gestured at a theater and an imagined community that went beyond the (English) Pale.

The wearing of native fabrics acquired a political as well as an economic meaning in the late—seventeenth century through its association with Molyneux's *The Case of Ireland's being Bound by Acts of Parliament, Stated.* The English Parliament passed the Woolen Act immediately after it rejected Molyneux's plea for parliamentary autonomy, and supporters of the bill made it very clear that they were bent on reducing Ireland to the status of a colony—a country that supplied raw materials to the motherland and depended on her for manufactured goods. When the Irish Commons began passing resolutions to encourage the use and wearing of Irish manufacture in the first decade of the century, then, their actions were an implicit form of anticolonial as well as economic resistance, and such resolutions themselves became a way of showcasing Irish grievances. In the same 1703–4 session that the Irish Commons asked for either "full enjoyment of our constitution" or a union, for example, they also passed a resolution advocating the use of Irish manufacture, and they pointedly mentioned the "discouragement of exportation" and the suffering of the poor of Ireland:

> That by reason of the great decay of trade and discouragement of exportation of the manufactures of this Kingdom, many poor tradesmen are reduced to extreme want and beggary.
>
> That it will greatly conduce to the relief of the said poor, and to the good of this Kingdom that inhabitants thereof should use none others than the manufacturing of this Kingdom in their apparel, and the furniture of their houses.[8]

Similar resolutions were passed again in the House in 1705 and 1707,[9] and as can be seen from a comment made by Swift in 1711, additional attempts by the English Parliament to restrict Ireland's manufacturing industry worked to further consolidate the Protestants of Ireland into an oppositional "Irish" political faction. In 1711 the English Commons proposed adding a new duty on Irish yarn, but, as Swift notes, the bill failed because of the lobbying that he and his "Irish" friends did in London. "All the Irish in town were there to consult upon preventing a bill for levying a duty on Irish yarn," Swift writes, "so we talked a while, and then all went to the lobby of the House of Commons, to solicit our friends, and the Duke [of Ormond] came among the rest; and Lord Anglesea solicited admirably, and I did wonders."[10]

If some of these "Irish" began advocating the wearing of native fabrics again in the 1720s, it was also because of the deterioration of the economic and political state of Ireland at that time. As James Kelly points out, the economic difficulties that led Swift to write his Irish tracts began toward the end of 1710 with poor harvests and the collapse of prices, and these difficulties grew over the next ten years.[11] By summer 1718 Bishop Nicolson of Derry was reporting, "[I] never beheld (even in Picardy, Westphalia or Scotland) such dismal marks of hunger and want as appeared in the countenances of most of the poor creatures that I met with on the road [to Derry]," and by 1720–21 conditions in the capital were so bad that Archbishop King was calculating that at least half of Dublin's population needed charity if they were to avoid starvation.[12] Tensions were further exacerbated by the outbreak of a new parliamentary row. In 1717 the English House of Lords overturned a decree by the Irish House of Lords in a legal dispute over land (the *Sherlock* v. *Annesley* case), thus raising once again the whole question of the legislative and judicial powers of the Irish Parliament, and as this legal case dragged on for the next three years, patriot sentiment ran high in Ireland. Irish peers, including Archbishop King and Viscount Molesworth, publicly reiterated Molyneux's arguments for Irish parliamentary and judicial independence,[13] and the Protestant people at large supported them. When the dispute began in 1717, Bishop Evans of Meath (an Englishman) noted, "[A]mong the common people (protestants I mean) from the least upwards hardly one of them but looks upon England to be their worst enemy, putting all hardships upon them, in respect of trade, etc,"[14] and in 1719 Bishop Nicolson of Derry wrote, "Mr Molyneux's book, burnt by the English House of Commons in 1698 is reprinted here and in everybodies hand."[15] Feelings were further enflamed by the English Parliament's passage of the so-called Declaratory Act (6 George 1, 1720), legislation that stated unequivocally that the king and Parliament of Great Britain alone had the power to make "Laws and Statutes . . . to bind the kingdom and People of Ireland."[16] Writing to Molesworth in May 1720, Archbishop King noted "the universal disaffection of all people" but particularly "the Whigs . . . after this enslaving act."[17]

When Swift wrote his *Proposal for the Universal Use of Irish Manufacture* two months after the passage of this "enslaving act," it was to articulate this disaffection and to outline a performative strategy, revolving around the practice of wearing Irish textiles, that would bring it into view. In a characteristically evasive move, however, Swift begins his tract by disavowing politics in favor of economics, and he suggests that the Irish Parliament should do the same; instead of amusing themselves with "great Refinements in *Politicks* and *Divinity*," politicians should concern themselves "a little, with the *State of the Nation*."[18] His proposal to the people of Ireland that they wear only their own manufacture and resolve "never to appear with one single *Shred* that comes from *England*" (16) also appears consistent with this modest economic emphasis, as does his appeal (which he couches in very loyalist terms) that both men and women in Ireland celebrate the upcoming royal birthday wearing Irish-made fabrics. "I hope, and believe," Swift writes, "nothing could please his Majesty better than to hear that his loyal Subjects, of both Sexes, in this Kingdom, celebrated his *Birth-Day* (now approaching) *universally* clad in their own Manufacture" (16).

But this text, and by implication the practice it advocates, also opens itself to a more subversive political meaning. Encoded in the emboldened letters of this pamphlet's full title—"A PROPOSAL For the universal Use OF IRISH MANUFACTURE, IN Cloaths and Furniture of Houses, Etc. UTTERLY REJECTING AND RENOUNCING Everything wearable that comes from ENGLAND"—is the notion that the wearing of Irish manufacture signifies a broader rejection of England itself. And this association gains strength from other hostile remarks that Swift scatters through the pamphlet itself—his criticism, for example, of English viceroys who were apt "from their *high* Elevation, to look *down* upon this Kingdom, as if it had been one of their *Colonies* of *Out-casts* in *America*" (21); his questioning (reminiscent of Molyneux) of whether men are bound in conscience to obey a law that "bind[s] Men without their Consent" (19); and his sarcastic enumeration of the wrongs "POOR England *suffers by Impositions from* Ireland" (18–19). By suggesting that the Irish elite appear at an official birthday celebration in Irish manufacture, Swift was also tacitly urging his compatriots to flaunt their political disaffection in the face of the London-appointed administration: their act would be another disavowal of "Everything . . . that comes from England."

If the wearing of Irish manufacture was about English disaffiliation, however, it was also about Irish affiliation, as Swift demonstrates when he works the allegorical tale of Arachne and Pallas Athene into the center of his tract, and this affiliation his writing suggests, was not just with the Protestant people of Ireland. In many ways, the Arachne–Pallas Athene story is a reworking of the "Injured Lady"–"Gentleman" allegory in Swift's earliest (and by the 1720s still unpublished) tract, *The Story of the*

Injured Lady (1707). In his 1707 tract Swift depicts the Irish-English political relationship as one of seduction and betrayal. An "unkind, inconstant Man" (England) has taken possession of the "Lady" (Ireland) "half by Force, and half by Consent," and then has proceeded "to shew his Authority, and to act like a Conqueror" after he had seduced her.[19] In what could be seen as the germ of his *Proposal for the Universal Use of Irish Manufacture*, Swift also uses clothing as a metaphor for Ireland's social and economic deprivation. "They that see me now," the "Lady" laments, "will hardly allow me ever to have had any great Share of Beauty; for besides being so much altered, I go always mobbed and in an Undress, as well out of Neglect, as indeed for want of Cloaths to appear in" (4).

In his *Proposal* written thirteen years later, the respective countries are now represented by a pair of women (a goddess and a mortal), not by a pair of lovers, but it soon becomes clear that the relationship is no less oppressive. For daring to compete with her in her spinning and weaving, Pallas Athene transforms Arachne, the young virgin, into a spider and enjoins her "to *spin* and *weave* for ever, *out of her own Bowels*, and *in a very narrow Compass*" (18), a state of degradation and misery that she shares with the "Injured Lady" who was also metamorphosed into a lowly "Sempstress" (8) at the end of her narrative. There is no explicit link made between the practice of wearing Irish fabrics that Swift advocates and this unfortunate female figure, but because the concept of weaving and clothing is central to both, the imaginative connection is clear. To wear native fabrics is to show compassion and empathy for the sufferings of Arachne/Ireland and to join in the condemnation of Pallas/England as Swift does himself when he writes: "I confess, that from a Boy I always pitied poor *Arachne*, and could never heartily love the Goddess, on Account of so *cruel and unjust a Sentence*, which however, is fully executed upon *Us* by *England*, with further Additions of *Rigor* and *Severity*. For the greater Part of *our Bowels and Vitals* is extracted, without allowing us the Liberty of *spinning* and *weaving* them" (18).

But who was the "Us" referred to in this sentence? What imagined community did "poor Arachne" signify? One obvious referent for the young weaver who suffers at the hands of a more powerful rival weaver was, undoubtedly, the still predominantly Protestant weaving community of the Liberties, a community that was suffering great hardship in the 1720s. Carole Fabricant has also persuasively shown that Swift was deeply concerned about the plight of the working poor who lived in the neighborhood of St. Patrick's Cathedral, championing their cause on more than one occasion.[20] But in his *Proposal* Swift also sympathizes with the mostly Catholic Irish population outside Dublin who were the victims of an inhumane landlord class, and it is this other Catholic population that was also, by extension, imaginatively represented by the practice of wearing Irish "stuff." "Country Landlords," he argues, "by unmeasurable *screwing* and *racking* their Tenants all over the Kingdom, have already reduced the miserable *People* to a *worse Condition* than the *Peasants* in *France,* or the *Vassals* in *Germany* and *Poland,*" and he goes on to state: "Whoever travels this Country, and observes the *Face* of Nature, or the *Faces,* and Habits, and Dwelling of the *Natives,* will hardly think himself in a Land where either *Law, Religion,* or *common Humanity* is professed" (21). In her dehumanized and impoverished state, "poor Arachne," and the figure dressed in Irish textiles who represents her, recalls these impoverished and wretched "Natives." In proposing the use of Irish manufacture, Swift imaginatively reaches outside the bounds of Dublin and its largely Protestant community, going beyond the Pale in both the historic and colloquial senses of the phrase.

It was undoubtedly because the *Proposal* signified on this double political register that it met with such a hostile reception by the government and its supporters. Shortly after its publication, the tract was presented to the Grand Juries of the City and County of Dublin as "false, scandalous, and seditious," and Chief Justice Whitshed ordered Swift's printer, Edward Waters, to be prosecuted. Whitshed also made it clear that he was determined to make an example of someone for this piece of audacity; when the jury returned a verdict of not guilty in the Waters case, Whitshed sent it back to be deliberated again, and after this happened nine times (the jury kept coming up with a verdict in the printer's favor), he deferred the case until the next year.[21] To cite the pro-government tract *A Defence of English Commodities Being an Answer to the Proposal For the Universal Use of Irish Manufactures* (1720), the author of the *Proposal* had clearly "awakened the Lion, and alarmed him with the Danger of his Whelps from *Ireland.*"[22]

Like the rebellious "puppies" of 1712, however, these "Whelps" did not give up their struggle with the British lion but instead transferred it to the playhouse; the legal case involving Waters was still undecided in April 1721 when Swift, with the help of Dr. Thomas Sheridan and the Smock Alley players, launched another campaign to wear Irish "stuff" from the stage of the Theatre Royal. At the time they launched this campaign, the administration and its supporters were also using the Theatre Royal to stage a new kind of neocolonial drama, the government play, and this context gave their Irish "stuff" performance an additional subversive valence.

Explaining the concept "government play" to a contemporary English readership who would have been unfamiliar with the term, Robert Hitchcock noted that "the manager of the theatre-royal in Dublin receives such a certain sum annually from government for the performing of plays on particular nights, such as the King and Queen's birth-day, his Majesty's accession, etc," and on such occasions, the "ladies are always complimented with the freedom of the boxes." Hitchcock also implied that these "government plays" or "government nights" had been a feature of the professional theater in Ireland since its founding in the mid-seventeenth century:

> [F]rom the earliest time they were considered as the most fashionable nights in the season, and consequently honoured with the presence of the lord lieutenant, or lord justices, for the time being; and so essentially necessary was the chief governor's appearance deemed on such occasions, that November 4th, 1714, the anniversary of King William the Third's birth-day, the tragedy of Tamerlane always appointed for that evening, was, by command, not to begin till an entertainment given by the lord mayor and city, at the tholsel, to the lord lieutenant, nobility, and gentry was over, that they might have time to repair from thence to the theatre.[23]

In *The Early Irish Stage,* however, Clark suggests that the government play is more properly understood as an invention of government in the second decade of the eighteenth century, and this reading is the more convincing one. As Clark points out, appearances by the Dublin Castle administration at the playhouse on holiday occasions greatly increased after 1713, and the first record of yearly payments to the theater dates from the early 1720s, an indication that the practice of subsidizing the theater began around this time.[24] That the government would formally institute such rituals at this time also makes sense in terms of the general emphasis that spectacle and ritual by the new Hanoverian rulers,[25] an emphasis that, as Hitchcock tacitly suggests when he alludes to the November 4 *Tamerlane* performance, was deemed "essentially necessary" in Ireland because of recent Irish patriot activity.

In *Imperial Eyes* Mary Louise Pratt points out that as European imperial powers (including Britain) came under pressure from colonial subjects abroad and from Enlightenment thinkers at home, they increasingly sought to represent their relationship with their overseas colonial subjects as one of benevolence and exchange. An anticonquest narrative, she notes, began to displace a conquest narrative in the representation of the colonial encounter, which was now idealized into "a drama of reciprocity."[26] A similar development, I suggest, occurred in Ireland in response to the Irish Protestant patriot critique of the first two decades of the century. To refute Swift's negative characterization of the state of Arachne/Ireland in his 1720 *Proposal*, for example, the writer of *A Defence of English Commodities* had emphasized the transformative and enriching effects of England's relationship with Ireland:

> They [the Irish] have been Metamorphosed, but into what? Not Spiders, but Men; they have been transformed from Savages into reasonable Creatures, and delivered from a State of Nature and Barbarism, and endowed with Civility and Humanity.
>
> *England* has adorned them with her Habits, Language and Manners, and let them into all the Benefits and Privileges of her Laws, Policy, and Government; and some of them shine at this Day, in the highest Places of Honour and Trust under her Authority.[27]

In this passage, the writer is specifically referring to England's impact on the native Irish, but a similar desire to demonstrate the benevolence and thus legitimacy of English rule was behind the cycle of entertainment that the government began providing for the Protestant gentry during their "Winter Season." From November to June every year, wealthy Protestant landowning families flocked into Dublin to take up their seats in Parliament, to attend Trinity College, and to do their business in the law courts or commercial establishments.[28] By entertaining this gentry with levees and balls at Dublin Castle, by attending their churches, by parading with them through the street, and by appearing with them at the Theatre Royal — events that occurred particularly on official holidays — the new (or returning) viceroy gave visible demonstrations of his and the London government's continued commitment to this elite's interest while also providing the gentry themselves with an opportunity to reaffirm publicly their loyalty and commitment to the crown. During the daylong celebration on the anniversary of the coronation of George II on October 11, 1733, for example, the "Nobility" was wined, dined, and entertained by the duke of Dorset in return for publicly demonstrating their support for the administration. As the following newspaper account reveals, the whole day was a drawn-out, elaborate "drama of reciprocity."

Thursday last being the Anniversary of their Majesty's Coronation, the great Guns were fired at the Barracks, and answered by Vollies from the Regiments in garrison, which were drawn out upon Oxmantown Green. At noon, there was a very numerous appearance of the Nobility and other Persons of Distinction at the Castle, to compliment his Grace the Lord Lieutenant on that occasion; after which his Grace, attended by the Guard of Battle-Axes and a Squadron of Horse, made a Tour around St. Stephen's Green. In the evening were Bonfires, Illuminations, and all other demonstrations of Joy. A Play was given by his Grace, for the Entertainment of the Ladies, and after the Play a Ball, and a magnificent Collation at the Castle.[29]

The common people of Dublin, too, were increasingly the object of displays of benevolence and paternalist largess, a sign that the government was increasingly concerned with the possibility of trouble from this section of the Irish population. On the occasion of the king's birthday on October 30, 1733, for example, the viceroy and "Nobility" observed the same rituals as they had on October 11, but after they withdrew into the castle for the evening ball, it was reported that "five roasted Sirloins of Beef, weighing 48 pounds each, eight Turkey Cocks, and 30 Sixpenny Loaves[,] . . . two Barrels of Ale and a Hogshead of Wine" were served up to the "Soldiers on Guard" on "long Tables in the Castle Yard"; while "several Hogsheads of Wine play'd from a Fountain made for that Purpose, amongst the Populace, who catch'd it, and drank their Majesties and the Royal Family's Health, with loud Huzzas and Acclamations of Joy." [30] Such dispensations of food and drink, it could be argued, were designed to portray the ruling elite (English or Irish Protestant) as anticonquerors and to elicit public expressions of gratitude and loyalty from the Irish "Populace" that would have the function of legitimating government.

The correspondence of Mary Delany (or Mary Pendarves, as she was then) also allows us to see the careful planning that went into such official entertainments. In a letter to her brother, Mary gives the following account of a ball that she recently attended at Dublin Castle on the anniversary of Queen Caroline's birthday, March 1, 1731.

The ball was in the old beef-eaters hall, a room that holds seven hundred people seated, it was well it did, for never did I behold a greater crowd. We were all placed in rows one above another, so much raised that the last *row almost touched the ceiling!* The gentlemen say we

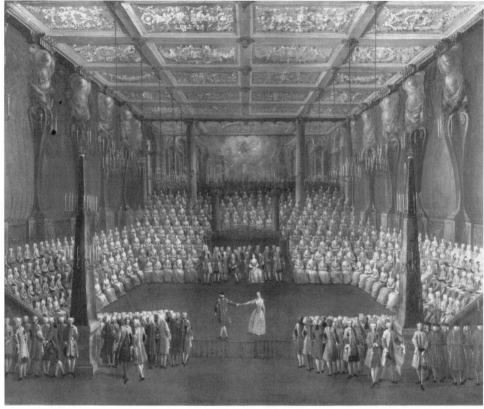

Figure 2. *State Ball at Dublin Castle, 1731*. Painted by William van der Hagen.
By permission of L. G. Stopford Sackville. Photograph courtesy of the Photographic Survey,
Courtauld Institute of Art.

looked very handsome, and compared us to Cupid's paradise in the
puppet-show. At eleven o'clock minuets were finished, and the Duchess
went to the basset table.[31]

William Van der Hagen's painting of the state ball that took place at Dublin
Castle on November 4, 1731, also makes apparent the ideological significance of this kind of seating arrangement (fig. 2). In Van der Hagen's picture, the spectacle of the seated women is arranged for the benefit of Irish
gentlemen who are standing in the foreground of the scene. These gentlemen spectators, like the seated ladies themselves, are ostensibly watching a
couple joining hands gracefully on the dance floor in the foreground. But

what the gentlemen are also observing—and because of its magnitude alone, this is clearly the more impressive and striking scene—is the political coupling that forms the background to this dance. Seated at the heart of this "Cupid's paradise" in the midst of all these beautifully dressed Irish ladies is the English viceregal couple (the duke and duchess of Dorset) and their entourage, so that the whole seating arrangement functions as a kind of masque that embodies the Anglo-Irish relationship as a happy union between an Irish elite and an English administration.

The "Play" that His Grace gave "for the Entertainment of the Ladies" (the government play) at the playhouse on such holidays nights was no less carefully arranged to produce an image of a happily united and radiant Anglo-Irish governing body, though the spectators at this show were the less privileged. By providing the boxes "free to the Ladies," the administration always ensured that the viceroy would sit in public in the company of a radiant "*Hibernia*," and as Theophilus Cibber reveals in a prologue he spoke at his benefit performance at Smock Alley in 1743, this scene could "awe and charm" humbler spectators like himself:

> When I behold such radiant Circles there,
> Enrich'd with all that's Good, or Wise, or Fair;
> While Wit, and Beauty, amiably unite
> I'm aw'd, I'm charm'd, and dazzled with the Sight;
> And own, no Kingdom, with *Hibernia* vies,
> For Elegance of Taste, and brightest Eyes.[32]

Viceregal command performances provided a similar opportunity for the administration to display its love affair with "*Hibernia*" in front of the people, as on such occasions the elite again turned up at the theater in all their splendor. Indeed, the substantial increase in the number of such performances in the second quarter of the century—the duke of Dorset, for instance, commanded approximately thirty performances during his term in office, and the duke of Devonshire commanded some fifty-four performances[33]—is explicable in terms of this political desire; the command performances allowed the administration to continue its political wooing of the Irish "people," both elite and nonelite. Speaking, for example, of the earl of Harcourt who arrived in 1772, Hitchcock writes, "At the commencement of his vice regency, he used every means to render himself popular, and amongst others, did not neglect that, of *courting it* at the theatre, which he visited once a week for some time."[34]

On at least some occasions the drama would have worked to complement these government plays or command performances, as can be illustrated by the plays of Charles Shadwell, the most important playwright at Smock Alley in the years immediately before Swift and Sheridan's 1721 staging. Shadwell was the son of the English poet laureate Thomas Shadwell, and he had moved to Ireland in 1713. By the end of his life he also consciously represented himself as an Irishman and as a supporter of the Irish Protestant nationalist cause; in a song he wrote in 1724, for example, he praised "the brave Drapier" for his achievement in fighting Wood's Halfpence and he toasted "The Protestant Int'rest Abroad and at Home / Our Friends in this City, and those on the *Comb*."[35] When he wrote for the Dublin stage between 1715 and 1719, however, he was a government employee—according to a notice in a Dublin newspaper, he operated an "Office of Assurance for the Support of Widows and Orphans" "by her Majesty's authority"[36]—and all the indications are that he was angling at this time for some additional kind of government-sponsored position in the theater. The 1720 tract, *A Letter of Advice to a Young Poet*, which alludes to Shadwell's recently published anthology of plays, sarcastically mentions "a certain Gentleman" who has "great Designs, to serve the Publick in the way of their Diversions . . . if he can obtain some *Concordatum Money*, or *Yearly Sallery*, and handsome *Contributions*," and this reference, as well as the statement that this gentleman had "travell'd full many a League, by Sea and Land, for this his profound Knowledge," suggests Shadwell.[37]

The politics of Shadwell's two most explicitly Irish plays—*Irish Hospitality; or Virtue Rewarded* (1717–18) and *Rotherick O'Connor, King of Connaught: or the Distress'd Princess* (1719–20)—also suggest that the playwright was proposing himself for an official position in the playhouse. The comedy *Irish Hospitality* was performed during a government night at the beginning of the politically troubled 1717–18 season, and in the prologue to this play Shadwell reminds the viceroy (Bolton) of the potential usefulness of the theater to an imperial state. He couches this reminder, however, in strictly moral terms. In "Great *Augustus Caesar's* joyful Days," he points out, the poet and the player worked together to teach "the *Roman* Youth" to hate "the Villain" and adore "the Truth," and he goes on to suggest that with adequate government patronage and himself as poet-playwright, the Irish stage could fulfill a similar pedagogical purpose in the present day:

We have a *Caesar* great as *Rome* could boast,
Whose Name is echo'd on each distant Coast

He has the Fate of *Europe* in his Hand,
He calls to Peace, and Kings obey Command.

. . . .

Were but the Poet, and the Player, then,
As great Performers as the *Roman* Men,
The Muses would resume this Land again.
Our Author has presum'd to break the Way,
And we present to-Night a Town-born Play.
He aims to mix Good-Nature with Delight,
And would, with Zeal, to virtuous Deeds incite.[38]

In the play itself, Shadwell also maintains this moral veneer as he dramatizes the story of the reforming Irish landlord Sir Patrick Worthy who
lives on his estate in Fingall (an area north of Dublin). At the beginning
of the play, Sir Patrick's well-being and that of his household and tenants
are threatened by a number of vice-ridden characters from among the
ranks of the gentry: Squire Clumsy, his beer-swigging brother; Lady Peevish, his superstitious sister; Sir Jowler Kennel, his sports-loving neighbor;
Sir Wou'd-be-Generous, another neighbor who attempts to murder Sir
Patrick out of jealousy; and (most important from the point of plot) his
own Oxford-educated son, Charles Worthy, who plans to seduce Winnifred Dermot, the daughter of one of Sir Patrick's native Irish tenants. By
the last act all these characters have come under the influence of the virtuous Sir Patrick, and in the kind of happy ending that is typical of sentimental comedy, all these characters mend their ways.

In creating a sentimental resolution for the Charles Worthy–Winnifred
Dermot seduction plot, however, Shadwell also transforms the Irish Protestant patriot's narrative of the "Injur'd [Irish] Lady" into a romance, and
by painting a rosy representation of the relationship between a contemporary Irish landlord and his native Irish tenants, he also implicitly puts himself on the side of the government and those who supported the political
and economic status quo. As we have seen in the discussion of William
Philips's *St. Stephen's Green,* idealized descriptions of Irish life could take
on a patriotic valence when they were used specifically to counter anti-Irish
prejudice. By the end of the second decade of the century, however, it was
mainly defenders of the English interest in Ireland who sought to minimize
the gravity of the economic condition of Ireland, while those on the Irish
patriot side increasingly voiced their concern about the evils of absentee
landlords and the dire suffering of the rural and urban poor. In 1721, for

example, Archbishop King (like Swift in his *Proposal*) related the proliferation of beggars in the capital to "the griping landlords who grind the faces
of the poor," but the vehemently antinationalist Englishman, Bishop Evans,
suggested that the suffering of the poor could be attributed to their own
laziness and the ineptness of city and church officials in distributing the
funds collected for charity. "Archbishop King," Evans wrote dismissively,
"may (possibly) much exceed in his account of the poor."[39]

There is no suggestion in this play that the native Irish family, the
Dermots, are idle, but there is an equally misleading portrayal of the
contentment and stability of Irish peasant life. "Your Father has been an
industrious Tenant, and Sobriety is the distinguishing Virtue of all thy
Brothers," Sir Patrick tells Winnifred when we first meet her (360), and
the glimpses we catch of these tenants' lives suggests that they have been
rewarded with prosperity for their industry. A scene set in "Dermot's
Cabbin" (the first recorded use of a native Irish setting on the Dublin
stage) shows Winnifred's mother, Shela Dermot, preoccupied with her
tasks of baking and bringing the plowmen their suppers (388–89), and
this native Irishwoman's only cause for complaint is that her husband
has not yet "let the Wheat be thresh'd out"(388) and that her daughter
still has "three Pound of the last Parcel of Wool to spin off" (389). The
end of this play, then, works to reinforce the image of a happy peasantry
and a benign ruling class. When Sir Patrick discovers his son's seduction
plans, he pretends he is going to marry Winnifred himself and has her
dressed in his daughter's jewels and finery (407), and this display of the
native Irishwoman's beauty has the desired effect of making Charles re-
pent his rakish ways and propose marriage. Whereas Swift's Irish "Lady"
is abandoned and neglected by her cruel English "Gentleman," Shadwell's Winnifred Dermot achieves happiness and wealth through her alliance with her gentleman from over the water (Charles has recently arrived in Ireland from Oxford).

In the prologue to *Rotherick O'Connor* Shadwell also overtly states that
this play has the purpose of reinventing English hegemony in Ireland. By
reminding his audience of the horrors of life under Gaelic rule and law, he
suggests, he will teach them a better appreciation and acceptance of the
present system of English government and a deeper contempt for old Irish
customs and laws:

Our Author tries by different Ways to please
And shews you Kings that never cross'd the Seas

He brings to View, Five Hundred years ago,
Heroes nurs'd up in Slaughter, Blood and Woe:
And Kings that Rul'd by Arbitrary Sway
Their slavish Subjects, born but to Obey
When *Brehon*-Laws cou'd reach the Subject's Life
And None, but Great Ones, dare support the Strife.

. . . .

Learn then, from those unhappy Days of Yore,
To scorn and hate an Arbitrary Power.
To Praise and Love those Laws that make you Free;
And are the Bulworks of your Liberty.
Adore the Prince who rules by milder Sway,
And, like good Subjects, lawfully Obey.[40]

As Wheatley notes, one of Shadwell's sources for this negative view of Irish kings and Irish law was undoubtedly Richard Cox's *Hibernia Anglicana* (1689–90), a history that "explicitly defends the Norman conquest as beginning the civilization of Ireland."[41] But the phrase "Five Hundred years" and the argument of the play itself suggest that the play also was a response to Molyneux's *Case,* the work that had become the source of the patriot defense in the ongoing dispute between the Irish and English lords. Molyneux had argued that he was defending the rights and liberties of a five-hundred-year-old "Nation" (88), and in 1719, as we have seen, the reprinted version of the *Case* was "in everybodies hand"; according to another contemporary observer, the arguments in this work were also being cited by Irishmen at this time as being "altogether unanswerable."[42] *Rotherick O'Connor* attempts, then, to explode this confidence in Molyneux's arguments by its counternarrative of the violent events surrounding the marriage of Eva and Strongbow and the first coming of the English (in reality, the Anglo-Normans) to Ireland in the twelfth century.

Molyneux argues in his *Case* that the native Irish civil and religious leaders *voluntarily* submitted to Anglo rule, and he also specifically lists "Rotherick O'Connor, King of Connaught, and Monarch as it were of the whole Ireland" among the native Irish kings who came to Dublin to swear loyalty when Henry came to Ireland in 1172 (28). This lack of conflict between the Irish rulers and the Anglo-Normans is also central to Molyneux's argument that this was no conquest and, consequently, that there was no difference in political status between England and Ireland:

For here we have an Intire and Voluntary Submission of the Ecclesiastical and Civil States of *Ireland*, to King Henry II without the least Hostile Stroke on any side; We hear not in any of the Chronicles of any Violence on either Side, all was Transacted with the greatest Quiet, Tranquility, and Freedom imaginable. I doubt not but the Barbarous People of the Island at that time were struck with Fear and Terror of King *Hen*. II's Powerful Force which he brought with him; but still their Easie and Voluntary Submissions Exempts them from the Consequents of an *Hostile Conquest*, whatever they are: where there is no Opposition, *such a Conquest* can take no place. (30–31)

The marriage between Eva and Strongbow is invoked in the *Case* to the same political end. In countering the argument that Ireland was a conquered country, Molyneux points to "the Stipulations between *Mac-Morrogh* [the king of Leinster] and the [Anglo-Norman] Adventurers, and especially between him and *Strongbow*, who was to succeed him in his Principality" (32–33), stipulations that included a marriage "Compact" with the king of Leinster's eldest daughter (27), Eva.

The play *Rotherick O'Connor* at first seems to acknowledge this patriot line of argument. As Strongbow berates the king of Leinster for his delay in fulfilling his end of the marriage bargain, for example, he specifically alludes to their "sacred Contract":

How can you fulfil your sacred Contract?
'Tis like you have forgot, that when you die
Your Kingdom must descend to me, and that
Your Daughter *Eva* was to be my Wife? (235–36)

At many other points, similarly, this play allows patriot sentiment to be aired. In response to Regan's expression of admiration for the greatness of Strongbow and the "Warlike Race of Men" who accompany him, for example, Eva articulates the contemporary Irish patriot's suspicion of English intervention:

When they have conquer'd all our Enemies,
Perhaps they'll then attack my Father's Friends,
And so, in Time, make Slaves of all this Island. (223)

And when Regan expresses his belief that Strongbow and his men belong to a superior civilization—"Their Country seems more civiliz'd than ours; / With Arts and Sciences they pollish all / The rude, the wild ungovernable Crew" (223)—Eva responds with an Irish patriot's pride:

> Regan, your Zeal for Strangers knows no Bounds;
> You have forgot you were in *Ireland* born
> Where pure Religion, by *St Patrick* taught
> Is still kept up with a becoming Zeal:
> Here we are govern'd by Nature's Dictates,
> Not by dissembling Art; which teaches Men
> To act quite opposite to what they think. (223)

Like *Irish Hospitality*, however, this play admits a patriot line of argument only to more effectively discredit it, and it does this by suggesting that in the last analysis the Anglo-Normans achieved their power in Ireland through war and conquest rather than "Compact." In the last act, when the conniving and cowardly archbishop of Tuam declares that the Catholic church will henceforth support Strongbow's "Right" to govern on whatever principle he wishes, the Anglo-Norman responds: "The Right of Conquest is the Right I own" (279). And in direct contradiction to Molyneux's argument that there was not "the least Hostile Stroke on any side," the Anglo-Normans in this play fight and kill two of the most important leaders on the native Irish side, Eva's Irish lover Regan and Rotherick O'Connor himself. The exchange between Strongbow and O'Connor, as the native Irish king lays dying, also leaves little doubt that this is a conquest; the Anglo-Norman overtly proclaims his status as undefeated conqueror, and the native Irish king is made to acknowledge his rival's victory:

> STRONGBOW: Well have you fought, but Death, at last's your Fate,
> None ever conquer'd yet the Earl of *Chepstow*.
> ROTHERICK: Thous has o'erpower'd me, and I must die. (287)

It is this kind of acknowledgment of English superior power that is also elicited from the audience at the end of this play as Strongbow encourages Eva to accept his marriage proposal. When she asks how she might reward him for being "the Protector of my Honour, " Strongbow replies:

Comply with my Request, and crown my Love;
Be a Parent to your sinking People,
Obey your Father, own yourself my Wife,
And let us to this Isle give lasting Peace. (288)

Peace between England and Ireland, this ending suggests, will be achieved when the Irish elite learn to "Comply," "Obey," and play a dependent (feminized) role.[43]

Thus when Swift and Sheridan reopened their "wear Irish stuff" campaign on the stage of Smock Alley the season after *Rotherick O'Connor* was performed, they delivered a message that ran directly counter to Shadwell's pedagogy and to the pedagogy of the government play. By giving voice to the complaints of the starving weavers and by conjuring up images of their "Stomachs sharp," they brought "poor Arachne" back into the public domain, providing a stark reminder of the poverty and misery that existed not only in the densely crowded streets of the Liberties but also in the cabins and cottages of rural Ireland. And by urging the audience to purchase their dress fabrics at Meath Street and the Combe, they implicitly encouraged the Irish elite to cast off their assigned dependent role and demonstrate Irish economic and political self-sufficiency.

Swift's suggestion that audience members imitate the native Irish fashion of the theatrical "Court" also carried with it the implicit suggestion that they reject the fashion set by the Dublin Castle court, and this suggestion acquired an additional subversive valence given the historic effort by successive Dublin Castle governors and their administrations to impose English dress and other cultural habits on the Irish people. In 1537 "An Act for the English Order, Habit and Language" explicitly forbade not only the use of the Irish language but also the wearing of Irish traditional dress and Irish hairstyles in an effort (as the drafter of this law straightforwardly admits) to erase the politically dangerous spectacle of Irish "diversity":

[There is] nothing which doth more contain and keep many of the [the king's] subjects of this his said land in a certain savage and wild kind and manner of living than the diversity that is betwixt them in tongue, language, order and habit, which by the eye deceiveth the multitude, and persuadeth unto them that they be as it were of sundry sorts, or rather of sundry countries, where indeed they should be wholly together one body, whereof his Highness is the only head under God. . . . Wherefore be it enacted . . . that no person or persons the King's subjects within this land . . . shall be shorn or shaven above the ears, or use the wearing of hair upon their heads, like unto long locks called "glibes". . . and that no person or persons . . . shall use or wear any mantles, coat or hood made after the Irish fashion.[44]

When the viceroy, Sir John Perrot, insisted in 1585 that Tirlough Luineach (O'Neill) and other Irish chiefs cast off their Irish robes and wear English clothing before they appeared before the Parliament that was then held in Dublin Castle, it was also undoubtedly because he wished to eliminate the spectacle of Irish cultural and political difference, and the reluctance of the Irish chiefs to wear these clothes also suggests that they recognized the ideological implications should they do so. A contemporary observer noted that English dress was "embraced like fetters" by the Irish leaders, and he remarked: "It is to be observed in the proud condition of the Irish, that they disdain to sort themselves in fashion unto us, which in their opinion would more plainly manifest our conquest over them."[45] The eighteenth-century Dublin stage also continued to facilitate this imposition of "English Order, Habit and Language" by embedding these impositions in dramas of reciprocity. At the end of Sir Robert Howard's *The Committee; or the Faithful Irishman* (1662), for example, the native Irishman, Teague, exchanges his traditional Irish wool mantle for a new suit of livery, and at the end of *Irish Hospitality*, Winnifred Dermot exchanges her humble dress for jewels and finery. In both cases this dress transformation is represented as a vast improvement in their condition, a fitting reward for virtue and loyalty. In effect, however, it involves entering into new conditions of subordination, and the power relation between the native Irish and the Anglo subject remains unchanged. Teague becomes a servant and Winnifred a wife; in the eighteenth century both of these kinds of subjects existed in a condition of dependency.

Although they were not advocating a return to a specifically Gaelic style of dress, Sheridan and Swift broke with this colonial legal and dramatic tradition and implicitly inserted themselves into the native Irish tradition of political dissent when they encouraged the Smock Alley audience to adopt the "stuff" of Meath Street and the Combe rather than the silks of Dublin Castle. By the eighteenth century the great mass of the Irish people had adopted English dress; the coat, waistcoat, and breeches, for example, were accepted by all classes of men, and poorer Irishwomen wore dresses and petticoats modeled on English fashions. However, the quality, expense, and color of the fabric worn still distinguished the dress of the rich and the poor, and as this economic distinction in Ireland generally broke along ethnic and religious lines, dress was still a marker of these differences. It was the descendants of the settlers who most often wore expensive, richly embroidered, brightly colored silks, satins, and printed cotton fabrics, while the great mass of the native people wore dark blue, black, red, or brown wool "stuffs" or, when wool was too expensive, cheaper, coarser fabrics such as ratteen or Connaught freize.[46] By suggesting that the wealthy patrons of Smock Alley forsake their "*Silks* for *Stuffs*" and wear "Ratteen," "Blew Shalloon," "*Irish Purple Plad*," "*Drugget*" and "*Crape*," Sheridan and Swift were tacitly suggesting that the Irish elite obliterate these marks of distinction and "go native" in the Theatre Royal.

The figure in Irish "stuff" retained its countercultural valence in the decades that followed, despite Dublin Castle's effort at appropriating this patriot trope. In October 1723, for example, Irish Protestants put on a display of Irish fabrics at Dublin Castle very much like the one Swift had advocated in his 1720 *Proposal*. As *St. James's Evening Post* related, on the anniversary of the king's coronation on October 20, "there was at the Castle a very great appearance of the Nobility and Gentry, who were all (as well as my Lord and Lieutenant and my Lady Dutchess) in new Cloaths made of the Manufacture of the Kingdom."[47] The timing of this display suggests that it was related to the developing Wood's Halfpence protest. A month earlier, the Irish Parliament had passed six resolutions denouncing Wood's patent as being "destructive of the trade and commerce of this nation and of most dangerous consequences to the rights and prerogatives of the subjects,"[48] and by wearing Irish manufacture, the Irish elite were continuing this protest, signaling their willingness to defend the Irish interest. As is evident from the above description, however, the new viceroy, the duke of Grafton, and his lady also adopted native fabrics on this occasion, and in so doing, it could be argued, they sought to strip this practice of its subversive valence and reduce it to a purely benevolent gesture of concern for the poor—a gesture on a par, for instance, with distributing food and drink to the populace on state holidays. Other governing couples obviously also found this a useful approach. In 1729, for instance, Lady Carteret formally requested ladies at the vice regal court to wear Irish damasks, and in 1745 Lady Chesterfield also adopted the practice.[49]

In his fifth *Drapier Letter* (1724), written during the Wood's Halfpence controversy, however, Swift himself also restored the political charge of this dress practice when he explicitly used the "stuff" metaphor to describe all of his controversial Irish writings to date. His 1720 *Proposal*, he wrote, was a "Piece of *Black and White Stuff* just sent from the *Dyer*"; his first Drapier's Letter was "*a plain strong Stuff to defend them* [poor people] against cold Easterly Winds, which then blew very *fierce and blasting for a long time together*"; the second and third letters were "kind of *Stuffs* for the *Gentry*"; and his fourth letter was "made of the best *Irish* Wooll [he] could get."[50] When the Irish gentry subsequently appeared in native fabrics, then, their dress was endowed with this political significance; the "Drapier" had put his indelible mark on Irish "Stuff." In 1724, too, the young Irish Protestant playwright and poet Matthew Concanen published Sheridan's prologue and Swift's epilogue in his *Miscellaneous Poems,* and by including a new text entitled "Answer to the Foregoing," he also restored the political antagonism implicit in this practice. Since attributed to Swift's close friend Dr. Delany, this "Answer" satirizes those who would oppose the "Irish Manufacture" campaign by putting their arguments in the mouth of a heartless belle who refuses to give up her foreign finery; it begins:

> The *Muses,* whom the richest Silks array,
> Refuse to fling their shining Gowns away . . .
> Far above Mortal Dress the *Sisters* shine,
> Pride in their *Indian-Robes* — and must be fine.
> And shall two *Bards* in Consort Rhyme and Huff;
> And fret these *Muses* with their Play-House *Stuff?:*
>
> The *Play'r* in Mimick Piety may storm,
> Deplore the *Combe,* and bid her Heroes arm:
> The Arbitrary Mob, in paltry Rage,
> May curse the *Belles* and *Chinces* of the Age;
> Yet still the *Artist-Worm* her *Silk* shall share,
> And spin her Thread of Life in Service of the Fair.[51]

This "Muse" who places herself "far above Mortal[s]" and who is pitiless toward the weaver also recalls Pallas Athene/England as she is depicted in Swift's *Proposal,* and it is this imperious English subject and her haughty supporters in Ireland who are also mocked above and in the lines that demand the banishment of the "*Wool gathering* Sonneteers" and "*Home-spun Witlings*":

> Hence then ye *Home-spun Witlings,* that persuade
> Miss *Chloe* to the Fashion of her Maid;

> Shall the *Wide Hoop*, that *Standard* of the *Town*,
> Thus act subservient to a *Poplin Gown?*
> Who'd smell of *Wooll* all over? 'Tis enough
> The *Under-Petticoat* be made of *Stuff.*[52]

Like the authorities who attempted to prosecute Swift's printer in 1720, this text suggests, this imperious subject tolerates no deviation from her "*Standard*" and no criticism from Irish patriot writers.

Concanen's close friend and collaborator, the Irish Protestant poet and playwright James Sterling, also disrupted government plays in the late 1720 and early 1730s with this kind of discourse. In a prologue written for October 30, 1731 (the king's birthday), for example, Sterling revived the persona of the heartless belle to attack those who opposed a bill then in the Irish Commons that would prohibit the wearing of gold and silver lace.[53] Spoken by his wife, Nancy Sterling, a player who had become known in Dublin as the "Irish Polly Peachum" for her successful portrayal of this role in the Smock Alley production of Gay's *Beggar's Opera*,[54] the prologue begins:

> Who now can doubt Hibernia's ample trade;
> So rich in Flanders-Lace, and French Brocade?
> Let grave wise Dons our gayety deride;
> And say that poverty still springs from pride!
> Yet which of us regards such snarling railers?
> Fellow; that poorly brag—they pay their *Taylors!* . . .
> To banish gold and silver their interest is,
> Who dress for court no better than a 'Prentice!
> Ladies and Beaux, all tremble at your doom!
> For birth-day suits they'll send us to the Comb! (28–29)

These lines, it is true, echo the sentiments and reproduce the central conceits of many contemporary antiluxury English social satires; like Pope's *Rape of the Lock*, for example, it focuses on the vanity of a belle to ridicule the vanity and love of luxury of a whole society. But when this speaker expresses her confidence that Hibernia's "trade" is fine and when she tells her hearers to exert their "British spirit" in the parliamentary area in defense of her cause, she also situates herself within a particular Irish political framework, marking herself as a supporter of the English interest in Ireland:

Exert, ye sovereign wives, against such laws,
Your British spirit, in the common cause,
Let each harangue here senatorial hector,
To vote for us—by a curtain-lecture! (29)

It was this English-identified political subject, then, that is also satirized in this prologue under the guise of advocating the wearing of Irish "stuff"— an attack that would have also worked to explode the romance of the government play.

In the prologue that he wrote for a performance before the returning viceroy Lord Carteret at the beginning of the 1729–30 season, Sterling also links the "wear Irish" motif to a description of the horrors Ireland was then suffering as a result of the third failed harvest in a row. And by putting Ireland's problems on show in this way, Sterling aligned himself with those other "Home-spun Witlings," Swift and Sheridan, who were still troubling the authorities with their Irish "stuff" at the end of the 1720s. In the *Intelligencer,* which Swift and Sheridan published in fall 1728, Sheridan stated that his explicit goal was to correct the "new cant" of those "vile betrayers and insulters . . . who insinuate themselves into favour by saying [Ireland] is a rich nation";[55] and a year later, in winter 1729, Swift was again trying to shock the government and its supporters out of their complacency with his savagely satirical *Modest Proposal.* Sterling's prologue, it could be argued, has a similar purpose beneath its overtly complimentary tone. In the opening lines of this dramatic script, for example, *Hibernia* is not a "beauteous Maid" who smiles at her returning lover but a dying father who is scarcely capable of raising his head to greet the new guardian of the land:

Lo! From the gloomy mansion of the dead,
Hibernia's genius rears his languid head!
Pours forth his sons upon the crowded strand,
And hails once more the guardian of our land. (131)

And the conventional compliment that a new golden age will follow in the wake of the viceroy's arrival is undercut in successive passages by the recurrence of antipastoral imagery; after issuing the prerequisite platitudes about future "plenty," the poet paints a picture of a present landscape filled with starving "swains," destroyed crops, deserted villages, and despair:

Lo! Cheerful plenty fills her horn again,
And faction vents its idle rage in vain!
Famine no more shall with pale looks appear,
To curse th'ungrateful glebe and blasted year:
The fiend no more shall drive affrighted swains
To seek new worlds from our deserted plains. (133)

It is in the context of this devastated economy that Sterling places his plea to "female patrons," including the viceregal consort Lady Carteret, to wear native fabrics; as he explicitly notes, the practice is an opportunity for women to show their patriotism and their solidarity with "their country's cause":

Beauty shall now exert its pow'r divine,
And each bright eye with keener lustre shine;
While female patrons vindicate our laws,
And plead in native silks their country's cause!
Thus may each blooming fair triumphant glow:
Still thus a generous emulation show;
Uncloath'd by *India* find more sure success,
And make ev'n beaux enamour'd of their dress;
Next Cart'ret's lovely consort blaze in charms,
And with her virtues crown each patriot's arms! (133)

When the gentry wore Irish "manufacture" to court and to funerals that year and when the "Ladies" appeared "dressed in silks of the Manufacture of this kingdom" at the playhouse for the government play on the queen's birthday (March 2, 1730),[56] it was not only at the request of "Cart'ret's lovely consort" but also at the request of Irish Protestant patriots like Sterling. He and his fellow "Home-spun Witlings" had woven a dense web of associations, political as well as economic, around this practice that could not be easily untangled.

The continued vitality of this patriot campaign in the 1730s and 1740s can also be measured by the reverse Arachne/Athene "Metamorphosis" that occurred in the Englishwoman Mary Pendarves, who came into contact with this circle of "Home-spun Witlings" in the early 1730s. Before she left for her first visit to Ireland in 1731, Mary gave the following account of her dress purchases in London: "I pick up by degrees the things I shall want for my Irish expedition; I have bought a gown and petticoat, 'tis a very fine blue satin, sprigged all over with white, and the petticoat facings and endings bordered in the manner of a trimming wove in the silk; this suit of clothes cost me sixteen pound; and yesterday I bought a pink-coloured damask for seven shillings a yard, the prettiest colour I ever saw for a nightgown."[57] It was undoubtedly these fine London clothes, too, that Mary wore for the queen's birthday ball, described above. By January 1732, however, Mary was beginning to realize that the expensive clothes she purchased in London were not winning her the approval of all her new friends in Dublin, a circle that included Jonathan Swift, Thomas Sheridan, and her future husband, Dr. Patrick Delany. From Dublin, she writes to a woman correspondent in England: "Mrs. Donellan and I have each of us made a brown stuff manteau and petticoat, and have worn them twice at the assemblies; pretty things they have produced; 'tis said now that people are convinced 'fine feathers do *not make fine birds.*' We '*adorn our clothes*'; other people are '*adorned by their clothes*'" (239). To wear "brown stuff," she was beginning to understand, was not only a sign of virtue but also a sign of belonging; it meant you were part of "us" and not "other people." By the 1740s she was also instructing others in the use of this fashion, including the new viceregal consort, Lady Chesterfield. In a letter dated August 24, 1745, she remarks how she intends to dress when she goes to Dublin Castle to pay her respects to Lord and Lady Chesterfield who had just arrived in Ireland. "I design," she writes, "to make my first visit in an *Irish* stuff manteau and petticoat, and a head the Dean [Delany] has given me of Irish work, the prettiest I ever saw of the kind" (240). And on three occasions at least during the 1745–46 season—on the birthdays of the king, the Prince of Wales and the Princess of Wales—she and large numbers of the Irish elite appeared at Dublin Castle and, it can be assumed, at the playhouse in the same material. On December 21, 1745, she writes: "The great folks at the castle continue to show great favor, but we pay them little attendance, no more than not to be remarked as backward. Everyone is to appear on the Prince of Wales's birthday in Irish stuffs, as they did on the Princess's. I have not yet bought mine" (240).

It is not clear if Mrs. Delany herself ever fully grasped the subversive political import of appearing in "Irish stuffs." But a short poem written by "a Lady" just after Lord Chesterfield had arrived in Ireland in 1745 leaves little doubt that many others in Ireland did. The poem is entitled "Ierne's Answer to Albion," and it clearly draws on the imagery and rhetoric of the Protestant patriot literary tradition. As a younger woman who suffers at the hands of a powerful older one, for example, Ierne is reminiscent of Swift's Arachne, and her complaints against Albion's Sons echo the complaints of Swift's Injured Lady:

> Sister, I sometimes have complain'd,
> That all my Wealth to you is drain'd,
> And you, as elder Sisters do
> Have only flounc'd and look'd a-skew;
> But if you'd have my Children fed,
> Your Sons should not eat all the Bread.[58]

If Ierne refuses to play her customary role in the viceregal court drama, it is also because, like Swift and the "Home-spun Witlings," she is resentful at England's political and economic treatment of Ireland. And if she insists that the viceroy adopt "Hibernian garments" before she sings his praises, it is because, like them, she sees these garments as a sign of commitment to Ireland's "sepr'ate Interest":

> You bid me now repine no more,
> For S[ackvil]e treads upon my Shore.
> Is he a God to sink or save,
> Or must I act the fawning Slave.
> He lands, and streight you Incense bring,
> But I must see before I sing . . .
> But if your C[hesterfiel]d appears
> Resol'vd to dry *Hibernia's* Tears,
> Not meerly sent to ride in State,
> To scheme a Tax, or give a Treat,
> But gently to unbind our Hands,
> And bid us Trade to foreign Lands,
> To put *Hibernian* Garments on,
> And bid *French* Fopperies be gone,
> To make our fainting Artists smile,
> And live the Guardian of my Isle,
> S[ackvill]e must do what few have done,
> Must make our sep'rate Interests one,
> Then shall my Harp, and Bards in Choir,
> Sing CHESTERFIELD, *The Land's Desire.*[59]

A demand for Irish political and economic equality and a sense of grievance at being treated as slaves, this poem suggests, were behind the lady in "Irish Stuff."

In this poem, however, this "Lady" also uses the metaphor of the mute singer and the silenced "Harp" and "Bard" to represent unfulfilled national aspirations, and in so doing, she also draws from a very different native Irish cultural repertoire. As I show in the next chapter when I examine playhouse music in the 1720s and 1730, the political ramifications of this kind of cultural borrowing by patriots was if anything more disruptive than the practice of wearing Irish "stuff" as native Irish music carried with it the memory of the Irish Catholic nation.

CHAPTER 3

"But *Drimin duh* is still in favour . . ."

Music, Memory, and the Irish Catholic Nation

> But Drimin duh is still in favour,
> Since we from Murphy beg and crave her . . .
> She, and old Eveleen a Rune,
> Are by the Muses kept in Tune
>
> Lawrence Whyte, A Dissertation on
> Italian and Irish Musick . . . (1740)

James Sterling's *Rival Generals*, which was staged at Smock Alley sometime during the 1722–23 season,[1] is clearly an Irish Protestant patriot work. The printed version of the play includes a prologue, "Design'd for King William's Birth-day," in which the heroism of the Venetian general in the play is compared to the heroism of William III at the Battle of the Boyne:

> *Both, a falling, bleeding State restor'd*
> *And Liberty sat perch'd on either Sword:*
> *The bloody* Var *is but a second* Boyne,
> *And* Remo*'s Fight, the* Battle of the Rhine.[2]

Sterling also dedicated his tragedy to the former Speaker of the Irish House of Commons William Conolly, and he specifically aligns his artistic efforts with the patriotic efforts of this well-known Irish Protestant political leader. "I must here congratulate my self, that I have first awak'd the *Irish* Muse to *Tragedy,*" Sterling writes, "and with some Vanity reflect, I have an Opportunity of presenting the first Tribute of this Nature to You, SIR, whose generous and national Temper naturally induces You to take into Your Protection the Product of Your Country, and to favour each laudable Design that may advance its Reputation and Improvement" (v–vi). The poem that Matthew Concanen wrote to honor his friend's achievement (Sterling had this poem printed with the play) also draws on the familiar Irish Protestant patriot image of the heartless lady to represent English dominance in the dramatic field. Like Pallas Athene in Swift's *Proposal for the Universal Use of Irish Manufacture,* the English stage is "a proud Mistress" who tyrannizes and oppresses her Irish counterpart:

> *Long had our Stage, on foreign Refuse fed*
> *To a proud Mistress bow'd her servile Head;*
> *Her Leavings treasur'd up, and curs'd the Land*
> *With broken Scraps of Wit at second Hand;*
> *While not one Muse arose in our Defence,*
> *Spoke our Resentment, or proclaim'd our Sense.* (viii)

In the lines that follow, however, Concanen configures English dominance in the dramatic field as the silencing of a native musical tradition and represents the patriot playwright, Sterling, as the bard who revives this tradition and restrings the Irish harp. For these images, he draws from a specifically Gaelic Irish cultural repertoire:

> *With scarce one native Note our Island rung,*
> *Her Bards untuneful, and her Harp unstrung,*
> *By you her home born Rage she now displays*
> *Inspir'd to merit independent Praise.* (viii)

In his historical drama, *Hibernia Freed,* which was produced in London and possibly in Dublin around the same time,[3] William Philips also brought a native "bard" and his harp onto the stage as part of the continued patriot effort to speak this "home born Rage." Philips's play focuses ostensibly on the period after the Danish conquest of Ireland in 1014 and on the attempt by the Irish monarch, O Brien (Brian Boru), to resist this foreign invader, but as Christopher Murray points out, the play undoubtedly takes its meaning from the 1720 Declaratory Act and the outpouring of Irish rage at the act's passage.[4] O Brien's critique of the "lazy *Dane*" in the first scene of the play, for example, is a barely disguised expression of Irish Protestant resentment at the ruinous economic sanctions that England was then imposing on Ireland; its aggrieved tone echoes the patriot prologues and epilogues discussed in the previous chapter:

> Fertile *Hibernia!* Hospitable Land!
> Is not allow'd to feed her Native Sons,
> In vain they toil, and a-mid Plenty starve.
> The lazy *Dane* grows wanton with our Stores
> Urges our Labour, and derides our Wants.
> *Hibernia!* Seat of Learning! School of Science!
> How waste! How wild dost thou already seem![5]

In addition to lamenting Ireland's economic and political hardships verbally, however, Philips uses a musical performance to enact this discord. The opening scene is set before O Brien's tent "on the Hill of Tarah, in the County of Meath," and before anyone speaks, Eugenius, the Bard, plays a tune on the harp (1). The harp music is broken off abruptly, though, when O Brien speaks, and in his first speech, images of musical dissonance are deployed to convey his (and by analogy, the Irish Protestant patriot's) grief at Ireland's present state of wretchedness:

> Enough, it will not be: vain is th'Attempt
> To calm my Sorrows by Harmonious Airs:
> Harsh is the Sound, and dissonant the Notes.
> Thy tuneful Harp, tho' guided by thy Art,
> Jars in my Ears, and swells my Griefs yet higher. (1)

In this chapter I discuss the implications of these kinds of Irish Protestant musical appropriations in the Irish theater in the first half of the century, and I suggest that these appropriations were important not only to the revival of native Irish music and culture but also to the revival of the Irish Catholic nation itself. As the example of *Hibernia Freed* reveals, Irish Protestant patriot writers were opening up a space for Irish music and Irish artists in their performances in an effort to articulate their own political and economic grievances, and in so doing, they also opened up a space for the return of the Catholic repressed. Ironically, however, Irish Protestant patriotism also worked to obscure this political and cultural revival through the kind of narratives it spun around the figure of muted bard and the unstrung harp. These motifs were soon transformed by Irish Protestant writers into a full-blown historical narrative about the contemporary dislocated state of Irish music, and as the political and rhetorical underpinnings of this narrative were forgotten, it began to be assumed that it reflected the actual state of Irish music and culture in eighteenth-century Ireland. Matthew Pilkington, it could be said, inaugurated this genre of musical historiography with his 1725 poem, "The Progress of Music in *Ireland*. To Mira." Pilkington traces the evolution of musical taste in Ireland from a past golden pastoral era when the village "Crowd" was transported by the harp music of the "Vagrant Bard," the blind Irish harpist Turlogh Carolan, to the present moment when "refin'd *Hibernia's* ravish'd Throng" stands transfixed by Italian singers and imported, ornate music. And he laments that this "improvement" in aesthetic taste signaled the demise, or at the very least the marginalization, of the native musical tradition:

> Th'awakened *Muse* thus rises, thus refines
> Improves with *Time*, and in Perfection shines
> The first rude Lays are now but meanly priz'd,
> As rude, neglected, as untun'd, despis'd:
> Dead—(in Esteem too dead) the *Bards* that sung,
> The *Fife* neglected and the *Harp* unstrung.[6]

A succession of writers down to the present day have reiterated this narrative of the dislocated state of Irish music, and it could be said that this narrative acquired an additional layer of authenticity with each reiteration. In his essay "The History of Carolan: The Last Irish Bard" (1760), for example, Oliver Goldsmith elevates Carolan to the status of a cultural great when he compares him to the Greek poets Pindar and Homer, but like the art of these literary giants, he also suggests that Carolan's music belongs to a defunct, more "natural" culture that has no place in the complex modern-day world.[7] And this theme of the incompatibility of Irish music and the modern is further developed in Joseph Cooper Walker's *Historical Memoirs of the Irish Bards* (1786). In the *Historical Memoirs*, the first work to deal in detail with the history of Irish music, Walker also celebrates Carolan as "a fine natural Genius,"[8] but again he characterizes the harpist as belonging to a bardic order that has been undermined first by the introduction of "English Customs and Manners" (156) and more recently and more thoroughly by the rage for Italian singers and music. After Italian music reached Irish shores, Walker argues, "[o]ur musical taste became refined, and our sweet melodies and native Musicians fell into disrepute" (158). Harry White's recent study, *The Keeper's Recital,* also takes Walker's *Historical Memoirs* as a beginning point for its discussion of the state of music in eighteenth-century Ireland. Walker's history, White writes, "allows us to establish a central feature of music in Ireland which was to affect both traditions (ethnic and colonial), namely, the dislocated status of the composer within the terms of Ascendancy thought."[9]

The eighteenth-century poetic, musical, and dramatic texts that I examine here, however, indicate that even after the political catastrophe of the seventeenth century, traditional Irish music survived in the underground culture of Dublin's displaced Catholic community. And by appropriating the music of the dispossessed, these texts suggest, Irish Protestant patriots created an opportunity for members of this community to remember and restore their nation's dreams and aspirations.

◆◆◆

Lawrence Whyte's "An Historical Poem, On the Rise and Progress of the Charitable and Musical Society, now assembling at the Bull's-Head in Fishamble-street, Dublin" (1740) provides a useful point of departure for this counternarrative of native Irish relocation and revival. In this poem (as the title suggests), Whyte traces the foundation and development of the Dublin Charitable and Musical Society, an organization that would soon gain international musical fame by sponsoring the first performance of Handel's *Messiah* in Fishamble Street Music Hall (the society moved from its customary meeting place in the Bull's-Head Tavern to the new Music Hall in 1740).[10] But in narrating the society's rise and progress, Whyte also obliquely tells the story of the rise and progress of the Catholic community after its *longbhriseadh,* or shipwreck,[11] at the end of the seventeenth century, and in this and other texts in his *Poems on various subjects* (1740), Whyte throws light on how this community kept its music and dreams alive in the heart of Protestant Dublin.

"An Historical Poem" traces the origin of the Charitable and Musical Society back to the moment during the reign of Queen Anne when Gregory Byrne, a Dublin shopkeeper, decided to meet for music and conversation with his "jolly Friends" (one of whom was Whyte himself) at the Cross-Keys Tavern in Christ Church yard, a busy commercial area on the south side of Christ Church.[12] The poem also indicates that these "jolly Friends" came from both sides of the political, religious, and cultural divide: there were "honest Whigs" as well as "Papists" and "Tories" and men with English as well as Irish-sounding names:

> To sit with jolly Friends, some Nights he [Byrne] fix'd,
> Where with his Liquor, Love and Mirth he mix'd,
> As *D..ll..g, P..k..r, Ed..gton,* and *Reed,*
> Your Bard made one, for so the Fates decree'd.
> . . . .
> There you might see old Alderman *M.. l..ne,*
> Who cou'd relate the Feats of forty one.
> There sate his Nephews *Ne..lls, Ree..s, T..gs,*
> With *Papists, Tories* and some honest *Whiggs;*
> If *F..s* came, then did *Greg Byrne* and he
> Compare their Systems of Philosophy,
> With some Remarks upon the new and old,
> From learned Authors, beautifully told. (218)

The music that this group created, Whyte's poem tells us, also reenacted the intercultural social condition of the group. Under the leadership of Pat Beaghan, another Dublin shopkeeper, the musical performances were a harmonious blend of different ethnic musical traditions, including the Irish one:

> In *Beahan*'s Days (our Governor for Life)
> *John* play'd the Flute, and *Billy* played the Fife.
> Some play'd the Fiddle, other vamp'd a Base,
> We sung the *Tinker,* or old *Chevy Case,*
> *Pat* smoak'd his Pipe, and gave us laws to boot.
> And Discord vanish'd from the Fife and Flute.
> Each night we shook off our domestick Cares,
> By *Irish, English,* or *Italian* Airs. (222)

In another of his poems, "The Broken Jug," Whyte also stresses that these musical and social gatherings retained their inclusive and carefree ethos as the group grew in size and moved from one tavern to another in the Christ Church–Fishamble Street area. By the time John Neal, a music publisher and owner of a music shop in Christ Church yard, took over the leadership of the club in 1723, after Beaghan's death, the Charitable and Musical Society (as the group was now called) was attracting people from every walk of life and every political, cultural, and religious background:

> While honest *Neal* the mallet bore,
> Who filled the chair in days of yore,
> There lawyers met, and eke physicians,
> Attorneys, proctors, politicians:
> Divines and students from the College,
> Men full of speculative knowledge:
> Captains and coll'nel's all in red,
> Who in the school of Mars were bred.
> Some beaux and prigs, with nice toupees,
> With wast-coats lac'd down to his knees;
> Some poets, painters, and musicians,
> Mechanicks, and mathematicians,
> For tradesmen there gave no offence,
> When blessed with manners or good sense;
> Some gentlemen, some lords and squires.
> Some Whigs, and Tories, and Highflyers;
> There Papist, Protestants, Dissenters,
> Sit cheek by jowl at all adventures,
> And thus united did agree
> To make up one Society.
> That some drink jill, and others beer,
> Was all the schism they had to fear.[13]

There is a kind of melancholic harkening back in these poems, however, that repeatedly disrupts Whyte's "jolly" tone and his overtly progressive narrative, and these narratives disjunctures, I suggest, speak to the larger disjunctures in the poet's own life and in the life of his community as a result of the seventeenth-century wars. At the time of writing, Whyte was earning a living by teaching mathematics in Dublin, and this job and his connections to prosperous Dublin Catholic merchant families (Cahils and Ferralls) would seem to suggest that he and his family had totally assimilated into the new order.[14] Throughout his poetic work, too, Whyte seeks to represent himself as someone who is gregarious, carefree, and uncritical, much like the character of the "Honest Jolly Companion" he describes in a bilingual poem in his later 1742 collection:

> Ni cáinim duine is ní thugaim mo slán fó aon;
> Má cáintear mise, ní thuigim gur náir dom é;
> Má bhíonn siad soilbhir, ní soilbhre cách ná mé,
> Is níl cáil ag duine, nach duine den cháilsin mé.

> I censure none, let who will censure me,
> I own my faults, since few from faults are free;
> Where folks are jovial, jovially I sit
> And with my humours, each man's humours hit.[15]

This use of Irish and the frequent allusions to Westmeath in his poetry, however, also reveal that Whyte remained deeply attached to his native culture and his native county (he came from old English Catholic stock from the vicinity of Ballymore, County Westmeath). And his long poem, "The Parting Cup, or the Humours of Deoch an Doruis," indicates that he continued to mourn the losses suffered by his family and the Catholic community. In the preface to his *Poems*, he casts "The Parting Cup" as a general representation of a traditional Irish way of life that has passed:

> The Parting-Cup, or the Humours of Deoghedorus, Etc. sets forth the great Hospitality and good Entertainment formerly met with in Irish Families, many of whom did not assume to be above the Rank of common Farmers, whilst some others who were second Brothers, or the Descendants of the Nobility and Gentry . . . turned Farmers also, and lived very hospitably; these retained the Title of Gentlemen, and were esteem'd as such, as least while they cou'd maintain it, till some Misfortune, or want of Industry reduced them to be Beggars, or Day-labourers, as a great many of them are at this Time, whose Misfortunes I cou'd not forbear to lament in the fourth Canto, together with the Cause of their Down-fall, with a word or two to the Absentees who spend their fortunes abroad, and are resolved that their Country shall never be a Penny the better for them.[16]

But it is clear that in telling the story of the "Down-fall" of the "Tribe of Deoch an Doruis" (the fictitious name he gives the Irish family in this poem), he is also relating the downfall of his own "tribe" as a result of his family's involvement in the seventeenth-century wars. Whyte's father had been transplanted to Connaught during the Cromwell plantation (though he subsequently found his way back to his native Ballymore); and his mother's family, the Daltons, lost most of their large landholdings in Rathconrath during the same period. Members of his family had also suffered losses in the more recent Jacobite wars: his half brother or uncle, Captain Thomas White, for example, was in Dillon's Regiment in King James's army, and he died in exile in the French service in 1705.[17]

The memory of similar losses, Whyte's *Poems* reveal, haunted the lives of many of the other "Papist" members of the original Cross-Keys Tavern group, and by rehearsing these losses, these members, like Whyte, also worked to keep the past alive and restore old hopes and dreams. The "old Alderman" mentioned in the opening lines of "An Historical Poem," for example, was James Malone, a bookseller who had been the State Printer to James II,[18] and judging from his and his nephews' ability to sit and drink beer with the "honest Whigs," it could be assumed that he and his family had accepted the new order. But Malone's propensity for relating the "feats of [16]41" also suggests that this assimilation was far from total. By rehearsing the Catholic version of this history at the tavern gatherings—his version of 1641, we can assume, would have been sympathetic to the rebels—Malone was covertly continuing his ideological assault on his old enemies, undermining what was one of the foundational narratives of the Protestant establishment. If the *"F..s"* mentioned in the next lines was the John Fergus, M.D., who is listed as one of the subscribers to Whyte's 1740 *Poems*, his conversation, it is likely, would have had a similar ideological thrust. Dr. Fergus, a Catholic and a Connachtman, was one of the most active collectors of old Irish manuscripts in Dublin in the eighteenth century, and he was also part of the Ó Neachtain circle of Irish scribes, scholars, and writers that was meeting in the nearby Liberties during the same period.[19] If he was the one discussing the writings of "learned Authors, beautifully told," then, it can be assumed his conversation would have included analysis of the merits of the works of the Irish bards.

Pat Beaghan and Tom Ryan, the club's first president and the owner of the Cross-Keys Tavern, respectively, were no less conflicted figures. As Whyte notes in the "Elegy" he wrote when Pat Beaghan died in 1723, the late "Governor" of the club had been a Jacobite soldier, and like many old soldiers, he was unable to forget his military past. In the daytime he played the role of the cheerful Dublin shopkeeper (the "Elegy" notes, for example, that Pat gave presents of almonds and raisins to the women who came into his shop). But by night he became the Homer of the 1688–91 wars, turning the Irish defeat into a stirring epic of "mighty feats":

> The Breach of *Cavan*, *Boyne*, and *Crum*
> Made him go off with Beat of *Drum*,
> To *Lymrick*, as a sure Retreat,
> Which Patt himself did oft relate,
> The mighty feats of Irish Arms,
> Their Battles, Sieges and Alarms,
> What past e'er since the Siege of *Derry*,
> At any place from that to *Kerry*,
> Did many Nights his thoughts employ
> And told at last the Fate of *Troy*
> How they at length gave up the *Town*,
> Lay'd *Swords* and *Pikes* and *Musquets* down,
> Which fix'd a *Period* to his Game,
> And then to Dublin, home he came,
> Where he was treated and liv'd better,
> By way of *Creditor* and *Debtor*
> When *Shop* was shut, and Business done,
> *Patt* never lov'd to be alone.[20]

Tom Ryan, the group's host, brought a similar if less romanticized repertoire of stories with him when he moved from the country to the city. Ryan now sold fine "Malt-Liquors" to make a living, but he was also a "Scholar," and when he was in the humor he would speak Latin and expostulate on the "*Summum Bonum*" or give detailed accounts of all the horrors of the recent Irish wars:

> He cou'd relate the Siege of *London-Derry*,
> Of all the Sieges, he omitted none,
> Including *Limerick*, *Anno* ninety one,
> He told the Battles fought by Horse and Foot,
> How many slain, how many hack'd and cut,
> The Numbers taken, and who ran away,
> Which Side was beated, or who got the Day.[21]

The kinds of contradictions and ambiguities that were apparent in the lives and discourse of Whyte and his circle, moreover, were characteristic of the Catholic middle class that began to emerge in Dublin and in other urban centers in the eighteenth century—a class that, like the Cross-Keys Tavern group, was attempting to negotiate between two cultural, political, and economic worlds. Writing to his brother in 1756, Charles O'Conor of Belanagare, one of the most important spokesmen for this emerging Catholic middle class, remarks on the bifurcated nature of his life as he moves between his family farm in County Roscommon and Dublin. "I spend one half the year reading, scribbling, and improving my grounds," he writes. "The other half I mix with men of all descriptions, accommodating myself to the manners of others far from expecting they should accommodate their manners to mine."[22] In his political life, too, O'Conor straddled two worlds. In his public writings he always presented himself as a Hanoverian loyalist and supporter of the political status quo, sometimes even creating the deliberate impression that he was a Protestant. But behind the scenes he worked tirelessly to effect the relaxation of the penal laws, and he was passionately committed to restoring a heroic Irish past and to rescuing Irish history from its Protestant detractors.[23] In a letter to a relative in Kerry in 1754, for example, he describes himself as someone whose "soul is on fire when he sees that the heroes of his native country are in no respect inferior to those of Greece and Rome except in the want of a historian whose talents would not be inferior to the task of doing them . . . justice."[24] If O'Conor was cautious about expressing his political concerns and his passion for the "heroes of his native country" in his public writings and public behavior, it was because he understood the tenuous position of the Catholic in contemporary Ireland. Advising his son about how to live in the "busy, elbowing scene" of Dublin in 1751, he writes, "[I]f you have any sagacity, you will make reflections on every incident and reap instruction and, whatever it be, strive to adapt it to the rank you are to fill hereafter: that of a Roman Catholic in a Protestant country, that of one in a low way, obnoxious to the laws."[25] It was this kind of awareness of the "low" status of Catholics that led him to advocate throughout his life a politics of indirection rather than confrontation as the way of advancing the Catholic position. "The mariner does not always steer directly to the place of his destination; he steers as the wind permits him," O'Conor wrote to his brother in the 1756 letter,[26] and he makes a similar point to his friend, the Dublin medical doctor and historian John Curry, in 1760 as he reflects on the necessity of paying a

Protestant writer (Henry Brooke) to write pamphlets in support of the Catholic cause. To gain an audience among Protestants who were predisposed through "education, custom, and party rage" to be antagonistic to Catholics, O'Conor suggests, a writer must use "not only art but a little honest artifice."[27]

Whyte's circle of Irish musicians, music lovers, and scholars were deploying a similar kind of art or artifice to earn a living and find an audience in early-eighteenth-century Dublin; indeed, Whyte explicitly points to the representative nature of his friends' experience in his description of Tom Ryan, the tavern keeper. Behind Ryan, he suggests, stands a whole section of the Catholic *"People"* who at that time were successfully negotiating the transition from country to town, from the old order to the new, through their "Sagacity" and "Wit":

> The Hills of *K[err]y, C[or]k, and T[ip]p[era]ry,*
> Producing *People* like him [Ryan] bright and airy,
> And from their Summits they come tripping down,
> To fill each City, and each Market-town
> Such as wou'd guard themselves from being bit,
> From these may learn Sagacity and Wit.[28]

As we have seen, however, these Irish Catholic migrants also brought into the heart of the Pale their *"Irish . . . Airs,"* and if we are to judge from *A Collection of the Most Celebrated Irish Tunes* (1724), which was published by John and William Neal, two of the original members of the Cross-Keys Tavern group, this music was as powerful a conduit of memory as the other imports, "Sagacity" and "Wit."

In his introduction to the *Celebrated Irish Tunes,* Nicholas Carolan notes that the collection is "the earliest body of Irish music to emerge from eight or nine thousand years of music making" in Ireland, and he points out that it appears to be a "first-hand collection": its forty-nine tunes can be traced to the repertoire of late-seventeenth- or early-eighteenth-century itinerant professional harpers, including Turlogh Carolan.[29] Not surprisingly, most of this music commemorates people and events that were important to the native Irish cultural and political tradition and, not surprisingly, too, includes lamentations for Jacobite leaders and Jacobite military defeats (for example, "Ld. Gallaways Lamentation"; "Gye Fiane [The Wild Geese]"; "Limbrick's Lamentation"; "Patrick Sarsfild"). As we know from the description of the entertainment offered by the "Deoch an

Doruis" family in Whyte's "The Parting Cup," many harp tunes were accompanied by songs lamenting the downfall of these heroes when they were performed in their original native Irish rural setting. Describing the harper who played at the gentleman farmer's revels, Whyte writes:

His Harp for Irish Hero's strung,
Their Fall he wept, and Zeal he sung; . . .

. . . .

His Lamentations sung and play'd
Compos'd for valiant Hero's dead
Who fell in Aughrim's fatal plain,
Manur'd with blood of thousands slain,
Recites the story to a truth,
The tragic End of Great St. Ruth,
The fate of *Gallway,* and Bophin,
Two chiefs, the noblest of their Kin

. . . .

Tyrconnell, Sarsfield, and the Rest,
With loud Encomiums he blest.[30]

Even if (as seems likely) the controversial lyrics were omitted when Whyte's friends played these elegiac tunes in a Dublin tavern, their music would have served to reactivate the memory of these Irish Catholic leaders and the associated political, economic, and cultural claims of the Irish Catholic people. As Bill Rolston points out in a recent article on music and politics in contemporary Northern Ireland, tunes have a significance or "aura" that can persist even when new lyrics (or, in this case, no lyrics) are set to the original tune. "The tune as a sign works not merely at a 'denotational' level, but also at a 'connotational' one," Rolston writes. "It conjures up feelings and emotions that are instantly retrievable by the audience when presented on later occasions with the sign."[31]

Even a more ostensibly celebratory tune like "Plea Rarkeh na Rourkough" (modern Irish: "Pléaráca na Ruarcach" [The Revels of the O'Rourkes]) could also be a vehicle for such subversive remembering. "Plea Rarkeh na Rourkough" is showcased on the title page of the *Celebrated Irish Tunes,* which specifically reminds readers of a recent performance of the tune by a visiting Italian composer and musician; the Carolan tune, it is stated, is "set with different divisions [for] Bass and Corus as performed at the Subscription Consort by Senior Lorenzo Bocchi."[32] For

Whyte and his circle, however, this tune would have had other cultural and political associations, and not all of these associations were necessarily productive of celebration. This Carolan tune was most likely first played by the harper himself at the Roscommon home of his friend and patron Charles O'Conor or at the home of one of O'Conor's relatives, the O'Rourkes, and the words that Aodh Mac Gabhráin (Hugh McGauran) composed to accompany it suggest that Carolan intended to honor his friends and patrons with this composition by recalling the revels of one of the most famous O'Rourke ancestors. As Donal O'Sullivan notes, the poem "Pléaráca na Ruarcach" "embodies the tradition of the Christmas festivities held in the Great Hall of his Castle at Dromahaire, county Leitrim, by the famous sixteenth-century Irish chieftain, Brian na Murtha O'Ruairc."[33] To remember O'Rourke and his revels, however, was also to recall a native Irish tradition of resistance to English colonial authorities and its brutal repression by the authorities. As the 1589 Calendar of State Papers for Ireland noted, O'Rourke used his "pléaráca," or revels, to thumb his nose at an English Protestant power. Commenting on "How naughtily O'Rourke hath always carried himself," the State Papers notes that at his revels the chieftain "caused a picture of Her Majesty to be drawn at a horse tail" and that he "kept his Christmas according to the Pope's computation" (i.e., the Gregorian calendar).[34] Subversive "play" in the broader political arena would also eventually cost this chieftain his life. O'Rourke waged continual war on the Elizabethan colonists in Ireland and provided assistance to the Spaniards stranded in Ireland after the Spanish Armada and for these actions he was eventually convicted of treason and hanged at Tyburn.[35]

◆◆◆

When Irish Protestant patriots put such Irish airs and songs into circulation, then, they provided an additional outlet for this kind of subversive remembering, and as evidenced by the appearance of the English translation of Mac Gabhráin's "Pléaráca na Ruarcach" in 1720, Swift and his friends were again among the first to get into the transgressive act. A number of recent studies have cited Swift's translation of "Pléaráca na Ruarcach" as evidence of a possible link between the dean and the circle of Irish scholars, scribes, and poets who gathered in the home of Sean and Tadhg Ó Neachtain in the Liberties in the first two decades of the eighteenth century. Mac Gabhráin, it has been pointed out, was part of the Neachtain circle, and Anthony Raymond, a Protestant clergyman and fellow of

Trinity College who was Swift's collaborator in this translation, was a friend of the Neachtains, lending them manuscripts and generally supporting their Irish studies.[36] In a poem of praise that Tadgh Ó Neachtain wrote for Raymond, he also noted the political impact of such translations by Protestant scholars; reflecting on what the "beloved professor" did for Ireland, for example, Ó Neachtain writes:

> He showed her [Ireland] to herself and to her people: he has shattered her dark covering of sorrow for her; he has left her as bright morning sun after the grey wrinkled frost of a spring day . . .

> He awoke her calling of learning, though this was difficult; also her speech and her fine way of life; he showed the majesty and vigour of her ancient people and their bondage under a band of foreigners.[37]

However, as we have seen, "Pléaráca na Ruarcach" was also the signature tune of the group that was meeting, together with "Divines and students from the College" (see "An Historical Poem" above), to play and hear Irish music in the taverns around Christ Church and Fishamble Street at this time. And in translating Mac Gabhráin's song, it could be argued, Swift and Raymond also helped to transmit the native Irish counternarratives that were being articulated in this tavern subculture.

There is no explicit reference to the counterclaims of the Irish dispossessed in the words Mac Gabhráin wrote for "Pléaráca na Ruarcach," but these counterclaims are encoded in the third verse in the description of the fight that breaks out between two guests at O'Rourke's feast. In the contentious exchange during this fight, one of the guests addresses the other as a churl ("a bhodaig") and vehemently reminds him that his (the speaker's) family is as ancient and as noble as any in Ireland, including the great aristocratic Old English family, the Kildares. No other context is given for this quarrel, nor is the ethnic identity of the two quarrelers specified, but as Leerssen notes, in seventeenth- and eighteenth-century Irish poetry, the conflict between Irish native and English settler was often represented as an opposition between an ancient, true nobility and a race of upstart boorish churls, and "it was this equation between 'Gaelic' and 'genuine' Ireland that was to be passed on to the late eighteenth-century Patriots and early nineteenth-century nationalists."[38] By creating an English translation of the following Mac Gabhráin passage, Swift and Raymond also participated (however unwittingly) in this nationalist transmission.

You Churle, I'll maintain
    My Father built *Lusk*,
The Castle of *Slain*,
    And *Carrickdhrumrusk:*
The Earl of Kildare,
    And *Moynalta*, his Brother,
As great as they are,
    I was nurs'd by their Mother
Ask that of old *Madam*.
    She'll tell you who's who,
As far up as *Adam*,
    She knows it is true.
Come down with that Beam,
If Cudgels are scarce,
    A Blow on the Weam,
Or a Kick on the A-se.[39]

By creating this translation, Swift and Raymond put the native Irish subject's critique of the upstart "*bodach*" or "churle" into wider circulation,
and they made this native Irish subject's historic memory of his family's
prior claim to the ownership of Ireland available to subsequent generations of English-speaking Irish men and women.

More immediately, these kinds of Irish Protestant appropriations made
it possible for a playwright such as Charles Coffey to include "Pléaráca na
Ruarcach" and other Irish airs in the dramatic works he was writing at this
time for the Dublin stage, and such musical translations, no less than the
written ones that Ó Neachtain describes above, helped to restore Ireland
"to herself and to her people." Biographers say little about Coffey's personal life and background other than that he was a hunchback and a "native of Ireland."[40] This last phrase, of course, could have been used simply
to indicate that he was born in Ireland, but it seems likely that in this case
it also meant he was of native Irish descent. Coffey (Ó Cobhthaigh) is an
old Irish surname, and one family branch of the Coffeys—a Country Westmeath branch—was famous for their bards. Perhaps not coincidentally,
there was also a Westmeath poet of this name (Aodh Ó Cobhthaigh) in the
Ó Neachtain circle at this time.[41] It is possible, then, that Coffey had first-
hand knowledge of the Irish musical tradition, though he could also have
acquired his knowledge of Irish music from attending the Neals' musical
evenings at the Bulls-Head Tavern. As noted in "An Historical Poem,"

there were "poets, painters, and musicians" at these gatherings, and in the mid-1720s Coffey was acting and writing for the Smock Alley playhouse, just around the corner from Fishamble Street.[42]

The syncretic form of Coffey's dramatic entertainment also suggests a continuity with the tavern counterculture. Like Whyte's poetry and the Neals' *Celebrated Irish Tunes*, his dramatic texts provide a bridge between the hidden Ireland—the Ireland of the rural hinterland—and the Protestant, English-speaking world of Dublin. At first view, it is true, Coffey's first play, *Wife or No Wife* (1724) could be mistaken for a typical contemporary English farce. It features a conventional May-December love plot (a dashing young military officer, Captain Gallant, is attempting to steal his former mistress, Lady Quibble, from her jealous old husband, Justice Quibble) and employs the standard farcical devices of disguise and mistaken identity to generate broad laughter in its audience. When Comick, Captain Gallant's servant, disguises himself as an Irish servant to gain admittance to Lady Quibble's house, it might also seem that Coffey is using a stock Teague character to get some of this broad laughter. After Comick first enters, for example, he is asked his master's name, but he is unable to remember it, and when Pert (Lady Quibble's servant) asks how long he has lived with his master, he replies with stereotypical Teague simplicity: "Fet I never reckon'd, but 'tis as long as he liv'd wid me indeed."[43] This literal-mindedness and lack of sense of time, like the ludicrous inconsistency known as the "Irish bull," also implicitly marks the native Irishman as a primitive—as someone without a sense of history or of the past.

When Comick sits down on the floor of the stage with a tankard of beer in his hand and sings "Pléaráca na Ruarcach," however, his song undercuts this stereotype. In enumerating the lavishness of the feast given by an Irish chieftain, the singer bears witness to the vitality and richness of the Gaelic culture that existed before English contact, and the very specificity of the details in the song testifies to the enduring place of that heroic past in the minds and memories of the common Irish people:

> Plaracanaroka, let all men remember,
> The like was ne'er known, nor never shall be,
> Six score and Forty Cows, Sheep were slaughter'd
> And all for to make us a Feast in one Day.
> Pails full of Bulcan we drank out of Madders,
> When we rised next morn we had a brave sport:
> My cloak it is singed, my Pipe it was broked,

My britches was stoled, they picked my Pocket,
Our Mantle and Kercher and Caps they are gone
Yeara, where are the Folk, let joy go with them.
Come change up your Tunes on the Harp to our Dancing,
And fill the Madders, bring a box of good Sneezing. (16)

Coffey's suggestion that "all men remember" these epiclike revels of an
Irish chieftain also had a deeper emotional charge than the equivalent lines
in the Swift-Raymond translation, as can be seen by comparing the opening lines of both texts. In the Swift-Raymond translation, a statement is
made in the first three lines about the noble and memorable nature of
O'Rourke's "noble Fare" but then is undercut by the fourth line: the claim
that this feast will be remembered by "those who were not [there]" transforms the whole into a typical "Irish bull":

> O Rouk's noble Fare
> > Will ne'er be forgot
> By those who were there.
> > Or those who were not.[44]

Coffey's second line, by contrast, is adulatory, and the later line "Yeara,
where are the Folk, let joy go with them" adds a plaintive note to the commemoration, suggesting that what has been lost is not just mantles, kerchiefs,
and caps but also a whole Irish community and its way of life. Again it is
tempting to speculate that this deeper sense of regret also came from Coffey's
personal familiarity with this community. When he inserted "Pléaráca na
Ruarcach" into a very similar drinking scene in *The Female Parson or Beau
in the Sudds,* a play he wrote for the London stage in 1730, Coffey had the
Comick of that play describe his song not only as "an *Irish* Tune" but also as
"a *Connaught* Tune,"[45] and this level of specificity suggests a knowledge that
comes from outside the English-speaking world. Significantly, Coffey also
dedicated *The Female Parson* to William, Earl of Inchiquin, a member of the
O'Brien family that was famous for its patronage of Irish poets and writers,
including some who were then part of the Ó Neachtain circle.[46]

When the ballad opera came on the Irish scene in 1728, it provided
Coffey with an even better vehicle for negotiating between an Irish Protestant and an Irish Catholic world and for mediating their competing political desires. As John Bender points out, the unique force of Gay's *Beggar's
Opera* lay in its synthesis of a multigenre structure with a widespread and

corrosive social satire. "Generic permutation and interchange are the rule in this work, which imitates, burlesques, parodies, and engages in every imaginable kind of oblique discourse, with an enormous range of genres, both established and emergent," Bender writes, and he notes that Gay "unleashes" this multigenred discourse on the fundamental institutions of society with devastating satiric effect.[47] Coffey's *Beggar's Wedding* reveals that this mixed-genre, formal structure could also provide a vehicle for negotiating an exchange between different kinds of Irish national and musical discourses and for unleashing a multivoiced (Irish Protestant and Irish Catholic) critique of colonial institutions.

The Beggar's Wedding was produced at Smock Alley in March 1729, just a year after Gay's ballad opera had taken Dublin by storm. In a preface to the Dublin edition of this work, Coffey acknowledges Gay's influence, but he also emphasizes the Irish difference of his dramatic and musical project. His intention, he says, was not to rival Gay but "to entertain or amuse the town with something of Irish birth," and he writes that he took "particular care to collect the most delightful Tunes, and such as were not made use of before." In asking for support for his work, he also stresses the Irish patriot implication of his dramatic effort: "Methinks 'twere a kind of cruelty indeed that an *Irish* Muse shou'd pass unregarded by those of their own Country, who have been so industrious to crown the *British* one with innumerable wreathes of every Blooming Laurel."[48] An analysis of *The Beggar's Wedding* substantiates these claims about the Irish difference and patriot relevance of this ballad opera. Thematically, as well as musically, this dramatic work takes its meaning from an Irish context, and it draws on both Irish dissenting traditions for its critique.

Beggars and what to do with them was a subject much discussed in Dublin in 1729, as three successive bad harvests and a worsening economy had brought record numbers of beggars into the Irish capital. Much of this commentary was extremely negative, reflecting the standard ruling-class belief that the poverty of the Catholic Irish was the effect of an innate moral degeneracy and idleness, but as Joseph O'Carroll notes, among some Irish Protestant social commentators in the 1720s and 1730, there was also a dawning awareness that poverty had its roots in the negligence of the ruling class and in the deeper social and economic structure of the country.[49] In 1723, for example, the Irish statute book directly attributed the increase in vagrancy and begging to the corruption of the parish beadles who were charged with controlling the beggars: "That great numbers of idle and vagrant persons do daily resort from the country to the city of

Dublin and the suburbs thereof, who by reason of the correspondence they do generally keep with the beadles of several parishes, and the neglect of such beadles in the performance of their duties, are permitted to beg in and through the city."[50] And in 1729 Swift famously used the problem of beggar women and their children in his *Modest Proposal* to indict a whole socioeconomic system that he considered predatory and cannibalistic, while James Sterling and the Smock Alley players used the stage to bring the plight of the poor to the public's attention.

The Beggar's Wedding, which is set in Dublin, takes some of its meaning from this kind of Irish Protestant patriot critique. Like Swift's *Modest Proposal,* for example, it is decidedly unsentimental about the Dublin underclass it chooses to represent; Chaunter and his gang of beggars, we soon learn, are all faking their various illness and disabilities, and most of them are engaged in petty crime of one kind or another. But like Swift's tract, also, this ballad opera suggests that there is a larger pattern of ruling-class corruption and mismanagement behind this kind of social problem, and it reserves its harshest critique for those who perpetuate this system of government. The opening scene of the play, for example, reveals Quorum, a Dublin alderman and justice of the peace, accepting bribes and receiving stolen goods from the very beggars he is charged with controlling, and after Quorum departs, Dash, his clerk, is allowed to soliloquize not only on this alderman's corruption but also on the corruption of all "Tyrants in Power":

> 'Tis the Devil to deal with one of those Tyrants in Power; especially if a Man be poor or any way dependant. . . . [I]f Perjury, Bribery, Avarice and Subornation be essential, my Master is certainly the most thorough-pac'd Rogue of this whole Brotherhood: But these are now by a long Habit grown so familiar, that they are rather esteem'd Virtues than the contrary. (17)

In a later scene, in which the beggar women discuss the joys of drinking and indulge their taste for a "hearty Bouze of *Uisquebagh*" (31), the theme of "Tyrannical Masters" is again taken up, with the same kind of hard-hitting attack on corrupt government that is apparent in many of Swift's Irish tracts:

> Mopsey. As you say, Charity is at a very low Ebb indeed, for between the Church Warrens and the Work-House we are greatly Sufferers! If at a Door we beg an Alms, they bid us apply to the Church, where half the daily Contributions stick to the Fingers of the Collectors.

Blouze. And if we offer to complain, we are immediately whipt into the Work-House, where we must work our Fingers to the bone, and be half-starved for our Labour, in order to enrich our Tyrannical Masters. (32)

The Irish music associated with the beggars in this scene, however, also adds another political dimension to this kind of complaint and to the drama's celebration of the beggars' final triumph over their "Tyrannical Masters." In his essay, "Music, Poetry and Polity in the Age of Swift," Frank Llewelyn Harrison argues convincingly that both the Irish ballad opera and the gentlemen's tune books provide evidence of "a crossing over of tunes between 'nations,' both from the indigenous Irish repertory and from the Carolan-country repertory, into that of ascendancy and urban circles" during the first half of the eighteenth century; and Harrison points to the occurrence of tunes from a native Irish "musical dialect" in *The Beggar's Wedding*, in particular, to support this claim. Six of *The Beggar's Wedding*'s fifty-six songs ("Captain McCan," "Highway to Dublin," "Lestrum Pone," "Molly St. George," "Ellen a Run," and "An Irish Tune") are identifiably Irish, he demonstrates, and two of them ("Captain McCan" and "Molly St. George") appear in the Neals' *Celebrated Irish Tunes*.[51] The editors of the *Sources of Irish Traditional Music, 1660–1855*, have recently added an additional nine tunes to this list ("Moggy Lawther on a Day," "Coal-Black Joak," "The Spring's A Coming," "Past One O''Clock," "There Was a Pretty Girl," "When First I Saw My Nancy's Face," "Abbot of Canterbury," "As I Gang'd Down to Yonder Town," and "Did You Not Hear of Boccough"), bringing the total of Irish tunes in this ballad opera to fifteen. And they have added two more to the list of tunes that may have come from the *Celebrated Irish Tunes;* "Past One O'Clock" is the same tune as "Ta me ma Chulla's na Doushe me," and "Did You Not Hear of Boccough" is the same tune as "Ye Bockagh."[52]

This crossing over of tunes from the native Irish tradition complicates not only the musical discourse of this opera but also its political import. The use of native Irish music infuses the "gentlemen and ladies of the rag" (as the beggars are frequently called) with an ethnic as opposed to simply a class identity, reconfiguring them as spokesmen for Ireland's dispossessed native gentry. As we have seen, in his prefatory remarks on "The Parting Cup," Whyte made an explicit connection between the "Beggars, or Daylabourers," and the old Irish gentry who had once led festivities in their rural communities; and in the fourth canto of this poem, he explicitly attributes

the emergence of a beggar class to the rapacity and anti-Irish prejudice of
the current ruling elite. After describing how Irish "Farmers" once "liv'd
like Gentlemen," he writes that these same farmers are

> Now beggar'd and of all bereft,
> Are doom'd to starve, or live by Theft,
> Take to the Mountains or the Roads,
> When banished from their old Abodes:
> Their native Soil were forc'd to quit,
> So Irish Landlords thought it fit,
> Who without Cer'mony or Rout,
> For their Improvements turn'd them out.
> Embracing still the highest Bidder,
> Inviting all Ye Nations hither,
> Encouraging all Strollers, Caitiffs,
> Or any other but the Natives.[53]

When the queen of the beggars, Mrs. Chaunter, sings "Then fill up the
glass" to the air of "Highway to Dublin" (31) and when her companion,
Tib Tatter, sings "By dint of Assurance" to "Lestrum Pone" (33) in the
above drinking scene, they introduce a native Irish note that causes their
complaints against "Tyrannical Masters" to resonate with Whyte's complaint. Irish music forges a link between the grievances of these "ladies of
the rag" and the grievances of a whole displaced native gentry class.

The Irish and Scottish music that is woven through this opera also ac-
centuates the subversive thrust of its final resolution. The central conflict in
this opera is, on one level, very like that of Gay's *Beggar's Opera*. It revolves
around the attempt by Chaunter, the king of the beggars, to arrange the
wedding of his son, Hunter, to his sweetheart, Phoebe, against the wishes of
Phoebe's father, the corrupt Dublin alderman, Quorum. The Irish and
Scottish music that is associated with Hunter from the beginning, however,
also gives a Jacobite underpinning to this young beggar prince's cause.
When Hunter first enters "with Musick" (a group of fiddlers) in the first
act, he sings a song to the tune of "Coal-black Joak" (24–25), a tune (also
known as "The Black Joke" or "The Black Joake") that was part of the
Scottish and Irish musical tradition,[54] and by associating this Scottish-Irish
musical dialect with this character, the opera however obliquely suggests a
relation between Hunter and another beggarly prince, Charles Stuart. The
medley of Scottish and Irish tunes that accompanies Hunter's restoration at

the end also politicizes what is otherwise a predictable ending for a comic opera. In the last act, a series of reversals ensure a happy ending for the drama: the beggars overpower Quorum's constables as Quorum tries to have them arrested (56), the alderman himself is exposed as a former convicted felon (58–59), and Hunter and Phoebe are united after the true identity of each has been revealed (Hunter, it turns out, is really the alderman's long lost son, while Phoebe is not Quorum's daughter but an orphan) (58–59). Like many comic operas, too, this one ends with a wedding celebration. As a prelude to Hunter and Phoebe's nuptials, Prince Grig and Tib Tatter (another two beggars) marry by leaping over crutches and by performing customary kissing rituals (the men all kiss the bride and the women the groom) (62). Many contemporary Jacobite songs and poems, however, also end with such scenes of social reversal followed by a wedding celebration between the Stuart claimant and his bride Ireland,[55] and by introducing a Gaelic musical subtext to this last scene—the last four tunes heard are "Ellen a Run," "Bonny Lad, come lay the Pipe down," "An Irish Tune," and "Did You Not Hear of Boccough"—this opera links itself to these subversive fantasies. To add Irish and Scottish music to the theme of a beggarly prince reclaiming his lost bride over the opposition of a corrupt law is to turn *The Beggar's Wedding* into a form of Jacobite *aisling*, or dream-vision.

It may have been because it encoded such subversive desires, too, that *The Beggar's Wedding* had such a problematic birth and such a short life on the Irish stage. As we know from Coffey's preface, the Smock Alley manager delayed the production for several months, and when the opera did appear, parts of the play—the drinking scene with the six beggar women and the beggar's wedding scene at the end of the play—were cut.[56] In this attenuated condition, *The Beggar's Wedding* received only two other performances on the Dublin stage,[57] and even then it was roundly denounced in some quarters for being overly "low." The author of the pamphlet *Doctor Anthony's Advice to the Hibernian Aesop: or An Epistle to the Author of the B———gs W———g* (1729), for example, suggested that Coffey lacked the dramatic skills necessary even for Madame Violante's Booth in Dame Street where pantomime and rope-dancing were then being performed; after first suggesting that the "Hibernian Aesop" should adapt his "Muse to *Dames-street* Stage," he adds "But ah / from thence you have been chas'd, / By *Punch*, of most distinguish'd Taste."[58] It was undoubtedly this kind of disparaging commentary, too, that chased Coffey himself from the Dublin stage; a year later he was in London writing for the English stage, and he spent the remainder of his life in England.

If Coffey was effectively "chas'd" from the Dublin stage, however, the Irish song and music he had introduced were not. The old Irish tune "Ellen a Run" (modern Irish: "Eibhlín a rún" [Eileen My Darling]), which Coffey had revived for Tib Tatter's song in the final act of his ballad opera, for example, was heard again two months later in "The New Epilogue Spoke and Sung by Polly Peachum [Mrs. Sterling] at her Benefit play *The Way of the World*" (this time with words in imitation of the original Irish);[59] and this melody and song continued to be performed regularly by singers and instrumentalists in the decades that followed. In 1741 the visiting London singer Kitty Clive advertised that she would sing "the celebrated Song Elen-a-roon" at the Aungier Street theater as a "Compliment to the Irish Ladies and Gentlemen, for the Civilities she hath received"; Mrs. Storer included it among the "favorite songs" she sang at Smock Alley in 1746; and the same year Mathew Dubourg, Master of His Majesty's Music in Ireland, published his variations on "Ellen a Roon . . . set for the Harpsichord."[60] The tune "Coal-black Joak" (or "The Black Joke/Joak") was equally durable. In February 1730 Mrs. Sterling sang a song to the air of "The Black Joke" in a new opera-epilogue at Smock Alley after a performance of Rowe's *Lady Jane Grey*. And in April of the same year, as part of the entr'acte entertainment at a performance of Farquhar's *Beaux Stratagem*, a dancing master named Pitts and one of his "scholars" advertised that they would dance "The Black Joak . . . in the characters of a Fingalian Man and Woman."[61] The latter entertainment may also have included local Dublin dances. Fingal is an area north of Dublin, but the term "Fingalian" had become a synonym for the Irish of the Pale ever since the seventeenth-century poetic satire *The Irish Hudibras or, Fingallian Prince*, and in this poem the local dances of the Fingal region of north Dublin are specifically mentioned. Describing a Pattren Day festival in the village of Lusk, the poet of *The Irish Hudibras* writes:

> Some Trip a Dance upon the Grass
> And every Culleen has his Lass . . .
> There was *O Threicy*, with *Old Darcy*
> Playing all Weathers at the Clarsey . . .
> Skipping of *Gort*, tripping of *Swords*,
> Frisk of *Baldoil* best he affords.[62]

To perform "The Black Joak" in "the characters of a Fingalian Man and Woman," presumably, was to imitate the dress and dance style of these

County Dublin natives—to bring the "skipping," "tripping" and "frisk[s]" of Gort, Swords, and Baldoyle (areas in Fingal) onto the stage of the Theatre Royal.

More important, the playhouse audience itself also began to get into the Irish musical act in the aftermath of *The Beggar's Wedding.* In his dramatic entertainments Coffey had used music to conjure up images of a carnivalesque Irish crowd that challenged structures of authority with its unorthodox behavior. Partly in response to his and other Irish writers' efforts, it could be argued, such a crowd also began to materialize in the playhouse and other musical venues in the 1730s, in this case disrupting the hegemonic drama with its improvisional pléaráca, or revelry. The anonymous poet of *The Upper Gallery,* a mock-heroic poem that was published in Dublin in 1731, provides us with the first picture of this crowd and its subversive activity. In this poem we follow the impoverished poet-narrator from the moment he finds the *"one fair Splendid"* (a shilling)[63] in his pocket that gives him the price of admission to the upper gallery of Smock Alley until he reemerges onto the freezing Dublin streets, and along the way we witness everything that this poet-narrator sees—from the "sudden lustre" of a young girl's legs as she slips on her way down to her seat in the upper gallery before the show (5) to the spectacle of the "brawny Chairman" panting "beneath his Load" as he bears wealthy patrons away from the playhouse at the end of the evening (14). It is the impromptu singing of the upper gallery before and during a play, however, that is the main focus of this poet's interest, and we soon learn that when he describes this singing as "sweet"—in his invocation he begs the Muse to help him "Sing . . . those sublime Abodes, /Where rais'd in graceful Pomp, the jovial Throng/ Sweeten the Intervals of Plays with Song" (4)—he is being highly ironic. As is evident from their reaction to the fops who dare venture into their region, the "Throng" that sits in the upper gallery is far from "jovial"; a deep hostility marks these audience members' relation with the beau monde:

> In the dim Shade we sit, a doubtful Race,
> Disguis'd each Voice, and cover'd ev'ry Face,
> Hid in the uncock'd Hat's wide spreading Round,
> Or sunk in some old Tie's immense Profound:
> Beneath, thick Coats their friendly Capes expand,
> And the Oak-Cudgel waves in ev'ry Hand.
>
> .   .   .   .

When'er some Fopling wou'd our Shade profane
By the white Ruffle, or the glancing Cane,
All fly his Touch, and with keen-stinging Jest
Torment the Wretch, who dares to be well-drest. (6)

This hostility also erupts into open conflict as soon as the theater orchestra strikes up the art music so beloved of these wealthier patrons, though
the conflict is now waged through the medium of music itself. When
the "Fiddles rise, / The wing'd Notes thicken, and the Music flies" (7), the
upper gallery attempts to drown out these orchestral sounds by singing
"gay native tunes" and "The Black Joke":

Pleas'd we elude the ling'ring Lapse of Day,
With jocund Catch, or am'rous Roundelay;
Our Tastes their throng'd *Hesperian* Notes confound,
Lost in a trackless Labyrinth of Sound;
Gay native Tunes assert their worthier Choice,
And the *Black Joke* resounds from ev'ry Voice. (8)

The poet of *The Upper Gallery* also explicitly attributes a nationalist meaning to this preference for indigenous music. From extolling "native Tunes"
and "the *Black Joke*," he moves directly to extolling the upper gallery's use
of native fabrics and to condemning the boxes and pit for their "foreign
Dress" and their failure to support Irish trade and Irish artists:

Our thick *Hiberian* Drab, at Midnight Hours,
Repels benumbing Frosts, and driving Show'rs,
Whilst those, who would sublimer Tasts express,
Shine in a useless and a foreign Dress,
Behold that radiant Circle of the Fair,
How the Pit brightens with a ruddy Glare!
Pernicious Pride! A publick curse they shine;
Hence Trade's depress'd, and starving Artists pine,
    "Each from our Battlements leans down his Head,
    "And then turns pale to see them look so red." (8–9)

What this poem suggests, then, is that the Irish Protestant campaign in
support of Irish manufacture that began with Swift and Sheridan in the
1720s was being taken up by a more socially diverse crowd in the upper

gallery in the 1730s. "Native tunes," like "*Hibernian* drab," had been invested with an Irish national significance, and a "doubtful Race" and less than jovial "Throng" was using both symbolic practices in the playhouse to contest a colonial culture and a colonial politics.

In *A Dissertation on Italian and Irish Musick, with some Panegryrick on Carrallan our late Irish Orpheus* (1740), however, Lawrence Whyte reveals that his kind of "doubtful Race" was also implicated in this subversive musical play, though to discern the presence of this other kind of ambiguously constituted Irish subject in the playhouse "Throng," it is again necessary to push against an evasive Catholic "art." Whyte does not explicitly state in *A Dissertation* that he is describing a scene in a playhouse or music hall. He subdivides his poem, rather, into musical sections: there is an introductory stanza entitled "A Prelude, or Voluntary," followed by three stanzas entitled, respectively, "Adagio," "Jigg," and "Recitativo."[64] The social types he describes in each of the last three musical sections, however, also correspond to the social types who would have frequented the boxes, pit, and galleries in a contemporary Dublin playhouse, suggesting that Whyte is doing his own playful musical variation on the standard descriptive playhouse poem. An elegant lady, "*Corinna*," is central to the "Adagio" stanza, "*Beaus*" and a "Country *Squire*" to the "Jigg" stanza, and the "*Vulgar*" including the poet and his friends (the "we" of the last verse) are central to the last "Recitativo" stanza. Musical allusions in the poem also suggest that Whyte has conflated three specific Dublin sites of musical performance during the mid-1730s — the Aungier Street theater, the Smock Alley theater, and the Crow Street music hall — to create his musical scene. In the "Adagio" stanza, for example, we are told that "*Corinna*" thrills to hear "*Hendal's* Notes" and that she goes into ecstasies "if *Dub——ge* but touch the String . . . and *Raffa* sing" (412), and later in the poem we are informed that "*Ariadne*," and Italian opera music in general, is taking the whole country by storm (413–14). Mrs. Raffa, a soprano who made her debut at Crow Street in 1733, sang Handel's *Acis and Galatea* at the Crow Street musical hall in 1734 and 1735, and for a government night performance at Aungier Street in March 1735, she sang an ode set to music by Dubourg.[65] At Aungier Street in 1735, too, *Ariadne in Crete*, the overture to Handel's opera, was performed for the first time.[66]

Like the poet of *The Upper Gallery*, then, Whyte suggests that in such musical venues, foreign art music is coming under attack from a patriot element in the audience. The elegant "*Corinna*" may swoon to hear the music of Corelli, Vivaldi, or Handel and the watching "*Beaus*" who court her may applaud her taste. But, this poet tells us, the "Country *Squire* dress'd like a

Hero" joins in a chorus "with the rest" (presumably in the gallery) to hear "The Black Joke" and other favorite Irish, English, and Scottish tunes, and he threatens to break the orchestra's fiddles if they refuse to comply with his request:

> The Country *Squire* dress'd like a *Hero,*
> Who'd rather hear *Lill'bolero,*
> And having neither Air nor Voice,
> Of *Bobbin Joan* wou'd make his Choice,
> And joins in *Chorus* with the rest,
> And cries *Encore!* to crown the Jest,
> Then out of time he gives a Clap!
> Huzza's! and then throws up his Cap!
> Cries damn you! play up the *Black Joke,*
> Or else you'll get your Fiddles broke,
> Then play *Jack Lattin* my dear Honey!
> Hey! *Larry Grogan* for my Money!
> Then rushes out with seeming Haste,
> And leaves that Sample of his Taste. (413)

A closer analysis of this passage also suggests that an emergent Irish Protestant patriotism is behind this little disruptive performance. With his preference for the bitterly satiric anti-Catholic song "Lill'bolero,"[67] the Squire is, on the one hand, a type of fiery Irish Protestant Williamite. But like Moore and the other Williamite "heroes" who disrupted the playhouse in 1712, this one also begins to blur the boundary between himself and the native Irishman as he elaborates on his rebellious desire. The phrase "my dear Honey" which he uses, for example, is generally associated with native Irish characters in English plays of the period,[68] and by voicing a preference for "*Jack Lattin,*" and "*Larry Grogan,*" the Squire suggests a further affinity with an indigenous people and culture as these two tunes acquired their names from a native fiddler and piper who played in the Dublin area in the first half of the century.[69] That the Squire had his counterpart in real life is also apparent from the account of Whyte's contemporary, John Bunkle. Looking back with nostalgia on the days of his youth in Dublin in the 1720s, Bunkle recalls Jack Macklean's famous Conniving House, a public house near Ringsend that was a favorite haunt of the "gentlemen of Trinity." And he also remembers with affection the music that he heard from Larry Grogan and Jack Lattin at this location: "Many a delightful evening have I passed in this pretty thatched house with the famous Larry Grogan, who played on the bagpipes extreme well, dear Jack Lattin, matchless on the fiddle and the most agreeable of companions . . . and many other delightful fellows who went in the days of their youth to the shades of eternity."[70]

In the last and longest section of *A Dissertation* where he specifically talks about the tastes of *"the Vulgar,"* however, Whyte also suggests that there was an Irish Catholic crowd behind this revival of indigenous music, and he hints that this music also serves to voice their political aspirations. In what can be construed as a nod in the direction of Pilkington's *The Progress of Music in Ireland*, Whyte first admits in this section that there has been a dislocation of music in Ireland caused by the influx of Italian opera and foreign performers, and he conveys the pathos of this disloca-tion by personifying Irish music as a woman who is being driven from her humble dwelling place among the common people by her rival, the war-bling *"Ariadne."* The passage below, for example, describes what happens to Irish song and dance when Ariadne arrives in the south of Ireland where Gaelic is spoken predominantly:

> She [Ariadne] flies to *Munster* for the Air,
> To clear her pipes and warble there.
> Poor *Cronaan*, being turn'd out of Play,
> With *Rinke Mueenagh* flew away,
> To the remotest part of *Kerry*,
> In hopes to make the Vulgar merry,
> But scare one Cabbin in their Flight,
> Wou'd give them Lodging for a Night,
> So taken with a foreign Jingle,
> *Tralee* despis'd them, likewise *Dingle*. (414)

But this dislocation of traditional song, Whyte also argues, is only tempo-rary. If the Irish musical muse has been driven out of her traditional dwelling place in the country, she has found a new home in contemporary opera. "Some old ones [songs] we have oft reviv'd,/ For modern Opera's contriv'd" (413), he writes, and he suggests that this Irish muse is also kept in tune by the demands of present-day Irish music lovers:

> But *Duimin duh* is still in favour,
> Since we from *Murphy*, beg, and crave her,
> Of him alone we must require

To do her Justice on the Lyre,
She, and old *Eveleen a Rune,*
Are by the *Muses* kept in Tune
Who many Centuries have thriv'd
And doom'd by fate to be long liv'd,
With many others we know well
Which do in harmony excel. (414)

Whyte does not explicitly tell us who these music lovers are who demand
to hear these old Irish tunes from Murphy (a harper who played in Dublin
between 1720 and 1740), nor does he state who it is who knows these old
Irish tunes so well. However, the other tunes that he praises as having
"preserv'd their Relish"—"Ta me mo choll," "Candun dilish," "Da mhi
Manum," and "Plankstys" and "Pléarácas" by Carolan (415)—all appear
in the Neals' *Celebrated Irish Tunes,* and this connection strongly suggests
that he is alluding to the group of Catholic migrants and Jacobite survivors
(himself included) who gathered in the taverns around Christ Church and
Fishamble Street to socialize and play music in the first half of the century.
That Whyte's kind of crowd—the "Tribe of Deoch an Doruis"—was
showing up and making their voice heard at the playhouse around this
time is also suggested by the record of benefits at the playhouse. By the
mid-1730s the Charitable and Musical Society was regularly sponsoring
benefit performances at Smock Alley for the relief of prisoners in the Four
Courts Marshalsea, and on at least one occasion Whyte himself wrote a
prologue for one of these benefit performances.[71]

   When Whyte states that "Duimin duh" (modern Irish: "Druimin
dubh" [Black Cow]) is "still in favour" among his kind of crowd, he also
hints that the Irish Catholic community of which he was a part was articulating its dream of political and cultural recovery through this music, though
this allusion would only be legible to someone familiar with the native Irish
musical and poetic tradition. In the popular Irish folk song "Druimin dubh,"
a brown- or black-sided cow is used as a metaphor for Ireland, and under the
cover of this conceit the singer laments his community's state of material and
cultural impoverishment and vents his desire for revenge against the English
conqueror. In Seán Ó Tuama and Thomas Kinsella's edition and translation
of this song, the second and third verses are as follows:

   'Níl fearann, níl tíos agam, fíonta ná ceol,
   níl flaithibh im choimhdeacht, níl saoithe ná sló,

ach ag síor-ól an uisce go minic sa ló
agus beathuisce 's fíon ag mo naímhdibh ar bord.'

Dá bhfaighinnse cead aighnis nó radharc ar an gcoróin,
Sacsanaigh do leadhbfainn mar do leadhbfainn seanbhróg,
Trí bhogaithe, trí choillte 's trí dhraighneach lá ceo,
agus siúd mar a bhréagfainn mo dhroimeann donn óg.

"I've no land and no home, no music or wine,
no princes to guard me, no scholars or troops,
only water to drink every hour of the day
with whiskey and wine on my enemies' table."

"Give me license to fight, or one look at the Crown,
and Saxons I'd clout as I'd clout an old shoe
through marshes, through woods, through thorn-trees in the mist,
—and that's how I'd cherish my dear Druimeann Donn!"[72]

To "beg and crave" "Drumin duh," then, is to beg to hear a tune with sub-versive political connotations, and for Irish-speakers like Whyte, such connotations would have survived even if different lyrics accompanied the tune. For the "Tribe of Deoch an Doruis," the Irish lyrics would have seemed a kind of ghostly echo to the English words whenever this song was performed in the playhouse.

The demand to hear the ancient Irish love song "Eveleen a Run" may have been no less charged, though this song is not explicitly political. In her analysis of eighteenth-century Irish popular song, Máirín Nic Eoin points out that the woman in the Irish love song was frequently "a site of representation on which are projected political yearnings and hopes," and in this sense she functioned as "a metonym for the oppressed Catholic population."[73] When Whyte links "Drumin duh" to "Eveleen a Rune" and when he transforms both these songs into female figures —"She, and old *Eveleen a Run*"—he hints that this song functioned in a similar symbolic fashion for his group of friends. "Eveleen a Run" is transformed, through her association with "Druimin duh" into a metaphor for the Irish Catholic nation, and it is the desires of this nation, Whyte implies, that are "kept in Tune" and restored each time this song is sung.

By 1745, then, an assortment of improperly interpellated colonial subjects—Irish Protestant patriots, members of an emerging Irish Catholic middle class, the religiously mixed "Throng" who sat in the upper gallery—had made their way into the theater. As this musical analysis shows, these improper subjects were attempting to reshape this institution in their own image. Sheridan was only partly exaggerating, in other words, when he later stated that at the time he took over the management of the Irish theater the playhouse was viewed as a "Common," a space presided over by "the Will and Pleasure of the People." And it was precisely because the theater had become something of a "Common" that it was the site of such a fierce struggle during the period of Sheridan's tenure. When the new manager tried to return the theater to its previous elite English "Owners" with his reform campaign, as we will see in the next four chapters, he met with fierce opposition from all sections of the Irish "People."

CHAPTER 4

The Gentlemen's Quarrel
and the Politics of the '45

In her influential study *Thomas Sheridan of Smock-Alley*, Esther Sheldon argues that a class issue—the relative status of players and gentlemen—was at the core of what she refers to as the "Kelly riot," a conflict that spread from the theater to Dublin streets, coffeehouses, the press, the university, and ultimately the courts, in spring 1747. According to Sheldon, the conflict began at the Theatre Royal on January 19, 1747, when a drunken young Galway gentleman named Kelly went behind the scenes during a performance and made unwanted sexual advances to some of the women players. Hearing the disturbance, Sheridan, who was playing the role of Aesop onstage, stopped the play and had Kelly removed from the playhouse by the theater guards. But the young man somehow managed to return to the pit, and when Sheridan next appeared, he struck Sheridan so forcefully with an orange that he knocked off his false nose. In the shouting match that followed between the two men, Sheridan then stated, "I am as good a Gentleman as you are" (or, according to other reports, "I am as good a Gentleman as any in the House"), and it was that assertion of gentility by a player, Sheldon argues, together with the fact that the manager subsequently dared to strike this gentleman—when Kelly went backstage again after the show to demand an apology, Sheridan soundly beat him with Aesop's oaken stick—that gave rise to the subsequent turmoil. The day after the incident there were fights between Sheridan and Kelly supporters in coffeehouses and other public places, and the day after that (January 21), when Sheridan failed to appear onstage to apologize, about fifty "Gentlemen" stormed the stage, ripping up theater property and clothing with their swords. After this riot, Sheridan shut the theater for two weeks.

Framing the events in this way, Sheldon then plausibly reads the humiliations suffered by the "Gentlemen" and their defeat in a court of law as a victory for democratic reform in the Irish theater. When the playhouse reopened on February 9, the "Gentlemen" were forced to leave the theater after the audience sided with the well-known municipal reformer, Charles Lucas, who called for a show of support for the manager. And on February 11, after another outbreak of violence in the theater, a number of the "Gentlemen" (Kelly, John Browne of the Neale, a Mr. Martin, and a Captain Fitzgerald) were conveyed by students to Trinity College and forced to apologize on their knees in the college yard. A Dublin court of law, according to Sheldon, provided the final say on this matter. Both Sheridan and Kelly had filed charges of assault against each other stemming from the January 19 incident, and both were indicted. When they came to trial on February 19, the jury quickly found Sheridan innocent of assault but found Kelly guilty. Sheldon concludes that this finding, which was accompanied by the justice's stern warning against intruders on the stage, helped Sheridan to transform the Irish theater into a more decent and orderly place. "Kelly's drunken behavior and his friends' destructive violence," she writes, "secured Sheridan the reform which gained him a place in stage history."[1]

In the first of the three letters he wrote under the pseudonym "A. Freeman, Barber and Citizen," however, Sheridan's most ardent supporter, Charles Lucas, suggests that ethnic, religious, and colonial tensions were at the heart of the conflict, and though his account reproduces the foundational colonial myth of English civility and Irish barbarity—this was a "Quarrel" between those "whose Ancestors came to subdue the Barbarity of the Natives of this Island" and the "Offspring" of those "Savages and Tyrants"[2]—it provides a better point of departure for analyzing the politics and structure of this theatrical event than Sheldon's exclusively class-based and theater-focused narrative. Central to Lucas's account is the notion that the Gentlemen's Quarrel registered an Irish Catholic resurgence, and this explanation can be supported by a fuller analysis and historical contextualization of this event. As I show in this chapter, the actions and words of the "Gentlemen" during this Quarrel can be understood in the context of a broader midcentury Catholic art and politics that was working to restore the social and political status of the marginalized Catholic subject. In the following passage from the first Barber's *Letter,* Lucas also provides us with insight into why the "Gentlemen" should have chosen this particular site and this particular moment to stage their countertheater:

> The first Cause of this Quarrel is well known, it is no more than this. *Sh...n*, or the Player, took upon him the management and Reformation of the Stage; chose the most Moral and Loyal Plays, and exhibited them, with great Decency and Regularity; to the Satisfaction of all Judges, not disaffected to our Government. To such indeed *Sh...n*'s choice of *Plays, Prologues, Epilogues, Songs*, with *Bonefires* and *Illuminations* upon particular Occasions, gave early Umbrage and a general, a declared Distaste to the Man. However *Sh...n* pretty well succeeded, and was growing in Favour with the Town, when he was look'd on with an envidious Eye, by some *Gentlemen*, who therefore resolved on his Destruction and that of the reformed Stage, in him. (3)

Sheridan's first season as manager (1745–46) coincided with the period of the Jacobite invasion of England and, as is indicated by the reference to his "Loyal Plays" and to his "choice of *Plays, Prologues, Epilogues, Songs*, with *Bonefires* and *Illuminations* upon particular Occasions," his theater participated in the campaign of intimidation that was directed at the Catholic community, particularly at its gentry leaders, during the tense period of "the '45."

❖❖❖

It is commonly claimed today that the period of the Jacobite rebellion in England was remarkable for the *absence* of Catholic harassment in Ireland. To explain this change, historians generally point to the British government's new policy of conciliating Catholics at time of war. Whereas previous viceroys at times of military threat had issued proclamations against the Catholic clergy and ordered the arrest of prominent Catholics, the earl of Chesterfield (the viceroy) met with leaders of the Catholic community and promised them his protection, and a number of Protestant bishops, including the archbishop of Tuam, wrote letters to their clergy and parishioners urging them not to take any offensive action against Catholics.[3] The readiness with which the Catholic gentry and clergy made public protestations of their loyalty during this period is also cited as proof of a new acceptance of the status quo on the other side. While Irish Catholics abroad played an important role in the Jacobite rising—there were officers from the Irish Brigade with Charles Edward Stuart during his invasion of England, and Irish soldiers fought with Scottish Jacobites at Culloden[4]—the leaders of the Catholic community in Ireland visited Dublin Castle and assured Chesterfield of their support. And the Catholic clergy, as reported by a notice in Dublin newspapers, urged their people "to behave themselves peaceably and quietly like good subjects, to avoid like true Christians all riots, mobs, drunkenness or late hours, to give no offence either in their words or actions to their neighbours, but to behave themselves so in every respect, as to be worthy of the favour and liberty they now enjoy."[5]

A closer look at the events, writings, and dramatic productions of this period reveals a less sanguine reality on both sides. Although it is true that Catholics were no longer subjected to the full force of the penal laws, the government and its supporters waged an intense ideological war against the Catholic community and its gentry during this period, and in so doing, it could be argued, they took their lead from Chesterfield, whose maxim was that the "popish religion and influence" could best "be undermined and destroyed by art."[6] In an October 24, 1745, letter to the duke of Newcastle, Chesterfield offers us additional insight into this undermining "art" as he reflects on the state of the "papists" and on his recent meeting with the Catholic nobility and gentry:

> The papists here are not only quiet, but even their priests preach quiet to 'em. The most considerable of 'em have been with me to assure me of their firm resolution not to disturb the government, and to thank me for not having disturb'd them, as usuall at this time. I told 'em very fairly that the lenity of the government should continue as long as their good behaviour deserv'd it, but that if they gave the least disturbance they should be treated with a rigour they had never yet experienc'd. I have very good intelligence of 'em, and I cannot discover that they meditate any disturbance.[7]

It is clear from this passage that the policy of conciliation did not preclude constant surveillance of the Catholic leadership, and it is also clear that the paternalist offers of government protection were laced with overt threats of retaliation if there was any lapse in "good behaviour." Chesterfield's address to a Catholic who was suspected of being an agent of the Pretender and who was "privately sent for to the castle" provides another example of this subtle coercive "art" at work. According to W. Ernst, the viceroy made the following speech to this Catholic gentleman: "Sir, I do not wish to inquire whether you have any particular employment in this kingdom, but I know that you have a great interest amongst those of your persuasion. I have sent for you to exhort them to be peaceable and quiet. If they behave like faithful subjects, they shall be treated as such; but if they act in a different manner, I shall be worse to them than Cromwell."[8] Ernst relates this incident as evidence of the viceroy's admirable ability to balance "lenity and prudence[,] . . . moderation and firmness" in his dealings with "the adherents to the exiled royal family,"[9] but it is better read as evidence of a policy of Catholic blackmail and intimidation. Unless this suspected Jacobite becomes an organ of the establishment, Chesterfield clearly suggests, the government *will* "inquire" into his affairs, an inquiry that in this case could lead to a capital charge of treason. The message for the whole Catholic community is no less double-edged; the alternative to being treated like "faithful subjects" is genocidal warfare, as the brief but loaded invocation of the name "Cromwell" suggests.

The Januslike face of Chesterfield's government is also apparent in his recorded reaction to the possibility of a rising in the western province of Connaught. Because the Catholic gentry of Connaught retained a greater percentage of their land and were more powerful than the branches of the Catholic gentry in other parts of the country, the province was always considered one of the greatest sources of danger to the Protestant state. This concept of Connaught also lies behind the following "good-humored jest" that Ernst relates in support of his claim that Chesterfield disapproved of intolerant zeal in any form. After his vice-treasurer Mr. Gardner told the viceroy in great alarm that he was "assured upon good authority, that the people in the province of Connaught were actually rising . . . Lord Chesterfield took out his watch, and with great composure answered him, 'It it nine o'clock, and certainly time for them to rise; I therefore believe your news to be true.'"[10] This posture of urbane skepticism about the Catholic threat is belied, however, by Chesterfield's words in a private correspondence in which he describes the additional precautionary measures he took in relation to both Connaught and Munster, the second province where the Catholic gentry was relatively strong. In a letter to the duke of Newcastle on September 21, 1745, Chesterfield remarks that he ordered a cantonment of the forces he had in Dublin so that "they may in eight and forty hours be got together, and form one corps, equally *a porte* of Galway or Cork, the two parts of this country where the papists are the strongest, and where, whenever there is an invasion, that invasion will certainly be made."[11]

The response to the invasion within the Irish Protestant community itself was no less double-edged. The very fact that the leaders of the established church, the bishops, were willing to enter into debate on the Catholic issue in newspapers and pamphlets during the period of the invasion bespoke a new willingness to rule through persuasion rather than coercion, and in many of their writings the tone is enlightened and tolerant. In his letter, for example, the archbishop of Tuam urges his clergy to visit their "popish parishioners" in their homes and "shew by friendly reasonings where their true interest lies," and he also attempts some of that friendly reasoning himself in his letter. The following passage, which addresses the question of how "the bulk of the Papists" are affected by the penal laws, was clearly meant to impress Catholic as well as Protestant readers with its logic:

> Do they [papists] not through his majesty's clemency, enjoy the free exercise of their religion, even at this very conjuncture, when they might expect to be restrained? Do they not resort publicly in great numbers to their Mass-houses, without the least molestation, as the Protestants do their churches? Is not the priest in every parish well known to the Protestant gentlemen, and tho' he be liable to prosecution, yet does any one lay hold of him, or disturb him so long as he behaves himself orderly and decently as becomes his character . . . ?[12]

But even this measured argument draws on images of physical coercion — the possibility of Catholics being "restrained," "molest[ed]," "prosecut[ed]," "la[id] hold of"—for its persuasive value, and this rhetoric of violence is explicit and pervasive in one of the most widely circulated anti-Jacobite tracts of the period, *The Farmer's Letters to the Protestants of Ireland* (1745).

The Farmer's Letters were written by Henry Brooke, an Irish Protestant who had already achieved considerable notoriety in England because of the banning of his play *Gustavus Vasa, the Deliverer of His Country*. This play was suppressed in London in 1739 under the English Stage Licensing Act for its suspected anti-Walpole and Jacobite tendencies,[13] but it brought him to the attention of a circle of English opposition writers and politicians that included Lord Chesterfield.[14] It is also possible that the play brought Brooke to the attention of patriots and opposition leaders in Ireland, for on December 3, 1744, *Gustavus Vasa* was produced for the first time at Smock Alley under the title *The Patriot*.[15] The mixed reception it received in Dublin would also seem to confirm that it was perceived as an antigovernment play. Mrs. Delany, for instance, writes (somewhat ambiguously), "I don't find it greatly approved of, but they say it is miserably acted," and a newspaper reports that when a different play was announced after the third performance (Brooke's benefit night), "The Patriot was loudly called for."[16]

In *The Farmer's Letters* of 1745, however, Brooke represented himself as an avid supporter of the Hanoverian administration, a switch in position that he explains by relegating patriot politics to the status of a minor family quarrel. His previous harangues "upon Corruptions in *England* and Grievances in *Ireland*," he writes in his first *Letter*, are "little Jealousies and Exceptions" that "only ruffle the Surface of Loyalty, and, like Family disputes, always cease on the Approach of a common *Enemy*."[17] A more likely explanation for this switch in politics, given Brooke's subsequent record of accepting payment from Catholic activists to write on their behalf, is that he had been bought off by Chesterfield's offer of the post of barrack master in Mullingar; Benjamin Victor, who was in a position to know, also explicitly states that Chesterfield gave Brooke this place in return for his "celebrated Farmer's Letters."[18] In either case, it is indisputable that Brooke brought his considerable knowledge of the Irish Protestant "Family" and its traditional lore to bear on his writing. In the effort to encourage Protestants to join the local militias (and this recruiting drive seems to be the central aim of *The Farmer's Letters*), he had recourse to the image of the bloodthirsty and rapacious Irish Catholic, an image that, as we have seen, would have been familiar to Irish Protestants from Sir John Temple's *The Irish Rebellion* (1646), Archbishop King's *State of the Protestants of Ireland* (1691), and the annual October 23 sermons.[19] A Jacobite victory, Brooke argues in his first *Letter*, would bring about the "utter Ruin" of Protestant homes and families and their personal liberties just as it did during the 1688–91 wars (1:3–4), and he returns again to the image of this ruined, violated hearth in the second *Letter* under the guise of reporting his [the Farmer's] own musings as he contemplates his "painfully improved" lands (2:2) and the fond wife and loving children who greet him on his return home each evening:

Is it possible that I should think with Patience on the *impending Ruin?*—To see my Fields in Flames, my House in a Heap of Rubbish, my Wife rent from my Bosom, and my Infants quartered by War! I will never survive to see such a Day of Horrors, and I only wish for a thousand Lives that I might die as many Deaths, in their Defence.

Have you then, my Countrymen, no such Properties to preserve, no Parents to protect, no Wives to cherish, nor Infants to defend? (2:2)

By discounting the law-abiding behavior of present-day Catholics and by dismissing their protestations of peacefulness as meaningless, Brooke clears the way for an all-out war on the Catholic community. "The Papists of this Kingdom, are particularly placid and peaceable, at this Season," the Farmer admits, but he argues that "so still and sullen a Calm" simply augers a "heavier Storm" (2:8) and that, finally, "arms" are the only solution:

> They [Papists] say to us, *had we lived in the Days of our Fathers, we would not have been Partakers with them, in their Oppressions and Massacres: But herein they confess themselves to be the Children of those Men,* by whom our Maidens were polluted, by whom our Matrons were left childless: by whom our Grandsires were butchered, and their Infants dashed against the Stones. Up then, my brave Countrymen! gird on your Arms! stand for your selves! be strong to defend your Rights, be valiant to repel the Invaders! (2:8)

After this passage, the Farmer goes on to state that these "brave Countrymen" would "commence no Violence against our *inmate Enemies,* while they prefer Peace to War, and the Administration of Justice to Rebellion," but the overall inflammatory tone of the *Letters* is better captured by a passage at the end of the first *Letter,* where he advocates total extermination of the lawless, rapacious Catholic enemy: "If we are Freemen, if we are Men—if we are Husbands, if we are Parents . . . we will arise! we will seize every Man his Sword! we will turn upon these Destroyers! these Enemies of Mankind! Nor will we be appeased, till we have swept this Invader with his Slavish Rout, from the very Face of the Earth they incumber" (1:8).

If *The Farmer's Letters* provide one measure of the scope and intensity of the Protestant rhetorical assault on the Catholic community at this period, *The Impartial Examiner* (1746), a paper reportedly written by a Catholic priest, the Reverend John Jones, provides another,[20] and in this paper it is possible to see something of the anxiety, fear, and resentment that lay beneath the expressions of loyalism by Catholic clergy and gentlemen during the '45. The full title of this paper alone provides an indication of the volume of anti-Catholic tracts rolling off the Protestant-controlled press in this period; *The Impartial Examiner* was subtitled *the Faithful Representer of the Various and Manifold Misrepresentations imposed on the Roman*

Catholics of Ireland, in the Several Charges laid at their Doors by the Scribblers of the Farmer's, Merchant's, and Drapier's Letters, and Charitable and Seasonable Advices, the Editors of the Magazines, and the Printers of the Journals, Courants, Occurrences, News-Letters, Gazettes, Pamphlets, and other modern Public Papers, Etc, which are daily printed in Dublin.[21] In the paper itself Jones verifies that there was such an outpouring of "misrepresentations," as he discusses and refutes the claims of the various tracts by the pamphleteers and newspaper editors alluded to in his title. These anti-Catholic tracts are too numerous to describe in any detail here,[22] but Jones's general remarks at the beginning of the pamphlet provide a sense of the intensity of this anti-Catholic rhetorical onslaught and a sense of how seriously the Catholic community itself took this attack. "*Modern Pamphleteers* do manage *the Cause of Religion* with such Scurrility, that they appear rather as *Leaders of a furious Mob*, breathing nothing but *Massacre* and *Plunder*, than *sober Advocates* for the *Christian Faith*" (6), Jones writes, and at a later point he states that these "*fiery Zealots*" not only make Roman Catholics "ridiculous in *their Faith*, but also by *Forgery* and *Scandal*, render them the most *odious Creatures* upon Earth, by painting their Morals and Practices in the very Blackest Colours" (10). He also suggests that these zealots are endangering Catholic lives with their rhetoric. Their misrepresentations are spread so widely among "the common People," he notes, that if it were not for the moderation of the viceroy and the Parliament, Catholics would be "torn to pieces, or stoned, as they walk down the street"(10).

A similar point about the life-endangering dimension of the anti-Catholic rhetorical assault is made by John Curry, the Dublin physician and friend of Charles O'Conor, in a pamphlet he wrote at this time. Curry's *Brief Account from the Most Authentic Protestant Writers of the Causes, Motives, and Mischiefs, of the Irish Rebellion on the 23rd Day of October 1641, Deliver'd in a Dialogue Between a Dissenter and a Member of the Church of Ireland, as by Law Established* was actually published in 1747. But in the advertisement of the tract, Curry states that his "Dialogue" was written "during the late Rebellion in Scotland, in vindication of the Roman Catholics of Ireland, against whom, not withstanding their quiet and dutiful behaviour at that Juncture, and indeed since the Revolution, many false, and scurrilous Libels were then published."[23] In his later *Historical Memoirs* (1752), in which he again justifies the publication of the 1747 *Brief Account*, he explicitly identifies these "scurrilous Libels" as *The Farmer's Letters*, and he elaborates on the inflammatory potential of the pamphlets in the context of the '45: "During the Scottish Rebellion in 1745 such (a) viru-lent Pamphlets were dispersed all over the Kingdom, against the Principles and Practices of Roman Catholics in general, and those of Ireland in par-ticular, as would certainly, at that juncture, have brought into imminent Danger, not only the Peace and Prosperity, but also the Liberty and Lives, of these People, had not the great Wisdom and Lenity of the (b) Govern-ment frequently interposed."[24] In footnotes to this passage, (a) is identified as the "Farmer's Letters" and (b) as the "Earl of Chesterfield, Lord Lieu-tenant," and these remarks would seem to suggest that Catholics looked to Chesterfield as their friend during these times. But in private, if we are to judge from Edmund Burke's remarks many years later, some Catholics were telling a different tale. In his *Letter to a Peer* (1782), Burke wrote of Chesterfield: "This man, whilst he was duping the Credulity of Papists with fine words in private, and commending their good behaviour during a rebellion in Great Britain, as it well deserved to be commended and re-warded was capable, of urging penal Laws against them in a Speech from the Throne, and stimulating with provocatives, the wearied and half ex-hausted bigottry of the then parliament of Ireland."[25]

♦♦♦

The Theatre Royal participated in this ideological effort to intimidate and contain the Catholic population, though like the Protestant state at large, it interlaced its shows of sectarian aggression with artful displays of benevo-lence and conciliation. During the 1745–46 season, three of the biggest stars of the London stage, David Garrick, George Ann Bellamy, and Spranger Barry, acted at Smock Alley, and during that season, the earl of Chesterfield commanded an unprecedented twenty performances at the theater.[26] The playhouse, consequently, was more of an English and court institution than it had been for many years; night after night it was a con-stant glittering spectacle of ruling-class power and ruling-class culture. Chesterfield's reported behavior on the occasion of Garrick's benefit per-formance also gives us an insight into the ideological function of these nu-merous shows of power. On the occasion of a viceregal command per-formance, it was customary for the patentee (dressed in regulation court attire and bearing two silver candlesticks) to receive the viceregal party in the vestibule of the theater and escort this party to the viceregal box. On the occasion of Garrick's benefit (and, undoubtedly, as an acknowledg-ment of this visitor's celebrity status), Sheridan shared this duty with the

English actor-manager; both men received Chesterfield and his lady with candles in hand, and both men escorted the couple to their box. According to Garrick's biographer, however, Chesterfield "took not the least notice of Mr. Garrick[;] . . . he spoke very kindly to Sheridan, but did not even return the salute of the other," reportedly because "his lordship, when in Ireland, had a mind to convince the people of that kingdom, that his heart was intirely Irish."[27] As in previous periods of political tension, the viceroy was using his appearance at the playhouse to present himself as the true, loving father of the Irish people.

Sheridan's "choice of *Plays, Prologues, Epilogues, Songs,* with *Bonefires* and *Illuminations* upon particular Occasions" and his "reformed stage" (to use Lucas's terms) worked to complement this viceregal theater. During the 1745–46 and 1746–47 seasons, Sheridan engaged Henry Brooke to write prologues and epilogues on significant anniversaries, and in what could only be interpreted as a show of support for Brooke's anti-Catholic stance, he also used Brooke's pseudonym "the Farmer" to advertise the new occasional pieces. The viceregal command performance to mark the duke of Cumberland's birthday on April 15, 1746, for example, was advertised with "a Prologue on the Occasion spoken by Mr. Sheridan, and an Epilogue by Mr. Garrick, written by the Farmer," and the command performance to mark the November 4 Williamite celebration in 1746 was advertised "With a new Prologue on the Occasion written by the Farmer, to be spoke by Mr. Sheridan."[28] A cursory glance at the first of these pieces indicates that they contained some of the same sectarian rhetoric as *The Farmer's Letters* themselves. Under the guise of paying tribute to William, Duke of Cumberland, the leader of the anti-Jacobite force in England in 1745, this epilogue engaged in a triumphalist celebration of the Williamite victors in the 1688–91 wars against the native Irish, and it rallied the members of the audience in the name of their Williamite ancestors and the blood spilled at the Boyne:

> O! did the gallant Cumberland but head
> Such troops as here our glorious William led!
> Bold names, in Britain's history renown'd,
> Who fix'd her freedom on Hibernian ground,
> Till death, embattled for their country, stood,
> And made the Boyne immortal by their blood.
> Such were your sires, who still survive in fame;
> Such are the sons who would achieve the same.[29]

The prayer in another part of this epilogue that Cumberland might be "the scourge of France, the dread of Rome, /The patriot's blessing, and the rebel's doom" was no less inflammatory. Roman Catholic and "rebel," the syntax of these lines suggest, are synonymous, and in praying for the "doom" of one, the speaker also implicitly prays for the doom of the other.

When news reached Dublin on April 28, 1746, of the overwhelming defeat of the Jacobite forces at Culloden, the manager also showed his alignment with the Farmer and the Protestant establishment by enthusiastically celebrating it. According to newspaper notices, the manager "ordered a large Bonfire before the Theatre, and a Barrel of Ale to the Populace, on Account of the Duke's Victory," and two days later, on April 30, the theater announced "A New Prologue on Occasion of the glorious and happy Victory lately obtained by his Highness over the Rebels in Scotland, to be spoke by Mr. Sheridan."[30] In a context in which "rebel" was being conflated with "Catholic," such displays would have been read by many in the Catholic community as implicit expressions of hostility, and at the very least they would have served as unpleasant reminders to the Catholic gentry of their own defeat in the 1688–91 wars. Later in the same season the theater provided a more explicit reminder of this defeat when, on the recommendation of Chesterfield, Sheridan advertised a benefit for the "distressed Widows, Orphans . . . of the Officers and Soldiers Defenders of Londonderry and Innniskillen, at the Time of the late Glorious and happy Revolution."[31]

Sheridan's well-publicized beating of Kelly less than a year after Culloden can be read as a continuation of this anti-Catholic and anti-native Irish campaign, though the ethnic and sectarian valence of this act becomes apparent only when it is viewed against the background of the social mores in contemporary Dublin and London theaters. In the first Barber's *Letter* mentioned above, Lucas represented Kelly's behavior at the playhouse on January 19 as so morally outrageous and offensive that the manager had no choice but to act the way he did. If Sheridan had Kelly escorted out of the theater by a guard, Lucas writes, it was because he had created such "open Outrages upon Decency itself, as are unfit for Citizens Ears" (3), and if Sheridan later beat Kelly with a stick backstage, it was as a last defense against his "unjust Abuses" (4). "[Y]et did the *Gentleman* persevere in his unjust Abuses," Lucas states, "till the other, as a Cat inclosed in a Corner, or a Worm trod on, *must have done* [my emphasis], used the best Means that Time and Circumstances would permit to defend and vindicate himself" (4). The *must have done* when applied to a theater manager's act of beating a "Gentleman" is misleading, however, as can be established by even a brief survey of mid-eighteenth-century attitudes in England and Ireland to the respective rights of gentlemen and players. Kelly's behavior on January 19 — coming drunk to the pit, climbing onto the stage, going behind the scenes, making unwanted sexual advances to a woman player, throwing an orange at an actor, and demanding a public apology from the player for real or imagined offenses — is, of course, indefensible by twentieth-century moral and social standards, and in mid-century London theaters when gentlemen or "beaux" behaved this way, they increasingly came in for criticism both from bourgeois reformers and from members of the gentry themselves. It is also worth noting that none of Kelly's supporters defended his behavior; the pro-"Gentlemen" pamphlet titled *A Serious Enquiry into the Cause of the Present Disorders of this City* (1747), for example, describes Kelly as an "unhappy Gentleman who drank too freely," and it calls for "a Reformation of Manners and Morals" in relation to this "great Vice" of "Drunkenness."[32] Because of the differential social standing of gentlemen and players, however, theatrical managers or players themselves generally could do little about these kinds of obnoxious behaviors other than plead with the perpetrators or complain in print of their treatment after the fact. When David Garrick was confronted by an aristocratic faction who hissed a play off the stage when he tried to end the practice of going behind the scenes at Drury Lane during the same 1747–48 season, for example, he took no direct action, legal or otherwise, against his gentlemen protestors. Instead, he tried to influence public opinion against this practice by writing satires and pleading in playbills and epilogues, and when these methods proved unsuccessful, he discontinued the practice of selling space on the stage and removed the structures that allowed audience members to sit there. Through such indirect and nonconfrontational steps, he finally brought an end to the practice of going behind the scenes in 1762.[33]

Players were equally at a disadvantage when it came to addressing other kinds of abuses and insults because of their perceived inferior social status. It is true that actors and managers increasingly tried to lay claim to a kind of bourgeois professional status by their behavior and self-presentation, and their defenders in biographies and pamphlets frequently tried to elevate their social status by styling them as either "ladies" or "gentlemen." But as Kristina Straub points out, the persistence of the old tradition of classifying players as "vagabonds" undermined this effort at social elevation, a failure that was evidenced in the many cases of physical and psychic violence toward actors throughout the century. Until the end of the century, Straub notes, London audiences demanded that actors go on their knees and apologize before the audience for real or imagined affronts, and throughout the period dissatisfied patrons continued to hurl fruit at players who displeased them.[34] The harsh treatment of the player was further legitimated, ironically, by the emergence of the discourse of "public rights" in the theatrical sphere in the wake of the 1688 revolution. As Leo Hughes notes, commentators throughout the eighteenth century repeatedly represented the public-player relationship as one of master-servant in an implicit attempt to shift power from the monarchy to the people in the theatrical as well as in the political domain. The reconfiguring of the player as a "servant of the public" (rather than as "the king's servant"), however, also gave the public new power to discipline the player, and it worked to reinforce the notion of the player's social inferiority. "'Tis the public that pays them their wages; and whenever they are disobedient, refractory or insolent, 'tis the public that must correct them," one writer rather typically observed in 1763.[35]

Dublin audiences shared the belief in the subordinate status of the player, and as the pro-"Gentlemen" pamphlet pointed out, in his earlier life Sheridan had been instrumental in leading an audience to discipline a player who had asserted that he was the social equal of a gentleman. In *A Serious Enquiry*, the anonymous writer reminds Sheridan that when he himself was still a "Gentleman" at Trinity College, a player named Este, who had been "born a Gentleman, and to an Estate of 800 l. a Year" but who had been "reduced to the Necessity of seeking for Bread upon the Stage," challenged Sheridan to a duel after the latter failed to pay him for some of his benefit tickets (14–15). Because Este was a player, the author of *A Serious Enquiry* writes, Sheridan felt it beneath him to respond to the challenge and instead formed a party to hiss the unfortunate player off the stage. Este temporarily won the audience over to his side when he humbly bowed and expressed his willingness to make any "Submission" the audience wanted if he had offended them (15). But, as this author notes, when the player went on to state that he was as much a gentleman as Sheridan and that he had the right to "call him to an Account as a Gentleman," he lost the support of the house and was eventually forced to make a public apology to Sheridan: "Mr. S... stood up in a Rage, said he was amazed at his Insolence, to put himself upon a level with any Gentleman, who, by the Place from which he spoke, was but a Vagabond and a Scoundril: the hiss immediately ensued: his attempt to set up for a Gentleman upon the Stage lost him the Friends which his Humility had gained, and he was never suffered to act again until the begged Mr. Sh...'s Pardon upon the Stage" (16).

Sheridan's behavior toward Kelly on the night of January 19, then, cannot be accounted for by referring to his own moral indignity at the abusive behavior of "gentlemen" toward players or by invoking the social norms of London or Dublin audiences on the question of the respective rights of players and gentlemen. His behavior becomes intelligible, however, when it is read against the backdrop of the inflamed anti-Catholic rhetoric of the previous year and in the context of the Tory if not Jacobite skeletons in his own family history. As we have seen, the Farmer had revived the image of the Irish Catholic as a murderous and rapacious "inmate Enemy," and when he had urged Protestants to "turn upon these Destroyers" and sweep them "from the very Face of the Earth," he did not exempt Catholics who had lived peacefully with their Protestant neighbors for many years. Though Brooke does not explicitly mention Irish families who had converted to the established church in this anti-Catholic tirade, there was a long history in Irish Protestantism of regarding converts in a similarly suspicious light. As noted in chapter 1, "converts" were objects of suspicion during Jacobite scares earlier in the century; the author of the pamphlet *The Conduct of the Purse in Ireland*, for example, reproduced a common Protestant view of "converts" in 1714 when he wrote:

> They [new converts] frequently after their Conversion retain their former intimacy with the Papists, and are as well and as cordially received by them as ever. They never make or endeavour to make any new Acquaintance or Alliance with the old Protestants; they rejoyce with the Papists, and when they are cast down, it is so with them also; good and bad News affect them and the Papists in the very same manner. And in a word, excepting that they sometimes go to Church, they remain in all respects to all appearances the very same Men they were before their Conversion."[36]

Thomas Sheridan was not a new convert, but he was descended from the old Gaelic O'Sheridan clan of County Cavan, and by all accounts some of his native Irish convert forefathers had suspect political leanings. There is some dispute over whether Sheridan was a descendant of Donnchadh Ó Sioradain, a native Irish convert and clergyman whose son, William Sheridan of Kilmore, lost his bishopric for refusing to take the Oath of Supremacy and Allegiance to William III in 1688–91.[37] But what is not in dispute is that in 1725 Sheridan's own father, the schoolmaster Dr. Thomas Sheridan, lost his living as a clergyman in Cork when he preached a sermon that was perceived as an attack on the Hanoverian administration.[38] That the manager's enemies were always ready to use this suspect family background against him is also apparent from *An Enquiry into the Plan and Pretensions of Mr. Sheridan,* a pamphlet that took issue with Sheridan's scheme in 1758—this was after he had lost his theater—to put himself at the head of a new "Hibernian Academy." As is evident from the following passage, the writer uses Sheridan's family's suspected Jacobite leanings to impugn his patriotism and to throw doubt on his fitness as an educator.

> In whom now may we not hope to meet with *Loyalty* and the *Patriot Soul?* . . . When *he* whose earliest and nearest Connections were with *those,* who were thought to make but light account of the Religious and Civil Liberties of mankind; *he,* whose first rudiments in Politics were received from *Persons* who in days of trial were far from being numbered among the foremost Friends of Freedom, takes the lead in loyal affection, and steps forth in vindication of Liberty? when even *he* gallantly adventures himself to rescue our Free-born Sons, by means of a tyrannical and debasing culture, principled in slavery and sunk into abjectness, and endeavours to render them useful Members of our Free Constitution?[39]

If Sheridan made an ostentatious display of his loyalism when he first took over the playhouse during the politically heated period of 1745–46, it was undoubtedly with the hope of putting these Jacobite ghosts to rest, and by attacking Kelly and his supporters in the playhouse and in the courts the following season, he made an even more public spectacle of his Protestantism and his difference from the Catholic community. The E. Kelly from Galway who was charged with assaulting Sheridan was a recent graduate of Trinity College,[40] and from this fact we can gather that he was legally a Protestant. So, too, were many of his supporters. John Browne of the Neale (County Mayo), who was identified by Lucas as the real leader of the "Gentlemen" faction, had conformed to the established church in the 1720s;[41] the "Captain Fitzgerald" who was among those forced to apologize in Trinity College yard was obviously a Protestant since he was in the army; and the "Mr. Martin" whom Edmund Burke describes as "the principal offender"[42] in the group was more than likely a member of the powerful convert family of Galway Martins.[43] Connaught convert families like the Kellys, Brownes, Fitzgeralds, and Martins, however, were precisely what the writer of the *Conduct of the Purse* pamphlet had in mind when he spoke of a class of "new Converts" who remained "in all respects to all appearances the very same Men they were before their Conversion." The highest level of conversions by Catholics to the established church, as Thomas Power points out, occurred in the counties of Galway, Mayo, Roscommon, and Clare where Catholic interest and a level of continuity with the past remained the strongest, suggesting that the conversions were simply strategies adopted by the old landed proprietors for evading the penal laws and holding on to their lands and their gentry status.[44]

That the "Gentlemen" retained their status as leaders of the Catholic community, despite their conformity to the established church, is also suggested by the popular reaction to two other quarrels, one that happened before and the other after this theatrical Quarrel. In 1733 Robert Martin, who was possibly the same "Mr. Martin" who supported Kelly in the Gentlemen's Quarrel, became involved in a fatal conflict with a Lieutenant Henry Jolly after the latter's friend, Captain Edward Southwell, hit Martin with spittle as the latter passed by the door of the Galway coffeehouse in which Jolly and Southwell were playing billiards. In the ensuing row, Martin fatally wounded Jolly, and for this act he was charged with murder. Because the authorities feared they would be unable to find a jury that would convict Martin in Galway—the only jury that could be assembled, according to one contemporary account, was made up of Martin's relations, "Papists," or absentee Protestants—they moved the trial to Dublin in January 1735, and Martin was escorted to the capital under armed guard. There, much to everyone's surprise, the jurors found the defendant not guilty, and this verdict elicited dramatically different reactions in Ireland's two communities. According to another contemporary account, the verdict gave "general offence to the Protestants of this Kingdom," but Martin's supporters in Dublin "showed their joy . . . by loud acclamations in the Four Courts and bonfires in the Popish quarters of the town."[45]

A similar celebration took place in Dublin in 1749 after the leader of the "Gentlemen," John Browne, was acquitted of murder in a case relating to another conflict involving members of the old and new elite. The year after the theatrical disturbance, Browne fought and killed a relative, Robert Miller, for attempting to implement a rule in Kilmaine's True Blue Club that would have excluded Browne and anyone who had "a great grandfather of the popish religion" (as noted above, Browne was a first-generation

"convert")[46] As the *Dublin Journal* reported, when Browne stood trial in
Dublin in 1749, he was attended by a "large Number of the Nobility and
Gentry," a group likely drawn from Connaught Catholic or convert families; and a self-exculpatory notice that Browne put in the same paper suggests that there were also boisterous populist celebrations in the Catholic
sections of the city after he was acquitted of murder (he was found guilty
of manslaughter). In this notice Browne denied that he had run "through
the Streets with a drawn Sword and Pistols in [his] Hands" or that he had
ordered bells to be rung and bonfires to be lit "to foment riots and public
disturbances in Town"; instead, he announced, he had endeavored "to pre-
vail on the Multitude to suppress their Joy."[47]

Kelly and the Connaught party, then, were clearly identified with the
native Irish Catholic interest even in Dublin, and it was because they had
this representative value, I suggest, that they made an appropriate target
for a manager who was anxious to publicly prove his loyalist political and
religious credentials. A satiric contemporary ballad called *The Down-Fall
of the Counts: A New Ballad to the Tune of Derry Down, Etc*, which recounts the humiliation suffered by the Kelly faction in the playhouse, the
college yard, and the courts, also makes it clear that the "Gentlemen" had
this broader ethnic and sectarian signification. The "Down-fall" of the
"Connaught Counts," as the first three verses of this song reveal, greatly
pleased those members of the Protestant public who yearned to see a native Irish Catholic gentry "all . . . beshit" and put back in their "Place" :

Oh! *Conaught*, dear *Conaught*, how it grieves me to tell,
What a direful Disaster our *dear Joys* befel,
With their Hats and their Feathers, and all their fine Cloaths,
And their Cursing and Swearing, that made them such Beaux.
                      Derry, down
What a Devil bewitched them to quit their own Place,
And come to this Town, to meet such Disgrace?
At home, for fine Blades they might easily pass,
And cut, by my Shoul, no small Figure at Mass.
                      Derry, down
With their Whores, and their Dice, and their Whiskey Content,
From Plays, one would think, they might surely keep *Lent*,
But there, by pretending to Courage and Wit,
In the Face of their Betters, they all were . . . beshit.
                      Derry, down

Catholic gentlemen never passively accepted their "Down-fall," and in the "Gentlemen's" behavior and discourse in the weeks that followed Kelly's beating, it is possible to see the complex of strategies—some traditional, some emergent—that the Catholic gentry deployed to cope with Protestant dominance and their own disempowerment at midcentury. For this analysis, Lucas's writing again proves instructive. In his first Barber's *Letter*, Lucas gives the following description of the "Gentlemen's" behavior at the playhouse on the night of January 21:

> The valiant Host with their chief enter'd the Theatre; by their matchless Strength, broke open doors, and with invincible Courage, abused women, beat a poor Taylor, the Ward Robe-keeper; with great Dexterity riffled Chests and Presses of Cloaths, and when they could not meet the Object of their Rage, such of the Gang as wore Swords, most bravely and manfully pierced the Dresses he commonly appeared in on the Stage. Not content with killing him in Effigy, they then openly vowed his Destruction in proper Person, and that nothing less should sate their Rage, than cropping him, and cramming his Ears down the Throat of the Female *Player*, that refused the Ringleader to gratify his Desires. (4)

Lucas also relates this performance to practices and behaviors that were "well known on the wrong side of the *Shannon*" (that is, in Connaught), and he argues that the purpose of such behavior on the part of these "Irish Gentlemen" was "to assert their *ancient* Right, not only to *Debauch*, but also to *Murder*, such of their Inferiors as they thought fit" (6). In 1740, however, when he wrote *A Description of the Cave of Kilcorny, in the Barony of Burren in Ireland* (a part of his native County Clare), Lucas paints a very different picture of the culture that existed west of the Shannon, and he also gives a far more positive account of the social relations between the surviving old elite and their "Inferiors" in the west of Ireland. In his *Description* Lucas reports that the "fabulous Natives" of North Clare tell "numberless romantic Tales" about the Cave of Kilcorny, including one concerning a race of very fine horses that often come out of this cave to eat the corn in the valley. "They [the natives] further add," he writes, "that many Stratagems have been tried to catch some of them; but with the loss of some Mens lives, they could catch but one Stone-horse, the Breed of which, being very valuable, they say is kept to this day by *O Loghlen* which with them is a Kind of titular King that they pay great Respect to."[48] Lucas himself came from Cromwellian settler stock, but what he demonstrates here, I suggest, is his familiarity with the counterculture of the displaced native gentry and also his awareness of the continued influence of this gentry over the minds and hearts of the common people. As Kevin Whelan has demonstrated, many of the descendants of the dispossessed or marginalized Catholic elite (a group that included Old English as well as Gaelic families) continued to maintain the lifestyle of their ancestors in the post-Williamite era, often blending traditional Irish notions of gentility with newer English ones, and through this everyday enactment of gentility, this "underground gentry," as Whelan calls them, retained their influence in their community and subtly challenged the power of the new Protestant elite.[49] This native gentry's resistance was also enabled and supported by popular cultural productions such as the "romantic Tale" described above. By ascribing the possession of a magical horse to O Loghlen (or O'Loughlin), the tellers of this tale restored prestige and status to the displaced hereditary ruler in their area, endowing him with the semisupernatural powers of an epic hero or king.

Lucas's familiarity with this subculture also surfaces in the above account of the "Gentlemen's" riotous performance on January 21. Beneath the irony, I suggest, it is possible to see the outline of the rural wedding or funeral game known as *Sir Sop or Sir Sopin, the Knight of Straw,* a folk drama that itself used an ironic structure to attack the new elite and revive the honor of a fallen "Irish Chieftain." As Alan Gailey notes, *Sir Sopin* is clearly a variation of the "Hero-Combat" mummer's play, a type of folk drama that is found in many parts of rural England. In this as in other such dramas, the theme of death and revival is central; two champions fight, and one dies but is subsequently revived through the intervention of a miracle-working doctor. It was undoubtedly this theme of the triumph of life over death, too, that made such a "game" appropriate for a wake or a funeral.[50] It is clear from Joseph Cooper Walker's description of *Sir Sopin* in 1788, however, that this folk drama also served a more specifically political therapeutic purpose in the Irish context. It was reworked by anonymous hands in a rural community, his account suggests, to heal the "wound" or dishonor offered the hereditary local leader by the new landed elite, and it served to magically restore this native leader to his former power and glory:

> The principal characters, are an Irish chieftain, who always takes his title from the Irish family of most consequence in the neighbourhood of the place where the play is exhibited, and an English chieftain, de-

nominated Sir Sop or Sir Sopin. Sir Sop is dressed in straw, with a clogad or helmet of the same materials on his head; but the Irish chieftain, who is the favourite hero, is clad in the best clothes that the wardrobe of his rustic audience can afford. When the characters appear on the stage they are separately attended by inferior officers and servants, who, like the ancient Greek chorus, stand at a respectful distance, while the chieftains converse. Sometimes, the chief officers are allowed to take part in the dialogue. With the drift of the plot I am not perfectly acquainted, but know that the catastrophe is brought about by an altercation which arises between our two heroes, and terminated in single combat. In this combat, Sir Sopin wounds his adversary, who falls, and a surgeon appears to examine the wound. Regaining his strength the Irish chieftain retires, followed by Sir Sopin. Soon after they enter again, and renewing the combat, Sir Sopin receives a mortal wound and is borne off the stage. The Irish Chieftain having thus gained the field, brandishes his sword and strides exultingly across the stage. Then pausing a while, he addresses himself to Heaven, offering thanks for his victory. This done, the curtain falls. The dialogue is extremely humorous, and interspersed with soliloquies, songs and dances.[51]

In creating Sir Sopin, the anonymous folk dramatists also drew on a distinctly Irish cultural and literary tradition. The use of straw costume and straw dress in folk plays was comparatively rare in Britain but was widespread in Ireland. As Alan Harrison has shown, there were continuities between this straw-clad mumming figure and the *crosán* or fool-trickster-demon figure of early Irish poetry and prose.[52] When rural mummers dressed the "English chieftain" in straw dress and clad him in a straw helmet, then, they transformed him into this grotesque, quasi-human figure and thus effectively "killed" him long before the dramatization of the fatal combat. The evidence would seem to suggest that this folk drama had made its way into the city of Dublin by the eighteenth century. When unnamed persons (Gilbert suggests they were Trinity College students who were Jacobite sympathizers) stole out at night and put a straw figure behind the figure of William III on the equestrian monument in College Green or when they dressed the statue of William with straw and "bedaubed [him] with filth" as apparently often happened in the early part of the century,[53] they were drawing on what was essentially a rural folk tradition that aimed at figuratively killing the rival Williamite elite.

The so-called riot on January 21, Lucas's account suggests, was another variation on this *Sir Sopin* satirical drama. Here, as in the original *Sir Sopin* play, the wounded Irish chief returns to avenge his honor, and as in the original drama, he stages a mock-killing of his enemy: like Sir Sopin or the "English champion," Sheridan is killed "in Effigy." Judging from George Anne Ballamy's reference to "stuffing," this mock-killing may have had a straw component; when the "dastardly ruffians" could not find Sheridan in person, Bellamy writes, "they revenged themselves upon the stuffing of Falstaff, which they stabbed in many places."[54] The vows of destruction and threats to have Sheridan's ears cropped can also be read in the context of the swaggering and "humerous" dialogue that happens in the *Sir Sopin* play after the "the Irish Chieftain . . . gained the field, brandishes his sword and strides exultingly across the stage"; and, as in the original folk drama, the point of this bragging dialogue would have been to restore the status and honor of an Irish gentleman who had suffered defeat and humiliation at the hands of one of the upstart new gentry.

When a group of Kelly supporters assaulted Lucas himself on Essex Bridge one night shortly after this "riot," it could be said that they were continuing this *Sir Sopin* drama, and if Lucas was subjected to this humiliation—reportedly the attack consisted of "giving him several Kicks on his A——, and soiling and besmearing his Scarlet Cloak"[55]—it was because, like Sheridan, he had publicly identified himself as a persecutor of the native elite. In his first Barber's *Letter*, Lucas had argued that the weakening of the penal laws was responsible for outbursts of native barbarity like the one in the Theatre Royal, and in the second *Letter*, he recommended that his "Fellow-Citizens" revive "the Power and Dignity of Constables" and confer that dignity on "Men of Ability" like himself in the next election.[56] While explicitly repudiating the confiscation and transportation methods of his own Cromwellian ancestors, he suggests that in this role of constable he would nevertheless be as effective as any Cromwell: "I shall gladly undertake to free the Town of *Rioters, Rebels* and *Conspirators* of all *Denominations*, without Transporting the Criminals, as was formerly the Custom, as I am well informed, from this and all the other Provinces, to *Connaught;* and thereby preserve the Peace and Welfare of this great *Metropolis*"(16). The motive behind the assault, then, was to punish Lucas for these not-so-veiled anti-Catholic and anti-Irish threats, as the "Mr. Francis Liberty," who supplies the above details on the Lucas assault, acknowledges in his bitterly ironic pamphlet, *A Letter of Thanks to the Barber For his Indefatigable Pains to Suppress the Horrid and Unnatural*

Rebellion, Lately broke out in this City; But by His Means, now happily almost Extinguished (1747). On the evening of the assault, Francis Liberty states, Lucas was drafting a proposal "for the more effectively enforcing the several Statutes made in this Kingdom . . . against IRISH GENTLEMEN of the true MILESIAN RACE, the Offspring of Savages and Tyrants, and for reviving the Power and Dignity of Constables" (5), and he had the "said Scheme" in his pocket and was on his way to a coffeehouse to consult with his supporters in anticipation of putting it before the Common Council of the city of Dublin when he was attacked (6). The implicit suggestion is that Lucas deserved what he got because he had revived colonial antagonisms and put himself in the role of the arrogant planter. Another anonymous text for this period, *A New Ballad on a Late Drubbing*, also makes this point, as it celebrates this (or another similar) attack on the Barber. In this version the assailant is identified as "H[alfpenny] B[rowne]" (John Browne), and Browne reputedly uses a stick to beat Lucas. But in suggesting that Catholics would rejoice in the news of this beating—"I hear many *Catholics* cry / The Cudgel deserves to be sainted"—and that the inhabitants of the Irish towns west of the Shannon would take heart from Lucas's fall, the anonymous author of the ballad also makes it clear that he perceived this attack as a legitimate response to renewed Protestant aggression:

> O publish it [the news of the beating] not in Athlone
> Tell it not to the Towns of the *Shannon*,
> Lest the Striplings of *Connaught* take Heart,
> And severally give him a Tanning.[57]

The author of the *Letter of Thanks* pamphlet is not content simply to legitimate the Kelly faction's acts. Under the guise of being a Lucas supporter himself, Francis Liberty also transforms Lucas and Sheridan's other citizen supporters into objects of ridicule, and in so doing, he and a number of other "Gentlemen" pamphleteers import into English a native Irish tradition of political satire that had its origin in the legitimation crisis of seventeenth-century Gaelic Ireland. Seventeenth- and eighteenth-century Gaelic poets and writers often represented the opposition between the English settler and the native Irish as an opposition between upstart churls and the rightful, old aristocratic owners of the country. As Vivian Mercier has demonstrated, this tradition of portraying the "new men" as ignorant churls and buffoons goes back to the great seventeenth-century Gaelic prose work, *Pairlement Chloinne Tomáis* (The Parliament of Clan Thomas), a social satire that savagely mocks the social pretensions of the upstarts (native Irish as well as English) who had replaced the old elite in positions of power.[58] And in this Gaelic satirical tradition, as Leerssen notes, the political and social ineptness of the "new men" is often explicitly related to their linguistic inability and to their ignorance of the tradition of classical learning. In these lines from Dáibhí Cúndún (a poet of the Cromwellian period), for instance, the new English settler is castigated for his failure to understand or appreciate "aon bheith gasda 'sa healadhnaibh saora" (anything intellectual in the liberal arts) (the translation is Leerssen's):

Ní fhoidhnid teagasg ar Laidin ná ar Gaeilge
Ná d'aon bheith gasda 'sa healadhnaibh saora

They do not tolerate the teaching either of Latin or Irish,
Nor of anything intellectual in the liberal arts.[59]

Behind the stylistic mimicry of *A Letter of Thanks*, I suggest, lies a similar Irish aristocratic *mepris* for the Cromwellianite settler and his descendants. In his first Barber's *Letter* Lucas had reminded his citizen readers that their ancestors and his own had come to Ireland "to subdue the Barbarity of the Natives of this Island" and to teach these natives "Manners as well as Arts" (5), and by invoking this history, he had located his and Sheridan's struggle in the broader context of the English civilizing mission. It is precisely this foundational myth of the barbarity of the Gaelic native and the civility of the English settler, then, that is challenged by the exposure of Lucas's demagogic and unsophisticated spoken and written style in *A Letter of Thanks*. The Barber's stylistic tics—his tendency toward repetition, his fondness for heaping up of synonyms within sentences, his habit of using italics, capital letters, dashes, and exclamation points for emphasis—are relentlessly reproduced and exaggerated in an implicit commentary on Lucas and his followers' lack of culture and learning and, consequently, on his and their inadequacy as social or cultural leaders. Mock-encomiastic passages like the following, for example, reproduce and ridicule not only Lucas's tendency to see Catholic revolutions and Jacobite conspiracies behind every minor disturbance but also the reformer's rhetorical style and that of his naive, impressionable followers:

My Friend! doubtless the *Vagrants* who would thus abuse thy Person, soil thy venerable Garment and endanger thy Posteriors with a Kick on the A—— would not scruple to bring in the *Pretender,* establish Convents, those Nurseries of Sedition, and overturn our happy Establishment!—Go on, thou brave Pillar of our *Civil Liberties!* Go on—continue, in Spite of *Tyranny* and *Oppression,* in Spite of those who were *so unanimously bent on the universal Destruction of all Opponents of their Lusts,* thy Efforts to restore and preserve our *Peace,* to unveil the *secret,* and punish the *open Invaders* of our *Rights,* the *Destroyers* of the *Public Tranquillity!* (10)

The short mock-heroic poem *The Farmer's Yard* can also be read in the context of this indigenous satiric tradition, though as it reveals in its subtitle—"A new Fable for Aesop"—its satiric object is the manager. Here the theatrical conflict between Sheridan and Kelly is recast as a conflict between a haughty gander and a "pert" goldfinch who tries to ravish "a comely *Goose*" after he spies her in a farmyard, and the court case that followed the theatrical conflict is represented as a hearing before the farmer in his yard (Gander's "dread *Majesty*" has to be appeased by appealing to the "Farmer's Laws" after this attempted ravishment of his goose).[60] Sheridan's speech in his own defense at his trial, too, is made an object of satire; in Gander's "grand Oration" before the court, the manager's style, his preoccupation with pedigree, and his grandiose claims about his own and the theater's importance are all ridiculed, with passing digs at his father's (Dr. Thomas Sheridan's) ambiguous politics. The following passage is representative.

> The Court now sat in proper Station,
> *Gander* begins his grand Oration,
> In Stile so pure, so *Ciceronian,*
> As might have vy'd with good *John Bunyan,*
> He shews the Nature of the Quarrel,
> Makes plain the Pris'ner's Scheme immoral,
> Tells, with what infinite Address,
> He *order'd* Goldfinch to *Duress,*
> And shews, th' *Utility of State,*
> That *Geese* should act the *Magistrate;*
> Defines a *Vagrant,* and deny's he's
> Of *Rank,* which he himself *despises;*
> He proves that all his *Geese* are *Swans;*
> He's one of *Jove's* and *Laeda's* Sons:

He who's the Haggard's great *Director,*
Who's still the *Capitol's Protector,*
Nay King he was, and many say 'tis,
A *Crimen Laesae Majestatis.* (6)

The ironic comparison to "good *John Bunyan*" also suggests that this is part of the native Irish anti-Cromwellian satiric tradition, and more specifically, the reproduction of legal argument and Latinate legal terms in this passage aligns this poem with those Gaelic poems in the Clan Thomas tradition that attacked the English legal and juridical system. Because of its role in undermining the old Gaelic order, the English system of laws was repeatedly the object of attack by Gaelic poets of the seventeenth and eighteenth centuries, and to convey the harshness of this system, these poets often mimicked the language of the courts, importing English legal terms into their Gaelic texts. Six lines from the anonymous poem "Tuireamh na hÉireann" illustrate this kind of satiric poetic production (again the translation is Leerssen's):

Is docht na dlithe do rinneadh dár ngéarghoin:
Siosóin cúirte is téarmaí daora,
wardship livery is Cúirt *Exchéquer,*
cíos coláisde *in nomine poenae;*
greenwax, capias, writ, replévin,
bannaí, fíneáil, díotáil éigcirt.

Hard were the laws that were made to our bitter pangs:
Court sessions and harsh legal terms,
wardship, livery and the Court of the Exchequer,
college tax in *nomine poenae;*
greenwax, capias, writ, replevin,
bans, fines, unjust indictments.[61]

When the poet of *The Farmer's Yard* introduces legal and juridical terms—"*order'd* . . . to *Duress,*" "*th' Utility of State,*" "*Magistrate,*" "*Capitol's Protector,*" "*Crimen Laesae Majestatis*"—into Gander's "grand Oration," he is engaging in a similar kind of satire, implicitly showing the illegitimacy of a court that, like the parliament in the original Clan Thomas satire, serves to elevate a boorish upstart (also conveniently named Thomas) above the native gentry.

That there was an audience for aristocratic Gaelic satiric wit in Dublin at the time of this Quarrel is also apparent from an incident that happened on the day of the Sheridan-Kelly trial. According to the account of Jack Pilkington, a young actor who would himself engage in satiric attacks on Sheridan and the Theatre Royal a year later, Kelly had engaged for his council one Peter Daly, Esq., "an excellent Hibernian lawyer, who value[d] himself on speaking with the accent of his native country." As soon as the cause was read over, we learn, this Hibernian lawyer also staged a mock–show of ignorance in front of the court to underline his contempt for the manager and his claim. Pilkington writes:

> Mr. Daly stood up, and said, my Lord, I am employed as counshill for — Kelly, Esquire; but I don't understand who thish Th —— s S —— n, Gentleman, is. Sh —— n's council answered, it was Mr. Sh —— n, patentee of the Theatre Royal in Smock-Alley. Oh! says he, I under-shand tish Mr. Sheridan the actor: well, I have heard of gentlemen shaylors and gentlemen taylors, but it is the firsht I heard of gentle-men actors and gentlemen merry andrews.[62]

With his deferential query and his broad Irish accent, Daly positioned him-self here initially as a kind of naive "Teague" who required instruction in the nuances and complexities of the social system, but this posture, it soon became clear, was merely a front. The mask of obeisance allowed this Hi-bernian lawyer the opportunity to subtly ridicule a legal and social order in which tailors, sailors, actors, and merry andrews could be designated gentle-men but — and this inference, as in much mock-satire, is left unstated — a member of an ancient Irish family could not.

If the "Gentlemen" drew from traditional populist and literary forms of na-tive Irish resistance for their campaign, however, they also drew from the ostensibly more accomodationist, urban and middle-class kind of Catholic "art"[63] then being practiced by John Curry, Charles O'Conor, and other leaders of the Catholic community as they responded to the "Manifold Mis-representations" (as the *Impartial Examiner* put it) that had poured from the Protestant press in 1745. And to the degree that they deployed their "art" to counter the negative stereotype of the Catholic subject and to challenge a history that cast the native Irish subject as a barbarian, it could be said that the "Gentlemen" participated in these writers' broader political and ideological project. As Thomas Bartlett points out, the midcentury pamphleteering of such writers as Curry and O'Conor marked a new, more aggressive phase in Catholic resistance, preparing the way for the establishment in 1756 of the Catholic Association, the first formal and organized effort to challenge the penal laws.[64] It is also clear, though, that the pamphleteers were able to adopt this more aggressive stance only by assuming dominant culture personas and by mimicking the dominant culture discourse. To explode the myth of the bloodthirsty Catholic savage of 1641 in the *Brief Account,* for example, Curry uses the persona of a "Member of the Church of Ireland" and sources from "most Authentic Protestant Writers." And in his *Impartial Examiner,* Jones assumes the persona and rhetoric of the detached Enlightenment Protestant observer to refute such supposedly "scientific" anti-Catholic studies as Walter Harris's *History of the Bishops of Ireland,* or the *History of the County of Down.* From behind these conventional masks, then, these Catholic apologists launched an attack that, in its own subtler way, was every bit as subversive as the satiric attacks that emanated from an "underground gentry" subculture. In Jones's "impartial" study, for example, Catholics are found to have all the qualities of good citizens — they make honest traders, loyal subjects, tender and loving husbands, and reliable servants (23–26) — and many Protestants are found to be lacking these qualities, and this difference is found to extend to the past as well as the present. Speaking of past Catholic uprisings, Jones writes that "ancient *Catholic Colonies* in Ireland were driven into these Rebellious Measures, partly by the Oppression of the *Protestant Natives,* and partly by the greatest *Provocations* that Flesh and Blood are capable of" (63), and he suggests that many contemporary Protestant "Writers and Teachers" are practicing a similar kind of oppression: they are "fiery zealots," leading "a furious Mob," and their language on October 23 and November 4 is full of violence, "Faggots, Axes, Hatchets, and Gibbets" (40).

The writers of the pamphlets *The Gentlemen's Apology to the Ladies* and *A Serious Enquiry* similarly assume mainstream personas and mainstream political and social rhetoric in order to attack their opponents' anti-Irish and anti-Catholic narratives, though the context here is ostensibly a theatrical dispute. In casting himself and the Kelly faction as a "Body of *Gentlemen,* who constantly devote ourselves to [the Ladies'] Service," John Browne, author of *The Gentlemen's Apology,* consciously positions both himself and the "Gentlemen" as men of feeling,[65] thus suggesting that both he and they accept the values and mores of the new bourgeois order. And in defining "the Gentlemen" as a body concerned to defend the rights of "*Citizens* . . . in Trade" (7) and the "Judgement and Rights of the Audience" (8), he continues to pay deference to this emergent bourgeois order by demonstrating his acceptance of the values of social equality and rights. But in casting Irish Catholic gentlemen as such civil subjects and good citizens, Browne also indirectly attacks the negative stereotype of the native Irishman perpetuated by the anti-Gentlemen faction and a whole tradition of anti-Catholic and anti-Irish writers. And when he attacks Sheridan for his "Train of continued Insults on the Town" and "his Industry to stir up his Audience to cut one another's Throats in his infamous Cause" (7), he replicates the Catholic pamphleteers' move of displacing the blame for social and civil tensions onto the self-proclaimed defenders of the establishment. Whereas Curry accused the Farmer of endangering the "lives and properties" of the whole Catholic population with their "virulent pamphlets," Browne suggests that Sheridan has "endanger[ed], not only the Lives of the whole Youth of the Kingdom, but the universal Peace of the City" with his "false, malicious, and groundless Insinuations" (7).

The writer of *A Serious Enquiry* (who may also have been Browne) similarly appropriates and estranges dominant discourse and dominant stereotypes in his lengthier investigation into the causes of the "Present Disorders" of Dublin. From the opening of the *Enquiry,* the writer portrays himself as a devout Hanoverian. "A milder Administration, a more indulgent Prince, a more publick spirited Ministry was never known," he writes in the second paragraph, and he goes on to note that there is no further fear of a foreign invasion because the "wise Measures" of their majesties, aided by Providence, has "baffled the deep laid Schemes of our Enemies, and the Glorious Duke of Cumberland has given us a lasting Pledge of Peace and Security at home, in the ever memorable Victory of Culloden" (3–4). From this loyalist beginning, however, the writer proceeds to construct a narrative of the theatrical uprising that refutes the Sheridan faction's narrative of savage Irish gentlemen and, by extension, all those other histories that portrayed the Catholic people as bloodthirsty barbarians. As we have seen, in the *Impartial Examiner* Jones wrote that "ancient Catholic Colonies in Ireland were driven into . . . Rebellious Measures, partly by the Oppression of the Protestant Natives, and partly by the greatest Provocations that Flesh and Blood are capable of " (63). The writer of *A Serious Enquiry* locates the gentlemen's uprising in the playhouse in a similar context of oppression by a player who has grown rich enough "to Farm the Play-House from the Proprietors " (6). In what could be read as a veiled critique of the benevolent settler image in Brooke's *Farmer's Letters,* he writes: "As soon as he became Master of the Play-House, he suffered the common Fate of them risen from low estate, and having mounted to the highest Pinacle of his Ambitions, the Government of the Play-House, he lost all Sense and Reason, imagining himself some of the Tyrants he so often acted, and thought to treat the Gentlemen as he pleased" (6). If the gentlemen rebelled, he goes on to argue, it was because they were unbearably provoked by this "Tyrant"; they had seen "one Gentleman dragged out of the Gallery like a Pickpocket, another taken by the Shoulder, turned out of the House like a Scoundril, and beaten like a Dog" and "the whole House manaced and threatened (Cane in Hand) by a Player" (12).

The depiction of a theater in which a "Body of Gentlemen" felt that "none of them were safe" (11) also serves as a veiled description of how a Catholic or "convert" gentry would have experienced the neocolonialist theater Sheridan created during the 1745–46 season, and in this writer's protest against Sheridan's intimidation tactics in the aftermath of the Kelly incident, we can read the gentry's veiled protest at the broader humiliations they suffered at the hands of government agents and Protestant writers during the same period. In support of the broader claim that the manager is a "Jehu" (11) who attempted to "suppress the Liberty of the Audience" (13), the writer argues that the manager sent for and intimidated the witnesses in the Kelly trial: "he made Examinations against a Number of Gentlemen of all parts of the Kingdom, and terrified them with fear of the Law, that we heard nothing in any part of the City for many Days, but that such a Person, or such a Person was found to be of the Party, and their Names were given into Justice" (13). And he adds that Sheridan attempted to "prejudice the Town against the Gentlemen indicted" and predetermine the outcome of the trial by publishing the affidavits of these witnesses in the *Dublin Journal* (14). As we have seen, the leaders of the Catholic community were similarly being "sent for" and subjected to "Examinations" and threats of "the Law" during this period, and they were also being harassed verbally by anti-Catholic zealots who sought to "prejudice" the Protestant population against them.

The complaints of Sheridan and Lucas after Kelly's defeat in the courts, moreover, testify to the effectiveness of this Catholic "art" in undermining support for the "reformed Stage" and, by extension, the Protestant sectarian state. Sheldon states that the trial on February 19 brought the whole theatrical drama to an end; after this judicial decision, we are led to believe, the opposition petered out and Sheridan emerged "more fixed in his position and stronger than before" (107). Sheridan's own words, however, clearly indicate that this was not the case. In a letter to the *Dublin Journal* of March 3–7, Sheridan expresses his concern that "the Party [against him] is rather encreas'd than diminished," and he laments the "inexorable Spirit" that still works to oppose him.[66] In the second Barber's *Letter* of March 3, Lucas also reveals that "free and well-affected Men" (i.e., Protestants of English descent) were now joining with the opposition: "It might be hoped, that this solemn Trial would have determined all Disputes finally, but instead "[t]he Masque is thrown off. . . . [T]hey [the Gentlemen] now openly and impudently declare themselves, and artfully skulking in the Shadows of *free* and *well-affected* Men in *Lucas's Coffee-House*, publickly beat up for Volunteers there, nay, actually impress some weak Men into their *detestable Association*" (6). In an effort to warn other "*free and well-affected* Men" against these kinds of shadowy recruiters, Lucas also elaborates on the method—what he calls the "little, low Artifice"—these recruiters use, and it is clear from this description that the success of the "Gentlemen" was due in no small part to their adoption of the kind of ostensibly assimilationist practices mentioned above:

> The very *Coffee-House*, that Men of their Stamp and Rank usually met in, would not now serve their purpose. Therefore, they [the Kelly faction] hold their Assemblies among *Protestant* Gentlemen, of the first Rank, for Loyalty at *Lucas's Coffee-House*, and tho, they only meet there, and it is known that since the TRUE GENTLEMEN discovered the vile Schemes of the *pretended Gentlemen*, or *Rioters;* these latter dare no more speak in the hearing or presence of the former; yet there, they still assemble, and from that adjourn to some Place of obscurity enough to pass unobserved, from that issue out APOLOGIES, ENQUIRIES, Etc. And impudently call themselves the TOWN! The PUBLIC! The GENTLEMEN at LUCAS's! To which Appellation the Chair-Men and Porters that wait there for hire, have an equal if not a better Right. (12)

By appropriating dominant cultural personas and discourse, this complaint suggests, the Kelly faction, like their Catholic counterparts in the broader political domain, were effectively destabilizing ethnic and sectarian boundaries (the lines between "True Gentlemen" and "Pretended Gentlemen") and opening up a space from which they could speak and attack their enemies. In his third and last Barber's *Letter*, Lucas again testifies to the successfulness of this strategy in blurring ethnic and sectarian distinctions when he complains that he himself had now become an object of suspicion to the government and to some members of the Protestant community. Browne, he writes, has used "all his arts and rhetoric, upon all degrees of people" to make the Barber "odious." . . . To *Roman Catholics*, he represented him as a *Cromwellian*, to the *Protestants*, as a rank *Jacobite*; to the men in power, as a seditious, rebellious libeller, a most dangerous member of society."[67]

If Lucas was susceptible to being represented as a "most dangerous member of society" to the "men in power," it must also be stated, it was not *exclusively* because of Catholic "arts and rhetoric." As I show in the next chapter, Lucas was staging his own populist Irish patriot counterdrama behind the cover of this Gentlemen's Quarrel, and as his increasingly radical brand of patriotism came to the fore in the two years following this disturbance, it further blurred the line between "True Gentlemen" and "Pretended Gentlemen" and opened up new opportunities for the marginalized Irish Catholic subject to speak.

CHAPTER 5

Attacking the Lucasian Stage

Edmund Burke, Paul Hiffernan,
and the Paper War of 1748

In a letter to Richard Shackleton, dated Dublin, January 14, 1748, a young Trinity College undergraduate named William Dennis announced that he and his two friends, Edmund Burke and Beaumont Brenan, were plotting a new "war" against the Theatre Royal and its manager in the interest of establishing a more tasteful and a more Irish stage, and he asked Shackleton to join in this campaign (see fig. 3). Dennis begins:

> *Arma virumque cano — bella horrida bella.*
> Nothing else to do, we the triumvirate talk of nothing but the subversion of the present theatrical tyranny; lend us your pen; you have often drawn it for your own and friends' entertainment; now do it for their assistance and the establishing taste in spite of Sheridan's arrogance or his tasteless adherents. Don't think this gasconade, for we love liberty and consequently hate French customs. No, we tread on firm ground with Irish resolution and perseverance, resolving to pull down Baal from the high places, and that by (what is esteemed uncommon) the force of Irish genius, and establish Irish productions in the place of English trash comedies and French frippery of dances and harlequins, which have been the public entertainments this winter.[1]

As he gives a fuller account of this proposed theatrical campaign, Dennis reveals that there is another force behind it, "one Dr. Hiffernan, a poet,

149

The College Buck.

Figure 3. "The College Buck." *The Hibernian Magazine,* October 1774.
By permission of the British Library. PP.6154k.

philosopher, and play-wright in this town" (316). Hiffernan became aware of the Trinity trio's existence, Dennis explains, after reading and admiring some of their writings (a prepublication copy of Burke's satiric pamphlet *Punch's Petition to Mr. Sh——n, to be admitted into the Theatre Royal* and a play script that Brenan was attempting to have staged), but he was not acquainted with any of them personally until he met Dennis in Cotter's print shop and discovered that Dennis knew these other two aspiring authors. In the course of discussing how Brenan's play might be brought to the stage (Sheridan had agreed to produce it that March, but the friends doubted that he would keep his word), the plan for launching a new war on Sheridan and his playhouse was born. Dennis writes:

> Then we talked about bringing it [Brenan's play] on the stage (without mention of the author) and he [Hiffernan] fancied it was practicable, and warrants the effecting it first by making a party of friends which he has secured already, which he calls an association in defence of Irish wit; then charging the town with a heap of papers on Sheridan, proving him an arrogant ass, and displaying his faults in the management of the theatre till having weakened his party so as not to fear opposition. These friends in the mean time may spread a favourable report of the play to prepare the town for its reception when they call for it in the playhouse, which desire of the audience to see it we hope to make general, so that Sheridan can't refuse bringing it on. (317)

Dennis also gleefully informs Shackleton that this group-conceived scheme—he describes it as "partly our contrivance and partly Hiffernan and mine, for (he) knows not either Burke or Brennan [*sic*]" (317)—was already being put into action at the time of writing, and he indicates that it was to be a guerrilla style of warfare. The manager was to be attacked from all directions by nameless opponents who would assume many different literary disguises to obscure their conspiracy:

> Burke's paper [*Punch's Petition to Mr. Sh——n, to be admitted into the Theatre Royal*] has paved the way; three hundred were sold yesterday. On Monday, Hiffernan in an expostulation from Punch displays Mr. Sheridan in a ridiculous but true light, which will take three papers. Next comes Brennan with a grave inquiry into the behaviour of the manager, which will be backed by Ned [Burke] and I; and thus we will persecute him daily from different printers till the

plot is ripe, and we have established liberty on the stage and taste among the people. (317–18)

I cite this letter at some length because it tells us how to read the seemingly unrelated anti-Sheridan, anti–Theatre Royal publications that began pouring out of Dublin printing shops in the early months of 1748. *Punch's Petition* is undated but Dennis's letter indicates it was published on January 13, 1748. In the months that followed, a "heap of papers" corresponding to the outline above went into circulation, though for whatever reason the coconspirators changed the order of the attack. On January 28 Burke and his Trinity friends began publishing a weekly periodical called *The Reformer*, whose first three numbers were devoted explicitly to attacking Sheridan's stage in what could be called a tone of "grave inquiry." And on February 18 Hiffernan and his "association in defence of Irish wit" began satirizing Sheridan and his supporters, Charles Lucas and George Faulkner, in what could be called the more "ridiculous," satiric tone of *The Tickler*. Rather than look at these publications as ideologically distinct productions (as they have been traditionally read), this Dennis letter suggests that we should read them as intricately interwoven assertions by two groups of Irish gentlemen sharing the same patriotic goals — freeing the Irish stage from foreign entertainments and replacing them with "Irish productions."

It is also clear from this letter that the campaigners saw their struggle as a battle between "Irish genius" and "Irish wit," on the one side, and foreign dullness, arrogance, and tyranny, on the other, and this formulation, I suggest, alerts us to yet another more politically subversive dimension of this patriotic campaign. As a number of scholars have noted, there was a class politics behind the "Wit"/"Dullness" aesthetic conflict in late-seventeenth- and early-eighteenth-century English literature; writers who defended "Wit" were also tacitly defending a traditional aristocratic order, and their attack on "Dullness" was a covert attack on the emerging middle class who were assuming the political and cultural roles formerly held by the aristocratic elite.[2] While this kind of defense of a traditional aristocracy could be considered conservative if not reactionary in England, it had a very different political valence in Ireland where the opposition between the old elite and the new rulers coincided with the opposition between native Irish and planter. In the Irish context a resurgence of Irish "Wit" could be read as a resurgence of a native elite. That the above attack on the Theatre Royal had this ethnic as well as class dimension was also suggested by Sheridan himself when, later the same year on the stage of Smock Alley, he labeled his persecutors a "Connaught"—that is, a "Gentlemen"—faction,[3] though in suggesting that his opponents were simply carrying on the previous year's Quarrel, he also characteristically told only half of the story. As I argue in this chapter, there were indeed continuities between this covertly waged paper war and the Gentlemen's Quarrel of 1747, but the immediate impetus for this campaign was Sheridan's support for the reformer Charles Lucas, who was then emerging as a new political force on the Irish scene. Behind the Burke-Hiffernan struggle to "pull down Baal from the high places" and dethrone Sheridan's "tasteless adherents," I suggest, was also the effort to pull down a new kind of populist Irish Protestant hegemony and a concurrent attempt to reassert the political and cultural leadership role of the traditional—Gaelic and Old English—Irish gentry.

◆◆◆

To establish the continuity with the 1747 Gentlemen's Quarrel, I turn first to *The Tickler*, Paul Hiffernan's main contribution to this paper war. If *The Tickler* is discussed at all today, it is solely in connection with the 1748–49 Dublin election campaign, and it is generally asserted that Hiffernan undertook its writing for purely mercenary reasons. The 1748–49 by-election became highly charged when Charles Lucas challenged the nominee of the city aldermen for one of two vacant Dublin parliamentary seats, and this political friction, it is suggested, provided a perfect opportunity for the ambitious, talented, but lazy Hiffernan. The *European Magazine,* a source that has been cited by all Hiffernan's biographers, states, for example, that this writer's "love of indolence and dissipation" made him unwilling to practice his chosen profession as medical doctor, but, it goes on to say, his "clever and caustic attacks on Lucas procured him, unfortunately, admission to the tables of persons of political celebrity, and not only of the latter, but those of all the leading aldermen who were the deadly enemies of Lucas."[4] However, that Hiffernan cites "the elegance and Politeness of the *BARBERS LETTERS*" as his literary model in the ironic dedication to Charles Lucas in the collected version of *The Tickler*[5] suggests that his hostility to Lucas had its source in the ethnic and sectarian tension of the "Gentlemen's Quarrel" of the previous year, and other internal evidence suggests that Hiffernan may well have written on the side of the "Gentlemen."

There are no pamphlets bearing Hiffernan's name from this dispute, but on the title sheet of the Royal Irish Academy copy of the *Letter of Thanks to the Barber* (1747), an anonymous hand has written "See *Tickler*

1748" over the phrase "By Mr. Francis Liberty," and the similarities of tone and content in these two works suggest that this attribution is correct. In *The Tickler,* as in *A Letter of Thanks,* there are repeated allusions to Lucas's attacks on Catholics, and both texts use a similar kind of mimicry to ridicule this reformer's arguments and by implication the arguments of all those zealous Protestant defenders of the sectarian state. "Have not the villainous Papists, the pest of society and dishonour of human nature, remain'd loyal in the late rebellion, for no other reason, but that you should not have an opportunity to display your talents in suppressing them?" a Lucas admirer is made to ask in a mock–letter of admiration to this new "CROMWELL" in the fifth issue of *The Tickler* (24–25), and in the seventh issue, *The Tickler,* like *A Letter of Thanks,* uses parody to ridicule Lucas's histrionic and self-serving anti-Catholic language. "He then who laughs at *C———s L–c–s,*" *The Tickler* writes, "insults the *metropolis,* affronts the most noble *province,* attacks the *kingdom,* intends to destroy the present happy *constitution,* subvert the *establishment,* and introduce popery, slavery, arbitrary power, the inquisition, Pope, Devil, and all,— Oh Lord! Oh Lord!" (52). When Hiffernan responded in his own voice to those who were criticizing him for unfairly satirizing Lucas in the sixth issue of *The Tickler,* he also explicitly mentioned the latter's attack on "a whole province" the previous year. "What could more justly deserve public satire than an incendiary apothecary, with whom nothing is sacred," he writes, "who, to the prejudice of his business and family, labour'd to exasperate a quiet people into rebellion; abused a whole province indiscriminately, stigmatized all English gentlemen in place here; be-rascalled the bishops; be-knaved the judges; damn'd the lawyers as dunces; and that forsooth he'd plead his own cause, loaded the lord mayor and aldermen with all the injurious epithets he could muster together" (45). The "whole province" that Lucas "abused," of course, was the Irish gentry–dominated province of Connaught, and in his anger at one who "labour'd to exasperate a quiet people into rebellion," it is possible to hear echoes of the Catholic pamphleteers, Curry and Jones, who raged against the Protestant zealots who tried to stir up the population during the '45.[6]

Hiffernan's family background, religion, and education also make it likely that he would have joined on the side of the Connaught gentry in the Quarrel. Hifferman was born in County Dublin of Catholic parents and had initially been educated for the priesthood, first attending a classical seminary in Dublin and then going at a young age with other Irish students to a clerical college in Montpellier in the south of France.[7] As an Irish Catholic clerical student in France, Hiffernan would have been part of the intelligensia of the Irish Catholic exile community, and as the Dennis letter above indicates, even when he returned to Ireland as a doctor (he abandoned his religious studies for a career in medicine), he was still recognized by his Irish contemporaries as a man of letters; Dennis refers to him as a "poet, philosopher, and play-wright," and by his own account he was part of "an association in defense of Irish wit." In the eyes of the traditional Irish "Wit" or man of letters, however, players and apothecaries were not suitable arbitrators of social behavior, and for such a man to have stood idly by when such social upstarts physically and verbally assaulted native Irish gentlemen would have been unconscionable.

It is also clear that Hiffernan's enemies saw him as one of the "Gentlemen" and as a closet supporter of the exiled Catholic community's cause. The bitterly anti-Hiffernan pamphlet, *A Narrative of the Barbarous and Bloody Murder of P..L H..ff..n, M. D. Committed by Himself on Monday, the 17th Day of October, Inst Being a LETTER from Mr. R..d D..ck..n of S..l..r C..t Castle-Street Dublin, to J..n B..ne Esq; at the Hague*, states as much. This pamphlet purports to be a letter describing Hiffernan's death, but it is really an excuse for launching a viciously sectarian and scatological attack on the author of *The Tickler*. An impoverished, dying Hiffernan is made to confess to his spiritual director, "Father Connor O'Shaghnessy" (who talks in "the high *Roscommon* dialect") that he is a priest, not a physician, and that all his high moral claims in his *Ticklers* were lies. In effect, he was driven to write against Sheridan out of spite for having his farce rejected, he admits, and he wrote against Lucas because he needed to make money and because the latter was "a violent Protestant."[8] From its opening and closing remarks, however, it is also clear that this letter is supposed to represent an exchange of intelligence from Catholic conspirators at home to their fellow conspirators abroad (the writer states at the beginning, for instance, that he is passing on the information regarding Hiffernan's death since he knows that "B——ne" is concerned with "everything that touches the Welfare of *our Community*").[9] And from the designation "*J..n B..ne Esq; at the Hague*" in the title, it is clear that the recipient of the letter is supposed to be John Browne of the Neale, the man who was identified by Lucas as the leader of the "Gentlemen" in the 1747 dispute. Browne had fled to the Hague in 1748 to avoid prosecution after he had killed a man in a duel earlier in the year.[10]

The involvement of Edmund Burke and William Dennis also suggests that this 1748 opposition was not simply the "remains" of the previous year's "faction" (as Sheridan stated in the above-mentioned denunciation) as the Trinity friends had been on the *opposite* side of the Gentlemen's

Quarrel the previous year. To understand their involvement, I suggest, it is necessary to look more closely at the nature of their support for Sheridan during the Quarrel and at the changes that had occurred in the Theatre Royal since that time. In a letter to Richard Shackleton on February 21, 1747, the young Burke had described Kelly and his supporters as rakes and bullies who respected neither the "ties of honour" nor "Religion," and he revealed that he was among the "100 well arm'ed" "Scholars" who had seized two of the "Gentlemen" (Captain Fitzgerald and John Browne of the Neale) from their lodgings on Castle Street early on the morning of February 13 and then forced them, along with Martin and Kelly, to kneel and apologize in the college yard.[11] Around the same time, Dennis, who was Burke's roommate, wrote a pamphlet titled *Brutus's Letter to the Town* supporting the manager and condemning his opponents. Kelly, Dennis argued, had "acted contrary to all Rules of Modesty and Good-breeding, breaking the grand design of Government, by infringing on the private Privileges of its Subjects," and he and his supporters had endangered the public by raising a "Tumult in the City, when [the Irish people] were scarce cool'd, when the apprehension of Civil War was just allay'd."[12] Dennis also concluded that the courts did the right thing when they found against the Kelly faction: "[T]he Magistrate spoke the sentiment of the Whole People, and defended the Privileges of each Member" (8). In a passing comment on Dennis's pamphlet in a letter to Shackleton on March 12, 1747, Burke commented that "[It was] a good thing I think."[13]

As is evident, the friends' opposition to the Kelly faction in 1747 had a traditionalist and conservative as well as modernist and liberal underpinning. In assuming the persona of Brutus to speak to the "Town" and in speaking a language of "Rights and Privileges," Dennis assumed a role and rhetoric popular with contemporary defenders of the new Whig order in England. But in arguing that the Kelly faction "acted contrary to all Rules of Modesty and Good-breeding," he also invoked traditional standards of gentry behavior as the norm by which their behavior should be measured and condemned. This traditionalist strand is even more pronounced in Burke. Although he endorsed his friend's pamphlet, he condemned the Kelly faction on the more conservative grounds of not respecting the "ties of honour or Religion," and the slight hesitancy in his remark about Dennis's letter suggests that he may have experienced his liberalism as a felt contradiction in relation to this conservatism.

These ideological contradictions can be attributed in part to the kind of English political education the young men were receiving at Trinity. As

J. G. A. Pocock has pointed out, the myth of an "ancient constitution" was at the core of English political thinking about liberties before 1688–89, and it continued to exist in an uneasy relation with concepts of contract, natural right, and reason even after the Glorious Revolution.[14] In the case of Burke (and perhaps Brenan about whom very little is known), this conservative strain can also be attributed to what Conor Cruise O'Brien has called the "Catholic" or "Irish" layer of Burke's own psyche.[15] As the son of a convert with close Catholic ties—he spent his early life among his maternal Irish-speaking Catholic relatives in Munster and retained contact with this community throughout his life—Burke absorbed a respect for traditional society that was lifelong. And as Seamus Deane has argued persuasively, these traditionalist pro-Catholic sympathies profoundly affected his political thinking, explaining his later negative reaction, for example, to such apparently different groups as the Irish Protestant Ascendancy and the French revolutionaries.[16] That such sympathies were already beginning to surface during the early years at Trinity is also evidenced by Burke's remarks on the defeated Jacobites in 1745. After noting in a letter to Shackleton on April 26, 1745, that many who had previously cursed the "pretender" and his supporters now "wish it could be terminated without bloodshed," he writes, "I am sure I share in the general compassion, 'tis indeed melancholy to consider the state of those unhappy gentlemen who engag'd in this affair . . . who have thrown away their lives and fortunes and destroy'd their families for ever in what I believe they thought a just Cause."[17]

It was this traditionalist Catholic and Irish layer, too, I suggest, that explains why Burke began attacking Sheridan and the Theatre Royal in winter 1747, even before Dennis and Hiffernan came up with their plan for an all-out theatrical campaign. There is no explicit mention of Lucas in Burke's correspondence in the 1747–48 period, though a passing comment in a joint letter by Burke and Dennis to Shackleton in May 1747 suggests that Burke and his circle may have been discussing Lucas and his Barber's *Letters* at this time. In this letter the two friends give Shackleton an account of the proceedings of their newly founded literary "Club," including Burke's mock-serious attempt to expel Dennis on the grounds that the latter "had a design of destroying the Club." In what could be read as an oblique comment on Lucas and his sectarian scare tactics, Dennis dismisses this charge of attempted subversion with the wry remark: "thus modern patriots urge every thing an introduction to popery and slavery, which they don't like."[18] Some fourteen years later, while Lucas was resuming his political career in Dublin after his years in exile, Burke explicitly expressed his dislike of Lucas and his brand of "mob" patriotism, and there are hints here, too, that this intense dislike stemmed from Lucas's Protestant zealotry. In a 1761 letter to Charles O'Hara, an Irish Protestant who also came from native gentry stock, Burke wrote:

> I own I am somewhat out of humour with patriotism; and can think but meanly of such public spirit as, like the fanatical spirit, banishes common sense. I do not understand that spirit which could raise such hackneyed pretences, and such contemptible talents as those of Dr. Lucas to so great a consideration, not only among the mob, but, as I hear on all hands, among very many of rank and figure. If any of them do it through policy, one may predict without rashness that he will give them room to repent it. I feel myself hurt at this, and the rather as I shall be obliged from decency and other considerations to hold my tongue.[19]

In this passage, Burke couches his dislike of Lucas's "patriotism" in purely functionalist terms; Lucas's kind of "public spirit" is the wrong kind, because it banishes "common sense." But the comparison of this "public spirit" to "the fanatical spirit" together with his statement that he is unable to speak freely about why he is "hurt" at Lucas's popularity strongly suggest that the underlying reasons for his antipathy to Lucas revolve around the latter's reputation (merited or not) as a Protestant zealot and anti-Catholic bigot, a reputation Lucas first acquired among Catholics as a result of his Barber's *Letters* of 1747.[20]

It is clear from the above comments, too, that Burke had the traditional Irish gentleman's dislike of upwardly mobile men like Lucas who had assumed a leadership role traditionally reserved for those of "rank and figure," and in a letter to O'Hara a week later, Burke uses paratheatrical imagery to express his contempt for this kind of plebian leadership. "If the latter mountebank should now descend from his stage," he writes, "it would be of great service to his character; which, if he returns to the usual unhealthy soundness of his intellects, will infallibly come to be known by the dullness of his admirers; and thus his medical quackery will cover the blunders of his political."[21] By labeling Lucas a "mountebank," Burke not only implies that Lucas is a quack (by this time he had earned a medical degree) but also associates his brand of populist patriotism with clowns, buffoons, and the "low" entertainments of the street or fair. Mountebanks often used professional clowns to attract audiences to their fairground or street stage, peddling their false wares with the aid of stories, tricks, and juggling. But this "mountebank" first began his ascent onto the political stage during the Gentlemen's Quarrel of 1747, and it is this ascendancy, as well as Sheridan's role in providing a platform for a Lucasian patriot act, I suggest, that we must also consider if we are to understand Burke's new-found hostility in 1748 to the manager and the Theatre Royal.

◆◆◆

In number of recent studies Sean Murphy argues convincingly that Lucas's political writing during the 1748–49 Dublin election campaign marked an important pivotal stage in the transition from what he calls "Anglo-Irish or Protestant constitutional nationalism" to the more radical, inclusive, and republican separatism of the United Irishmen.[22] Much of the political analysis in Lucas's twenty election addresses conforms to traditional "commonwealth" ideology, but Lucas also attempted to show that the British constitution was also the birthright of the Irish, and in so doing, Murphy suggests, he went further than his Irish Protestant nationalist predecessors. In his tenth election address of January 1749, for example, the reformer reiterated Molyneux's claim that Ireland was not a conquered or dependent colony, but he also moved beyond Molyneux's brand of Protestant nationalism, Murphy claims, when he stated that "there was no general rebellion in Ireland, since the first British invasion, that was not raised or fomented by the oppression, instigation, evil influence or connivance of the English." He took his critique of the "mother-nation, England," even further in his eleventh address during the same month, Murphy suggests, when he argued that the native Irish in medieval times had been treated as badly "as the Spaniards . . . used the Mexicans . . . or as inhumanely as the English now treat their slaves in America." This kind of sympathetic identification with the plight of the colonized hinted at an inclusive Irish nation that transcended "the Anglican and dissenter sections of the population"—a nation that had a "common interest in resisting English domination."[23]

In tracing Lucas's emergence as a spokesman for this broader nationalism, however, Murphy brackets his involvement in the theatrical dispute of 1747, suggesting that he was temporarily derailed from his patriot career by the unusual events of 1745: "The obsessiveness of the anti-catholic propaganda in Lucas's Barber's Letters of 1747 was . . . uncharacteristic, and it is likely that like many of his co-religionists he had been affected by the scare attendant on the Jacobite Rising of 1745."[24] I argue, however, that the Barber's *Letters* articulate the same ambiguous patriotism as Lucas's other writing and, moreover, that Lucas intervened in the playhouse conflict of 1747 precisely to jump-start his stalled reform campaign. In 1742 Lucas had represented the barber surgeons' guild on the common council of the Dublin Corporation, and he and James La Touche, a wealthy Dublin banker, undertook a campaign to limit the oligarchic powers of the lord mayor and aldermen in the upper house while restoring the ancient rights of the lower house, the sheriffs, and the commons. This campaign led to frequent disruptions of Corporation business in the period 1742–44, and it ended with the removal of Lucas and La Touche after the two filed an unsuccessful lawsuit against the aldermen in 1744.[25] Lucas's involvement in the theatrical Quarrel of 1747, then, was an attempt to find another platform for his reform campaign, and if we are to credit *An Apology for the Conduct and Writings of Mr. C——s L——s, Apothecary,* one of the many anti-Lucas tracts that appeared later during the 1748–49 electoral campaign, the apothecary's own theatrical experience inclined him to this venue. After Lucas became bankrupt early in his life, the anonymous author of *An Apology* states, he fled to England and spent a brief period writing for the London stage, and when his play was not accepted, he came back to Ireland and turned orator and patriot, "now disdaining to follow the humble Business he was bred to, and vehemently aspiring to the Illustrious Character, if not of a Poet (which he found he was not to expect) at least of an Orator, and Patriot; he was perpetually deafening his Wife, and Family with the most exorbitant Praises of the ancient Sages of *Greece,* and *Rome;* with the glorious (as he call'd it) Immortality of their Names, and with frequent ejaculatory Wishes, mix'd with the strongest Hopes, that the like Blessing might be hereafter granted to his own."[26]

Whether or not this account accurately traces the genealogy of his political impulse, Lucas certainly enacted the role of "Orator" and "Patriot" when he helped to expel the "Gentlemen" from Smock Alley on February 9, 1747. As Benjamin Victor's eyewitness account reveals, Lucas's intervention constituted the second disruptive performance at the playhouse on that night. The play *Richard III* was first interrupted by the "Gentlemen" in the boxes who cried for a "Submission" as soon as Sheridan appeared, but when Sheridan came to the edge of the stage and expressed his willingness to comply with the audience's wishes, he was interrupted a second time as "a CITIZEN, then well known for his Struggles for Liberty in the City [Lucas], rose up in the Pit, and asserted the Rights of the Audience and the Freedom of the Stage."[27] Little attention has been paid to this second performance, but I suggest it was every bit as subversive as the "Gentlemen's" act. What Lucas provided when he stood up was, in effect, a minidrama on constitutional theory and practice, with the audience on the receiving end of his pedagogical project. Lucas first gave a speech, the gist of which was (as he later reported) "*That it was no longer his* [Sheridan's] *Quarrel, that he was no Aggressor, and that he should not give up the Public Right by making a base submission to Lawless Rage and Tyranny.*"[28] He then suggested that like other disputes this one should be determined "by the Majority," and at the end of the speech he asked for a show of hands from those who were "for preserving the Decency and Freedom of the Stage."[29] As Victor observes, Lucas judged that "when they [the anti-"Gentlemen" faction] should come to know their Numbers and Superiority, they would silence or turn out their Opponents," and his calculations proved correct. "He was heard with great Respect, and saluted with Shouts of Applause," Victor writes, "but on the Division, the Numbers were so great against the Rioters, and, withal, appeared so animated for Action, that the Majority suddenly went off, and left the Performance of that Night in quiet."[30] If, as Jim Smyth points out in *The Men of No Property*, popular politicization is "a dynamic process" that is "shaped by action, by experience, and participation in public affairs,"[31] then it is clear that this Lucasian performance provided such a politicizing experience. Under the guise of upholding the status quo, Lucas taught a socially mixed audience a subversive lesson about the strength of sheer "Numbers" in determining the outcome of social conflict, and through his mini-drama he gave all sections of the audience, including the humbler social stratum in the upper gallery, the experience of participating in a democratic exercise.

Under the guise of pleading the manager's case in the three Barber's *Letters*, too, Lucas put himself in the public spotlight while simultaneously engaging in fund-raising for his next political venture. When he dwells on the plight of a "poor, *persecuted Refugee*" who has contended for "the RIGHTS and LIBERTIES of a FREE PEOPLE" (13) in his second Barber's *Letter*, Lucas is ostensibly pleading the case of the manager who suffered losses of revenues because of the closing of his theater during the disturbance. And in asking his readers to join him in subscribing to a "SOCIETY FOR SUPPORTING IMPOVERISHED OR OPPRESSED FREEMEN OF DUBLIN" in the final paragraph of his third Barber's *Letter* (20), he is also ostensibly raising funds for the manager and his "reformed" stage. At an earlier point in this third *Letter*, he explicitly identifies Sheridan as one of the "innocent oppressed" who would benefit from such contributions and with him "a reformed, a free stage, the king's theater too" (13). However, in the opening sentence of this third *Letter*, Lucas also casts *himself* as one of "innocent oppressed" who deserves moral and financial support (3), and after narrating the many trials he has suffered at the hands of the "Gentlemen" in the first three pages, he explicitly conflates his case with the manager's. He (Lucas) is a "no less innocent and worthy citizen, who by being basely attacked, assaulted, abused and threatened by the *Gentlemen*, had . . . made one common cause with Mr. *Sheridan*'s" (6). In asking his readers to consider "how far it is incumbent on the public in general, the citizens of *Dublin* in particular, to support the man, who regardless of all perils, losses and expences, bravely defended the rights and liberties of free-subjects" (11), Lucas also tacitly reminds them of the losses he suffered in his earlier campaign on behalf of Dublin "rights and liberties," and in urging them "to recompence the losses and expences sustained by any man in the service of the public" (13), he also solicits their moral and financial support in his own upcoming political campaign. In the second *Letter* he had announced his intention to run for the position of constable in the next election, and in this third *Letter*, he again reminds readers of this upcoming campaign: "It is enough that I have escaped and am determined to spend the last gasp of my breath in the service of you, whose free generous spirits are, and ever must be, my best support against oppression and tyranny" (5).

By encouraging his plebian readers to support him in a war against "oppression and tyranny" in the playhouse, Lucas was also tacitly telling them to assert their former control over the theatrical realm, and in so doing, he, no less than the "Gentlemen" faction, was working to undermine Sheridan's "reformed stage." In service to his self-appointed task of "freeing" Smock Alley from the control of "the People" and returning it to its previous (elitist and English) "Owners," Sheridan had begun to wage war not only on the "Gentlemen" who invaded the stage but also on the upper gallery crowd who were also beginning to think of the playhouse as their own. The manager began this war in December 1745 when he placed an announcement in the *Dublin Journal* attempting to dissuade his more affluent patrons from allowing their footmen into the Great Room behind the boxes during a Garrick performance—"[E]veryone," he announced, should "give Orders to their Servants to stand without"— and by January 1746 he was intensifying this war with repeated notices announcing that the management might have to "shut up the Gallery" and have "Servants . . . entirely excluded, unless they behave[d] themselves better for the future."[32] By December 1746 he was threatening to place additional guards in the upper gallery to prevent this section of the audience from putting on their antihegemonic musical demonstrations. He accused the upper gallery of throwing apples and stones at the theater band, and for several months he ran a notice warning, "[P]roper Men will be placed to mark the Offenders, who will certainly be prosecuted the next Day to the utmost Rigour of the Law; and a Reward of three Guineas will be paid by the Manager, upon the Conviction of any Offender."[33] That this intimidation campaign was beginning to work by 1747 is evident from the comments made both by the manager and his opponents during the theatrical Quarrel of 1747. "The Upper-Gallery which us'd to be constantly so noisy, Mr. *Sheridan* contriv'd to make one of the quietest Parts of the House," Sheridan himself boasted in *A State of Mr. Sheridan's Case* in 1747,[34] and the writer of *A Serious Enquiry into the Cause of the Present Disorders of this City* testified to the same state of affairs even as he denounced the manager as a tyrant. Sheridan's "Act of Power" in ejecting a "Gentlemen Attorney" from the gallery, this writer complained, "has so terrified the Town, that no one has since dared to hiss in the Galleries" (8).[35]

When in the opening paragraph of his first Barber's *Letter* Lucas urged his "Citizen" readers not to remain "idle Spectators" but to go to the playhouse and become actively engaged in determining the outcome of "the controversy . . . between some who call themselves *Gentlemen*, and the Players of *Smock-Alley*" (1), he was implicitly telling them to resist this silencing and this attempted exclusion, and the slippages and instabilities attendant on the term "Gentlemen" add a further subversive charge to his call for mobilization in the playhouse and in the city at large. As noted in the last chapter, Lucas identified the "Gentlemen" as the offspring of native Irish "Savages and Tyrants" in the opening pages of his first Barber's *Letter,* and because he gives tyranny this native Irish Catholic face, he represents his act of popular mobilization as ultimately conservative and loyalist. After making disparaging remarks about the idle "*Coshering*" lifestyle of "IRISH GENTLEMEN," Lucas writes, for example, "Look out for such, weed them from among you, my Brethren, and keep Peace and Decency in your City; not by Force, but by exerting the Strength of your Constitution, by exercising your wholesome Laws" (2); with this charge, it could be said, he reminds his Protestant readers of their duty to undertake the English civilizing mission. However, in urging his readers to "Look out *for such*" (my emphasis), he encourages his readers to think analogically as well as literally about "the Gentlemen," and in this and subsequent

Barber's *Letters,* he elaborates on the term "Gentlemen" in such a way as to suggest that he is advocating a resistance to *all* kinds of social, economic, and political tyranny, no matter what the source. In the penultimate paragraph of the first Barber's *Letter,* for example, Lucas broadens his definition of "Gentlemen" to include all those wellborn customers who threaten tradesmen when the latter try to call in an "old Debt" (7) or who insult ordinary citizens and their families in shops or coffeehouses (8). Thus when he urges those who "are not in their Sense, *Gentlemen*" to go to the playhouse and monitor and if necessary "crush this Pest of Society" (8), the thrust of his rhetoric is to suggest that tradesmen use the playhouse as a site of a resistance to any kind of social or economic oppression. That his call has this broader social and economic significance is also apparent from the following inflammatory passage in his third Barber's *Letter* in which he explicitly denounces "gentlemen in general":

> I shall not ask you, whether you can approve the tyranny set up by *the Gentlemen* in your city? or their looking upon all men of professions or trades, as *Slaves* and *Hirelings;* bound down to *passive Obedience,* and *Non-Resistance,* to their employers? These are positions, your generous, free souls must detest. You well know, that *gentlemen in general* [my emphasis] have as great, or greater dependence on us, than we on them. It is well known, that tradesmen may, and do, live by tradesmen—Can the gentlemen say as much? (11)

In arguing, as he does in his second *Letter,* that "Every breach of the Laws of Society, is Rebellion" (4), Lucas similarly widens his definition of "Rebellion" so that it could apply to "gentlemen" of any ethnic or religious background, and in suggesting that "He . . . who knowingly persists in a violation of the Laws of his Country, is a worse Enemy, and a more dangerous Rebel to our free Government, than the Slave who for mercenary Views, draws the Sword with intent to subvert our happy Establishment, and set up a hateful Pretender" (4), he also explicitly states that such elite lawbreakers are greater threats to national security than are Jacobites. By reminding his readers in the same letter of the connection between the "Gentlemen's" faction and the Wood's Halfpence affair, too, he slyly hints that this greater threat may come from the English metropolitan center itself. When Lucas displaces the blame in this *Letter* from Kelly—the latter is now a "young Gentleman" who suffered "from the ill Effects of too much Liquor and *bad Company*" (10)—to an "infamous old crafty *Traitor* and

Conspirator" (5) who "utters and avers seditious Falsehoods with the same Solemnity, that he swore *Stamped Leather* was the *current Coin* of this Kingdom" (9), he is apparently referring to John Browne, who had testified for the government in the 1720s in the Wood's Halfpence affair. At another level, however, this displacement encodes the message that the greater threat of oppression comes from an external English rather than an internal Irish power, and by referring his readers to Swift's *Drapier's Letters* for a fuller knowledge of this "President" [Browne] of the Kelly faction—"You may see some out-lines of his Portrait in the *Draper's* [*sic*] Letters before Mr. F[aulkner] curtail'd it"—Lucas further gestures at the broader Irish Protestant nationalist dimension of his proposed resistance. As Bryan Coleborne points out, for Swift and other patriots at the time, Browne was the prototype of the "dunce as enemy of the state . . . which momentarily existed in the unity of opposition to the coinage, [and] which momentarily embodied a rare glimpse of another political and social order."[36]

In the third Barber's *Letter*, there are also hints of that more inclusive attitude toward the native Irish that Murphy mentions, though it is important to note that Lucas extends his sympathies only to the "poor Irish" and not to the native gentry. In response to the charge, for example, that he "represent[ed] all the *poor, conquered Irish,* without exception, as a *base, barbarious, savage* people, whose very *names* are *hateful* to *English* Protestants" (15), Lucas writes, "I never did nor can look upon the *Irish* as a *conquered People*" as "[t]hey voluntarily submitted to the Kings and laws of *Britain*" (16). Even as he makes this claim he again explicitly justifies the dispossession of the native Irish elite on the grounds of rebellion—"For breaking solemn engagements, it is, that some are turned out of their ancient possessions" (16)—and he again justifies his statements about "*ancient Irish Barbarism*" by referring to that "set of People, who vainly boast their ancient pedigree from illustrious *Irish,* or imaginary *Spanish* kings; who like their *Ancestors* keep their subjects, or tenants, in the most abject dependence and slavery" (16). If Lucas's enemies successfully represented him as a "Cromwell" to the Catholics, as "a rank Jacobite" to Protestants, and as a "seditious, rebellious libeller" to the "men in power" in spring 1747, then, it was not entirely because of their "arts and rhetoric" as he himself claims in his third Barber's *Letter*.[37] It was also because of the uniquely populist nature of his brand of Irish patriotism, a political ideology that led him to support the claims of "poor" Irish Catholic peasants and Irish Protestant tradesmen and "citizens" while at the same time denouncing the claims to power of either the English or the Irish gentry.

In winter 1747 Lucas went public with these attacks on the gentry, and as *The Tickler* makes clear, with Sheridan's cooperation and support, he again used the playhouse as a staging ground for his campaign. Lucas's next venture into the political arena after the Gentlemen's Quarrel occurred in December 1747 when he presented his *Complaints of Dublin* to the earl of Harrington at the King's Bench, shortly after the latter arrived in Dublin to take up the position of viceroy. The *Complaints* (first delivered as an oral statement and later published as a pamphlet) was ostensibly Lucas's protest at the abortive treatment of his lawsuit in 1744. In effect, however, the reformer used his lawsuit as an opportunity to attack tyranny in all its forms, and he managed to infuriate gentlemen on both sides of the ethnic and religious divide. In questioning the decision of the justices in his lawsuit, for example, Lucas stated that this decision laid "the foundation for the heaviest oppression this nation ever knew, the subjecting one free Kingdom to another, by pronouncing that Ireland is subject to Laws made in England against the consent of the People or Parliament of Ireland,"[38] and it was undoubtedly to show their displeasure at these remarks that Lucas was told not to come back to court again. In criticizing the government's importation of "English clergy" from "fallen Oxford," he made comments on the "unnatural, illegal Government of the STUARTS" and on Oxford University's reputation for courting Jacobites—"the *imaginary Progency* of their *late Invaders,* rendered yet more savage by *foreign Popish education*"—that equally infuriated Catholic gentlemen like Hiffernan.[39] In the fourth issue of *The Tickler* (published on March 11, 1748), Hiffernan referred to the *Complaints* as "the late petulant production of a delirious brain" (19), and more than a year later he was still brooding on Lucas's negative remarks on the Stuarts in this text. Noting that the present English king was himself related to the Stuarts, Hiffernan wrote in a July 1749 *Tickler:* "What must he [the king] think of his identified friend LUCAS, (*see complaints* of Dublin) where he calls the STUARTS, *unnatural,* and *illegal,* etc."[40]

At the very time that Lucas was alienating gentlemen on all sides of the political spectrum, Sheridan, who owed Lucas a debt for coming to his rescue during the previous year's Quarrel, was openly showing support for him (the Harrington administration, in any case, showed no interest in patronizing the theater). And by all accounts, Lucas was no less overt in showing his support for the manager and his theater. In his retrospective accounts of his career as manager, Sheridan makes no mention of his relationship with the controversial Lucas, and when he talks of his own "reform" campaign, he is always careful to insist that it was impeccably loyalist. During the 1747–48 season, however, the manager was living as a lodger at Lucas's house in Ormond Quay, and according to *The Tickler*, he and Lucas were working in tandem to promote each other's careers. The first issue of *The Tickler* (February 18) lists an "Apothecary" among the "commanding Officers" of Sheridan's "attendant Clappermen" and "noisy hirelings" at Smock Alley at this time (1), and the fourth issue (March 11) portrays Lucas as loudly applauding patriotic passages from Addison's *Cato* to draw attention to himself (2). A mock-letter from Sheridan to *The Tickler* in the third issue (March 3) also suggests that the manager was permitting Lucas to insert his trademark speeches about "Liberty" and "the Constitution" into plays at this time ("But sure, sir," the manager is made to say in defense of such interpolations in his recent revival of Beaumont and Fletcher's *The Loyal Subject*, "you'll allow such absurdities to be pardonable, when done in a view to shew one's love to the CONSTITUTION" [17]); and in the seventh issue of *The Tickler* (May 13), it is suggested that Lucas took a benefit at the playhouse "under pretext of a private person in distress; and that to enable him to prosecute his iniquitous schemes" (49).

These charges could perhaps be dismissed as mere partisan invention if it were not that other independent sources confirm them. On May 4, 1748, Sheridan gave a benefit "for the Support of a Person in Distress," and a *Dublin Journal* notice relating to this benefit stated that "Charitable Contributions and Benefactions [were] to be received for the Use of the distress'd Object, by Mr. Charles Lucas, at his House on Ormond Quay."[41] An anti-*Tickler* pamphlet from spring 1748 also confirms that the playhouse was serving as a rallying place for Lucas and his supporters during this period. After ironically praising Hiffernan for his "Spirit in mounting to the upper Regions [the upper gallery]" at a recent performance so that he "might be exalted above that haughty *Charley* who 'perk'd it at the same time in the Boxes' and was saluted with a loud Clap," the anonymous author of *Mr. Nobody's Anti-Ticklerian Address to Mr. Lucas* informs Hiffernan that a similar enthusiastic reception will attend Lucas "whenever he shews his Face there."[42] This author also finishes with an ominous warning to the "Tickler" to "[be]ware pumping," and he hints that if Hiffernan continues to offend the Trinity College "Lucasians," he may have his ears nailed to the college gate.[43]

The symbiotic relationship between Sheridan's theater and the Lucasians during the 1747–48 season also explains the piece Hiffernan himself would later term his "mock heroic description of a ridiculous *Apotheosis*" (46), a satiric attack that is arguably *The Tickler*'s most memorable piece of writing. This "ridiculous *Apotheosis*" is embedded in a letter in the fifth issue of *The Tickler* that purports to come from a concerned Lucas admirer. After expressing his regrets at Lucas's lack of opportunity to display his "great man" status like his hero Cromwell, this admirer advises Lucas to jump off Essex Bridge into the Liffey as a way to gain immortality and simultaneously revenge himself on a thankless city. The ensuing "ridiculous *Apotheosis*," then, is this admirer's envisioning of this scene. Dressed in an incongruous assortment of clothes and props—a mourning suit that Sheridan wore as Antony in *All for Love*, the truncheon belonging to the Ghost in *Hamlet*, a wig previously worn by his neighbor, the beggar Hack-ball—Lucas is imagined leading a grotesque "patriot procession" from his house on Ormond Quay to the equestrian statue of George I on Essex Street (26). The manager's "*free clappermen*" form the vanguard of this procession, and they are followed by the players with "sullied truncheons, rusty shapes, and high embowr'ing perriwigs" and by Sheridan himself, dressed in Hamlet's black suit. The rear guard, meanwhile, is formed by "*J—ks—n* and his constables" who "with protended staves keep a *clear stage*, and prohibit the desiring crowd to encroach on the decorum of the piece," and at the last moment the parade is joined by "poor Brass" (Faulkner), who carries a copy of *Clarissa* that he intends to offer to Lucas so that he can model his style on it in the other world (26–27). When this motley crew reaches Essex Bridge, Lucas and Sheridan exchange melodramatic speeches of farewell, and then cheered by his "beloved citizens," by the "nocturnal nymphs of the bridge" (prostitutes), and by such well-known Dublin street characters as Hack-ball (king of the beggars), Crow (a runner for the playhouse), and Millcushion (a reputed idiot), Lucas jumps off the tail of the equestrian statue into the Liffey, his "train, high flying in the wind . . . like to that of a portentous comet" (27–28). Miraculous portents also occur in the wake of this event: "At this great deed, voices are heard in air, innoxious flames play around *Boyle's* noseless face on *Ormond*-quay and, (O astonishing!) the wooden man in *Essex*-street cries *Huzza*. From *Essex* up to *Island*-bridge, and back again, the replicated shouts of bellowing crowds resound along the concave banks" (28).

Like Pope's *Dunciad* to which this vision is obviously indebted, this mock-heroic description functions as both a theatrical and a political satire. During the 1747–48 season, "low" English comedy, pantomime, and French dance were particularly prevalent at Smock Alley, and in the first issue of *The Tickler* Hiffernan had railed against such entertainments as he disputed Sheridan's claim to have established a "well-regulated stage" (2).

This scene of "more than tragic pomp" (as the Lucasian admirer puts it) is a composite of these forms of theatrical "corruption" (6). The comical costumes and wigs, the farcical leap from the tail of the equestrian statue, the voices in the air, the "innoxious flames," the speaking wooden man—all are reminiscent of the pantomime that Hiffernan had deplored as he took aim at Henry Woodward's "motley dress of *Harlequin*" and his "most low-lived preposterous tricks" (2); while the long drawn out final scene between Sheridan and Lucas on Essex Bridge—a scene marked by repeated embracing, copious weeping, and long drawn out, bombastic speeches of farewell—recalls Hiffernan's critique in the same issue of the manager's "languid state of expiring," a form of tragic acting that "screamingly burlesquest all vehement passions" (3).

But this Lucasian street theater, with its supporting cast of armed constables and players with truncheons, is also a metaphor for the nightmare upside-down world of Hanoverian Ireland as this world was perceived by marginalized Catholics like Hiffernan—a world in which apothecaries and players could rise to power while native gentlemen were excluded and insulted. Writing on English Augustan poetry of the same period, Michael McKeon argues that the overwhelming preference in this poetry for the mock-panegyric and mock-heroic was symptomatic of "an extended crisis in the authority of public leaders," and he suggests that the crisis was provoked by the Hanoverian rulers' abandonment of this "crucial principle of genealogical legitimacy."[44] The abandonment of the principle of genealogical legitimacy in Ireland, however, brought a much deeper crisis, because it was accompanied not just by the overthrow of a monarch but also by the overthrow of most of those who were the hereditary leaders of that society. As noted in the last chapter, native Irish writers registered this crisis in the Clan Thomas genre of satirical writing that depicted the leaders of the new order as buffoons, churls, and vicious clowns. This "mock heroic description of a ridiculous *Apotheosis*" in *The Tickler* belongs in this native Irish tradition of writing; by associating Lucas with theatricality, Hiffernan underscores what he takes to be the inauthentic and dangerous nature of his brand of populist leadership. In the last *Tickler*, which appeared on October 20, 1749, after Lucas had fled the country, Hiffernan also makes this theatricality/false leadership analogy explicit when he equates Lucas's abilities (as Burke would later) with those of the "*mountebank*": "for what difference can there be betwixt holding forth on a *street-stage*, or before our corporation audiences," he asks, "which, the doors open'd, are composed of the eructations of the street." In his concluding paragraphs he again uses theatrical imagery and borrowed dramatic lines to sum up what he considers Lucas's failed and false political effort. Lucas was a "bellowing phantom, [a] poor player, that strutted, and fretted his hours in halls, and now is heard no more," Hiffernan writes, "TRUTH's mock-standard bearer, whereon, to sickly and deluded eyes, appear'd RIGHTS, LIBERTY; but to the eyes of reason, glared in bloody characters, DISSENTION, INCENDIARY."[45]

◆◆◆

Burke's first pamphlet, *Punch's Petition to Mr. Sh———n, to be admitted into the Theatre Royal,* which was written in winter 1747, articulates a similar vision of an upside-down world dominated by buffoons to the exclusion of the true elite, and, like *The Tickler,* this piece of writing functions as both a theatrical and a political satire. Punchinello, the persona Burke adopts in his first pamphlet, is of course a character from the commedia dell'arte. Unlike other characters from the commedia, however, Punch has no set role or social position, an indeterminacy that has allowed many different cultural and social groups to embrace him as their own. As Allardyce Nicoll notes, Punch is "a characterless dummy which could be dressed up in any way a particular actor—or a particular public—desired"; thus "a Neapolitan can claim the Polcinella of his stage as the very symbol of Naples' spirit[,] . . . a Frenchman can assert that Polichinelle is an expression of the Parisian populace [and] Punch may be the title of an English periodical."[46] As soon as the puppeteer Randall Stretch set up his "Great Booth" at Dame Street in Dublin in the early 1720s, the Irish also began claiming Punch as their own, much to the dismay of the Smock Alley players. In the prologue to the mock-puppet show farce, *Punch turn'd School-Master* (1721), a play Dr. Thomas Sheridan wrote to satirize the new taste for puppet shows, we find Griffith complaining that Smock Alley "was almost empty grown / From the first Moment *Stretch* appear'd in Town," and a decade later Mrs. Sterling was still castigating "Footmen and Beaux" from the stage of Smock Alley for preferring their "wooden brethren" and "Seignior *Scaramouch* and *Punchinello*" to the more rational joys of Shakespeare and the legitimate theater.[47]

Contemporary Irish commentary on Punchinello also suggests that this puppet signified differently in different kinds of social and cultural contexts and that it was used to articulate different kinds of political desires. From the description of a puppet show (probably Stretch's) in Swift's poem "Mad Mullinex and Timothy" (1728), for example, it is clear Punch delighted the puppet-booth audience because he was an agent of disruption, an anarchic figure who thumped his nose at authority figures and made a farce of conventional morality and manners:

> Observe, the Audience is in Pain,
> While *Punch* is hid behind the Scene,
> But when they hear his rusty Voice,
> With what Impatience they rejoice.
> And then they value not two Straws,
> How *Solomon* decides the Cause . . .
> You e'ry moment think an Age,
> Till he appears upon the Stage
> And first his Bum you see him Clap,
> Upon the Queen of *Sheba's* lap.
> The Duke of *Lorrain* drew his sword:
> Punch roaring ran, and running roar'd,
> Reviles all People in his Jargon,
> And sells the *King of Spain* a bargain.
> *St. George* himself he plays the wag on,
> And mounts astride upon the *Dragon*.[48]

In the hands of an Irish Protestant patriot writer like Swift, however, the puppet also became a vehicle for attacks on bad politicians and bad government, as the larger context of this poem reveals. The "Timothy" alluded to in the title of this poem was the Irish M. P. Richard Tighe, and throughout the poem Swift ridicules Tighe for being a Whig fanatic, a man who is obsessed with "*Popish* Craft," with "the *Pretender*," and "With Plots; and *Jacobites* and Treason" (774, 775). In comparing Tighe's behavior to the disruptive antics of Punchinello, Swift then continues and expands this satire. As Ehrenpreis notes, "[W]hen Swift compares Tighe to Punch in the puppet show, he implies that the machinery of government in Ireland has for its true function that of a farcical entertainment, diverting the people from their real problems."[49]

> Thus *Tim*, Philosophers suppose,
> *The World consists of Puppet-shows;*
> Where petulant, conceited Fellows
> Perform the part of *Punchinelloes;*

So at this Booth, which we call *Dublin,*
Tim thour't the *Punch* to stir up trouble in;
You Wrigle, Fidge, and make a Rout
Put all your Brother Puppets out,
Run on in a perpetual Round,
To Teize, Perplex, Disturb, Confound.
Intrude with Monkey grin, and clatter
To interrupt all serious Matter. (777)

In deploying Punch as a vehicle for this kind of antigovernment satire, Swift was also continuing an Irish patriot tradition that had begun a few years earlier with the anonymous *Punch's Petition to the Ladies* (1724). In this earlier poem Punch asks the ladies for help after the Irish secretary of state and master of the revels, Edward Hopkins, refuses to let Stretch put on his show unless he paid the government a large sum.[50] Behind the image of the tyrannical "Vander Hop" who "invades [the puppet booth] without pretence and right, / Or any law but that of might,"[51] however, is also the image of the money-grabbing English place seeker who was so frequently the object of patriotic satire; indeed, Hopkins (who was an Englishman) had been explicitly satirized as such an extortionist in an earlier pair of satires (one of which was by Swift) revolving around his attempt to exact a similar license fee from the Smock Alley players in 1722.[52] The patriot thrust of the puppet show conceit in *Punch's Petition to the Ladies* becomes more apparent when Punch offers to pay the required government license fee using Wood's Halfpence. As "mimic men," Punch states, it is appropriate to pay in "mimic coin" (295), an ironic comment on the political position of the Irish subject who is forced to accept this debased currency and by extension a debased political position.

When Burke has his Punchinello petition for admittance to Sheridan's Theatre Royal because of this stage's "great Similitude" to Punch's own,[53] then, he is continuing this patriot tradition of satire, though, as we will see, he also adds a more subversive native twist to his patriot protest. As noted above, the Dublin stage was dominated by harlequins and French dancers during the 1747–48 season. In having Punch emphasize the continuity between these kind of entertainments and those he offered in his puppet booth, it might seem that Burke is using Punch as many mid-eighteenth-century conservative English writers and critics did—to satirize the "low" taste of contemporary audiences that increasingly demanded spectacle, pantomime, song, and dance in their theatrical entertainments. Commenting on William Hogarth's "A Just View of the British Stage, or Three Heads Are Better Than None," for example, Scott Shershow writes, "[B]y midcentury the puppet could serve as a visual emblem not just for the process of performance itself, but also for a broad spectrum of paratheatrical entertainments seen as invading and polluting a theater that had finally achieved the legitimacy to which Jonson had so painfully aspired a century earlier."[54] By inserting an "ingenious Native" element in the following protest in *Punch's Petition to Mr. Sh———n,* however, Burke complicates what could otherwise be read as a straightforward defense of an aristocratic principle of heredity:

> But he [Punchinello] trusts as you [Sheridan] value yourself on the Love of your Country, that you will encourage an ingenious Native preferable to a Foreigner, as your Petitioner is descended from the Ancient British Harlequins, who have had Possession of this Stage long before these Italian Performers were heard of, and that it is not his want of Merit, but his being Body and Soul of Irish Manufacture, which makes him neglected, he being able to shew more Feats of Agility, and has besides that advantage over them, that to his admirable Postures he adds his admirable Wit, a Quality they don't even pretend to.

As an "ingenious Native" and "admirable Wit" who is simultaneously of "Ancient British" descent and "of Irish Manufacture," the Punchinello in Burke's text suggests the position of the Catholic (Old English and Irish) gentleman and writer; and it is the "neglect" of this class—their exclusion from the theatrical, cultural, and political domain—that is also indirectly protested here. This Punchinello act of ventriloquism, it could be said, allows Burke to complain of the ascendancy of the new elite and the marginalization of the old gentry while simultaneously concealing his Catholic sympathies.

The voice of this "ingenious Native" also sounds, however obliquely, in *The Reformer,* the weekly periodical that Burke began editing and publishing on January 28, and the anti-Lucasian satire woven through this publication makes explicit the political referent for this Punch's attack on the Theatre Royal's dull foreign "Harlequins." In the essays in the first three issues of *The Reformer,* Burke and his friends launched the kind of "grave inquiry into the behaviour of the manager" mentioned in Dennis's January 14 letter, and as this letter promised, the inquiry takes issue with every aspect of Sheridan's playhouse. Ireland has become an "Empire of

Dulness" that forces "Men of *Genius* and *Spirit* to rise up,"[55] *The Reformer* argues in the opening paragraph of its first issue, and in this and the next two issues, it suggests that Sheridan's theater has played a key role in promoting this national decline. The poor quality of the manager's theatrical entertainments, the low talents of his players, and the barbarism of his audience have all promoted a general depravity of taste and morality.[56] *The Reformer* also hints, however, that it has an anti-Lucasian agenda when it states in the first issue that its objective is "the restoring Taste, to its long usurped Rights, and to discountenance domestic Petulance, and all foreign Immorality, and Dulness" (2). The referent for "Domestic Petulance" is ostensibly those "pert and ignorant Coxcombs" who, like Sheridan, refuse to recognize "such Productions of our own as promise a Genius" (2). But in the immediate political context, it also suggests the upstart Lucas who was then daring to "usurp" the "Rights" of the elite both in the playhouse and in the political domain at large.

The Hack-ball advertisement that appeared after the "grave" essay in this first issue also made the Lucasian valence of this theatrical attack more explicit, and if present-day readers have consistently missed this political subtext, it is undoubtedly because the advertisement is not reproduced in Arthur P. I. Samuels's edition of *The Reformer,* the only readily available copy of this work.[57] In real life Hack-ball was Patrick Carregan, the reputed king of the many homeless beggars who roamed Dublin in the eighteenth century.[58] When *The Reformer* published an advertisement in its first issue announcing that a print of Hack-ball, "the Head of the *Mendicant* Order, and of obstreperous Fame in this City," was being published by subscription so that posterity would have "the Remembrance of so illustrious a Personage," it was clearly being satirical, and the allusion to a "Fellow Citizen of *some Eminence* [who had] to pay the entire Expence himself" for a similar "Print" would have identified Lucas as the butt of this satire. In 1747 Lucas had commissioned a portrait of himself from the painter William Jones, and this portrait was subsequently sold as a print by the engraver Andrew Miller.[59] Entitled "Charles Lucas—A Free Citizen and sometime one of the Commons of Dublin," this self-commissioned print depicted Lucas as he wished to be seen by his fellow citizens (fig. 4). The reformer's somber but well-cut dress, his wig, his upright posture, his serious gaze, and his gesture of placing his right hand on his breast all suggest patrician virtue, and the pamphlets in the picture further identify him as a champion of liberty and as a defender of the rights of the people. In his left hand, for instance, Lucas holds a pamphlet with the words "State

Figure 4. Charles Lucas: A Free Citizen and sometime one of
the Commons of Dublin / Wm. Jones Pinxit 1747; Andw. Miller fecit."
Courtesy of the National Library of Ireland.

of the Case of the Freemen and Citizens of Dublin" on it, and the words
"Develina Libera" are clearly visible on a pamphlet that lies on the writing
table behind him.[60] In keeping with this depiction of patrician virtue, too,
the arms of the city of Dublin appear on a Roman archway in the background of the picture. When *The Reformer* announced that Hack-ball's
print would be adorned "with the Arms of his most Antient Family, with
several emblematical Figures of the remarkable Actions of his Life," and
with Latinate inscriptions, then, it was taking aim at this print, and in the
event that readers missed the Lucas allusion, they are told at the end of the
advertisement that they "may contemplate the great Original, at his *sympathetic Residence* on ORMOND QUAY" (3).

Figure 5. *The Tickler*. Frontispiece.
By permission of the Folger Shakespeare Library.

Later the same year, it should also be noted, Hiffernan provided a visual counterpart to this Hack-ball satire in the "Curious Frontispiece" that
accompanied his collected edition of *The Tickler*,[61] and in this parody of
the Jones-Miller print, Lucasian politics and the paratheatrical are again in-
extricably intertwined (fig. 5). In Hiffernan's frontispiece, the classic background of the original Jones-Miller print is replaced by a floor in a criss-

cross pattern that is reminiscent of Harlequin's costume, and while Lucas wears the same clothes and wig and still stands before a writing table, his splayed legs and his perplexed look—he now points his finger to his lips in a state of puzzlement—suggest plebian ignorance and foolishness. The clown who shares the frame with Lucas then further underlines this asso- ciation with "low" culture and rough buffoonery. At one obvious level, this clown is a representative of the author himself. The clown's physical characteristics resemble those that Hiffernan assigns himself in his self- portrait in the seventh issue of *The Tickler*,[62] and his activity—he is tick- ling Lucas with a feather—clearly designates Hiffernan's own satiric art in *The Tickler* papers. At another level, however, this clown also functions as a commentary on Lucas and his political ambition: behind the patrician front, this visual juxtaposition suggests, is the figure of a lowly fool.

The Reformer offered a similar unflattering image of Lucas in its Hack- ball advertisement, and it is clear from the reaction that contemporaries grasped its specific satiric intent. In *The Reformer Reform'd*, a pamphlet that appeared the same day as the first issue of *The Reformer*, a writer who signs himself "Tom Telltruth" responds with indignation to the paper's at- tacks on Sheridan and his stage, and, though this "Tom" is clearly no fan of Lucas, he also finds fault with the Hack-ball advertisement for its satire on "a certain noted Citizen": "So stupid a Piece as your Advertisement, deserves little Notice, as 'tis neither instructive or diverting, and the Whipe given therein to a certain noted Citizen, for whose Sake, the whole seems to have been contrived, is very poor, as he deserves more severe Satire, than you are able to afford him, you should have let him alone, till a fairer Opportunity."[63] It is also clear from Dennis's letter to Shackleton on Feb- ruary 4 that the manager's supporters suspected Hiffernan of being the au- thor of this paper, an identification that speaks to the ideological similarity in the writings of Burke and Hiffernan at this time; as far as their contem- poraries were concerned, the satire of the one was indistinguishable from the satire of the other:

> I send you enclosed the second number of the Reformer, with this comfort that the generality of the town likes it I believe, by the sale which was about 500 to-day. The first number the town bought near 1000 of: we have set out *bonis ominibus*, and I hope shall continue the same. Hiffernan who was heretofore a friend of Victor's, has lost his acquaintance on the suspicion of being the author. Sheridan is much piqued, and his friends . . . vigorously oppose it, and damn it as

earnestly as they do taste every night at the playhouse in the applause they bestow upon dulness.[64]

It was undoubtedly to allay these suspicions of involvement with the native-identified, Catholic Hiffernan (as well as to sustain the sales of both papers) that the Trinity campaigners decided to stage a fight between *The Reformer* and *The Tickler* in the following weeks, and undoubtedly also it is this mock-fight that has shaped the perception that these two publications have no political interest in common. In his very first *Tickler* of February 19, Hiffernan accused the author of *The Reformer* of being another one of the manager's "noisy clappermen" (1), and in a "Postscript to the Reformer" in this same issue, Hiffernan explicitly states that the only thing he contributed to *The Reformer* was the mock–Hack-ball advertisement. After reprinting the Hack-ball advertisement in its entirety (and thus, of course, reiterating the insult to Lucas), he writes, "This advertisement was sent by the *Tickler* to the *Reformer*, and was the only thing of his [that had] appeared in that paper," though Hiffernan adds, "he has been often undeservedly complimented on that head" (7). Burke, in turn, claims to be shocked at *The Tickler*'s charges of partisanship of any kind, and he implies that he has no knowledge of the Tickler's identity. In the fifth issue of *The Reformer* (published on February 25), he describes how he heard a newsboy crying "A Letter to the Reformer" on the street and found to his horror that in this letter he was being accused of being a Sheridan supporter: "[H]ow great was my Surprize! When I found the Author of this Paper (who calls himself the TICKLER) accused me with being one of the Manager's Partizans, an Accusation so much the more disagreeable, as I had with the utmost Caution avoided giving any Room for a suspicion of Party."[65]

Beneath the surface of this mock-conflict, however, *The Reformer* continued a subversive interplay with *The Tickler* and also continued to lend its support to Hiffernan's renewed "Gentlemen's" campaign against Sheridan, Lucas, and the Theatre Royal. In the essay in the fifth issue, the "Reformer" describes his experiences as he anonymously visits various Dublin coffeehouses, a round of visits he undertook, he claims, explicitly to ascertain whether the public shared *The Tickler*'s view that *The Reformer* was a "Party" paper (1). In most sites he visits he encounters indifference and apathy rather than hostility, but circumstances take a dramatic change for the worse when he enters the last, most socially diverse coffeehouse. There he hears a "clever tall Fellow" (2) publicly praising the manager and denouncing the author of *The Reformer* as a "Scoundrel, who was tempted to write thus for the sake of a Dinner," and when the author steps forward and expresses his belief that such thoughts were "unworthy of a Gentleman," the speaker threatens to hit him with a "Cudgel" (3). The "Reformer" then feels it prudent to withdraw on hearing from a bystander that "this angry Person was one of the Manager's Partizans, who had it in his Commission to abuse all who dared dislike his Proceedings" (3). But the victorious Sheridan supporter goes "boisterously vapouring all over the House" until people from every walk of life in the coffeehouse (politicians, tradesmen, lawyers, divines, gentlemen, critics, beaus, pedants) are drawn into the controversy, including, as the "Reformer" tells us, "A little Gentleman, with a black Wig, and of sower Aspect, whom I took to be either a Physician or Apothecary, [who] said it [*The Reformer*] was so malevolent, that the Authors ought to be purg'd for the Spleen" (3). Under the guise of disproving *The Tickler*'s claim of partisanship, *The Reformer* thus figuratively reenacts the Kelly "riot" of 1747, with the role of the manager played by the "clever tall Fellow," the role of Lucas played by the "Apothecary" who demands that his opponents be "purg'd," and the role of Kelly played by the "Reformer" himself; and by depicting the Sheridan-Lucas camp in this negative light, this paper lends its support to the overtly political campaign that Hiffernan was undertaking in his paper. Like *The Tickler* (and before that the "Gentlemen's" texts), *The Reformer* suggests that a universe dominated by Sheridan, his "sower" "Apothecary," and their supporters is a nightmare world of violence and disorder; here, as in Hiffernan's mock-apotheosis, the "Cudgel" serves to intimidate and silence gentlemen who dare criticize these new political and cultural leaders. As another hidden signifier of its relation with Hiffernan, this fourth issue (like six other issues of *The Reformer*) carries an advertisement for subscriptions to *Reflections on the Structures and Passions* by "P. H. M. D" (Paul Hiffernan, M. D) (4), a philosophical work that Hiffernan published later that year. As in the first issue of *The Reformer* and *The Tickler*, a seemingly insignificant advertisement undermines the two papers' overt assertions of mutual animosity and instead points to their shared political and cultural goals.

In issues four through nine of *The Reformer,* Burke also articulates the gentry alternative to Lucas's populist patriotism, and in so doing, he brings out the Irish nationalist agenda that is always implicit in Hiffernan's Lucasian satire—an alternative that this Catholic gentleman (like his counterparts O'Conor and Curry) can never speak without undermining his loyalist cover. In a recent essay in which he reconsiders the politics and content of Burke's paper, Thomas O. McLoughlin argues persuasively that *The Reformer* is not just a plea for a better theater but "a plea for a humane and Irish-based socio-economic order in which Arts and Sciences have a central position," and he also notes that *The Reformer* sees the involvement of the upper classes as the key to this change.[66] This argument is also borne out by an analysis of the central issues of this paper. *Reformer* 4, for example, roundly denounces the "Nobility and Gentry" for not patronizing Irish "Manufacture" (either commercial or artistic);[67] *Reformer* 7 condemns the "Great" for callously indulging in their "Pageantry" and "luxurious lives" while the poor peasants live in unprecedented squalor and poverty;[68] and *Reformer* 9 paints a picture of a "Nation sinking into Ruin and Misery, while whose those who are bound to promote its Advantage, by Birth, Gratitude and Interest, are spending its Revenues in a Country which despises us, or laying out their Income among our Enemies for Fopperies, which would be better retrenched, or equally well supplied at home."[69] However, in arguing that these kinds of protests take their meaning *exclusively* from an Irish Protestant patriot tradition of dissent—the tradition of protest established by Molyneux, Swift, Berkley, and Madden[70]— McLoughlin overlooks the dialogue between the "Reformer" and "Asper" in the central sixth issue of *The Reformer* (there were thirteen issues in all), a dialogue that suggests the Reformer's critique derives equally from a native gentry source. The Reformer describes Asper as his "Friend" and as a "Man of good Sense and a sincere Lover of his Country," and he devotes most of his essay in this sixth issue to expounding Asper's views on the poor state of "polite Literature in this Kingdom."[71] Details in this exposition, however, leave little doubt that "Asper" is a pseudonym for Hiffernan,[72] and it is Hiffernan's native Irish gentry brand of alienation that is apparent in his gloomy description of the present ruling class. In Asper's critique of a "Gentry" who have lost the "Taste of true Glory" and who neglect the "fine Arts" because they are "constantly employed in the Study of accumulating Wealth, or idly spending it" (1), for example, it is possible to hear the complaint of the traditional Gaelic writer against the mercenary "new men" who have displaced the old elite, and in his description of the consequences of this neglect, it is possible to catch another glimpse of the upside-down, nightmare world of both *Parliament Clann Tomas* and *The Tickler:*

> How many good Things have been the Objects of the publick Censure? How many of the vilest have met general Approbation? Else sure *Fustian* playing would never be term'd *Genius, Faction, Spirit;* nor

a Set of leaden-headed Fellows, the lowest of Mankind, set up for Men of Taste; nor Books the vilest in their nature (here he mentioned *Clarissa* and some other modern Pieces) be accepted and universally read. These things shew the Flood of Barbarism to be at the highest, and 'tis vain to oppose it. There is a Fatality in all Things, some Ages shine with the Light of Science and Virtue, while others are buried in the grossest Darkness. These mutally and naturally succeed each other as Night does Day; and when it comes to any Nation's Turn to fall into Ignorance, Experience shews it can no more be avoided than the Change of the Seasons. (1–2)

"Fustian," "Faction," and the "leaden-headed Fellows" who approve *Clarissa* are also scarcely disguised references to Sheridan, Lucas, and Faulkner, the triumvirate who ruled over the empire of dullness that *The Tickler* describes, and if there was any doubt about this identification, *Tickler* 3, which appeared on the same day (March 3) as *Reformer* 6, depicts "the *lying Chronologer*" (Faulkner) boasting to Sheridan of his ability to make "my foolish country-men swallow the most stupid of stupid works *Cl..rissa*" (16). "Fustian" was also the name Hiffernan would later use to represent Sheridan in his 1749 mock–puppet play, *The Election*, and in this same play, as we will see, he gave Lucas the equally "factious" name of "Firebrand."[73] Though the Reformer responds to Asper's tirade with a mild disclaimer, countering his "melancholy Prospect" with remembrances of "the many Societies we see formed for the Support of Useful Trades and Charities" (2), he nevertheless acknowledges the validity of his friend's vision. "[T]he more I considered it, the more Reason I had to fear the Truth of my Friend's Assertions," he writes. "The *Desire of Lucre* is become almost the general Spring of Action, and it has never produced any but mean ones" (2). With this acknowledgment and with the insertion, more generally, of this double-voiced discourse, Burke makes an oblique comment on the nature of his own socioeconomic and cultural critique throughout this paper. Behind his discontent, he suggests, is the discontent of a dispossessed native Irish Catholic gentleman and a marginalized native Irish "Wit."

As we have seen, however, the much-vilified Lucas had also spoken out against the "Great" on behalf of the dispossessed from an alternate Protestant populist patriot perspective, and it is this point of intersection between a Catholic-identified gentry patriotism and a Protestant-identified populist patriotism that I wish to focus on in the next chapter as I examine the drama of these warring camps. The Burke-Hiffernan paper war of 1748, I will suggest, turned into the Capel Street theatrical opposition of 1748 and 1749, and a comparison of its theatrical productions and the ongoing Lucasian drama at the Theatre Royal shows that even as these two groups of patriots bitterly attacked each other, there was some common ground between them. Most significantly, both groups shared the belief that Irishmen themselves knew what was best for Ireland.

CHAPTER 6

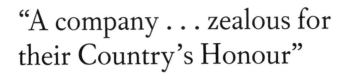

"A company . . . zealous for their Country's Honour"

The Capel Street Opposition of 1748–50

From its beginning the Capel Street theater had served as a site of opposition to Dublin's Theatre Royal. This little playhouse (also called the City Theater or the New Theater) had been hastily slapped together by the actors who were rejected when the Smock Alley and Aungier Street companies joined forces in 1743, and as William R. Chetwood notes in his *General History of the Stage*, it thus had a countercultural thrust from the beginning. "The Theatre was built," Chetwood writes, "like an aggrieved People in the State of Rebellion; their Forces raised in a Hurry, neither well cloathed, armed, paid; their Fortifications so slightly thrown up, that they did not promise a long Defence. . . . [T]his hasty Building was erected in the great Cause of Liberty!"[1] When Francis Whetson, a Dublin cabinetmaker, took the playhouse again in December 1747 (the initial company did not stay long), he continued its tradition of opposition and unorthodox play. Whetson's version of the Jason and Medea story, *The Sorceress, Or the Disobedient Daughter*, for example, was advertised as being performed by "artificial comedians"—four-foot-high puppets—and "Mr. Punch," who played the role of "Jason's Man," was billed as the main attraction.[2] In advertising that *The Sorceress* would be performed "with all the Sinkings, Flyings, Decorations . . . interspersed with several diverting Interludes of Dancing, too tedious to insert," Whetson also took an oblique jab at Sheridan, whose advertisements for the Theatre Royal were becoming increasingly verbose and long-winded.[3]

From early March 1748 until it was closed in 1750, the Capel Street theater was engaged in its fiercest struggle to date with Smock Alley. Although our knowledge of this opposition is sketchy, all the evidence suggests that it was mounted as part of the ongoing Burke-Hiffernan campaign to overthrow an emerging plebian reform movement and replace it with a gentry-led reform movement. *The Reformer* was still going strong in March 1748, but, as McLoughlin notes, there was a decided change in its tone and style around this time. From the eighth issue on, the "puckish" humor that was subservient in the early issues begins to displace serious inquiry as the dominant approach, and the paper now begins to mimic the affected style of the very fops it previously had denounced.[4] However, when McLoughlin reads this change as Burke's despairing "surrender" of his reforming cause—he compares the mood of these last issues to the darkly comic mood at the end of Pope's *Dunciad*[5]—he accepts *The Reformer*'s own explanation for its shift in style and overlooks the more obvious strategic reason. *The Reformer* certainly presents its decision to abandon "dull Reasoning" in favor of giving "Chocolate" as a despairing acquiescence to the "reigning Humour" and folly of the town,[6] but Burke and his fellow conspirators consciously adopted this kind of grave moral tone to obscure their connection to Hiffernan and his aggressively partisan satire in *The Tickler*. The resigned and despairing rhetoric that precedes the shift to smart humor in the eighth issue can be read as a continuation of this diversionary tactic, one designed to obscure the paper's connection to the dancing Punchinello who was then bringing *The Tickler*'s subversive campaign to the Capel Street stage under the guise of giving "Chocolate."

The "Chocolate" stage of the Burke-Hiffernan campaign began when Samuel Foote, a player and puppeteer who was already acquiring fame for his mimicry and satire in London, returned to Capel Street in the first week of March 1748,[7] bringing with him a version of his *Diversion of the Morning; or a Dish of Chocolate*. This form of entertainment first had been given the previous year in the Haymarket theater, a playhouse that had many of the same marginal associations as the Capel Street theater, and in it, under the pretext of inviting his friends for "Chocolate," Foote mimicked the actors of the London patent theaters and other well-known English public figures.[8] There are no surviving scripts of Foote's Capel Street entertainment, but the speed and intensity of the counterattack from Smock Alley and from Faulkner's *Dublin Journal* suggests that Foote had adjusted his "Chocolate" to fit the politics of the Dublin scene and, specifically, to fit the views of the Burke-Hiffernan faction who, I argue, were his Irish sponsors and supporters. Foote's performance opened on March 7, and by the next issue of the *Dublin Journal* (March 8–12), Woodward was announcing that he would "treat his Brother Atall [Foote] with a Dish of his own Chocolate" on the Smock Alley stage. On five other occasions during the month of March, Woodward responded to Foote's "Chocolate,"[9] an indication of just how seriously the Theatre Royal was taking this attack. The *Dublin Journal*'s willingness to support Woodward in this "Chocolate" war and its indignation over the Capel Street performances also suggest that Faulkner and possibly Lucas may have been the target of Foote's satire. After the latter departed Ireland at the end of March, Faulkner's paper proclaimed that Woodward's satire was "greatly superior to Mr. ATALL's," and it printed an extract from Woodward's "Chocolate" that labeled Foote's "dancing Punch" a national insult—a characterization that would make particular sense if the patriot, Lucas, had been the focus of attack. This piece begins

> My indignation, Sirs, at length is o'er,
> *ATALL* is fall'n—and Nonsense reigns no more!
> Nor more shall wou'd-be Satire spit its Rage,
> No living Puppet dares disgrace the Stage:
> Short liv'd Encouragement *Britannia* gave,
> Polite *Ierne* scorn'd the mimick Slave;
> Her well-bred Sons no dancing Punch delights,
> The wooden Mimick her Contempt excites!
> Her Judgment soars above such Monkey-Parts,
> And loaths the Venom of Ill-natured Arts![10]

The Reformer's support for Foote and the Capel Street theater during this period and its engagement on the anti-Sheridan side in the "Chocolate" war suggests that this "dancing Punch" was carrying on his satiric campaign at the behest of the Burke-Hiffernan faction. As noted in the last chapter, Burke had begun his campaign on behalf of the excluded "ingenious Native" by speaking through the mask of Punchinello, and in the planning stages of this campaign, as Dennis records, the leader of the Irish "wits," Hiffernan, announced his intent to satirize Sheridan in "an expostulation from Punch." The same Burke-Hiffernan faction, all the evidence suggests, were pulling the strings of the "dancing Punch" at Capel Street; the voice that "spit its Rage" through this "living Puppet" was the aggrieved voice of a marginalized Irish gentry. Even before Foote arrived in Ireland, *The Reformer* provided advance publicity for his performances,[11] and it puffed this upcoming show by noting that this "polite Entertainment" had run "upwards of Fourscore Times at the Opera-House, in the *Hay-market*, and Theatre-Royal at *Covent-Garden, London*" (4). By formally renouncing "dull Reasoning" in its eighth issue on March 18, *The Reformer* also freed itself to join in the "Chocolate" war on the side of Foote against Sheridan and his Theatre Royal supporters, and as we can see from this engagement, there is a clear continuity in tone and style between this "Chocolate" satire and the satire in *The Tickler*. The first sample of "Chocolate" in *The Reformer's* eighth issue, for example, is a letter from an imaginary foppish Theatre Royal supporter, Sir Dilberry Diddle, to his friend Jacky Wagtail in which Sir Dilberry argues that the manager and his players are far better mimics than Foote; Woodward, Dilberry boasts, has the "most inimitable Faculty of yelping like a Lap-Dog," while Sheridan provides "the double Delight of a Hero and Harlequin" (2). As we have seen, *The Tickler* also used a mock-letter from a foolish admirer to ridicule Lucas and his Theatre Royal supporters in its famous "mock-apotheosis" fifth issue; to give "Chocolate," it would seem, was to play the role of "the Tickler" under a different name.

The mock–editorial note that follows this letter provided another way for *The Reformer* to puff Foote's performance and to subtly inform its supporters and the supporters of *The Tickler* of the larger political and cultural purpose behind Foote's Irish visit. Commenting on Sir Diddle's letter, *The Reformer* writes: "By this Letter 'tis easy to perceive Mr. *F———t's* coming hither at such a Season was at the Instigation of *Jacky Wagtail*, in order to supplant *Mr. Sh———n* in the Favour of the City, by exhibiting Entertainments still more monstrous and incoherent than the other could furnish them with" (2). Though this statement appears to be critical of Foote, its hint that the English entertainer was in Dublin to overthrow Sheridan would have credentialed him with the manager's opponents, as would *The Reformer's* subsequent revelation that the English player refused Sheridan's invitation to join him in his "new fangled Folly" at Smock Alley (3). Other letters, supposedly from readers, similarly served as an excuse for puffing Foote and the Capel Street opposition. In a letter immediately following the above note in the eighth issue, "an Admirer of Mr. *Foote's* Entertainment" advises "Mr. *Reformer*" to go and see this "excellent Player" and "ingenious Satyrist," and the writer concludes this letter with the following witty and flattering epigram on Foote:

Foote's Action, Satyr, and Grimace,
Are surely of celestial Race;
Since by all Authors it is given,
That Momus is the FOOTE of Heaven. (3)

The "Spectator" who claims in the ninth issue that he "equally frequent[s] both Houses" (4) is no less laudatory. On the topic of "Ridicule," he writes, "no body has ever more happily exercised this useful Weapon than Mr. *Foote*," and because "shewing and convincing Persons of their Errors, is frequently the most effectual Means to *reform* them, and the more so, when it is not maliciously or ludicrously done," he wishes that Foote's performances meet with "the Success they deserve" (4).

By the time this last letter appeared in *The Reformer*, the "Foote" who was delivering "Chocolate" on the Capel Street stage was the young Jack Pilkington, and the presence of this player and his mother at Capel Street at this time further links this theatrical opposition to the Burke-Hiffernan campaign and the "Gentlemen's Quarrel" of 1747. "Younge Atall" or "Foote the Second," as Jack Pilkington billed himself, began giving "New Chocolate" and "Tea" after Foote himself left Ireland at the end of March, and the author of these new satiric skits, it is generally recognized, was his mother, Laetitia Pilkington. It has also been argued that a humiliating in-cident involving forged theater passes at Smock Alley earlier the same sea-son was the reason for the Pilkingtons' participation in this "Chocolate" war. As Laetitia later revealed in her *Memoirs,* Sheridan had her son ar-rested when the young man attended the playhouse using passes that he had counterfeited, a forgery she describes as insignificant since Victor usu-ally provided them with free passes. She also notes with indignation that she herself only narrowly escaped arrest (she had also used a forged pass) thanks to the intervention of "a Gentleman" who had escorted her out of the playhouse.[12] It was to avenge these insults, Lawrence suggests (and Sheldon repeats his hypothesis in her study), that the Pilkingtons took the Capel Street stage after Foote left at the end of March 1748; the whole campaign, it is implied, was a fit of personal pique.[13] Arch Elias notes in his edition of Laetitia Pilkington's *Memoirs,* however, that on at least one oc-casion during that month the Pilkingtons shared the boards at Capel Street with part of the "Gentlemen" faction of the previous year, and he suggests that Laetitia became involved in this dramatic alliance with the "Gentle-men" because of her pro-Catholic sympathies and her close friendship with the leader of the "Gentlemen," John Browne.[14] A closer look at the background of the Pilkingtons supports this more political reading; it suggests, moreover, that the Pilkingtons' satirical attacks should be read as a continuation of this native gentry form of resistance.

Jack and his mother occupied much the same socioreligious "border zone" as John Browne or Edmund Burke did. They were Protestants by birth and education, but their family maintained a close social connection with their Catholic maternal relatives, the Meades. It is also clear from their writings that both mother and son took pride in this kinship with the old aristocracy, seeing it as a source of status and gentility. The first piece of family information Laetitia provides in her *Memoirs* (the first volume of which was published in February or March 1748), for instance, is that her great-grandfather was the earl of Killmallock, the ancestor of the great Jacobite leader Patrick Sarsfield, and she proudly informs her readers that on her mother's side she was "descended of an antient, and honorable Family, who were frequently inter-married with the Nobility" (10). Throughout her narrative she expresses sympathy for Catholics and Jacobites with a boldness that is not common in midcentury English writing. For example, she comments that a young lady whom she saw kissing a picture of Charles Edward Stuart was probably a Catholic and that "it [Catholicism] is a Religion that *Patrick Sarsfield*'s Niece can never hate, let who will take Offence at it" (277). In his autobiography Jack also repeatedly draws attention to his kinship with the old aristocracy. While describing a boyhood visit to his Cork relatives, for example, he recounts a family coachman's comment that he had an "affinity . . . with all the Meades family, and several of the nobility and gentry,"[15] and he uses a description of a visit to Shane Castle in the north of Ireland on another occasion to slip in an account of his genteel Irish ancestry. At Shane Castle, he writes, he was introduced by a friend who "assured Mr. Oneile that [his] mother was descended from as noble a family as any in Ireland; but the adherence of her ancestor, Patrick Sarsfield (Lord Lucan, son to the Earl of Kilmallock) to King James the second, whose General he was during the wars in Ireland, and who accompanied him to France, and afterwards lost his life in Flanders, had impaired the fortune of the family, but not in such a manner as to deprive those who conformed to the present establishment of estate and dignity" (134).

It was this native gentry "dignity" and pride, I suggest, that Sheridan offended when he laid rough hands on Jack and threatened his mother in full public view in the playhouse, and the Pilkingtons' grievance was undoubtedly enhanced by their awareness of the manager's treatment of their friends in the "Gentlemen" faction the previous year. Neither of the Pilkingtons was in Dublin in 1747 when the Kelly incident took place, but they arrived soon enough afterward—in May 1747[16]—to have heard of the affair. From subsequent comments, it is also clear that they were both sympathetic to the "Gentlemen." In his *Real Story*, as noted in chapter 4, Jack repeated the sarcastic joke about "gentlemen actors" that Kelly's "Hibernian lawyer" made at the expense of Sheridan during the trial, and like the "Gentlemen's" defenders, Jack also suggested in his memoirs that all the disturbances that happened under Sheridan's reign were the effect of Sheridan's arrogant nature and his unwillingness to recognize his social betters. About the later 1754 theatrical uprising, Jack writes: "[T]he many disturbances Mr. Sh——n's capricious, splenetic and haughty temper has . . . occasioned in Dublin, and his frequently affronting persons superior to him in birth and fortune, as if he supported the town, instead of the town supporting him, at length cured them of their partiality to this theatrical bashaw, and encouraged them to take arms and tare [*sic*] the house down about his ears" (170). Laetitia makes no direct comment on the 1747 Quarrel in her *Memoirs*, but her subsequent outspoken support for John Browne when the latter was again at the center of a social and legal controversy in 1749 leaves little doubt that she shared her son's pro-"Gentlemen," anti-Sheridan sentiments. When Browne returned to Dublin in 1749 to face trial for murder, Laetitia visited him frequently in jail and wrote admiringly of both the man and his writing—Browne was courting her with love poems at this time—in her correspondence to a mutual friend, Lord Kingsborough.[17] In her *Memoirs* she was also outspoken in defense of the controversial Browne: "[My] polite *Roman* [Catholic]! my Friend, beloved by all, but the malicious and unworthy, who prosecute you for no other Cause, but that you excel in Courage and Learning" (320).

The similarities between Laetitia Pilkington's account of her son's ejection from the theater and the "Gentlemen's" account of Kelly's ejection suggest that she saw Jack as another type of Kelly. In the 1747 pamphlet *A Serious Enquiry*, the writer (who may well have been Browne) had argued that the "Gentlemen's" riotous behavior was retaliation for Sheridan's public humiliation of a gentleman. On that occasion, this pamphleteer writes, the "high and mighty" manager, "size[d] the poor Gentleman [Kelly] by the Shoulder and crie[d] out to the first of his Slaves he met, Here take this Fellow, and turn him out of Doors" (10). In her *Memoirs* Laetitia Pilkington described her son's 1748 arrest in similar terms and with a similar sense of outrage at the public humiliation of a person of gentle birth:

The first Act was scarce begun, when a Person entered, and as the House was thin of Company, tapt my Son on the Shoulder. I did not apprehend the Cause of it, but began to grow uneasy when I found him stay a full Hour; at length he returned, and informed me, that he had been, at the instigation of Mr. *Sheridan*, arrested by two Constables, from whom he was only delivered by the Sollicitations of Mr. *Victor.* This greatly astonished me, as I thought Mr. *Sheridan* ought to have had a little more Respect for the Son of a Clergyman. (328)

The scathing poetic satire that she sent "his Mightiness" [Sheridan] a few days later (and which she later published in her *Memoirs*) was also the verbal equivalent of the gentlemen's riotous behavior in the playhouse in the aftermath of the Kelly incident. If the "Gentlemen" killed Sheridan in effigy on that occasion, then she does likewise with her pen, first by attacking the reputation of everyone in his "motly Race"—his father, mother, and all belonging to him, she suggests, are tyrants, whores, and crooks (328)—and then by imagining Sheridan himself suffering the ultimate indignity of the hangman's noose. The last verse of her poem reads

> Oh may I live to hail the Day,
> When the glad Players shall survey,
> Their Tyrant stript of all Command,
> High on the well fixt Ladder stand.
> And taking thence, one glorious Swing,
> How will they spout, "God save the King'"?
> Then shall those Cloaths, in which disguise,
> You'd seem a Lord to vulgar Eyes,
> Did not thy base and abject Mien,
> Betray the Beggar's Brat within,
> Be by thy Kinsman Hangman worn,
> And still a Scoundrel Thief adorn. (329)

Interestingly, too, one of Burke's 1748 campaign partners, Beaumont Brenan, includes a similar imaginary gallows scene in his Sheridan satire, *The Stage or Coronation of King Tom,* as he ridicules the manager's acting in death scenes:

> Behold great *Tom,* in life's remotest stage,
> His soul departing with heroick rage . . .

Not real murtherers more confusion breed,
When to appease some tyrant, hundreds bleed;
Or gallows' heroes, pendant to a spring,
The cart withdrawn, plunge down and gently swing;
The pitying throng a just compassion shew,
And shout as if each breast had felt the blow.[18]

This poem was first printed in this form in 1753, but as we know from a remark by Burke in 1747, a version of it (now lost) was first printed around the time of the Gentlemen's Quarrel.[19] It is possible that Laetitia Pilkington was personally acquainted with this poem and its author since, as Elias points out, Brenan wrote a poem in 1748 admiring Pilkington's literary skills, particularly her ability to ensnare men with "am'rous Billets."[20] At the very least, it could be said that Pilkington was drawing from and participating in a larger countercultural tradition of satire that was circulating in Dublin at this time, a form of writing that was designed to avenge insults done to the honor of the descendants of "antient" Irish families.

From Jack Pilkington's later cryptic comment that Foote had "Cause" to be friendly to him in Ireland,[21] it is tempting to speculate that Jack himself was the "Jacky Wagtail" who, according to *The Reformer,* was the immediate instigator for Foote's Irish visit. Jack Pilkington would certainly have had the opportunity to get to know Foote during the 1746–47 season when both of them worked in Drury Lane,[22] and if he had been instrumental in bringing Foote's act to the attention of the Burke-Hiffernan faction, it would explain Jack's later sense that the English player was indebted to him. That a benefit for Jack was announced as early as March 19–22[23] also suggests that he and his mother were involved in Foote's "Chocolate" act from the beginning; Irish artists with native gentry sympathies, this benefit indicates, were literally providing the background support for the English "dancing Punch" from the moment he opened at Capel Street. It is also tempting to speculate that this pair of Irish artists were part of that anonymous "association in defence of Irish wit" that Hiffernan mentioned to Dennis at the outset of the anti–Theatre Royal campaign.[24] As Elias points out, Laetitia Pilkington was well known in Dublin as a "Wit,"[25] and if we are to judge by some of the satiric remarks directed against Mrs. "PILL-KILL-TONGUE" in the newspapers at this time, the "New Chocolate" she and her son began dishing out at Capel Street after Foote departed was every bit as hard-hitting and controversial as the "wit" in *The Tickler.* In a letter to the *Dublin Journal* on April 19–23, for example, a correspondent who calls herself "Justitia" reminds Woodward that Mrs. Pilkington has not only "pelted" him "with so much Dirt" but also "MANY OTHERS she is as great a Stranger to," and in the name of this offended "Publick," this correspondent urges Woodward to retaliate with all his force.[26] The advertisements for the Pilkingtons' "New Chocolate" also hint that the mother-son team may have earned this kind of "Publick" animosity by targeting the same well-known Dublin figures as *The Tickler*. As part of one of their entertainments, for instance, the Pilkingtons announced that "Foote the Second" (Jack) would take off "three celebrated Originals of the City . . . in a picturesque Manner,"[27] and in the contemporary contest this reference would suggest that they were satirizing Sheridan, Faulkner, and Lucas, the triumvirate who were the comical antiheroes of *The Tickler*.

In sharing the stage with the group of players who were putting on a benefit performance for an "unhappy young Gentleman in the Marshalsea" in the last week of April, the Pilkingtons also underscored their connection both with the "Gentlemen" and the ongoing Burke-Hiffernan campaign. The only detailed advertisement for this benefit appeared in the eleventh and twelfth issues (April 7 and April 14) of *The Reformer,* and this fact, as well as the content of the notice itself, suggests this connection:

> For the enlargement of the unfortunate young Gentlemen, confin'd in the Marshalsea of the Four Courts (who met with the fatal Disappointment at Smock-Alley Play-house, occasioned by the Dispute that happened there on the 21 of January 1746) will be acted at the Theatre in *Caple-street,* on Thursday, the 21 of this Instant, the celebrated Comedy (never acted here before, and now acting in London with great Applause) called the FOUNDLING; the part of Sir *Charles Raymond* to be performed by the unfortunate young Gentleman, young *Belmont* just arrived from London, and *Faddle* by the Author of a new Comedy, called the Devil turn'd Methodist (which is now in Rehearsal). To which will be added a new Farce called the *Lady's Physician,* the part of Sir *Solomon Wronghead* to be performed by the Author, who never appeared on any Stage before.[28]

As is indicated by the allusion to the "Dispute" on January 21, 1746 (1747 N. S.) this benefit performance took up some unfinished business from the Gentlemen's Quarrel of 1747. The play on January 21, 1747, had also been scheduled as a benefit "For the Enlargement of a young Gentleman confined in the Marshalsea of the Four Courts,"[29] but because of the Kelly "riot" on that evening, the play had been canceled, thus the "fatal Disappointment" of the "unfortunate young Gentleman" who, it appears, was still confined in debtor's prison a year later. In his first Barber's *Letter,* Lucas had also implied that the timing of the "riot" on a later benefit night—at the performance for the Hospital for Incurables—was deliberate and further proof of the savagery of the native gentry. "This [benefit night] was thought a favourable Opportunity for the Faction, and regardless of Promises, regardless of the Ladies, regardless of the Charity," Lucas wrote, "a Tumult was raised" (7). By putting on a benefit for the debtor who had lost out because of the "riot" and by allowing the prisoner himself to take the lead role—subsequent notices suggest that a debtor named Galbraith played the role of Sir Charles Raymond[30]—the Capel Street company were making reparation to this individual and also implicitly showing that, contrary to Lucas's claim, they had concern and compassion for the less fortunate.

If, as seems most likely, the *Lady's Physician* (the "new Farce" that was advertised for that evening) was an early version of Hiffernan's *The Self-Enamour'd; or the Ladies Doctor,* this entertainment would also have served as an apology for the "Gentlemen" while bringing their spokesman—Hiffernan himself—to center stage. There is no character called Sir Solomon Wronghead in *The Self-Enamour'd; or the Ladies Doctor . . . by P. H. M. D* (Paul Hiffernan, M. D.), a play that was published in Dublin in 1750 with the notice that it was "now Acting at the City-Theatre in Caple-Street."[31] However, the central character, Floridor, certainly qualifies as a "wronghead" by his rakish behavior, and that he pretends to be a physician during the play makes it even more likely that he and Sir Solomon were essentially the same character and that the anonymous "Author" who played the lead role in the first version of this farce was Hiffernan. In an attempt to evade detection by Justice Morose as he pursues Morose's daughter, Floridor disguises himself as "Doctor Chronic," a "Ladies Doctor," a part that Hiffernan, a doctor himself, would have found easy to play even if (as *The Reformer*'s advertisement implied) he had "never appeared on any Stage before." Other internal and external clues also suggest that *The Lady's Physician* was an early version of *The Self-Enamour'd.* The complimentary remarks to "Stanhope" who "now rules here" (29) in *The Self-Enamour'd* (see below) suggests that the play was first written in 1748 while Harrington (a Stanhope) was the viceroy, and the gap in publication in *The Tickler* between March 18 and April 29 suggests that Hiffernan may have been rehearsing this Capel Street production during this period. In *The Tickler* of March 18, Hiffernan announced that he was under "an indispensable Necessity of going to the Country" and that he would cease publication of his paper "until next Term" (30).

As a play that preaches the inherent goodness of "Gentlemen" and the triviality of a young rake's misdeeds, this *Self-Enamour'd* farce would also have served the ideological interests of Hiffernan and his "Gentlemen" circle as they struggled to recover from the anti-Catholic assaults of 1745 and from Lucas's diatribe against them in 1747. While much of the humor of the play derives from the antics of the rake Floridor (or Sir Solomon Wronghead in the 1748 production), the spectator is constantly being asked to view his follies and the "Follies of the Town" (14) through the eyes of Truewit and his young protégé Thinkwell, two gentlemen whose names are indicative of their orthodox moral attitudes. It is these characters' moral perspective, not the rake's, that prevails in the end. After Truewit has saved the young man from falling victim to a fortune hunter, Floridor promises "a sincere Repentence" and urges "each self-enamour'd Youth" to learn from his mistakes and value friends like Truewit. In dedicating his play "to the Ladies" and in stressing in his prologue that he wanted to raise a "moral" rather than a "ridiculous, unmanner'd" laugh, Hiffernan also asserts his own identity as a "Truewit," and in so doing, he again answers the charge of native Irish barbarism in such texts as the Barber's *Letters*. A passing reference to an untrustworthy apothecary made by Floridor in the role of Doctor Chronic also slyly indicates that this is the play's larger therapeutic agenda; Floridor states that his role is to protect the "Ladies" from "purchasing Health at the price of a Nauseous Draught from a rascally Apothecary" (42).

As it seeks to rehabilitate "Gentlemen," however, this farce also introduces a patriot note that is at odds with its conservative moral and social message, and in this patriot note, it is again possible to hear the dissenting voice of the native Irish writer or "wit." The following exchange during the second act of *The Self-Enamour'd*, during which Truewit and Thinkwell reflect on the Irish landscape (the setting has changed to "A View of the Ring"), serves to illustrate the play's double-edged political discourse:

TRUEWIT: How beautiful is yon spreading Plain, richly checquer'd with a gay variety of rural seats, skirted by Wicklow's lofty Hills, and enliven'd by a Prospect of our great Metropolis!

THINKWELL: Thrice happy Land! were its Inhabitants convinced of
               their own Happiness, and would encourage those ele-
               gant entertainments, prepared by native Hands, they
               hunt after abroad with parricide Expence.

TRUEWIT: Behold the generous Monument of that great Man, of
               whom, in glorious opposition to Swift's famed line "I
               hate the Viceroy, but I love the Man," was unani-
               mously said, "We, thru the man, the Viceroy love."

THINKWELL: What heart but gladdens at the laurell'd Name of
               Stanhope; revered in war, and on Parnassus loved,
               and now rules here, the favourite Effluence of the Best
               of Kings. (29)

There are two political perspectives in this scene, and these perspectives are
at odds with each other. While the foreground perspective gives us a politically orthodox view—we are encouraged to contemplate the glories of the
viceroy and the British monarchy who are represented in heroic terms if
not godlike terms—the background perspective shifts to a nationalist and
implicitly confrontational view. We are invited not only to take pride in the
beauties of the Irish landscape and in the grandeur of the capital but also to
critique those "Inhabitants" (in this case the ruling Protestant elite) who
destroy Ireland by their wasteful economic practices and their refusal to patronize the work of "native hands." As we have seen, however, this duality
of perspective is characteristic of Irish Catholic "art" at this period; writers
of native descent and Catholic ancestry typically launched their attack on
the Protestant establishment from behind a protective loyalist front.

     The dissenting voice of the native Irish "wit" sounded even more
forcefully in the anti-Lucas play that Hiffernan staged at Capel Street the
following year during the next phase of this anti–Theatre Royal literary
and dramatic campaign. Ironically, this disruptive voice began to resonate
with the voice of the Lucasian hero who was launching his own patriot attack from the stage of the Theatre Royal.

◆◆◆

In August 1748 Lucas announced his intention to run for a Dublin parliamentary seat that had just opened up. According to the mock-advertisement
that appeared in *The Tickler* on September 8, 1748, Sheridan immediately
threw his weight behind his candidacy:

NYCTICORAX, our great Tragi-Comedian, or Comi-Tragedian . . .
is coming to Town to make interest for his friend *Charley*, who has
furnish'd him with a pathetic discourse on *Liberty*, that he is to de-
claim in all companies he can have access to. In recompense *Charley*
has promised, on the decease of our present representative, to have
him brought into the house, and then *England* mind your hits, as you
forsooth, never look'd on our *Nycti* as a good player. He expects, on
the occasion, no small number of votes, as he intends to make all
Freemen's wives and daughters, *Free-women* of his house.[32]

That Sheridan staged Henry Brooke's new ballad opera, *Jack the Giant
Queller*, on March 27, 1749, at the height of the election campaign, also lends
weight to *The Tickler's* claim that the manager was making "interest for
his friend *Charley*." As Jacqueline Hill points out, Brooke was Lucas's chief
propagandist in this election campaign,[33] and the new dramatic piece that
Brooke composed for the Smock Alley stage bore an obvious relation to his
campaign writing. In the series of letters that the Farmer wrote to the "citizens" at this time, for example, Brooke often represented Lucas as a type of
messianic figure who had emerged from his humble background to deliver
Ireland and other oppressed nations from bondage: "Can any Good, I then
said, come out of Galilee?" he asked in one pamphlet. "I now can answer
Yes. . . . While the *American, African* and *Asian* Worlds groan under universal bondage[,] . . . while even in *Britain* the Terms Liberty and Patriotism are
secretly ridiculed as *chemerical* . . . it is to *Ireland* alone . . . to . . . carry Life
and Health anew throughout the whole system."[34] Jack Good, the peasant
hero of Brooke's ballad opera, has a similar messianic mission. This "Good"
also rises from a humble background to rescue Princess Justice and his native land from the control of corrupt giants (Plutus [Wealth], Galligantus
[Power], Rumbo [Violence], and Blunderbore [Wrong]); and he also brings
"Life and Health" to the whole political system by ridding his land of these
giants. The political intent of this ballad opera would also have been clear to
anyone who read the *Dublin Courant* at this time. The theatrical advertisements for *Jack the Giant-Queller* generally appeared on the same page with
one of Lucas's election campaign addresses, in which the reformer cast himself as a kind of giant queller for the Irish people, vowing "to vindicate those
Rights and *Liberties* of which you have been stripped, and for which I have
hereto, contended, against the highest Powers in a lower Sphere."[35]

Like Lucas's tenth and eleventh electoral addresses,[36] however, this
Lucasian musical fiction signified in a way that went beyond the struggle

for the rights of the Protestant electors of the city of Dublin, and it was its very excess of meaning, I suggest, that made this dramatic work so controversial. For many in the Dublin playhouse, for example, the opening scene of the ballad opera in which peasants run across the stage from all directions complaining that the giants have eaten up all their houses and farms would have conjured up an image not of Dublin's electoral dispossessed but of Ireland's (predominantly Catholic) rural dispossessed, and the subsequent scene in which Jack tells his mother why he has to leave home and undertake a mission to destroy these giants would have reinforced this broader connection through its invocation of the vision of an "ancient madam." Jack describes the appearance of his vision as follows:

> The three last nights as to my bed I hied me,
> Methought, an ancient madam stood beside me;
> Her kerchief with her eyes and nose was slubber'd,
> Her gown was tatter'd and her cheeks were blubber'd:
> > "Jacky," she cried—and sure she was no other—
> > "I am, my child, thy true and loving mother!
> > "My farm that was so fenc'd, is run to ravage!
> > "My bleating flocks devour'd by Giants savage.
> > "Up, Jacky, up, have at the raggamuffins!
> > "For thee I've chos'n, to give these blades their bussings."[37]

As Luke Gibbons points out, the Irish peasantry frequently used "enigmatic female figures who hovered between the other world and everyday life" (Queen Sieve, "Dark Rosaleen," "Cathleen ni Houlihan") to represent Ireland and to articulate their hopes of deliverance from Williamite confiscations.[38] For those familiar with this tradition—and there were many such theatergoers in the Dublin playhouse at this time—the visionary "ancient madam" would have had a similar political resonance, adding a populist if not Jacobite thrust to Jack's mission.

That *Jack the Giant-Queller* drew some of its music from Gaelic ballads that made use of these kinds of personifying abstractions would also have given it an additional subversive resonance. As Jack is about to leave his mother's cottage to begin his liberationist quest, for example, Grace, his sister, sings a farewell song to him to the tune of "Oroo Dremendoo" (30–31) (or "Drimin duh," as it was called elsewhere), a song that, as we have seen, articulated Irish Catholic political resentments and aspirations.[39] And a similar subversive dialogism would have operated in the next song that Jack's mother sings to the tune of "Grania Mucil" (32) or "Grania Meuel."[40] This tune takes its name from a historical figure, the fiery sixteenth-century Mayo chieftain Grace O'Malley. But as Máirín Nic Eoin points out, Grania is another symbolic figure for Ireland, a female signifier like those mentioned above that served to channel the discontent and political yearning of the most economically oppressed classes in Ireland.[41] The native Irish populist resonance of such songs would have been harder to miss, too, if, as Grattan Flood suggests, a piper accompanied these Irish airs during this first 1749 performance.[42]

Even when the Irish tunes had a less directly political association, they would have continued to add a native Irish and populist charge to Jack's rebellion. When this ballad opera shows Jack marching into court at the head of a crowd of shepherds, shepherdesses, and beggars to overthrow the giants, it would have configured, at one level, the image of the Protestant freemen of Dublin uniting behind Lucas in his election bid, and Brooke wrote this kind of dramatic scene, undoubtedly, with the intention of inspiring such a grassroots rally among Dublin voters. But by weaving an indigenous Irish musical dialect through this scene of confrontation, this ballad opera also unwittingly transformed this uprising into an image of a broader Irish rebellion: in the last act, for example, as Jack defeats the giants and frees Princess Justice, he sings songs to the tunes of "Pudreen Mare" (76), "Sub roo roo" (77), "Boghil-beg-buee" (78), "Ballin a Mony oroo" (80), "Larry Grogan," and "See Shees egus whoeslum" (Sín síos agus suas liom"),[43] and these tunes would have given a native Irish populist subtext to his act of liberation. The lyrics of the last song in *Jack*, too, would have accumulated meaning from this musical context; after all these native Irish populist airs, the hero's final rallying call would have sounded dangerously like a rallying call to all the poor people of Ireland, Catholic as well as Protestant, rural as well as urban. This last song begins

> Arise, arise, arise,
> Each shape, and sort, and size
> Of HONESTY, where ye lye,
> Unheeded on dank or dry;
> From cottages, shades, and sheds, to Court,
> My Brothers of Worth and Want, resort!
> Arise to labour, arise to play,
> For VIRTUE dawns a new-born day! (90)

Dublin Castle's decision to ban *Jack the Giant-Queller* after only one performance suggests that the authorities saw the broader political implications of this call to "Arise," and the conflicting explanations that theater historians subsequently provided for this act of censorship further testify to this opera's double meaning. In his theatrical history, for example, Victor states that the ballad opera was prohibited because it contained "two or three satirical Songs, against bad Governors, Lord-Mayors, and Aldermen," but Flood states that it was shut down because "a few of the songs were regarded as Jacobite."[44]

It might be expected, then, that the anti-Lucas play, *The Election*, which was staged by a group of "Gentlemen" at Capel Street two months later, would contain a defense of "Governors, Lord-Mayors, and Aldermen" and a clearly anti-Jacobite message, but analysis of the play reveals it was every bit as antigovernment as *Jack the Giant-Queller*. If *The Election* has this subversive thrust, I suggest, it was also because the "Gentlemen" who staged it were part of the same group of Irish "wits" who had launched the attack on Sheridan and Lucas the previous year, and this group had strong ties to a native Irish gentry counterculture. From some of the pamphlets that appeared in the aftermath of the 1748 campaign, it would appear that the Capel Street opposition initially conceded victory to Sheridan and his Smock Alley supporters. In *A Letter to the Admirers of Mr. Sh———n*, which appeared in 1748, a writer who was almost certainly Hiffernan ironically praises Sheridan for overcoming "two powerful parties, form'd for his ruin" (presumably the "Gentlemen" party of 1747 and the Burke-Hiffernan party of 1748).[45] And in *A Letter to Mr. W–dw–rd, Comedian*, signed by "T. S." (though likely written by Laetitia Pilkington), the writer similarly sarcastically praises Woodward for overcoming his "Competitors in Caple-Street" and earning more money in Ireland "than any Person of real Genius." In the characteristic mock-heroic style of the Irish "wits," this pamphleteer also lauds King "Tommy" for importing such low foreign entertainers to Ireland and creating a new era of dullness:

For now the Time is come to mock at Form:
To Ireland now assemble, from every Region Apes of Idleness.
Have you a Ruffian that will swear, drink, whore, dance,
And commit the oldest kind of Sin the newest Way?
Be happy he shall trouble you no more;
Ireland shall double gild his treble guilt:

Ireland shall give him Office, Honour, Might,
For Tommy now is King.[46]

Even as this second writer concedes defeat, however, she warns Woodward that "the *Irish* will not be imposed on" and that some "ignorant Persons of Quality" have taken a dislike to him, and it was almost certainly
some of these same "Irish" "Persons of Quality" that reopened Capel
Street in 1749. In the *Dublin Courant* of February 28–March 4, 1749, Hiffernan announced that "a company of Gentlemen, zealous for their Country's Honour, by encouraging theatrical productions in this Kingdom, have
taken Caple-Street Playhouse," and he indicated that various novel arrangements were being adopted to encourage this new kind of theatrical
venture, including giving their "Emoluments in whatever Channel they
please" to those who wish to preserve their anonymity "thro Modesty, or
regard to their Rank."[47] On the face of it this latter stipulation seems to
be an attempt to attract more genteel writers, and perhaps also more
women writers, but it can also be read as an indirect way of encouraging
native Irish involvement in this patriot theatrical undertaking. Anonymity,
as we have seen, was the desired condition for gentlemen (or gentlewomen) of native Irish extraction who were "zealous for their Country's
Honour."

It is not surprising, then, that the one surviving new play that came
out of this 1749 Capel Street undertaking was written anonymously and
performed by an anonymous cast. The *Dublin Courant's* announcement
simply states that on "May 10 will be performed by a Company of Gentlemen a new Comedy called *The Election*," and the same paper's announcement for the benefit night on May 24 stated that the author is "but little
known in this City."[48] In other ways, too, the author of this play attempted
to conceal its origin. There is no record of *The Election* even being acted in
London, but when it was published in 1749 it was advertised as "now acting in *London* with great Applause" and the place of publication was given
as London.[49] The play similarly attempted to establish an English identity for itself by setting its scenes in London and by drawing heavily from
the English dramatic tradition, both elite and popular. Like Ben Jonson's
Bartholomew Fair, The Election has a "Poppet Man" called Leatherhead
who introduces the show (though he does not interpret it, as Jonson's puppeteer does), and it also features Dick Wittington, the lord mayor of London, a popular character in English puppet shows since at least the early
seventeenth century.[50] The names of two of its other principal characters,

Firebrand and Fustian, as well as the idea of a satirical play about an election, would seem to have come from Henry Fielding's *Pasquin. A Dramatic Satire on the Times: being the Rehearsal of Two Plays, a Comedy call'd The Election; and a Tragedy call'd The Life and Death of Common Sense* (1736), while the idea of a puppet show being performed by live actors—the play was advertised as being performed by "a Company of Gentlemen"— would seem to be derived from Fielding's *The Author's Farce with a Puppet Show called the Pleasures of the Town* (1729).

Despite these borrowings and these efforts at concealment, there is little doubt that *The Election* takes its meaning from a specifically Irish debate about political and cultural leadership, a debate that the Gentlemen's Quarrel of 1747 had initiated and that Lucas's strident election campaign had revived. The internal evidence also suggests that Paul Hiffernan wrote the play, and the similarity and tone of this drama and *Punch's Petition* and *The Reformer* indicate that metaphorically (and perhaps also literally, if we are to credit the old tradition about Burke's engagement on the anti-Lucas side in the 1749 election campaign),[51] Edmund Burke was behind the scenes of this performance. Like *The Tickler*, for example, this three-act comedy portrays Firebrand (Lucas) and his supporters Fustian (Sheridan), Puff (Faulkner), and the City Commons as venal, ignorant fools who are threatening to bring about the "the utter Dissolution of the Society" (7) with their desire to assume a leadership role in political and cultural affairs, and like *The Tickler* also this play achieves much of its satiric effect through rhetorical mimicry and parody. Firebrand's long "Oration" in the first act (17–20) and his written "Address" in the second act (26–29), for example, parallel the satire on Lucas's election speeches and addresses in many of the later *Tickler*s, and the satire on Fustian's pride (39), his method of performing dying scenes (31–32, 37–38), and his political interpolations (36–38) mirror *The Tickler*'s attacks on Sheridan. In Act 2 of *The Election*, for example, as Firebrand and Fustian discuss the bathetic lines Fustian proposes to introduce into Edward Young's *The Revenge*, Firebrand asks his friend to insert anti-Aldermen satire into his performance, and Fustian agrees to do so in his next comedy:

> FIREBRAND: . . . But now, *Fustian!* Your Hand's in, I'll tell you how you can oblige me with your Fancy; turn them Devils who roam the Earth into *Aldermen*, for, methinks I shou'd be glad to see them damn'd, tho' it were only in Description.

| FUSTIAN: | O Sir, it would be destroying the Dignity of Tragedy, to put particular Satire in it; but have Patience till the next Comedy I alter; and you'll see how I'll handle them. |
| FIREBRAND: | Well, pray let it be soon. (35–36) |

In a later scene in the same act, Hiffernan also satirizes the closeness and what he considers the inappropriateness of this relationship between a populist political campaigner and a stage manager when he shows these two characters exchanging inflated compliments and repeated kisses:

FIREBRAND:	You are the *Shakespear* of the Age.
FUSTIAN:	And you the *Demosthenes*.
FIREBRAND:	When you act, the whole House is in one Uproar.
FIREBRAND:	And when you harangue, the whole City is ready to run mad with Transport.
FIREBRAND:	You have no Enemies, but such as are Blockheads.
FUSTIAN:	And the greatest Men of the Age, glory in being your Friends.
FIREBRAND:	But of all Friends, I love you best, *Fustian*.
FUSTIAN:	And I you, *Firebrand*.
FIREBRAND:	Then as a Token of our Amity, let us kiss, for surely never were two Hearts so closely united.
FUSTIAN:	Agreed—(*here they kiss*)—again, and again, dear *Firebrand!* (40–41)

As McKeon points out, the notion of virtue in the eighteenth century always retained something of the old Roman notion of *virtus,* "the civic virtues of the independent, uncorruptible, arms-bearing citizen."[52] When Hiffernan depicts Sheridan in the embrace of Lucas, he is suggesting, through the imagery of homosexuality, that the manager and his company have lost this virtue/*virtus* and have become politically dependent and corrupt.

As in *The Tickler,* there are a number of references that suggest that the animus for this satire derived both from the present parliamentary election campaign and from the Gentlemen's Quarrel of 1747. In the second act, for example, as Puff the printer (Faulkner's representative) tries to warn Fustian to moderate the "puffs" he submits to his newspaper, a conversation takes place between the three principal protagonists that suggests that the author sees the parliamentary conflict of 1749 as a continuation of the Gentlemen's Quarrel:

PUFF: . . . I met just now *Punchinello* from the other House, who [be]rated me on Account of your last Copy of Verses; he called me, numskull, Puppy, meddling Fool, Wooden-headed Rogue, (and so forth) and wondered why to gratify a Vagabond, I would asperse so near a Relation.

FUSTIAN: How! had *Punch* the Impudence to call me a Vagabond? By the L——d I'll have him before my *Lord Chief Justice* for the Insult; for I'd have the Rascal to know, that notwithstanding I condescend to play, more for my own Amusement, than, to divert the Publick, that I am still a *Gentleman.*

FIREBRAND: Aye, he must be as great a Blockhead, as *Punch* himself, who can doubt that after all I have written to prove it.—But now I talk of writing, *Puff*, I have the prettyest pen'd *Address*,—such a Whapper,—I-gad if you don't get your Wife a *Capuchin* out of the Profits of it, I'll be content to go naked all my Lifetime— Shall I read it to you? (44)

Fustian's threat to bring Punch to court for calling him a "Vagabond" is, of course, analogous to Sheridan's decision to press charges against Kelly in 1747, and Firebrand's mention of his writing to "prove" Fustian's gentleman status is a not so subtle reference to Lucas's Barber's *Letters* of the same period. Firebrand's seamless segue from these *Letters* to the present parliamentary "Address" in his last sentence also suggests a continuity between this earlier quarrel and the present ongoing parliamentary struggle, and it implies that the Lucas-Sheridan-Faulkner trio are involved in both conflicts for the same materialistic reasons—for "capuchin[s]" and "profits."

As is clear from the above passage, this play also follows Burke in using the impudent Punchinello as a figure for the politically problematic native Irish gentleman, and like Kelly and a whole dispossessed native ruling class, this Punchinello figure creates a disturbance with his refusal to acknowledge the gentleman status claims of the new elite. Like the "Gentlemen," too, this disruptive figure will not be excluded from the theater, nor will he be silent during the hegemonic play. In the play's epilogue Punch appears on stage, having, by his own admission, "broke loose at length" from his captors—he begins his address to the audience with "*Well Gallants! I've broke loose at length to tell / What strange Disasters have poor*

Punch *befel*" (63)—and in bitter tones he personally berates the elite of the town for standing idly by as "true Wit," as represented by himself, is "hunted down" and "cramp'd":

> *Can ye bear then, ye* Royst'rers *of the Town,*
> *To see your once lov'd Actor hunted down?*
> *When a vile Player, through his own Default,*
> *Had half this City's Rage upon him brought;*
> *Beaus, Belles, and Scholars, did at once unite,*
> *To this Fellow's fancy'd Merit Right.*
> *But when true Wit, as just as e'er was stamp'd*
> *Is by a set of sordid Schemers cramp'd,*
> *Not one of you will set your Throats a Bawling,*
> *Or brandish Stick to keep his Cause from falling.*
> *So well this strange Inconstancy of you,*
> *Does prove, Alas! This Observation true,*
> > *"Excess of Merit makes the Brave to fall,*
> > *"And proves more hurtful than no Parts at all."* (68)

Punch's bitterness, this passage suggests, derives from a specific betrayal, namely, the decision of the "Beaus, Belles, and Scholars'" to support Sheridan (the "vile Player") against the "Gentlemen" in the 1747 conflict. But when Punch berates his genteel audience for their silence as "True Wit" was being "cramp'd" by a "set of sordid Schemers" and when he alludes to the "hurtful" "fall" of "the Brave," he also seems to be referring to the larger political betrayal that resulted in the marginalization of native Irish writers and native Irish gentlemen. The sense of betrayal that is expressed in the last eight lines of this passage echoes the "hurt" that Burke expressed later in his letter to Charles O'Hara as he pondered Lucas's reputation "among very many of rank and figure," a hurt based on the belief that the Barber's social acceptance also involved a tacit acceptance of anti-Catholic and anti-Irish bigotry.[53]

This critique of the current Irish Protestant elite is also apparent in the play itself, and in the sense that it openly voices this critique, it could be said that Punch or a native Irish gentry "wit" has indeed "broken loose" in this work. After the above speech, Punch states that the only solution to his present predicament is to "turn Poet" and to vent his "venom'd Rage" in "stingless Satyr" (68), but he also reveals that he is profoundly indifferent about which party he joins, even indicating at one point that he is thinking of writing "senseless Song" for Sheridan's stage and political diatribes for Lucas's party:

> *If Lucas will admit me of his Party,*
> *I will espouse his Cause with Rancour hearty;*
> *Call all Men Knaves, and Jacobites to boot,*
> *Whose Maxims don't with his own Notions suit . . .*
> *The great Arcanum now in Madness lies*
> *Then since the fashion 'tis, the Town shall see,*
> *I will write Things more crazy still than he:*
> *Lords, Commons, Bishops, in my madding Rage,*
> *Will I expose as Villains of the Age;*
> *Judges and Aldermen, with Libels mawl,*
> *Or write dull Traps to hamper Gallows-Paul.* (69)

But if that fails, he states in his concluding lines, he will go to the other side:

> *But if fastidious they will not admit;*
> *To prop their sinking Cause my stronger Wit;*
> *(For there are Fools, and Plenty in this town,*
> *Who think no Nonsense current but their own)*
> *For t'other Side then will I be a Stickler,*
> *And write down Essays to support the Tickler.* (69–70)

It could be argued that this expression of political disillusionment is itself merely a pretext for a display of this "stronger Wit," a clever pose of disinterestedness adopted for the purpose of artfully disclosing the true identity of the author. According to an anti-*Tickler* pamphlet from the period, Dublin newsboys had ominously dubbed Hiffernan "Gallows-Paul" after the notorious highwayman and thief catcher Paul Farrell who was killed by Dublin street gangs in 1734,[54] and through this allusion to "Gallows-Paul" and to "the Tickler" in the last line of the epilogue, Hiffernan wittily signs his name to the play. But the radical satire in the play itself suggests that Punch's disaffection and cynicism is not a mere pose, and it appears at times that Hiffernan is writing in support of Lucas's "Cause." *The Election*'s portrayal of the representatives of the establishment, the lord mayor and aldermen, is every bit as negative as that of Firebrand and his supporters, and in creating such a negative portrait of these authority figures, the play comes to resonate with *Jack the Giant-Queller* and other Lucasian texts. In the opening scene of *The Election*, for example, Wittington and the aldermen are "discovered sitting with Bottles of Wine before them, as at the End of a great Feast" (11), a setting that immediately hints at a government based on appetite and greed, and the ensuing conversation among the members of this governing body works to support this impression. Whittington begins discussing "Business" only after the aldermen's " fat Bellies are with Capon lin'd" (11), and the main thrust of this political "Business," this scene reveals, is to protect these "Bellies" (the aldermen's own privileges and power) from plebian incursions. In explaining the necessity of opposing Firebrand, for example, Whittington states: "For if by Chance he wins the Day, / He'll take our Custard, and our Rights away" (11).

Firebrand's conversation with the aldermen in this scene also allows us to see their arrogance and indifference to the suffering of the people, and in permitting Firebrand to articulate the complaints of the starving citizenry in the next passage, this play further blurs the boundary between itself and a Lucasian text like *Jack the Giant-Queller:*

FIREBRAND: Well may you tremble, Slaves! And knock
        each Knee,
    When you myself, and injur'd Brethren see.
    Those meagre Looks which all our Wants
        proclaim,
    Are but the Marks of what shou'd be your Shame.
    Well may we stalk, like Sprites about the Town,
    When your vile Feasting keeps our Bellies down;
    For, had each starved Citizen his Due,
    He'd look as rosey, and as plumb as you;
    But while like Beasts, you batten here alone,
    You both consume our Pasture, and your own.

WHITTINGTON: Peace! Peace! My Friend, and do not be so hot,
    Your Hunger, and your Rage we value not,
    The Law but gives us, what we well deserve,
    We feast by Charter, while by Rules you Starve.
    (13–14)

If Hiffernan comes to resemble Lucas at such moments, it could be argued, it is because he is here emerging from behind his loyalist cover to express his real sentiments about the rulers and people of Ireland. There is an excess of animosity in the comparison of the aldermen to "Beasts" who consume "our Pasture" that suggests this is the author's true view of government, and there is a degree of harsh realism in the portrayal of the "starved Citizen[s]" who wander the streets like "Sprites" that suggests identification with the plight of the mass of the Irish people.

The cynicism that underlies the restoration of ruling-class power at the end of the play also bespeaks the native Irish gentry's sense of deep alienation, and in so doing, it preaches an implicit message of political resistance if not actual rebellion. Firebrand is defeated, *The Election* reveals, only because the aldermen outdo him in deception, corruption, and the ability to manipulate public opinion. In return for abandoning his election campaign, the aldermen secretly offer Firebrand a "Place" as "Collector of a certain Tax called *Drivel-Money*" (56), and as they describe this office, it becomes clear that their strategy for managing social unrest is not only bribery but also the stirring up of sectarian animosity. In describing "the *Drivel Tax*" one of the aldermen says: "'Tis a Cess, has been much litigated, of late Years, by a Set of sturdy *Papists*, who think, they have a Right to cough, belch, spit out, or blow their Noses, equal with other Poppets of a loyal, and Protestant Denomination. Now Sir, considering the Terror, you usually go cloathed with, and the extreme Vehemence, with which you urge all Processes, we thought we could not do better, than by lodging such an Authority in your Hands, put you in a Condition of retrieving it (56–57). The "*Drivel Tax*," this description suggests, is the "intrusion money" or "quarterage" that nonfreemen had to pay if they wished to carry on trade in any Irish town, a levy that Catholics bitterly resented and, as the century went on, increasingly resisted paying.[55] This is not the full extent of the aldermen's Machiavellian maneuvering, however. After Firebrand accepts their bribe and turns his back on the Commons (he pretends he has gone insane), he discovers that the paper that supposedly contained the "Place" offer is blank, and the aldermen foil any subsequent chance he might have of winning back his supporters by publicly exposing his acceptance of this place (63–64). The play ends, then, with the defeat of Firebrand as the Commons kick their erstwhile hero out of the town hall, and while the aldermen exit to the tavern to make themselves "merry with Laughing at this event" (66), Whittington, as "Father" of the "People," hypocritically brings the whole proceedings to a close with a short prayer for continued "Peace":

May Peace continue still our Isle to bless,
And Faction ever meet the like Success. (66)

After the exposure of the city rulers' corruption and sectarianism, this prayer is richly ironic, as is Whittington's description of himself as "the Father of my People." If the city fathers have triumphed, this puppet show play suggests, it is only because the powerful are better at playing the game of deception than their plebian counterparts and "Faction" continues under the surface at all levels of Irish society.

A shared distrust of government and a shared sense of resentment at the mismanagement of Ireland, then, linked these two groups of Irishmen who were vying with each other for control of the social, political, and cultural terrain in the late 1740s, though in the heat of this struggle, neither side acknowledged this common ground. As I argue in chapter 7, however, a new display of imperialism on the part of King "Tommy" and the administration in the next five years would dramatically change this situation, leading to the emergence of a new nationalist bloc in the playhouse and in the country.

CHAPTER 7

Staging the Nation

The "memorable Night of the Subversion of the Theatre," 1754

Benjamin Victor, an eyewitness to the event, suggests that the "riot" that nearly destroyed Smock Alley on March 2, 1754, was exclusively the work of "Patriot" gentlemen who wished to avenge themselves on Thomas Sheridan for the latter's sponsorship of the Beef-stake Club, a social organization that drew most of its members from the "Court" party.[1] According to Victor, this resentment first surfaced when James Miller and John Hoadly's adaption of Voltaire's *Mahomet the Imposter* was staged at Smock Alley on February 2, 1754. On that occasion the pit was filled with "Leaders and Chiefs of the Country Party," and these gentlemen disrupted the play by demanding an encore of Alcanor's speech condemning senatorial corruption and by loudly applauding other lines spoken by this patriotic character (161–63). When the play was repeated on March 2, however, the actor who was playing Alcanor (West Digges) refused to comply with the audience's request for an encore of one of these patriotic speeches on the grounds that, as he put it, "his *Compliance would be greatly injurious to him*" (167), and it was this refusal and the manager's failure to appear and explain it, Victor suggests, that provoked the "riot." According to Victor, after the patriots had called in vain for Sheridan for some time,

> Two of their Leaders (Persons of Gravity and Condition) rose up from the Middle of the Pit, and went off over the Boxes. *That was the*

agreed Signal; and the Grace for falling to was as follows: A Youth in the Pit stood up, and cried out, *God bless his Majesty King George,* and three Huzzas! and at the End of the last Huzza, they all fell to demolishing the House, like Lions devouring their Prey; and the Audience part was all in Pieces in five Minutes. (170–71)

In his 1758 *Humble Appeal,* however, Sheridan suggested that the opposition he encountered on what he called the "memorable Night of the Subversion of the Theatre" was set in motion by the "numberless Enemies" he had made during the Gentlemen's Quarrel of 1747,[2] an argument that adds a native Irish Catholic dimension to this opposition. And in a pamphlet entitled *A Vindication of the Conduct of the late Manager of the Theatre-Royal Publick. Humbly address'd to the Publick* (1754), which he published in the immediate aftermath of this remarkable night, the manager added yet another social element to the mix when he suggested the "Mob" was involved. When he refused to appear before the audience on the night of March 2, the manager wrote in this *Vindication,* he was motivated by fear of the "incensed Mob" in the galleries,[3] and the subsequent destruction of the theater, according to him, was brought about not only by the "Gentlemen" in the pit but also by a "Mob" from the street:

> When the Gentlemen were withdrawn, the Mob forced their Way into the House, Part of whom plundered and stole whatever they could carry away, others drew the large Grate in the Box room from it's [*sic*] Place in the Floor, and heaping the Benches and Wainscot upon the Fire, would soon have consumed the House, and probably that whole Quarter of the Town, as the Buildings stands so close there, had not this Sight roused six of the Servants belonging to the Theatre to a desperate Courage: At the immediate Hazard of their Lives, they assaulted and drove the Mob out of the House, extinguished the Flames, barrricadoed the Doors, and afterwards dispersed the Mob, by firing out the Windows upon them.[4]

All three of these narratives, I suggest, are necessary to an understanding of the makeup of the "enraged Multitude"[5] that stormed Smock Alley on March 2, 1754. The opposition that Sheridan encountered that night was an overdetermined one, shaped not only by the parliamentary "Patriots" of 1754 but also by the Catholic or crypto-Catholic "Enemies" he had made during the Gentlemen's Quarrel and the Burke-Hiffernan campaign of

1748–49 and by a Dublin "Mob" that had been politicized by Charles Lucas's populist patriot campaign during the same period. To understand how and why these previously antagonistic forces came together with such explosive force on that night, it is also necessary to provide a political framework that is missing from all these narratives and a fuller account of Sheridan's behavior during the five years preceding this event. The drama on the "memorable Night of the Subversion of the Theatre" took place against the backdrop of a larger national staging, and by 1754 "King Tommy" (to use the nickname given the manager by his opponents) had positioned himself firmly on the antinationalist side.

◆◆◆

Sheridan began setting the scene for his own downfall and his playhouse's destruction during the 1749–50 season when he attempted to shut down the two kinds of patriot theater that had emerged in Dublin in the 1740s: the Lucasian one in his own playhouse and the "Gentlemen's" one at the Capel Street theater. As noted, the government itself shut down the Lucasian ballad opera *Jack the Giant-Queller* in spring 1749. Far from being intimidated, however, Jack's real-life counterpart, Charles Lucas, seemed to be inspired to new heights of boldness by this attack from the "Giants," and as his struggle with the authorities intensified in the summer of that year, he began to rally around him precisely the kind of rebellious crowd envisaged in the last song of the suppressed ballad opera. In June 1749 Lucas began publishing what is sometimes described as Ireland's first radical newspaper, *The Censor, or, the Citizens Journal,*[6] and the same month he made an appearance before the lord justices at Dublin Castle during which he renewed attacks on "evil ministers" (a thinly veiled reference to the viceroy, the earl of Harrington) and the English Parliament. In response to this piece of audacity, the lord justices issued a warrant for the arrest of his printer, and both houses of the Dublin Corporation issued censures against Lucas himself. Fifteen of the city's twenty-five guilds rallied around him, though, publishing statements supporting him and condemning his critics.[7]

There was no evidence of a diminution of this populist support either in the fall when the authorities accelerated their persecution. On October 3, immediately after Harrington arrived back in Ireland, Lucas turned up at Dublin Castle with a new list of complaints, and in response to that, at the instigation of the viceroy, the House of Commons filed a complaint against him. When Lucas made his way to Parliament on October 16 to answer this complaint, however, he went like the hero of Brooke's ballad opera rather than as a defendant. Like Jack Good on his way to "Court," he was accompanied by a large trail of supporters, who continued to support him even after the Commons found against him and declared him an enemy to his country. The Lucasian crowd also continued to make its presence felt even after the reformer fled Ireland later that month to avoid imprisonment. When the viceroy embarked for England some six months later, for example, he was sent off with groans from an angry quayside crowd of Lucas supporters.[8]

There are indications, too, that this crowd may have included (as the last song in *Jack* put it) "each shape, and sort, and size" of Irish subject. On October 22, 1749, the Sunday before the long-awaited election, Catholic priests urged their congregations not to "join in any mob, tumult or meeting . . . or even to appear about the place of the election, as they have no manner of concern therein," an injunction that, as Murphy suggests, would hardly have been necessary if Catholics were not suspected of being involved in election activity.[9] The pamphlet Charles O'Conor wrote in support of Lucas on September 30, 1749, provides other evidence that Catholics were involved in this election campaign, and it also throws light on why some Catholics at least were interested in allying themselves with Lucas. By posing as a Protestant Lucasian supporter in *A Counter-Appeal to the People of Ireland* (1749), O'Conor was able to go on the offensive against Sir Richard Cox and the Reverend William Henry, two writers who were bitter opponents not only of Lucas but also of Catholicism, and under the guise of refuting the anti-Lucasian arguments of these writers, he was able to pen a bold defense of native Irish political and cultural traditions. In opposition to Henry's argument that ancient Ireland was closer to "an hell of devils, than a habitation of men" (part of Henry's argument for continued dependence on Britain),[10] for example, O'Conor depicts preconquest Ireland as "the Throne of *Liberty,* the Emporium of *Literature,* and the Sanctuary of *Christianity,*" and by tracing Ireland's "ancient Government and Religion from their source," he represents this old Irish nation and religion as "the *freest,* and . . . the *purest* that ever existed in the World."[11] Because the argument in this pamphlet brought the two Irish dissenting traditions — one Protestant and one Catholic — into alignment, it also had an explosive political charge. On October 12, 1749, Michael Reilly wrote from Dublin to O'Conor in the country: "Your inflammatory *Counter Appeal* has been roared about the streets here all this day and so inflaming it is that Walter Harris, the historian, told the printer Kelbourne he would be summoned to the bar of the house and sent to Newgate; for that is of a more dangerous tendency than all Lucas's papers together."[12]

Even as these kinds of explosive cross-religious alliances were being generated, however, Sheridan was backing away from his involvement in patriot politics and taking steps to distance himself from his old friend Lucas. On September 16, 1749, just before the new theatrical season was to start, he placed the following notice in the *Dublin Journal:*

> As I find there have been many Reports raised, during my absence from Town, that I was the Author of several Pieces lately published in Dublin, and had a share in many more; I think it necessary to assure the Publick that I neither wrote, nor was privy to the Writing of any Paper whatsoever Relative to the present Dispute. A Manager of a Theatre will always find Employment enough before him, without stepping aside to engage in matters out of his Sphere. While I have the honor of being in that office, the faithful Discharge of my Duty shall be the sole object of my Ambition, nor have I leisure or Inclination to attend to anything else.[13]

It seems likely Sheridan repudiated his friend primarily out of fear for his own position and safety. The banning of *Jack the Giant-Queller* the previous March after only one performance was not only a financial blow; it was also an unmistakable indication that the government regarded Lucas as a danger, and the arrest of Lucas's printer a few months later demonstrated that the authorities were willing to prosecute anyone who supported him. When the manager publicly stated he had no "Inclination" to help Lucas, then, he was distancing himself from these political suspects in much the same way he had distanced himself from suspect Irish Catholic "Gentlemen" during the '45, and in so doing, he undoubtedly hoped to put himself and his theater on securer ground. But this loyalist strategy was only partly successful at that time, and it was even less successful in the tense political atmosphere of 1749. By seeming to align himself with the government against Lucas, Sheridan added the Lucasian crowd to the ranks of his still active "Gentlemen" enemies, and by repressing Lucas's theater later the same season, he created more common ground between these two patriot camps.

The records on Capel Street during the 1749–50 season are again sketchy, but the numerous performances of *The Self-Enamour'd* and the inclusion of an entertainment that resembles the earlier "Chocolate" performances—"A Dish of Irish Sage Tea"—suggest that Hiffernan and some of his group continued to hold sway there.[14] The attacks on "King Tommy" and his foreign artists and "low" entertainments also continued from this quarter during the 1749–50 season:[15] indeed, if anything, these attacks became more strident and pointed at this time. In the *Play-House Journal* (January 18, 1750), for example, an anonymous writer (very likely Hiffernan) accused "the *French* king, of Smock-Alley" of deploying his "low artifices" to "stifle the [Capel Street] company before existence and dirty efforts to suppress them since"[16] and of generally intimidating the audience while accommodating the government. "None of the audience dared to offer the least insult to him, or the meanest of his musick," the *Play-House Journal* complains, "but, as for the government, they might make as free with it as they pleased." The larger charge against Sheridan, however, is that he is being unpatriotic in attempting to quell this rival theater. A Capel Street prologue, which the *Play-House Journal* also published, suggests that in working to stifle the little city theater the manager is working not only to repress a more traditional kind of English drama but also Irish musicians and a "home-bred wit":

> Thus, without aid of pomp, of song, or dance,
> From *heavy* HOLLAND, or *fantastick* FRANCE;
> Without one *foreign fiddler* in our band,
> But all collected in our native land,
> We strive to please—and, fairly, own our wants
> We have not pockets for *exotick* plants—
> 'Tis hard, indeed, if *Shakespear's* manly muse,
> Must stoop for aid—to *Madam* VANDERSLUYS!
> How must illustrious *Johnson's* laurel face,
> Wither and shrink—beneath a *dancer's* shade! . . .
> Must *Fletcher, Dryden, Congreve,* all submit—
> And *foreign scrapers* trample *home-bred wit?*

In spring 1750 Sheridan answered this last question in a resounding affirmative when he took out a twenty-one-year lease on the Capel Street theater and shut it down. With this autocratic gesture, he lent credence to the "Gentlemen" faction's claim that he was indeed "King Tommy," a theatrical tyrant who was determined to "trample *home-bred wit.*"

Complaints about theatrical tyranny and about the repression of native talent are also found in the pamphlet *A Full and True Account of the Woefull and Wonderfull Apparition of Hurloe Harrington, Late Prompter to the Theatre-*

Royal in Dublin (1750), though these complaints take their meaning from a very different kind of political and cultural crisis. As suggested in chapters 5 and 6, the Capel Street group's sense of alienation can be seen in the context of the larger legitimation crisis caused by the displacement of the native Irish elite; King Tommy's nightmare upside-down world, where "Apes" and "Ruffian[s]" flourish[17] and "home-bred wit" dies, was also a metaphor for a larger Irish world that has descended into chaos because it has lost its traditional leaders. The writer of *A Full and True Account* shares this nightmare vision, though his alienation derives from the displacement of a new kind of Irish Protestant populist leader in the person of Charles Lucas. The Hurloe Harrington mentioned in the title of this pamphlet had been a prompter at Smock Alley in 1749, but in September of that year the unfortunate Mr. Harrington had thrown himself out his window while in a feverish and delirious state.[18] That this prompter had the same name as the viceroy opened up a golden opportunity for smarting Lucas supporters, as this pamphlet reveals. Posing as the Reverend Parson Fitz-Henery who is writing a letter to the archbishop of Canterbury to confirm their shared belief in ghosts and other supernatural occurrences, the author of *A Full and True Account* uses the conceit of a theatrical haunting by the dead Harrington to launch a searing critique of the earl of Harrington and his supporters for their treatment of their hero in fall 1749.[19] The first action of this baleful Harrington ghost, for example, was to insist that there would be no "Play" (i.e., no parliamentary business) unless "the principal Actor [Lucas] be directly turned out," and after that was accomplished, this Harrington spirit ran rampant through the town, attempting to "break the Spirits of all the stubborn People here."[20] As a result, Parson Fitz-Henery writes, "the People in general . . . are in the most inconceivable Distraction and Confusion. They are running in wild Tumults thro' the Country and thro' the Streets of this City. They cry, *"there is no Law, no Justice to be had, no fair or free Election, since this damn'd Ghost has first appear'd"* (21). Most of the thirty-two-page pamphlet is an expansion on this theme — exposing how the Harrington "spirit" has penetrated and corrupted all Irish political institutions, including the House of Commons, the Tholsel, and the army. Members of all of the aforementioned institutions, the writer of the pamphlet argues, have been "prompted" to abandon their patriotic duties in return for places and promises of advancement.

In one paragraph, however, the author turns from these overtly political considerations to a consideration of the state of the Theatre Royal itself, and he suggests that it is here that the "Harrington" spirit is most in evidence:

Now, if any Body yet remains in Doubt of the Certainty of this Apparition, let them but go a few Nights to any Part of the *Theatre;* there the *Prompter* seldom fails to appear in one shape or other; and there their Doubts are most likely to be removed—Sometimes, he *prompts* the Manager to attempt Characters quite out of the Reach of his Genius and national Disposition. . . . There, he will be found to *prompt* the *chief Musician* to play *Italiano Piano* to *Irish* Ears; There, he *forces* a hopeful young Officer to quit the Camp, and act upon the *Stage;* and there, he fills the *Galleries* with common *Soldiers,* every one of whom confesses the *Influence, Direction* and *Command* of the *Ghost* of HARRINGTON, the *Prompter.* (27)

It is clear from this paragraph that by spring 1750 embittered Lucasian supporters had come to see the manager and the theater in much the same negative light as their old enemies, the "Gentlemen." The *Play-House Journal*'s charge three months earlier that "none of the [Smock-Alley] audience dared to offer the least insult to him [Sheridan] or the meanest of his musick; but, as for the government, they might make as free with it as they pleased," is repeated here in the image of a stage dominated by the Harrington spirit and the presence of the military. And the Capel Street paper's claim that the Theatre Royal and its manager preferred "foreign fiddlers" to native ones is echoed in the charge that Smock Alley's "chief *Musician*" imposes Italian music on "*Irish* ears." Here, as in the Burke-Hiffernan pamphlets, Sheridan's theater is represented not only as a repressive institution but also as one that is unpatriotic and anti-Irish.

The upper gallery's attack on Smock Alley's theater orchestra and its general hostility to Sheridan during this 1749–50 season can also be read in the context of this new attack on the neocolonial stage. Almost from the moment that the Smock Alley doors were opened in fall 1749, the manager had trouble with the upper gallery. "Evil minded Persons," he complained in the *Dublin Journal* in October, were throwing "Stones and other Things at the Band of Musick, to the great Disturbance of the Audience, and Peril to the Musicians,"[21] and despite the offer of a reward for the apprehension of these evil persons, the upper gallery attacks continued during the following months. By January Sheridan was taking more direct steps to stop them; he doubled the price of the galleries for one night, for example, and he issued a threatening notice in the *Dublin Journal* that he would continue these higher prices unless the gallery offenders were detected and apprehended. When Sheridan reopened the Aungier Street theater in February 1750, significantly, it was without an upper gallery (it had been combined with the middle gallery), and as Sheldon suggests, this innovation was undoubtedly in response to the trouble from the upper gallery in the other playhouse.[22]

At one level these attacks were a continuation of the musical war that had commenced in the 1730s when a boisterous upper gallery crowd first began to drown out the theater band with their singing of "gay native airs" and their calls for traditional Irish ballads.[23] The timing and focused nature of this campaign also suggests that, like the writer of the *Play-House Journal* and the writer of *A Full and True Account,* the less affluent Dubliners who sat in this part of the theater were weighing in on the current dispute between Sheridan's "foreign" band and the "native" musicians—a dispute that clearly had broader nationalist overtones. During the previous 1748–49 season, Sheridan had replaced the troop of English harlequins and French dancers that he had brought in for the 1747–48 season with a band of twenty-two instrumentalists and at least five singers from London. This band was headed by the violinist Signor Pasquali, and it included the well-known composer Mr. Lampe.[24] Reaction to this band of newcomers, it would appear, was mixed from the outset. The *Dublin Journal* hailed them as "the best Band of Instrumental Performers ever heard in this Kingdom,"[25] but a notice in Lucas's paper, *The Censor,* on June 3, 1749, hints that they were not universally welcomed. After announcing a benefit at New-Garden in Great Britain Street for the "Hospital for poor, pregnant Women," Lucas's paper noted that there would also be a benefit in the Old Bowling Green in Marborough Street, "for the Support of the unemployed, native Musicians of this Kingdom," an indication that this influx of foreigners was already creating difficulties for local Irish musicians.[26]

These tensions between "native" and "foreign" musicians came to a head at the beginning of the 1749–50 season when it became known that Sheridan had made arrangements with the Charitable Musical Society to provide the services of his theater band for a concert every Tuesday of the season, in place of the regular musicians who had been playing with the society for many years. On October 2, 1749, a pamphlet entitled *The Political Manager: or the Invasion of the Music-Hall, set Forth* accused the manager of allowing his *"foreign* Band of Musick" to displace "a better, and a stronger Band of *Natives,"* and of forcing "every Institution, however generous, patriotic, or charitable" to give way to Smock Alley.[27] The reaction to this attack suggests also that there was a deep split in the Charitable Musical Society itself between those who supported the "established Band" and those who supported Sheridan's "foreign Band." At the end of

September 1749, a group that called itself "the established Band of Musicians (Natives of this Kingdom)" and that claimed the support of gentlemen who were part of the original Bull's-Head Tavern group twenty years previously, placed notices in the *Dublin Journal* announcing a subscription for a new series of Friday night concerts at this tavern location.[28] But in a letter to the *Dublin Journal* on October 6 (the day these concerts were set to begin), a defender of the new arrangement depicts its critics as a "Set of malevolent Spirits, that are ever prone to Divisions and Discontents," and this writer justifies the Charitable Musical Society's decision to engage the foreign entertainers by arguing that the "NATIVE ESTABLISHED MUSICIANS" exacted exorbitant salaries for their performances.[29]

When the upper gallery fired stones and other missiles at Sheridan's band during theater performances in fall and winter 1749, then, they were weighing in on the part of these "NATIVE ESTABLISHED MUSICIANS," and in so doing, I suggest, they were also demonstrating a nationalist spirit that had been shaped both by the "Gentlemen's" campaign and by Lucas's campaign during the previous two years. Ten years later Lucas's running mate, La Touche, would argue that the new level of national awareness demonstrated by the lower orders at midcentury was a function exclusively of the 1749 election campaign. Since "the Rebellion of the Year 1749," he wrote, "you might hear the lowest Tradesmen call themselves *Free Citizens* with more than Roman arrogance . . . [and be] so wrong-headed as to talk of *National Rights,* of *Liberty,* of *worthy Representatives.*" From that point on, La Touche argued, these humbler citizens "[have] read newspapers and even the votes of the Commons, and have more than once been audacious enough to crowd the Streets about Parliament House, even when they are armed with Soldiers up to the Doors of the House" and to "talk of *instructing their own* [parliamentary] *members.*"[30] A Catholic or crypto-Catholic gentry faction working against Lucas during the same period, however, had also brought the issue of "native" political and cultural rights to the foreground, and if the upper gallery crowd were now "audacious enough" to instruct their theatrical ruler on these topics, it was undoubtedly because some of them would have read the pamphlets and periodicals of this faction.

If the multiple reasons Sheridan offered for the growth in his "enemies" around this time reflected his genuine understanding of this opposition, it was also not surprising that he failed to foresee the more serious attack by the "enraged Multitude" five years later. At the end of the 1749–50 season Sheridan was embroiled in yet another heated musical controversy after he refused to allow his band of musicians to play for a benefit concert. The concert in question had been organized and advertised by the well-known Dublin philanthropist Dr. Bartholomew Mosse, who assumed he had secured the theater band when Pasquali consented to the engagement. Sheridan refused to honor this agreement because he had not personally agreed to it, and this failure to support a local charity event—the audience turned up, but the band did not—was read by many as another example of the manager's arrogance and contempt for the Irish public at large.[31] In an attempt to defend himself from these charges, the manager published a twenty-six-page pamphlet entitled *A State of the Case in Regard to the Point in Dispute between Mr. Mosse and Mr. Sheridan* in April 1750, in which he tacitly reveals the degree of opposition that he and this theater were now facing. As Sheldon points out, "the last ten pages are taken up with near hysterical complaints that he who had done so much for the public should have to take time so often to defend himself, innocent as he invariably was."[32] Even as he attempted to answer the question of why he had so many "enemies," however, Sheridan showed no awareness that this growing antagonism was shaped by his own support for government and for "foreign" over "native" culture, and by continuing down this political and cultural path in the next five years, "King Tommy" put himself and his theatrical "Citadel" in the eye of the next political storm, the so-called Money Bill Dispute of 1753–54.

◆◆◆

At the narrowest level, the Money Bill Dispute refers to the conflict that arose between the administration and the Irish House of Commons in December 1753 when the latter asserted its right to allocate a surplus in the treasury without prior royal consent. Historians generally agree, however, that this conflict was part of a much broader political struggle that had been brewing for some time, and many see the Irish public's support of the patriot side as a defining moment in the emergence of the Irish nation. According to C. Litton Falkiner, the conflict began in 1751 when the duke of Dorset arrived back in Ireland with a mandate to reassert English authority by taking power from the Speaker of the Irish House of Commons, Henry Boyle, and his cadre of supporters in Parliament, the most notable of whom were the Gore family, led by the prime sergeant Anthony Malone and the earl of Kildare and his relatives. From the first 1751–52 parliamentary session, then, there were clashes between this Boyle party and the Castle party, led by the primate George Stone and the viceroy's son Lord George

Sackville; and by the time Dorset returned to Ireland in 1753, the public was beginning to see this conflict in national terms. The Speaker's party was viewed as the defender of the Irish interest against an English party, headed by the Englishman Primate Stone.[33] Like the Wood's Halfpence crisis in the 1720s, a difficult economy exacerbated these political tensions. A severe winter in 1752 and a rise in food prices created hardships for country gentry and urban poor alike, and these hardships, as Declan O'Donovan notes, created discontent at every level of Irish society. On the streets in 1753, disgruntled weavers attacked ladies wearing imported fabrics or shops carrying foreign materials, and in the opposition newspapers there were renewed complaints about English restrictions on Irish trade, absentee landlords, English placemen, and the "gentlemen and ladies of the first fashion and distinction" who imported luxury goods without paying duty.[34] As O'Donovan points out, this last criticism may well have been directed specifically at the Dublin Castle coterie, which, under the duke of Dorset's leadership, was engaging in unprecedented displays of wealth and grandeur. In a letter in winter 1751, for instance, the bishop of Derry noted that "the duke of Dorset has had the most shining assemblies ever seen in Ireland, everyone endeavouring to outdo another in equipage and grandeur."[35]

When Boyle and Malone refused to insert a royal "consent" clause into a bill dealing with the allocation of a surplus in the Irish treasury in November 1753, then, their act of resistance was shaped as much by these extraparliamentary pressures as by their own political desires, and the larger representative function of their resistance became apparent on December 17 after they secured the rejection of the altered money bill by 122 votes to 117 (the bill had been returned from England with the consent clause inserted). On the night of the victory itself, the "Patriot" members (as those who rejected the bill were now called) were escorted to their homes in triumph by a huge crowd bearing torches and carrying sheaves of burning furze on pitchforks, while members of the court party were forced, for their own protection, to leave the House through a back door and make their way through side streets.[36] In the weeks that followed, people at every level of Irish society and in every part of the country demonstrated their support for this patriot opposition. Dublin chairmen, it was reported, refused to carry any fare to the castle, and middle-class and upper-class members of Irish society showed their appreciation of this opposition by sending numerous addresses of thanks to the Dublin papers, by drinking toasts in newly founded Patriot clubs, and by striking special medals in honor of the Patriots.[37]

There were also signs that this resistance was the work of a community that was coming together across ethnic and religious lines. Anthony Malone, the man who many credited with masterminding the parliamentary opposition, was himself a man with a foot in both ethnic and religious worlds. Though his father had been a member of the English bar with a large practice at Westminster, Malone came of native Irish stock and had close ties to the Irish Catholic community (his wife, for instance, was Catholic). These "popish connections" were sufficient to make Primate Stone, for one, suspect that the parliamentary opposition had a broader nationalist agenda.[38] The massive "Patriot" literature that began pouring out of the presses in support of the parliamentary opposition also hints at this more inclusive nationalism. The majority of these opposition tracts, it is true, drew their arguments and their imagery from an Irish Protestant nationalist tradition. The patriot pamphlet *The True Life of Betty IRELAND . . . Together with Some Account of her elder sister BLANCH of BRITAIN* (1753), for example, resembles Molyneux's *Case* in using a sibling rivalry allegory to critique England's treatment of Ireland during this and other periods of history (Blanch of Britain is Betty Ireland's older haughty and tyrannical sister), and it resembles Swift's *Injured Lady* in configuring Ireland as an unfortunate young woman who has been repeatedly mistreated by a series of Englishmen.[39] However, from the long pamphlet *Hibernia Pacata: or, A Narrative of the Affairs of Ireland from the Famous Battle of Clontarf, where Brian Boirom defeated the Norwegians, till the Settlement under Henry II* (1753), it is evident that patriot writers also borrowed from a native Irish historical tradition for their allegorical depiction of the recent power struggle. There is clearly much that is tongue-in-cheek about the use of the material in *Hibernia Pacata;* in an obvious satire of Irish antiquarianism, for instance, it is stated that the history is based on "an *Irish* Manuscript written by *Dermic Macshaglin*" that was discovered by a Doctor Godfrey in "the Ruins of *Bermingham* Tower" and that it was translated from the Irish by a "Father Neri of Tuam."[40] Nevertheless, in choosing to tell the history of Henry Boyle's struggle with Stone and the castle party through the allegory of Brian Boru's struggle with "Galesius" and the Norwegians and in electing to use a native Irish king as a model for contemporary patriotic virtue—Brian, it is said, was "the first who had united *Patriotism*, and *Loyalty* together"[41]—this pamphlet tacitly validated the native Irish nationalist tradition and gestured at the possible convergence of both kinds of resistance. In a less obvious way, Beaumont Brenan, a member of Burke's old triumvirate, also hinted at this convergence in his poem *The Patriots*

(1754). By putting Malone at the head of the "Race of Patriots" he celebrates in this poem and by referring to all the patriots as defenders not just of "Hibernia" but also of *"Erin's* Cause"—"They call them factious who in *Erin's* Cause, / Dare plead her Rights and justify the Laws"—he implied this was as much a native Irishman's as an Anglo-Irishman's struggle.[42] "Erin," of course, was the Gaelic Irish name for Ireland.

While this new kind of Irish political opposition was emerging in the world outside the playhouse, Sheridan was more closely aligning himself with the court and the "English interest," and, more important, he was using his dramatic art to help the viceroy to stage his spectacles of power. As was evident from the "shining assemblies," and the increased spending on coaches, dress, equipage, and castle renovations, the duke of Dorset was attempting to use spectacle as part of his plan to restore the prestige and status of the administration. The rise in the number of viceregal command performances at the playhouse during the tenure of this viceroy (for example, from four during the 1749–50 season to twenty-four during the 1751–52 season)[43] can be read in a similar ideological light; as in earlier periods of crisis, the administration was turning to the playhouse to court the Irish elite and to showcase its presence and power. It is also clear that Sheridan did everything he could to assist in this government endeavor. As his granddaughter, Alicia Lefanu, later wrote, Sheridan was always "assiduous in paying his duty at the castle,"[44] and he showed this sense of "duty," too, in more direct ways by putting his stagecraft to work for the castle. For the duke's first appearance at Smock Alley in October 1751, for example, Sheridan had the house specially illuminated with wax,[45] and in the prologue he composed and spoke on this occasion, he hailed Dorset as a type of Apollo who was coming to illuminate and guide the benighted "natives" of Ireland:

> At length the day is come, our tedious night,
> At length is broke by a *meridian* light
> The darken'd *natives* of the northern zone,
> Not with more joy behold the rising sun . . .
> Parent *Hibernia,* heav'n protected isle
> Thro' time's dark cloud what joyful prospect smile?
> Just is the loud applause that fills thy land,
> When *George* commits the reins to *Dorset's* hand.[46]

The "darken'd *natives*" image, of course, also worked to support the administration's view that Ireland was a dependent colony, and in stating that

Dorset had received the governing "reins" from the king, the prologue underlined (just as the viceroy had done in his opening speech to Parliament in 1751) the importance of the principle of royal consent. The ode that Sheridan's assistant, Victor, wrote for the birthday night celebration at the castle at the end of the same month had a similar ideological thrust. In depicting Dorset as a husband who was coming in response to a "suppliant" Hibernia's prayer before the English throne, this poem again reinforced the notion that Ireland (like a wife) was in a subordinate position vis-à-vis England, and in framing this relationship as a romance, it also continued to mystify this subordinate relation as a drama of reciprocity:

> There suppliant lies,
> With lifted eyes,
> HIBERNIA! like a beauteous maid!
> With smiles she pleads, Her loyal deeds,
> And asks a DORSET to her aid.
>
> Our King has heard *Hibernia's* pray'r;
> Again resigns her to a *Dorset's* care:
> *Ierne's* choice — her best support —
> Hail, fav'rite of *Britannia's* court![47]

At a grand ball at the Aungier Street theater in March 1752 Sheridan converted the playhouse into a kind of exotic landscape that suggested visually the benevolence and godlike transformative powers of the Dorset administration. The floored-over pit was illuminated with twelve hundred large wax candles and decorated with grottoes, fountains of perfumed water, statues, "Orange Goves, Myrtles, Bays, Jessamins, Trees in Blossom and full grown, Fruits of all Sorts," and the ceiling was painted to show the rising sun driving away the moon and the stars — another reminder of the "*meridian* light" that had broken Ireland's "tedious night."[48]

During the politically heated 1753–54 season, Sheridan and his troop continued to demonstrate their support for the administration and the "English interest" through their behavior inside and outside of the playhouse. A special prologue (this time spoken by Sheridan's leading lady, Peg Woffington) was again composed to greet Dorset on his first appearance at Smock Alley, and at another glittering ball in November 1753, Victor again composed a flattering ode while the Smock Alley scene painter, Joseph Turner, did the decorations and painting.[49] As one of the anti-Sheridan pamphlets that appeared after the 1754 disturbance sarcastically noted, the Smock Alley players were by this time an integral part of the castle circle, fulfilling the roles formerly held by "Poets" and "Wits":

> We are now Company for the best Lords of the Land; who prefer our Conversation before that of the greatest Wits or Proficients in any one Science whatsoever. We have Access to great Men's Chambers, when other honest Artists are forced to wait in their Halls. All Topicks of Conversation turn upon us only. We are allow'd to excel even in Merit the Poets whose Verse we rehearse and live by. In short, we are the only Set of Men, now-a-days, worth admiring.[50]

The ostentatious lifestyle of Sheridan and Woffington at this time further identified them as part of the castle set. Alicia Lefanu's account of the elaborate feasts that Sheridan provided for his guests at his ornately decorated house in Quilca substantiates Victor's claim that in 1753 the manager was turning his family home in Cavan into "a palace in miniature,"[51] and if we are to credit another later source, at this time Peg Woffington had also "launched out into extravagance, keeping a coach and pair, and an open house where she gathered around her the choicest wit and merriest spirits of the town."[52] At the recently founded Beef-stake Club, too, Sheridan and Woffington consorted with the leaders of the court party (including Lord George Sackville), drinking toasts and making remarks that were openly antipatriot.[53] And as John Watkins later noted, the manager continued these weekly assemblies "even when they were openly complained of as injurious to the nation, and intended to render the theatre an engine of government."[54]

If there was a blurring of the boundaries between the theatrical and the political in the satires that began appearing from patriot pens in fall and winter 1753, then, it was because there was this symbiotic relationship between the castle and Smock Alley, and insofar as they had this double focus, these literary attacks prefigured the actual attack on the theater in March. In fall 1753, for instance, a patriot satirist uses the conceit of a mock-playbill to render his opinion of the upcoming parliamentary session and the Theatre Royal; by configuring this upcoming session as a farcical entertainment that was to be performed "by command" (October 9 was the day set for the opening of the new parliamentary session), this writer takes aim at what he takes to be the autocratic and inept nature of the administration in Ireland while also hinting at the farcical nature of the "command" performances at Smock Alley:[55]

By special Command

For the Benefit of Ireland,

Now in Rehearsal, and will be performed,

At the GREAT BOOTH

IN

COLLEGE-GREEN,

On *Tuesday* the 9th of *October*, 1753

A *Tragi-Comical Farcical Entertainment*, not acted these three

Years, called,

COURT AND COUNTRY

WITH

THE HUMOURS OF ROGER DE COVERLY

All the Parts will be disposed of to the best Advantage, with entire new Dresses, all

of IRISH MANUFACTURE and other Decorations suitable to the Play.

To which will be added, a Pantomime Entertainment, call'd,

THE GROANS OF THE BARRACKS

The Part of Gimcrack to be performed by

VANTRYPE

The celebrated Dutch Architect, (being the last Time of his performing there)

With several Pieces of Machinery, Scenery, Sinkings, Flyings, bowings, Cringings,

entirely new in this Kingdom:

The Dead Man brought to Life or D———t in a Cradle:

The Principal Characters in the Play will be printed in the

Bills the Day of the Performance.

Places, Pensions and Promises to be had at *Caiphas*'s in

H-nr-ta-Street, or a Friarius's Office in the C———le Yard, on

the Days of the Rehearsal.

N. B. If they are not bespoke before the Day of Performance; they will

be all engaged.

VIVATREX[56]

The broadsheet *Political Fire-Eating* (1753) also draws on an actual Sheridan-sponsored paratheatrical entertainment as a vehicle for its political satire. Toward the end of November 1753, Sheridan engaged Mr. Powell, the "celebrated Fire-Eater from London," to perform his fire-eating feats on the Smock Alley stage in the role of Pluto in the pantomime *The Necromancer, or Harlequin Dr. Faustus,* and on December 4 Powell repeated these feats at the Capel Street theater, which by now was also under Sheridan's control.[57]

When the writer of *Political Fire-Eating* argues that the viceroy brought Mr. Powell over from London to assist with a bill "with certain *f–n Alterations*" that "is to rammed with coals of fire down the throats of the people in an experiment quite disused since the days of William Wood" and when he states that all gentlemen in Parliament must attend the little theater in Capel Street to hear lectures and receive "proper Combustibles" in anticipation of "the grand Performance . . . at the great Cock-Pit on or before *Christmas-Eve*,"[58] he is taking aim at such "low" entertainments as well as the altered money bill that, he implies, the administration will try to force parliamentary member s to accept at the end of December. In the minds of patriots, such texts suggest, the realms of the political and the theatrical had become indistinguishable.

Like the patriot pamphlets described earlier, these mock–theatrical texts emanated from every part of the social spectrum, and they draw on different dissenting traditions for their material. In 1754, for example, the "independent electors of the antient, loyal, and ever memorable town of Inniskillen," like many other Protestant bodies across the country, offered an address of thanks to Kildare, Boyle, Cox, and other members of the patriot opposition, to which they added forty original toasts and three anti-government satires. Two of these satirical pieces were attacks on a proclamation against the printing of seditious libels that was issued by the Dorset administration in February 1754,[59] and one was titled *A Proclamation by his Grace Hack-ball, King of State Mendicants in the Kingdom of EUTOPIA.*[60] As already noted, Burke and Hiffernan had first made use of the Hack-ball conceit in *The Reformer* and *The Tickler,* and the image of the king of the Dublin's beggars was invoked to ridicule Lucas and his "mob" followers. In this mock-"Proclamation," however, Hack-ball is invoked to satirize the administration itself and to ridicule its attempt to suppress the patriot opposition. While the government proclamation aimed at suppressing patriot pamphlets on the grounds that they misrepresented the administration, this mock-proclamation issued by "his Grace, Hack-ball" aimed at suppressing pamphlets by government apologists (John Brett, Christopher Robinson, David Bindon, Gorges Howard) on the grounds that they "misrepresent the Patriots of this Kingdom." And while the original proclamation was issued from the chambers of Dublin Castle, this proclamation was issued from the "Council Chamber at the Sign of *Caiphas,* in *Back-Lane.*"[61]

A member of the Burke-Hiffernan campaign, Beaumont Brenan, also lent his voice to this patriot attack when he republished *The Stage or Coronation of King Tom* in 1753. This mock-heroic poem on Sheridan and his stage originated in the "Gentlemen's" campaigns of 1747 and 1748, and some version of it had been printed during that period. However, the phrase "for some years" in the opening lines of the poem suggests that Brenan had also revised and updated his satire to suit the current political context; the absolutist and usurping theatrical prince depicted in these lines is not only the tyrant who attacked Kelly and the "Gentlemen" but also the newly empowered favorite of the Dorset court:

> Now for some years unrival'd and alone,
> Has *Irish* TOM usurp'd the stage's throne,
> A Prince as absolute in his domain,
> As *Lewis* once, or greater *Charlemagne*
> Each trembling slave before their monarch stands,
> And wait implicitly his high commands.[62]

In the political context of 1753, too, the subsequent description of a "whole fabric" dominated by "farce" "folly" and "tinsel'd Vagrants" also reads as a veiled satire on the viceroy and his administration; at a literal level the "dome" in the following lines is Smock Alley, but this dome can also be read as a reference to the Irish House of Parliament (the poem *The Speaker* [1713] mentioned in chapter 1, for instance, used the term for this building):[63]

> There stands a dome devoted to wit and sense,
> While sense and wit to favour held pretense.
> Now farce and folly the whole fabric sways,
> Exprest in fustian and indecent plays.
> Since by kind licence of the powerful great,
> 'Tis grown the Players' not the Muses' seat.
> Here tinsel'd Vagrants in gay pomp appear,
> To charm the eye, unmindful of the ear. (22)

The antigovernment pamphlet *The Secret History of the two last Memorable S..ss..ons of Parliament* (1754) also suggests that the common people were joining in these attacks on "the powerful great," just as they had during the 1749–50 season. On one occasion during the 1753–54 season, according to this pamphlet, several of the court party, namely, "Briarius [Lord George Sackville], Lord Venal and several other unclean Birds," assembled at Crow Street Music Hall to attend "a Superb Entertainment at the Expence of the Nation," and while there, these courtiers concocted a scheme for ridiculing the patriots: "They wrote a Catalogue of scandalous illnatur'd Toasts against the Patriots of I[relan]d, erected one of the Mob, who could read, upon a Butcher's Block, and when they had order'd the Populace three Barrels of Ale and plenty of Spirits, a numerous Mob surrounded the Block, and Lord Venal order'd the Toasts to be read with an audible voice and drank round."[64] This attempt at creating an antipatriot populist demonstration with the aid of the customary bribe of free drink failed dismally when the "Mob" spontaneously rewrote the script: "The Mob too sensible of the obligations they ow'd the protectors of their Country, inverted the Tables on their Enemies, and the first Toast they gave was, disappointment to L[or]d G[eorge] S[ackville]. This Spirit of gratitude in the People, put the unclean Birds under a necessity of drinking the Refuse of the Populace, whose favour they often pitifully courted, tho' they inveigh'd against the Patriots for being admir'd by them."[65] The complaints that began appearing in newspapers early in 1753 also suggest that this kind of countertheater was occurring in the playhouse itself. In a letter sent to the *Universal Advertiser* on March 13, 1753, a writer who calls himself "Philo-Dramaticus" but who sounds remarkably like Sheridan inveighs against two groups whom he suggests are creating disturbances in the playhouse at this period: first, those ""worthless and ill bred Domesticks" who, as they keep places in the boxes before and during an entertainment, offend "Ladies of the first Distinction" with their "offensive Effluvia of Porter and Tobacco" and "other Indecencies of Behaviour"; and second, the "select Junto" who repair to the "exalted Regions of the Theatre" and tipple on their "Cargo of strong Liquors" during the performance. In calling for the manager to put "an immediate and effectual Stop to such irregular Proceedings for the future," this letter writer then hints that these groups should be banned from the playhouse or at least be more rigorously disciplined in the interest of affording more "rational and instructive Entertainment."[66] An epilogue entitled *Bucks Have at Ye All,* which was first spoken by the popular comedian and mimic Thomas King in 1754 and which afterward became one of the favorites of the Dublin galleries, throws a different light on these populist disturbances and complaints. In the following lines, King readily acknowledges that the upper gallery repeatedly disturbed the play:

Ye *Bucks* above, who reign like Gods at large—
Nay, do not grin,—but listen to your Charge!
You who, resolv'd to change the Scene of Raillery,
Out-talk the Players, in the *Upper Gallery;*

You need not to your Wit such Succours bring
As—*is it Weight?*—and chatt'ring to *Tom King* . . .

Your Judgment is so fierce—your Wit so loud,
That, 'pon my Soul, I'm sure it must be good.
Behold I bow me to your grand Decree,
And own your Justice—th'o you *groan* for me.[67]

But in these lines King also suggests that these disturbances were more often displays of "Wit" and "Judgement" than drunken boorishness, and the editor of the collection in which this epilogue appears, James Love, confirms this reading when he indicates that these exercises of "Wit" were often directed at political targets. In an explanatory note on the word *groan* in the last line above, Love writes, "The Spirit of the Times, in Party Matters, boiling over amongst the lower Order of People to great Excess; a rude and daring Liberty was taken by the *Upper Gallery* of calling to account the People of Fashion, and distinguishing them with Marks of Contempt or Approbation—Noblemen, Gentlemen, nay even the Ladies themselves were called upon by name, as they entered the Boxes, and saluted with a *Clap* or a *Groan*."[68]

The carnivalesque performance that occurred during the first staging of *Mahomet the Imposter* on February 2, then, was a continuation of this patriot countertheater. As Sheldon points out, this first performance of *Mahomet* took place at Smock Alley on February 2, 1754, the very day that the administration announced the proroguing of Parliament.[69] This parliamentary suspension was the administration's response to the Irish Commons' refusal to pass the amended money bill in December 1753, and it had been prefaced by the dismissal of Malone, Thomas Carter, and other prominent leaders of the opposition (Boyle remained, however).[70] These patriots needed an alternate forum, then, to signal their continued defiance of the castle and their continued commitment to the patriot cause, and from Victor's statement that "the Pit was filled very soon with Leaders and Chiefs of the Country Party," it is clear that they fixed on the playhouse. In *Mahomet*, too, they found a script that voiced their rage at those who had betrayed their country and sided with government. The first major disruption that Victor records, for example, occurred when the "Party in the Pit" loudly demanded that West Digges, who was playing the role of the senate leader Alcanor, repeat his "If, Ye Power divine" speech, which occurs during the following exchange in Act 1:

PHARON: Say is the Senate Sound?
I fear some Members of that rev'rend Class
Are mark'd with the Contagion, who, from Views
Of higher Power and Rank, or canker'd with
The gangerous Defilement of a Bribe,
Worship this rising Sun, and give a Sanction
To his Invasions.

ALCANOR: If, ye Powers divine!
Ye mark the Movements of this nether World,
And bring them to account, crush, crush these Vipers,
Who, singled out by a Community
To guard their Rights, shall, for a grasp of Oar [*sic*]
Or paltry Office, sell them to the Foe![71]

By forcing this repetition, the opposition leaders effectively dislodged this speech from its original dramatic context and appropriated it for their own political *agon*, transforming the fiercely unyielding Alcanor into a figure of the patriot opposition and the corrupt Mecca senate members who support the "imposter Mahomet" into the Irish parliamentary members who supported the viceroy.

The audience also continued to invest Alcanor's lines with an anti-court meaning through their applause and groans during the remainder of the play, and like the broader patriot opposition at this time, this audience opposition was a cross-class operation. While the pro-patriot report that appeared on Feburary 8 in the *Dublin Spy* emphasizes the pit's contribution to the subversive play—Digges was "encor'd in a spirited speech, and Bravoes thunder'd from the Pit," this paper reported[72]—a hostile item that appeared in the *Dublin Journal* in the next issue after the first *Mahomet* disturbance points to the upper gallery as the source of disruption. In *An approved Receipt to make an English Tragedy in the present Taste*, a piece that is clearly intended to satirize the audience's behavior at the *Mahomet* performance, readers are told:

Take the Words *Liberty, Patriot, Country, Tyranny, Oppression, High-Priest, Priest-craft, Bribery, Corruption, Pensions, Placemen;* of each an equal quantity. Take out of the Dictionary as many Words as will make up two thousand Words of English Verse, but take Care that at least one of the above-recited Words be in each Line. Divide these into five equal Parts; between each Part let there be a Chorus of Groans in the Upper Gallery.—Your Tragedy will do, depend on't.[73]

The upper gallery, this attack suggests, was every bit as active as the pit, rewriting the drama with their "Chorus of Groans" to make it applicable to the Irish political situation.

As *An approved Receipt* implies in its ironic title, however, this Irish audience also made a mockery of "English" tragedy by such interventions, and it is this parodic remaking of the hegemonic English text that must also be considered if we are to understand the full subversive thrust of the February 2 performance. The tragedy *Mahomet the Imposter* was based on Voltaire's *Mahomet, ou le Fanatisme,* a play that had been first staged in France in 1741. Because of pressure from religious supporters in Paris who saw the play as an attack on the Catholic Church, however, Voltaire was forced to withdraw the piece after only three performances,[74] and when the two English Protestant clergymen, James Miller and John Hoadly, adapted this play for the London stage, they drew attention to this censorship, noting in their prologue that Voltaire's "Tragic Muse," with its indictment of religious fanaticism and tyranny, had to travel to England to be heard:

> On English *Ground she makes a firmer Stand,*
> *And hopes to suffer by no hostile Hand.*
> *No Clergy here usurp the free-born Mind,*
> *Ordain'd to teach, and not enslave Mankind;*
> Religion *here bids Persecution cease,*
> Without, *all Order, and* within, *all Peace;*
> Truth *guards her happy Pale with watchful Care,*
> *And* Frauds, *tho' Pious, find no Entrance there.* (Prologue)

A letter to the *General Advertiser,* which appeared shortly before the first English production of the play at Drury Lane in April 1744, also encouraged London theatergoers to read the religious and political differences between England and France into this play and to view these differences against the background of the most recent struggle for hegemony in Europe, the War of the Austrian Succession (1741–48). "It is not doubted but these very Sentiments, which in France, prevented the Representation of this piece, will, in England speak loudly in its favor . . . especially since so audacious an attempt has been lately made by the Common Enemy of Europe to establish at once a Civil and Spiritual Tyranny over those injur'd Nations, by the old Mohametan and Roman Arguments of Fire and Sword."[75] *Mahomet*'s popularity with London audiences during the second half of the eighteenth century, when Britain's competition with France for world dominance rose to its highest pitch, also suggests that London theatergoers continued to read this play in the light of this international struggle.[76] Like Rowe's *Tamerlane*, *Mahomet* could be interpreted as a conflict between a religiously and politically tolerant Protestant Britain and a politically intolerant, fanatical Catholic France, and this interpretation, of course, worked to justify Britain's imperial enterprise.

When the Smock Alley audience identified the tyrant Mahomet with the viceroy and the "English interest" in Ireland in 1754, however, they turned the whole ideological calculus of this play on its head, and the far-reaching subversive political effect of this inversion can be illustrated by looking at the central exchange between Alcanor and Mahomet in Act 2, Scene ii. Here Mahomet admits that he has destroyed the empires of Persia, India, Egypt, and Turkey, but he also defends his policy of ravishing the globe "from North to South" (22) on the grounds that a new and better political and religious structure is rising in the place of these ruins: "On this Wreck of Nations Let lov'd *Arabia* rise: A new Religion, New Laws, new Ties, and a new God are wanting, To rouse the slumb'ring World to Deeds of Glory" (22). In his reply Alcanor then questions the arrogance and presumption of these claims, and on the London stage where there was a tradition of reading the differences between England and France into this play, his question would have served to interrogate Catholic France's imperial aspirations while also implicitly demonstrating the contrasting righteousness of the English political and religious position:

> At thy Nod, then,
> The Face of the Creation must be chang'd.
> By Menaces and Carnage, modest Thou!
> Would'st force all Mortals to believe alike:
> What right hast thou receiv'd to plant new Faiths,
> Or lay a Claim to Royalty and Priesthood? (23)

In the Smock Alley audience's rewriting of this play on February 2, however, Mahomet was reconfigured as the viceroy, and it was thus an English ruler's religious and civilizing claims that were exposed as mere pious imposture by this exchange. Because this play served as a broader allegorical defense of British imperialism, such an exposure also had implications that went beyond the immediate Irish situation. Alcanor's question "What right hast thou?" would have reverberated in the Dublin playhouse on this occasion as an interrogation of the whole British "civilizing" mission that served as the ideological underpinnings of British global expansionism.

Sheridan's decision to stage a second performance of this play but also to prevent any repetition of speeches, then, was an attempt to restore this text to its original salutary British meaning, and as far as his patriot critics were concerned, this effort further identified him with those parliamentary "Vipers" who were willing to sell out "the Community" for power and money (see Alcanor's speech above). Many of the manager's critics later explicitly suggested that he revived *Mahomet* a second time with the deliberate aim of producing a public confrontation with the patriots on the expectation that the castle would reward him with a pension and provide him with a way out of his approaching bankruptcy. A passage from *The Curtain Lecture: or, The Manager Run Mad. A Dialogue between a Stage-Director and his Wife*, a satirical poem that appeared four years after the "riot," gives the gist of these charges in a speech supposedly delivered by Mrs. Sheridan:

> That second of March, that terrible night!—
> I ne'er to be sure shall recover the fright,
> 'Twas then my mad *Tommy* committed the deed;
> Then drowning in debt, he snatch'd at a reed.
> 'Twas then amidst factions mad *Tommy* wou'd wrestle,
> And vainly suggested great hopes from the Castle
> What folly! What pride! The effect still evinces
> How wisely you'd lean'd on the favour of princes.
> A pension, no doubt, some hundreds a year,
> The D..ke was to give—nay, frown not my dear.
> Your hopes were all rais'd as high as the steeple,
> Your friends you affronted, you spurn'd at the people.[77]

Three days after the "riot," the *Universal Advertiser* also reported that the "unpopular proceedings" at the playhouse on March 2 stemmed from "a project hatch'd at the Beef Stake Club to serve as a foundation for a *private* Bounty from the Public or founding Criminal Prosecutions," a reading that gives Sheridan's behavior an even darker complexion.[78] This report suggests that Sheridan was working with the courtiers not only for his own material advantage but also to create a snare to legally entrap some of the patriot leaders.

The provocative attacks on the patriot crowd that appeared in the *Dublin Journal* in the days before the disturbance also lends credence to the suspicion that this was a deliberately staged confrontation. Between the first and second performances of *Mahomet*, the manager or others working in support of him repeatedly used the *Dublin Journal* to criticize the crowd who had disrupted the first *Mahomet* performance while at the same time lauding the conduct of Sheridan as manager. *An approved Receipt* was followed by two other letters in the same, deliberately inflammatory anti-patriot vein. On February 9–12 a writer signing himself "Theatricus" denounced all those members of the audience who came to the playhouse "to give Vent to Party Principles," and he asked all "true Patriots" to "exert themselves in support of the Manager" who has established "the only free Stage now in the World." And in a letter in the February 19–23 issue, "Hibernicus" repeated this request for support for Sheridan while denigrating the kind of native entertainment favored by the patriot crowd. All the recent improvements in the Irish capital (the building of elegant homes, the decline in absentees), Hibernicus argued, can be attributed to "the conduct of the present manager"; before his arrival "our whole Diversions consisted of a miserable, unfrequented Theatre, and a Six-penny Concert at the Bull's Head Ale-House in *Fishamble Street*."[79]

Patriot writers, not surprisingly, countered these attacks in other papers and pamphlets, and as they publicized their side of the story, they also encouraged patriots to show up at the playhouse at the next March 2 repeat performance of *Mahomet*. The pamphlet *A grand debate between court and country*, for example, repeated the *Dublin Spy*'s pro-patriot account of the February 2 disturbance for the express purpose of letting "the Reader . . . into the Nature of the Quarrel between the Politiest Audience in the World, and a Saucy Impudent Manager of a Theatre" (7), and by reprinting several other speeches that were applauded that night—for example, Alcanor's speech requesting that heaven enable him to "Pluck the spoil from the Oppressors, / And keep his Country as he found it—free"—this pamphlet provided an advance patriot script for the next *Mahomet* demonstration.[80] In *Remarks on Two Letters signed Theatricus and Hibernicus*, too, a writer calling himself "Libertus" specifically identifies Sheridan as the author of these two letters on the basis of their "Insolence and Vanity,"[81] and in the course of denying Sheridan's claim that he had created a free stage, this writer also pointedly reminded the "People" of their tradition of using the playhouse for patriot protest. "The Theatre," Libertus wrote, " . . . has ever been the very Place where the People have distinguished their Patriot Spirit; and when their Remonstrances have been, by ministerial Influence, obstructed to the *Powers that be*, this has always the *Succedaneum* they have made Use of, to shew their Sense of whatever Grievance or Oppression they have laboured under" (5). By invoking the case of the London stage and by suggesting that their failure to challenge a corrupt ministry and its supporters would result in the loss of larger political freedoms, this writer also created an added sense of urgency to the upcoming *Mahomet* performance. "But what was it that lost the Theatres in *London* their Liberty, but the uncontroul'd Power of a corrupt Minister of State, who procured to the Lord Chamberlain the Authority of licensing Plays, either in the Whole or in Part?" Libertus points out, and he concludes, that "if the gallant Patrons of Liberty, do not upon all Occasions support even the Freedom of the Stage, the Loss of this may perhaps, in a short Time, be the least Grievance or Oppression they may have reason to lament" (7).

In the opening paragraph of *The Signs and Groans of Mr. Sh———n*, a pamphlet purporting to give a full account of the "Comical Farce" that was "acted" at Smock Alley on March 2, there is also an implicit acknowledgment of the effectiveness of this kind of patriot publicity.[82] "The House filled before six o'Clock," this pamphlet begins, "and it seems what brought so many together was to enjoy the Pleasure which others, at the first Performance, had said they received; this was a Motive sufficient to induce Persons of all Conditions to come to the Performance" (3). In the three succeeding paragraphs, this pamphlet also points to what may have been the immediate catalyst for the large turnout, namely, the rumored attempt by Sheridan to silence Digges before this performance. In the *Vindication* that he published two weeks after the "riot," Sheridan went to great pains to dispel the notion that he had in any way threatened Digges or the other members of the cast before the March 2 performance, and he made this claim by reprinting a speech he supposedly read to his players at a green room meeting on March 1. Though this speech inveighed strongly against the practice of repeating speeches at the request of the audience on the grounds that it would lead to the theater becoming "a Scene of Riot and Disorder," it also stated that the players were "entirely free" to act as they thought proper, and this sentiment was specifically repeated in remarks addressed to Digges at the end of the speech. "You have now heard my Arguments upon that Head," Sheridan says he told Digges. "If you think they are of weight, I suppose you will act accordingly; if not, remember I do not given any Order upon this Occasion, you are left entirely *free to act as you please.*"[83]

In reference to this green room meeting, however, *The Signs and Groans* pamphlet reported that "it had . . . been given out by some Persons that the Manager had taken *Digges's* answering to the Encore, in very great Dungeon, and had threatened him [Digges] with the Forfeiture of his Sallary if he dared answer to the Encore" (4), and from the pseudopolitical language and the allusion to the issue of *"Consent"* in this pamphlet's account of the green room discussion, it is clear that many saw Sheridan's behavior at the meeting as directly analogous to the viceroy's recent attempt to coerce the opposition into signing the money bill. Sheridan had resolved that there was a "Country" faction in his company, this pamphlet states:

> And he accordingly ordered it to be resolved in a Committee of the whole House, that no Actor whatever from the highest to the lowest shou'd presume to answer his *Encore,* and be it resolved by the Authority Aforesaid, that it be entered in the Records of the House, that whatsoever Actor or Actress, shou'd presume to answer an *Encore* tho' the whole World was the Audience, that he or she so offending shou'd be discharged.
>
> And be it further resolved that the Reasons of this Resolution are to prevent so untheatrical a Proceeding, in an insolent Audience from coming into Precedent without the *previous Consent* of the Manager. (4)

Other pamphlets that appeared in the wake of the March 2 theatrical uprising also suggest that Sheridan's treatment of his players was seen as directly analogous to the government's attempt to intimidate the Irish patriot opposition, even if they do not specifically mention Digges. In *An Epistle from Th——— S Sh———n Esq; to the Universal Advertiser,* the following words are put in the mouth of Sheridan (or "Thomas, *Rex Theat,*" as the manager is named in this pamphlet) as part of his mock-defense:

> And Query, if a certain V———y, who shall be nameless, did not in imitation of me, endeavour to govern the Inhabitants of this Isle, as I have those whom Providence has committed to my Guidance. Is it not plain, then that an eye has been had to my system of government, and will it not, think you, one Day, be used as a Regulator of the Grand Machine? . . . Have I not, in my small Sphere, given an excellent Speci-

men of the Salutary Effects of passive Obedience and Non-resistance, ruling my Vassals with a Rod of Iron, and obliging them in the most abject Manner to truckle to their Sovereign?[84]

It is also clear from *The Signs and Groans* that the audience read Digges's refusal to repeat the "If ye Powers divine" speech on the night of March 2 as proof that he had been intimidated by Sheridan. According to Victor, when Digges heard the request for an encore of this speech, he "seemed startled, and stood some Time motionless" before stepping out of character to say that much as he would like to accede to their demands, *"his Compliance would be greatly injurious to him."*[85] The author of *The Signs and Groans,* however, writes that the audience interpreted Digges's remarks to mean that "he was obliged to sign the Resolution of the Manager's Privy-Council, and that therefore he hoped that the audience would not insist on his disobliging the *Sultan*" (5), an explanation that again transforms the "Manager" into a figure for the autocratic administration that had tried to impose the amended money bill on the Irish Parliament. In another mock-self-defense entitled *Mr. Sh——n's Apology to the Town; with the Reasons which unfortunately induced him to his late misconduct,* this comparison is more explicitly developed, and under the guise of condemning Sheridan's tyranny, the tyranny of the government is again exposed and condemned. In this satire the manager is made to proclaim:

> I am not only Lord of my own House, but every Thing that passes there, even to the Spectators Judgments: to manage Playhouses of late is not only become the Director's Province but to manage Audiences also; and he who dares to dispute this Prerogative will make, I am afraid, but a *Money-Bill* Affair of it, that is to be turned out of his *Place;* for by my Connections with these Powers who are at Variance with those who call themselves Friends to their Country, I am able at any Time, to have a Posse of Soldiers, or Constables, to overawe any who shall dare but to whisper they are of the same Opinion with the Patriots aforemention'd—Tremble, then, O Ye Sons of Liberty and Turbulence, I will make you swallow such Stuff as I please to ram down your Throats, or you shall be represented as Enemies to good Government, and his M——y's mild Administration.[86]

A passage in *The Play-house Prorogued,* another anti-Sheridan pamphlet that appeared after the disturbance, also strongly suggests that others saw

this attempt to suppress Digges's speech in the context of the recently issued proclamation against seditious libels. "Now surely, it will be granted,"
this pamphlet satirically argues, "that the passage in *Mahomet* was a direct
Libel . . . and might if repeated again, have turned things topsy-turvey, to
the great Damage of the State, as well as Discredit to the Manager's Reputation for Politics."[87]

The response to this act of theatrical coercion was analogous to the national response to recent acts of government coercion; as in the larger political domain, resistance in the theatrical domain came from above and
below and from both sides of the cultural and religious divide. After Digges
gave his faltering explanation, for example, the audience called on the manager to appear and make an apology, and when he failed to appear after
an hour of these calls, *The Sighs and Groans* pamphlet explains, "the Wags
in the Gallery begun their Raillery to entertain the House, and called upon
him by his beloved Title of Thomas Sh———n Esq; come on the Stage—
but this tho' repeated as in Court three times, was also rejected" (5). The
first attack on Sheridan that evening thus was launched by the least affluent
patrons of the playhouse, and the content of this "Raillery" aligns it with
the subversive play of the Kelly faction in the 1747 theatrical dispute; the
term "Esquire," of course, denoted the status of gentleman, and Sheridan
had first laid public claim to this gentry status during the Gentlemen's
Quarrel of that year. Other pamphlets both before and after this disturbance also display these "Gentlemen" sympathies, suggesting that there
was a Catholic presence in this opposition. Commenting on the manager's
claim that he had created a "free" stage as a result of this 1747 confrontation
in *Remarks on Two Letters,* for example, "Libertus" writes, "What bombas-
tical Declamation here! What vain Puffing about an Affair, which was acci-
dentally brought to pass by the drunken Frolick of a giddy young Man!"
(7), a statement that essentially reiterates the view of Kelly proposed by
John Browne and other "Gentlemen" apologists. And in another implicit
vindication of the "Gentlemen's" position during this Quarrel, the writer of
Mr. Sh———n's Apology cites the audience's constant "indulgence" of the
manager's "numberless Impertinences, Broils and Confusions" (3) as the
principal reason for the manager's haughty conduct on the evening of
March 2—an indulgence that has taught him to say: "We are no more that
tame Passive Race, that will suffer raw young Gentlemen to lord it over us,
and subject us to such Concessions as the meanest of Slaves would not fail
to kick at" (5). In linking this mock-defense of Sheridan to a mock-defense
of Samuel Richardson and Henry Brooke—"he who dares dispute this Po-

sition will be as little qualified for polite Company, as if he shou'd assert the author of *Pamela* or *Grandison* was not a fine Writer, myself the best Actor the Stage ever produc'd, or *Hall Br——ke* the Glory of the Age he now lives in"—this anonymous author also identified himself with the Irish "Wits" who had attacked the manager and his supporters in 1748. Richardson, as noted earlier, was a favorite object of satire of Paul Hiffernan in his *Tickler*, because Faulkner had puffed this author's novel in his newspaper, and in his recently republished *The Stage or Coronation of King Tom*, Brenan identified Brooke (the "*Hall Br——ke*" in the above passage) as the goddess of Dullness's first great love. Addressing Sheridan in this poem, the goddess of Dullness says, "Not all regard to *B——ke*'s pen is due / Some sparks of love remains, dear child, for you."[88]

This kind of raillery from the gallery soon gave way to a more specifically Irish Protestant patriot political theater, one that would seem to have drawn its inspiration from the tracts, addresses, and toasts emanating from patriot bodies all over the country. After Sheridan failed to appear, *The Sighs and Groans* reports, a number of different theater personnel filed on the stage in a vain attempt to pacify the audience, and with their appearance, there was a brief interlude of physical farce. The "Knight of the Black Wig," as this pamphlet terms Carmichael the prompter, was "saluted with some Freedoms" that made him "glad to get off in a whole Skin," and the "redoubted" Sowden (Sheridan's assistant manager at this time) was similarly "repulsed" for "thinking that he had to deal with the tame spirited Audience at *London*" (6). On discovering that Sheridan had stolen away from the house, however, the audience went back to a more political theater, the whole house joining in a series of "Claps" and "Groans" that took their meaning from the current parliamentary crisis and from an increasingly outspoken Irish Protestant patriotism. The first claps, for example, were conventionally loyalist ones: "The King," "Prince of Wales," "The Duke and the Army," "The Royal Family." But these were immediately followed by claps for all who had defied the attempt to insert the royal consent clause into the money bill or who had attacked his majesty's administration in word or deed during the recent crisis: in order, these claps were for "Lord Kildare and Liberty," "Roger the Speaker, and Ireland," "Lord Carrick," "Mrs. Hamilton," "Lord Tyrone," "Anthony," "The outed Members," "The Smith that refused to shoe a Courtier's Horse," "The Country Writers," "The Dublin Spy," and "The Universal Advertiser" (7). The "Groans," similarly, were directed at the representatives of His Majesty's government in Ireland and at all those who supported it, though these

powerful government figures were named more cryptically, often identified only through the nicknames the opposition writers had used in their
writing. There were "Groans," for example, "For Reynard" (Dorset), "For
the Cub" (George Sackville), and "For Caiaphas" (Primate Stone), as well
as ones "For All Indorsers," "For the No-honest Man," and "For the Hangman that burns the News-Boys Papers, Etc. Etc" (8).

The physical assault on the playhouse thus took its meaning from a
kind of multivoiced Irish anticolonial theater, and with this act of physical demolition, it could be argued, this audience also completed the subversive rewriting of *Mahomet* that they had begun on February 2. In the fourth
act of *Mahomet*, the patriot senator Alcanor learns that the "Citizens are
rous'd, and all in Arms" (59), and in a climactic moment in the fifth act,
these enraged citizens, led by Zaphna (one of Alcanor's children), come on
stage to confront the tyrant Mahomet with the body of their murdered hero
(65). This populist resistance finally comes to naught in this play; convinced
by Zaphna's sudden death that Mahomet has divine powers, the people are
intimidated and leave the stage in defeat (68). When the "Gentlemen" with
the assistance of the "Mob" laid Smock Alley to waste on March 2, however,
they rewrote the hegemonic script, turning the British hegemonic play into
an Irish "Comical Farce." On that evening, as *An Epistle from Th———s
Sh———n Esq to the Universal Advertiser* sardonically notes, King Tom himself was "forced to retire with as much Precipitation as *Mahomet* . . . from
the blood-thirsty Citizens of *Mecca*"[89] and, more important, an aggressive
English administration was symbolically routed by an audience that was beginning to stand for the whole people of Ireland.

CHAPTER 8

Rehearsing Revolution

Patriots, "Paddies," and the
"Aggregate" Riot of 1784

English, English is the cry! away with English! anything but English
will go down with us!

Freeman's Journal, July 3–6, 1784

Under the heading "Irish Affairs" in its July 1784 issue, the *Gentleman's
Magazine* gave its London readers three items of news from the Irish capital. The first concerned an attack on a master tailor who had violated the
tenets of the anti-importation movement:

> *Dublin, June 21.* Saturday se'night a number of persons, about seven
> o'clock in the morning, assembled in a riotous manner before the
> house of Mr. Alex. Clarke, master taylor; and eight or nine of them
> having forcibly entered, they stripped him quite naked, and with a
> brush b-smirred him with tar, assigning, as their reason, that he was an
> importer of English cloth.

The second concerned the public rebuff that the viceroy, the duke of Rutland, delivered to municipal officials on receiving a petition from an "aggregate" meeting of Dublin freeholders and citizens:

Dublin, July 6. The High Sheriffs waited on his Grace the Lord Lieutenant with the petition of the aggregate body of the inhabitants of the city of Dublin to his Majesty, requesting his Excellency that he would be pleased to transmit the same. He returned the following answer: "Gentlemen at the same time that I comply with your request, I shall not fail to convey my entire disapprobation of the contents, as casting unjust reflections on the laws and Parliament of Ireland, and tending to weaken the authority of both."

The third concerned the uproar that occurred during a command performance at Smock Alley Theatre a few days later, a disturbance so intense that the viceroy withdrew from the playhouse:

Dublin, July 9. The play of Douglas being ordered by his Grace the Lord Lieutenant, on the rising of the curtain the audience cried out for the volunteers' march, which on his Excellency's entrance was played accordingly. The play, or more properly the clamour, now began, and choruses of groaning, hissing, and shouting, with whistles, cat-calls, horse-legs, and geld-horns, all kept in tune by the trunk-maker, thundered through the house, and made the drama a complete farce. The manager was called upon: "I am," said he, "the servant of the public, and wish to know whether it is your will the performance should continue." The propriety of this speech was universally approved, and the play was suffered to go on, but with frequent interruptions. A few scenes were acted, and the catastrophe introduced. The entertainment concluded a few minutes after eight, when the Viceroy withdrew, but not unnoticed, the former music attending him to the castle. (550)[1]

In including this theatrical disturbance in its account of disruptive events in the Irish capital, the *Gentleman's Magazine* tacitly pointed to the continuity between what was happening in the theatrical and the economic and political arenas, and it underlined this connection again in a later issue that summer when it used a theatrical metaphor to describe what it represents as the near–state of chaos in Dublin city. In its "Advices from Ireland" column in August 1784, the magazine informed its readers, "Not a day passes but some outrage or other is committed either by the military, the mob, or the volunteers; so that Dublin is at present the theatre of riot and licentious delinquency."[2]

In this chapter I argue that the Dublin playhouse was implicated in the larger "theater of riot" that was being played out throughout the Irish capital in summer 1784, though I suggest that this "theater" was something other than "licentious delinquency." In tracing the process by which the Dublin preindustrial "crowd" was transformed into the revolutionary underground of the United Irishmen, Jim Smyth points to 1784 as a crucial turning point: "1784, with its alliances of catholics and radicals, Volunteer-reformers and 'the people,' and in the way in which the lower classes were politicized by meetings, petitioning, the press and collective experience, anticipated the 1790s."[3] The carnivalesque drama on July 10,[4] I suggest, was played out against this incipiently revolutionary background. It was staged by the same "aggregate body" that had presented the controversial petition to the viceroy on July 6, and it was linked more broadly to the anti-importation riots and other antigovernment demonstrations organized by Volunteers, patriots, and "the mob" during the highly turbulent period of 1779–84.

Before beginning the analysis of these events, however, I want to focus on the continued history of anticolonial resistance in Dublin playhouses in the decades after the *Mahomet* "riot," because this history helped to create the conditions of possibility for the revolutionary drama of the 1780s. As Antonio Gramsci has argued, for collective man to assert himself in history, he must first attain a "cultural-social unity," because it is only through that unity that "a multiplicity of dispersed wills with heterogeneous aims, are welded together with a single aim, on the basis of an equal and common conception of the world."[5] Dublin playhouses in the second half of the century proved such welding sites for the ethnically, religiously, and socially divided subjects of the Irish capital. Between 1754 and 1779 audience members, playwrights, and players used these spaces to challenge English hegemony, and their alternate "cultural-social" imaginings created the "aggregate" subject that drove the imperial subject out of the theater in 1784.

Contrary to what government supporters indicated, the "enraged Multitude" that stormed the stage in 1754 did not fade away in the years after the *Mahomet* disturbance. In a letter from Dublin to London in March 1755, Victor tried to reassure the recently departed Dorset administration that

the half-empty house that greeted another revival of *Mahomet* at the opening of the 1754–55 season was proof of the demise of "that monster party,"
but the details he provides on this performance are hardly reassuring. Victor reveals, for example, that *Mahomet* was back by public demand, having
been called for by a number of anonymous letters, by a petition from several Trinity College students, and by a "unanimous request" from the audience. And he also indicates that despite the poor house this controversial
play was enthusiastically received by "young *patriots* . . . [who] encored
their favorite speech, which they enjoyed."[6] A passage from the Fitzgeralds' correspondence during the same season also suggests that in the post-
Mahomet era the "mob" was continuing to use the playhouse to call political leaders to account, and it indicates that the struggle between the Irish
political elite and the castle was still being waged, though now more subtly,
in this site. In a letter to the countess of Kildare on May 10, 1755, James
Fitzgerald, Earl of Kildare, gives the following account of the mixed reception he received when he and the new viceroy, Lord Hartington, appeared at a recent Smock Alley performance: "There was a clap at the playhouse a night or two ago for the Lord Lieutenant; and after, a very great
one for me, which was *encored*. But somebody said No, for I was seen in the
Primate's [Stone's] coach. I came with the Lord Lieutenant thro' the town
in it, when he landed" (155).[7] Stone, of course, was the leader of the court
party in the previous year's conflict, and by appearing in his coach, this audience member was implying, the earl had compromised his patriot credentials. In a response to that comment five days later, the countess of Kildare also interprets this intervention as an expression of "mob" sentiment,
and from her reply it is clear that she and her husband were no less politically interested in using the playhouse to demonstrate their standing with
the Irish people to the incoming administration. "Your being with Lord
Hartington in the Primate's coach must surprize the mob vastly," she writes,
and then she adds, "I am glad, however, my friends huzza'd for you as well
as him [Hartington]; for I don't see why it shou'd hurt him at all, and dare
say it did not, but it shew'd him what a favourite you are with the people,
which I think there was no harm in."[8]

The Kildare exchange sheds light on the complaints in *A Letter to
Messieurs Victor and Sowdon, Managers of the Theatre-Royal*, a pamphlet
that was also written in 1755. The anonymous author writes to deplore
the "amazing Insolence, the terrible Outrages, Scurrility, and Obscenity,
which every Play-night assail our Ears from the Ruffians in the Upper
Gallery," and he warns the managers that unless they put an end to this

"Barbarism, the "civilized Part of Mankind" would refuse to patronize the theater. This decline, he also suggested, had already begun, as this behavior had prevented "many Persons of Distinction, of both Sexes" from attending the theater.[9] The earl of Kildare's anecdote suggests, however, that it was more likely the upper gallery's bold practice of voicing its political opinion of the members of the ruling class that was keeping many of them away. Like Sheridan, who stayed in London for two years after the *Mahomet* incident, many "Persons of Distinction" had reason to fear the retribution of an increasingly politicized Dublin crowd.

In the next two decades, a socially diverse patriotic crowd also continued successfully to foil every effort by the government and its supporters to regain control over the Irish theater, a resistance that began with the opening of Crow Street in 1758. As early as 1756 there had been talk in Dublin of building a new theater under the management of Spranger Barry, a Dubliner who had already made a name for himself on the London stage, and by winter 1757–58 a large new theater was being built at Crow Street, the money for this enterprise raised mostly by subscription.[10] While the theater was being erected, the proprietors of the Smock Alley and Aungier Street theaters petitioned Parliament to confine theatrical entertainment to the existing united theaters, and in January 1758 Sheridan took up the fight, first petitioning Parliament to buy his lease and theatrical property and then amending his proposal to ask that in the event the new theater was opened, it should be put under his control with one company playing in both houses.[11] The supporters of Crow Street objected fiercely to this proposal. According to Sheridan's comments, this opposition was a continuation of the patriot, anticolonialist opposition of 1753–54. "The new theatre had been built in opposition to me, upon party principles," Sheridan wrote to Samuel Richardson in March 1758, and he goes on to link these "party principles" to a broader anticolonial and anti-British resistance:

> The great spreaders of corruption are not content with the plenteous harvest which they reap in England: they are sowing the seeds of it here, and in all the British colonies. It is amazing to think how warmly some men of high station in London have interested themselves in raising and supporting this new theatre, merely to keep up a factious spirit: they have written many letters, with their own hands, to persons in power here, in favour of the undertaking. There have not been wanting also some good men of high rank, who have written to others in my favour. My Lord Primate is my fast friend; the Speaker of the

House of Commons is inclined to serve me, but I have not as yet such a weight of interest with him, as to be sure of his strenuous endeavours in my cause. Now, my good Mr. Richardson, I think it is in your power effectually to secure him to me, and consequently to ensure success. When he was last in England, he received such civilities from the great and worthy Speaker of the English House of Commons, that three lines from him to Mr. Ponsonby would make him exert his utmost influence.[12]

This letter also reveals that Sheridan's supporters in this struggle came from the antipatriot or court side. The "Primate" who was Sheridan's "fast friend" in this affair was George Stone, the defender of the "English interest" during the Money Bill Dispute of 1754, and the "Speaker" whose influence Sheridan was trying to secure at this time was John Ponsonby, a member of a family that also had been prominent on the court side during the 1753–54 parliamentary conflict.

The failure of Sheridan's proposed bill and the opening of Crow Street, then, marked another symbolic victory for the patriot faction, and by framing the conflict in the familiar patriot language of public "rights" and "liberties," the defenders of Crow Street helped to further redefine the theatrical institution as one that belonged to the citizens of Dublin rather than the castle. The anonymous writer of *The Case of the Stage in Ireland* (1758), for example, argued that the "rights" of "THE BODY COPORATE OF THIS ANCIENT AND MOST LOYAL . . . are so inseparably connected with Mr. Barry's, that he cannot be injured, without doing them a wrong," and this writer went on to argue that by preventing the lord mayor of Dublin from exercising his "indisputed privilege . . . of licencing a theatre for the entertainment of the citizens," Sheridan's bill constituted "an immediate violation and infringement of the rights, liberties and franchises of the body corporate of the city of Dublin."[13] That Dublin's "citizens" had a new sense of ownership over the theater after this dispute is also evident from contemporary descriptions of the decade-long theatrical rivalry that followed the opening of Crow Street. The prologue to George Stayley's farce, *The Rival Theatres: or, a Play house to be let* (1759), reveals that apprentices, newsboys, shoeshine boys, barbers, footmen, and chambermaids were now participating in the debate about the relative merits of Crow Street and Smock Alley, and by agreeing that "Smock-Alley must go down," these humbler members of Dublin society again implicitly aligned themselves with the patriot opposition:

There's scarce a 'Prentice, but neglects his Trade
To talk how This, *and* That, *and* Th'other Actor play'd.
The bawling Boys *have tack'd it to their* News,
And judge of Marplots—*as they clean your* Shoes.
The Politician *throws* Gazettes *away,*
And Prussia *now*—*lies vanquish'd by a* Play.
The prating Barber, *while the Lather dries,*
Looks in your Face,—*and tells* Theatric Lies;
While you as eagerly attend on him,
And laugh, and stare, and cry—shave, shave on, Tim . . .
Behind your Chair, *see list'ning* Footmen *wait,*
Nor hear the hungry' Guest,—demand a Plate.
And mincing Chamber-Maids, *throughout the Town,*
Are all agreed,—Smock-Alley must go down.[14]

Two subsequent attempts to introduce monopoly bills in the 1770s met
with similar resistance. When Sheridan again proposed a theatrical monopoly bill in 1772 with a view (as he put it) to enclosing the theatrical
"common" and establishing the best theater "in the British dominions,"[15]
Crow Street supporters again cast this as an infringement on the citizens'
liberties, both individual and public. They put a notice in the Dublin papers, for example, warning "All Lovers of the DRAMA, and Enemies to
MONOPOLY and OPPRESSION" to suspend their judgment until they
had read an "impartial and candid Account of the present State of the Stage
in this City . . . by which they will clearly see the great Danger of vesting
the Management of their Amusements in one Person," and they petitioned
Parliament in defense of the property of "Spranger Barry, Esq. against the
Invasion intended by Thomas Sheridan, Player."[16] When Robert Jephson,
the master of the horse at Dublin Castle, and the English stage manager
George Colman introduced a similar bill in 1779, opponents also explicitly
linked the issue of theatrical freedom to the larger issue of Irish national
freedom. Castigating the Irish Parliament for even considering a proposal that would "reward the prostitute tools of their [the government's]
wretched measures" by encroaching on the theater, a correspondent of the
Hibernian Journal writes: "With the language of freedom and redress in
their mouths, can they [the Irish lords and Commons] for the pecuniary advantage of a petty scribbler adopt, themselves, the measure of tyranny?
The obscure subaltern [Jephson], who devotes his little talents to support
the infamous measures of a former Administration, should not be an object

of encouragement to a patriotic Parliament, especially when he dares to demand their assent to an act of injustice."[17] A correspondent who signs himself "an Observer" in a letter to the *Freeman's Journal* in January 1780 similarly objects to giving control of the Irish stage to *"half starved courtiers or obsequious players,"* and he warns that a "restraint was mediated and disguised in that *job*, to the freedom of Irish sentiment." "If the Theatre be so much the school of manners, and the instructor of life," "an Observer" writes, "may we not be fearful that our instructions will be *passive obedience* and our school doctrine *non-resistance*, if the regulation of the Theatre is to be subordinate . . . to courtly ordination?"[18]

During the 1770s, patriots used the playhouse itself to articulate their opposition to an administration that had become more transparently imperialistic. During the viceroyalty of Lord Townshend (1767–72), patriot opposition in Parliament led to the rejection of yet another money bill, and that defeat, as Bartlett notes, convinced the British government to place power more squarely in the hands of the castle administration; from Townshend on, Ireland would have a *resident* viceroy who would rule Ireland directly, a change that obviated the need for Irish "undertakers" in the House of Parliament. However, these political reforms also exacerbated the very conflict they were meant to resolve, because they laid bare the political inequity of the Irish-English political relationship. As Bartlett points out, "Ireland's constitutional subordination could scarcely have been made more explicit, and for that reason more capable of being resented."[19] This resentment manifested itself in the outpouring of satirical writing against "Sancho," as Lord Townshend was called by Irish patriots in the early 1770s.[20] But it was also apparent in the letter "Libertus" wrote to the *Hibernian Journal* on January 31–February 3, 1772, in which he urged Dubliners to use the occasion of yet another revival of *Mahomet* to demonstrate their political discontent. Through a cross-referencing that reveals that a countercultural theatrical history was being transmitted from one generation of Irish patriots to the next, Libertus cites the protest of the Irish lords during the *Tamerlane* controversy of 1712, and he uses this example to argue that theatergoers should not be afraid to attend the current revival of *Mahomet*. The play may indeed have been "forbidden by some Message from the Castle, or by the Whisper of some State Tool," he acknowledges, but citing the dissenting lords in 1712, Libertus argues that this prohibition did not constitute a "legal Suppression." Looking back to the more recent "riot" of 1754, he also argues that if ever a protest was justified "it was upon that Occasion; when the *Desire* [of repeating Alcanor's speech] was prompted by a *Love of Patriotism*, and the *Refusal* made through a *servile Fear of offending bad Men in Power*"; and, like his namesake who wrote in 1754 urging "the people" to use the playhouse for political protest, this Libertus urges his fellow countrymen to applaud *Mahomet* even at the risk of displeasing the viceroy and "the Sycophants of the Castle." "Yes, my Countrymen," he writes, "be so loud in your Applause, that your numerous shouts may reach the Castle, and in spite of the Circling Glass appall the Junto of Oppression."[21] Judging from a passing remark in *Roach's New and Complete History of the Stage, from its origin to its present state* (1796), Dublin audiences responded to this call. Referring to the actor West Digges, who appeared in this and subsequent revivals of *Mahomet* during the 1770s and 1780s, Roach writes: "This last gentleman having appeared again in Alcanor in Mahomet, was encored by the spirited Irish, in the very speech which occasioned the riot in Sheridan's time; which he immediately repeated."[22] It was undoubtedly this kind of patriot climate, too, that encouraged the reformer Francis Dobbs to write *The Patriot King; or Irish Chief* for the Dublin stage in 1773. As Wheatley notes, Dobbs uses the character of the Irish king, Ceallachan, to dramatize his concept of a leader who (unlike "Sancho") practices private virtue for the public good, and in the union of Ceallachan and a Danish princess at the end of the play, Dobbs configures his dream of an Ireland where "Catholics and Protestants, Gael and Saxon, would share Irish identity in an independent kingdom."[23]

The continued decline in theatrical attendance by the viceroy and the elite in the 1760s and 1770s also testified to the strength of this patriot opposition in the playhouse. In 1788, in *An Historical View of the Irish Stage*, Hitchcock remarked that "government" nights at the playhouse "continued fashionable till Mr. Barry and Woodward's management [1758–67]," but since that time, he noted, "they have been, in every respect, the very reverse of what they were originally intended for, and at present, few persons of credit resort to the theatres on such nights."[24] Command performances went into a similar decline around this time, if we are to judge by a 1768 letter telling Garrick that Spranger Barry's takings at Crow Street were down "near a thousand pounds" because of "the Lord Lieutenant's not coming once a week, as was the custom."[25] As theater historians have noted, the elite's increased interest in gambling and in private theatricals undoubtedly contributed to this fall-off in attendance.[26] But according to "Observator," a regular columnist in the *Freeman's Journal* in 1777, the decline in attendance by "the Great" was also linked to "the pernicious effects of party on our entertainments in 1753, as well as certain recent instances," and to the audience's general failure to show a "becoming respect" to their "rulers." "Before such things [parties] appeared in our Theatres, they were regularly attended by the Great; There our Viceroys and persons of distinction formed frequent and brilliant circles, consequently business was benefited, and a pleasing unanimity appeared," Observator writes. "But of late, our Chief Governors honour us not in these places with their presence. Tho' the reasons are guessed at, yet the loss to traders is acknowledged. Whatever therefore may be our sentiments of government measures, let us ever pay a becoming respect to our rulers, when they appear in our joyous assemblies."[27] Other reports from the 1770s add weight to Observator's claim that the "Great" were avoiding the playhouse because of their fear of an increasingly politicized theater audience. As is evident from the *Hibernian Journal* of July 1774, even a normally popular member of Parliament like Luke Gardiner could find the theater uncomfortable if he did not do enough to uphold the "Irish" interest to the satisfaction of his Dublin constituents. "Mr. Gardiner," the paper noted, "was severely abused in Crow Street playhouse by the People in the Galleries, on account, it is supposed of his not taking an active part against the bill (which passed the Commons here, and was thrown out by the Privy Council on the other side) respecting the New Custom House."[28]

As the "Great" retreated in the face of such pressure, Dublin's lower socioeconomic orders increasingly stepped into their place, and their ascendancy in the 1770s and 1780s also helped to accelerate the changes that were taking place in the theater, making it a more representative and a more Irish space. In a letter to the *Freeman's Journal* in March 1778, an irritated theatergoer asked the manager for extra guards on an upcoming government night as prospective audience members "have every reason in the world to apprehend the mob may wish to intrude into the boxes, to shake hands with their party-coloured brethren (sweeps, butchers, sailors, etc) who the papers announce are to honour *that* part of the house with their company on the above night."[29] By 1782, it is clear, these "party-coloured brethren" were a regular presence in the boxes. A disgusted correspondent to the *Hibernian Journal* that year writes: "The Boxes which were wont formerly to be the appropriated and distinguished circle for the real Nobility and Gentry are now become the most heterogenous hemisphere of the house. Such a hodge-podge, higgledy-piggledy mass never occurred, I am certain, in any human display of former times. Francis Street, Bride's Alley, Potatoe Row, and all the scriveners' offices in town, vomit forth their sons and daughters, bedizened to outshine, in this bright meridian, the too-long unrivalled lustre of their *equals* in Merrion Square."[30] By the 1780s, moreover, this " hodge-podge, higgledy-piggledy mass," like the Dublin "mob" in general, would have been predominantly Catholic, and it is the ascendancy of the lower-class Irish Catholic subject that Samuel Whyte both acknowledges and deplores when he creates the figure of "Paddy" in his 1779 poem *The Theatre*.[31] Paddy, the newsboy who translates the theatrical advertisements to his illiterate working-class companions in the following street scene, is a figure for the working-class Irish Catholic theatergoer who was now beginning to exert his pressure on the stage and the players.

> With more address our Stagers buy esteem,
> And all our prints with their perfections teem.
> Where rang'd sedans each morning line the street,
> Paddy, a second Stagyrite! you meet,
> With News in hand, perch'd on his half-drawn pole,
> The seeds of learning pregnant in his soul,
> As round him his unletter'd comrades stand,
> Spelling the play-puffs to the listening band:
> Shoeboys and scavengers their work suspend,
> And shrill-voiced sweeps their rambles, to attend.
> Ladies may wait, and angry footmen call,
> They see not, hear not, or they curse them all.
> Wondrous, O Thespians! must be your renoun,
> In sweat, foot, dirt, thus bandied thro' the town!
> Who can dispute, when oracles so pure
> Announce perfection, and success ensure?[32]

But Paddy, "perch'd on his half-drawn pole" above the listening crowd, is not just an avid theatergoer but also a kind of performer himself, and it is the productive effect of this kind of player's performance that must also be taken into account when considering the changed nature of the theater in the post-1754 period. Whyte himself obviously intended his readers to view Paddy's theatrical "spell" in wholly negative terms; the entire cultural, social, and economic order, he implies, is disrupted (work is abandoned and "Ladies" are forced to "wait") when this kind of unorthodox subject dares to perform his street theater. Another way of reading this scene is to say that Paddy is playing the role of translator in a divided world—that he is, in effect, acting to bridge the gap between literate and oral culture, between the world of the Irish elite and the world of the common Irish people. As we will see through a brief examination of their performances, the "Paddies" who dominated the Dublin stage in the second half of the century played such a mediating role; they, no less than the patriot crowd in the audience, laid the ground for the revolutionary drama of the 1780s.

◆◆◆

Charles Macklin is the first case in point. As an Irish Catholic who was born on a small farm in northern Ireland but who had spent some of his teenage years as a "badge-man," or servant, at Trinity College in Dublin,[33] Macklin had a familiarity with both Irish Catholic popular and Irish Protestant patriot culture. The special epilogue that he wrote for the Dublin premier of his two-act farce, *Love a la mode*, in 1761 reflected this dual perspective. In this epilogue Macklin launched a sardonic attack on a "*Britannia*" that would mock the Irish for their speech while overlooking the errors of its own Cockney speakers, and in increasingly nationalist tones, he urged "the Sons of Ireland" to resist the cultural imposition of their arrogant neighbor (I cite extracts from this epilogue at some length because to my knowledge this epilogue has not been reprinted since it appeared in the *Dublin Magazine* in 1762):

> *Hibernia* too, in this politer age,
> Has long been only laugh'd at on the stage:
> Her harmless follies have been painted forth,
> Without the smallest mention of her worth;
> And every genius would his wit employ,
> To joke with *Paddy*, or to banter *Joy*:
> Her very *accent* swell'd the comic song,
> And every phrase was nationally wrong.
> As if *Britannia* could herself conceal,
> Her thoughtless slips of *winegar* and *weal*.
> For *breakfastis* had ne'er prepar'd the *toastis*,
> Or bruis'd her *these here fistis* with the *postis*.
> Ye sons of Ireland, whersoe'er ye sit,
> For once take off the manacles from wit;
> And let these lords of beef and pudding know,

That merit springs in *every* soil below.
Some native spark of heav'nly fire confest,
Glows to divine within the *Indian's* breast,
Swells unconfin'd from Britain to the Pole,
Expands, exalts, and dignifies the soul . . .

For once here *Irish* excellence display'd is,
That they can *Love*—they leave it to the ladies;
That they can *Fight*, each honest Briton knows,
And bravely too—they leave it to their foes.
Fair *Science* long has led them to explore,
The deep researches of her mystic store;
Their *genius* too impartial truth declares,
If BACON'S yours, an USSHER has been theirs;
And SWIFT or STEELE the sacred beam secures,
Though deathless POPE and ADDISON were yours.
Then, nobly just, O ratify their claim,
The equal heirs of liberty and fame:
Their warmest hopes no highter can ascend,
Then calling *Britain*—Sister—Guardian—Friend.[34]

On one level, this call to resist British linguistic imperialism was directed at those "Sons of Ireland" of native Irish descent, those "Paddies" and "Joys," who heard their accent ridiculed almost every time they attended an English comedy at the theater;[35] and if Macklin was able to identify with these audience members, it was undoubtedly because as a struggling young actor in provincial English theaters he had personally experienced the pain of being laughed at for his accent. According to James Thomas Kirkman, when Macklin played the role of Friar Lawrence for a company in Bristol, he was told by the manager "that if he could cut three or four inches more of the brogue from his tongue, he could speak the part well," and this prejudice persisted even after the young Macklin took six months of elocution lessons. "With the judicious his Irish accent was an objection which they allowed his acting, in a great degree, counterbalanced," Kirkman writes. "[W]ith the lower order, his being an Irishman was an objection, however admirably he might act."[36] By the middle of the century, however, Irish Protestants were also being affected by this kind of linguistic prejudice, and thus Macklin also addresses these other "Sons of Ireland" in this epilogue.

As David Hayton notes, the stereotype of the blustering Irish army officer and the fortune-hunting Irish blade that appeared in so many eighteenth-century English comedies began to gather within its scope not only the Catholic gentlemen of Ireland but also the Irish Protestant gentry, and this new Irish gentleman stereotype had many of the linguistic characteristics of the humbler native Irishman. "Verbal eccentricities," Hayton writes, "could drop from gentlemen as well as peasants: ignorance could be as amusing in a squire as a bogtrotter, if not more so."[37] As writers in the emergent field of elocution began to codify the rules for "proper" English pronunciation, even the less accented speech of the Irish Protestant gentry was increasingly stigmatized and deemed aberrant. In his 1762 *Course of Lectures on Elocution*, for example, Thomas Sheridan wrote that all dialects except the court dialect were "sure marks either of a provincial, rustic, pedantic, or mechanic education; and therefore have some degree of disgrace annexed to them," and he specifically identified the "idiom" of "Irish gentlemen" (a phrase that cuts across religious lines) as a dialect that needed correction.[38] To many Irish Protestants, British linguistic imperialism was as repugnant as political and economic imperialism, and by midcentury some of them were beginning to express their repugnance with that same mixture of resentment and Irish pride that characterized Irish Protestant nationalism. The anonymous author of *An Essay on the Antient and Modern State of Ireland* (1760), for example, roundly denounced Sheridan for his statement that Ireland had no great orators,[39] and he also condemned those "dramatick Scriblers, (probably of our own degenerate Growth)" who denigrate Irish accents. "I am at a Loss," this author writes, "to know why a Man should become a standing Jest for his Ignorance in an alien Tongue, almost the constant Fate of our Countrymen in *Britain,* where, whoever is not smartly expert in the *English* Language, is immediately denominated a *Teague,* a *Paddy,* or I know not what, in the Stile of Derision."[40] This resentment was linked to what an English visitor to Dublin in 1764 derisively terms "*Hibernian importance*" or "*Dublin assurance,*" a growing pride in Irishness that extended to matters of language. "The inhabitants of Dublin have the ridiculous vanity of pretending to speak better English than those of London," this writer notes with obvious incredulity in a pamphlet titled *Hibernia Curiosa,* and he goes on to say that "an Englishman can hardly spend a day in Dublin, if he much frequents the coffee-houses without finding this the topic of conversations somewhere, in one or other of them, the superiority of the Dublin English to that of London."[41]

Macklin also made an explicit appeal to this sense of "*Hibernian impor-tance*" or "*Dublin assurance*" in his Irish Protestant listeners. Even as he made his argument for the "merit" of the indigenous Irish and indeed all other non-British peoples—"Some native spark of heav'nly fire confest . . . Swells unconfin'd from Britain to the Pole"—he celebrated the "*Irish* excel-lence" of Protestant political and cultural leaders like Ussher, Swift, and Steele, and in so doing, he also implicitly positioned his call to "take off the manacles from wit" within an Irish Protestant national tradition. Given the Irish reaction to his first dramatic production in Ireland, it is clear that this double-edged discourse worked. Soon after the first performance of *Love à La Mode*, Macklin wrote to an English friend that the play was "in much higher reputation here than ever it was in London," and later in the same season he wrote, "Sans puff, the stream is with us. Love à la mode is the rage."[42] It was undoubtedly this sense that "the stream" was with him that inspired him to repeat his strategy and his linguistic theme in the first play he wrote for the Irish stage, *The True-born Irishman or the Irish Fine Lady* (1762). In this farce Macklin again weds an Irish Protestant to a na-tive Irish form of nationalism, and he makes this play's native Irishman (a role he played himself) the spokesman for a new Irish-English hybrid form of political and linguistic community.

The plot of *The True-born Irishman or the Irish Fine Lady* revolves around the rivalry between the Irish tenant farmer, Murrogh O'Dogherty, and Count Mushroom, the London agent of O'Dogherty's absentee En-glish landlord; the count is attempting to backmail O'Dogherty's wife into becoming his lover in return for renewing O'Dogherty's expiring leases, and O'Dogherty is attempting to foil this plot and secure his wife and his lands. At one level this romantic and economic rivalry functions as an al-legory of the ongoing castle-patriot struggle, and indeed it was read as such in its own day. In his *Memoirs of Charles Macklin*, W. Cooke states that contemporary Dublin audiences believed the satire on Count Mush-room was an attack on Gerard Hamilton (also called "Single Speech Hamilton"), the secretary to the earl of Halifax, lord lieutenant of Ireland, and that the "opposition courted him [Macklin] for caricaturing a person, who from his office, generally becomes obnoxious to them."[43] Cooke does not mention it, but the patriot opposition also had a particular reason for being pleased with this caricature as it was generally believed that Single Speech Hamilton had used his legendary eloquence to persuade Irish M. P.'s to pass the government's latest money in November 1761.[44] O'Dogherty's critique of his wife's "London vertigo,"[45] which leaves her vulnerable to Count Mushroom, then, functions as a critique of an Anglophile ruling elite that was so easily seduced by this kind of English eloquence, and the Irishman's demand that the "Irish Fine Lady" forgo her "London English" in favor of "good, plain, old Irish English" (111) functions as a demand that the ruling elite see through this English rhetoric and remember their patriotic duty to Ireland. It is a request, too, that parallels the request made by Jonathan Swift and other patriots that the "Ladies" forgo foreign finery and put on plain Irish "stuff," though the terrain is now linguistic and cultural rather than economic.

> O'Dogherty. And as to yourself, my dear Nancy, I hope I shall never have any more of your London English; none of your this here's, your that there's, your winegars, your weals, your vindors, your toastesses, and your stone postesses; but let me have our own good, plain, old Irish English, which I insist is better than all the English English that ever coquets and coxcombs brought into the land. (111)

Ironically, in the context of 1762 O'Dogherty's overt denunciation of parliamentary patriotism in the first act would also have worked to confirm his status as a true patriot. In 1756, after Boyle and other leaders of the Money Bill opposition sold out to the government in return for places and titles, there was widespread popular disillusionment with parliamentary patriotism (Boyle's effigy, for example, was hung in public by a "mob" of a thousand).[46] When O'Dogherty suggests that his "poor country" is better served by "an honest quiet country gentleman who . . . establishes manufactories, or that contrives employment for the idle and industrious," than by "courtiers, and patriots, and politicians" (87), then, he distances himself from these false patriots while also expressing his commitment to an earlier Swiftean kind of economic patriotism.

However, as a tenant farmer of native Irish descent whose social and economic survival is dependent on working out a new lease with an absentee English landlord, O'Dogherty is also a figure for the Catholic (or convert) middleman or big tenant farmer, and it is the potential alliance between this kind of subject and the patriot subject that is also suggested by the action and dialogue of this play. For O'Dogherty's attack on his rival, it is clear, Macklin draws not only on a patriot tradition but also on the native Irish popular tradition of resistance that would have been part of the playwright's own heritage. In the following exchange, for example, in which O'Dogherty ironically thanks Count Mushroom for honoring the Irish people with his intention to settle among them, the "True-born Irishman" replays, to some extent, the conflict between the "Irish" and "English Chieftain" in the traditional folk drama *Sir Sopin, or the Knight of Straw;* here as in the original folk play, the upstart representative of the English landlord class (Mushroom's father was a London pawnbroker [88]) is transformed into a figure of ridicule, and the spokesman for the native Irish gentry emerges triumphant through his superior show of wit:

COUNSELLOR: Upon my word, sir, the people of Ireland are much obliged to you for your helter skelter, rantum scantum portrait of them.

O'DOGHERTY: Indeed and that we are: and so you like us mightily.

MUSHROOM: I do upon honour, and I believe I shall marry one of your women here, grow domestic, and settle among you.

O'DOGHERTY: Orra but will you do us the honour?

MUSHROOM: I really intend it.

O'DOGHERTY: Faith then you will be a great honour to us, and you will find a great many relations here, count: for we have a large crop of the Mushrooms in this here country. (92)

When Macklin has O'Dogherty's brother-in-law, Counsellor Hamilton, join with this "True-born Irishman" in mocking the new "mushroom" gentry, however, he also rewrites the *Sir Sopin* script in a way that is politically significant for Irish nationalism. The Hamiltons, as J. O. Bartley points out in his textual note on Counsellor Hamilton, were Scottish planters who had come to Northern Ireland during James I's plantation of Ulster, and this history should have put Counsellor Hamilton on the side of Count Mushroom.[47] In this scene, however, the descendant of the settler joins with the descendant of the Irish native in an attempt to defeat the rapacious British metropolitan subject, a dramatic reconfiguration that provides a model for a different kind of Irish political subject and a different kind of united Irish resistance.

Mrs. Diggerty's decision at the end of the play to abandon her English name in favor of her husband's "fine sounding Milesian name" (111–12) also prefigures this kind of Irish unification, though to see the generative potential of her act, it is also necessary to understand the tensions over names in Ireland at this time. As noted in earlier chapters, Irish Protestant writers in the first half of the century had deemed that the mere mention of an Irish-sounding name was sufficient to prove the disloyalty and immorality of its bearer. "Sound but their Names," Lucas had written of the Kelly faction in 1747, "their very Names to *Protestant* Ears, sound *Rebellion, Treachery, Murder, Rapine, Riot, Debauchery,* and every Vice that can deform human Nature."[48] To divest themselves of these negative associations and to allay Protestant fears about their political intentions, many native Irish, including Macklin and his two actor-playwright friends, John O'Keeffe and Robert Owenson, had anglicized or suppressed the "O's" and "Macs" in their names.[49] And according to the daughter of Robert Owenson, Lady Morgan, it was not until the Catholic emancipation bill had passed that such Irish gentlemen could resume "that suspicious cognomen . . . without fear of being suspected to have any intention to resume the estates or principalities along with them."[50] An anecdote that Kirkman tells about an Irish friend who came to Macklin's London lodging looking for "young Charley Mac-Laughlin" makes it clear, however, that many of these same Irish gentlemen secretly held on to their Irish names among their Irish acquaintances. Macklin, according to his biographer, told his confused landlady that "that fine mouthful of a word [McLoughlin] was the *true Irish* for *Macklin*," and he added, "[I]f any of [his] countrymen called here, they would inquire after me by the name of McLaughlin."[51] And from a poem that John O'Keeffe wrote after an Englishwoman insisted on calling him "Keeffe" rather than "O'Keeffe," it is also clear that many of these "true Irish" deeply resented the loss of their Irish names and longed for the day when they could openly resume their "O's" and "Macs." The first and last verses of O'Keeffe's long poem give its flavor:

> You say not mine the letter O,
> Though to my name I add it,
> Where Shannon glides, and shamrocks grow,
> My ancestors all had it

> Biography is apt to err,
> Why credit such narration?
> Historic truths if you prefer
> Accept true information.

As many had, St. Patrick knows,
Of land, lost snug possessions,
The Irish wisely dropp'd their O's,
That mark'd them old Milesians. . . .

Yet Bryen, Leary, Kelly, Toole,
Keeffe, Callaghan, Byrne, Connor;
As party feuds began to cool,
Soon reassum'd this honour.

To ancient names their O's return,
Their right admits no query,
O'Keeffe, O'Bryen, and O'Byrne,
O'Kelly, and O'Leary.

Of my poor O, I'm full as proud
As Knights of Stars and banners;
Pray grant it me, as you're endow'd
With kindness, sense, and manners.[52]

Such sentiments were also common in the Gaelic literature of the day, though they were generally voiced there in more strident and more overtly political tones. From the seventeenth century on, Irish poets used roll calls of Gaelic names to evoke the Irish people who would rise up and overthrow the Saxon yoke,[53] and in verses like the following from the poet Owen Roe O'Sullivan they manifested their contempt for the new order by ridiculing and cursing settler names:

Lysight, Leader, Clayton, Crompton *is* Coote,
Ivers, Deamer, Bateman, Bagwell *is* Brooks,
Ryder, Taylor, Manor, Marrock *is* Moore,
Is go bhfaiceam-na traochta ag tréin-shliocht Chaisil na búir.

"*Is*" in the above lines means "and," and the last line can be translated "And may we see the boors routed by the mighty descendants of Cashel."[54]

The speech that O'Dogherty gives after his wife has agreed to revive his old Irish name finds its meaning from this literature and culture of the Irish dispossessed. Like the Gaelic poets of the period, the "True-born

Irishman" uses a list of Irish names as a metonym for the displaced native Irish people, and like them, too, he ridicules the names of the "upstarts and foreigners, buddoughs [churls] and sassanoughs [Englishmen]" who have robbed his people of their names and land:

> Ogh, that's right, Nancy—O'Dogherty for ever—O'Dogherty!— there's a sound for you—why they have not such a name in all England as O'Dogherty—nor as any of our fine sounding Milesian names—what are your Jones and your Stones, your Rice and your Price, your Heads and your Foots, and your Wills, and Hills and Mills, and Sands, and a parcel of little pimping names that a man would not pick out of the street, compared to the O'Donovans, O'Callaghans, O'Sullivans, O'Brallaghans, O'Shaghnesses, O'Flahertys, Gallaghers, and O'Dogherty's—Ogh, they have courage in the very sound of them, for they come out of the mouth like a storm; and are as old and as stout as the oak at the bottom of the bog of Allen, which was there before the flood—and though they have been dispossessed by upstarts and foreigners, buddoughs and sassanoughs, yet I hope they will flourish in the Island of Saints, while grass grows or water runs. (111–12)

But here, too, Macklin adds a new political twist to this traditional Irish motif when he makes the restoration of O'Dogherty's name and honor contingent on Nancy Diggerty's consent (just before the above speech, he asks her to address him only by his Irish name and she agrees). The native Irishman's dream of social, economic, and political restoration is dependent on the cooperation of the descendant of the settler, Nancy's involvement suggests, and the category of "buddoughs" and "sassanoughs" is consequently redefined to encompass only "upstarts and foreigners" from the English metropolitan center. This new kind of Irish imagined community is also briefly realized on the stage when everyone from the native Irish servant girl (Katty Farrel) to Lady Kinnegad and her aristocratic friends join with the O'Doghertys in mocking Count Mushroom in this last scene (the count is discovered dressed in women's clothes, cowering in a portmanteau). Ireland's ethnic and religious divide has been bridged, this ending suggests. If in the past Ireland was an "Injured Lady," now, as the last line of the play states, "*The fine Irish Lady's mended*" (121).

The Dublin audience's positive reaction to *The True-born Irishman* suggests that there was a basis in reality for this dramatic imagining of a new kind of "mended," intercultural Irish community. Despite its overt nationalism, the play was greeted with "thunders of applause" when it was first performed, causing at least one shocked observer to charge the whole audience with being closet Jacobites. In June 1762 the theater critic for Exshaw's *Gentleman's and London Magazine* wrote of the play: "Yet while we pay the tribute to merit, shall candour be sacrificed to indiscriminate panegyric, and is not something due to truth and impartiality? We must say some things there are that gave offence . . . to decency; but strange to say! they were received with thunders of applause. The men clapped, the women tittered, and enjoyed the joke to the utmost, they swallowed it with avidity, and not even covering their faces, they shewed their affection for the BAD OLD CAUSE."[55] The play's differing fate on the London and Dublin stages in the years after this performance highlights the growing difference between theatrical audiences in the two capitals in the second half of the eighteenth century. Macklin altered *The True-born Irishman* in a number of minor ways in an attempt to make it palatable for an English audience, but when he brought it to London in 1767, as his friend John O'Keeffe noted dryly, "John Bull, pit, box, and gallery, said No!"[56] The reaction to the play was so negative that Macklin felt it necessary to go before the audience and personally apologize for his work, and after that disastrous first night the piece was withdrawn.[57] Nevertheless, *The True-born Irishman* continued to be enormously popular with Irish audiences throughout the rest of the century, a difference in reception that one writer attributed to differences in local and national taste. *The True-born Irishman,* an anonymous commentator wrote in 1773, "ceases to be represented in this kingdom, though acted with great success in Ireland: nor is it to be wondered at, why it should not be palatable to an English audience; for though it abounds with great humour and observation, the ridicule is *local,* and the dialogue, for the most part, *national.*"[58]

John O'Keeffe, who came from the same social and cultural background as Macklin and who played with Macklin on at least one occasion in his *True-born Irishman,*[59] was no less adept at incorporating local humor as well as Irish dialogue and music into his dramatic creations, and through his syncretic entertainments he also worked to mend the divisions in Irish society. O'Keeffe (or Keeffe as he was then billed) made his acting debut at Crow Street in 1767, and from then until 1781 he played in Dublin theaters and in various regional theaters around the country.[60] During his time as an actor and strolling player, he also wrote a number of comic pieces that drew on popular culture and local occurrences for their inspiration and material. He noted in his *Recollections,* for example, that during his first years at Crow Street, he wrote a play about the "franchises," the spectacular street pageant put on each year by Dublin's guilds, and he also describes how he hired a boat in Cobh to paint an India ship then docking in Cork harbor for a scene in *The India Ship,* a play (not extant) he wrote for the Cork stage.[61] *Tony Lumpkin's Rambles through Dublin,* which the *Hibernian Magazine* later described as "a kind of histrionic interlocution" and as O'Keeffe's "chief d'oeuvre in dramatic writing in Ireland,"[62] was also clearly a vehicle for introducing local humor, places, and events. It was first presented, starring O'Keeffe himself, as *Tony Lumpkin's Rambles through Cork* in Cork in 1773 and then later on the Dublin stage as *Tony Lumpkin's Frolics Thro' Dublin . . . With a humorous and descriptive View of the Streets, Theatres, Coffee-Houses, public Buildings, etc.*[63]

These locally inflected pieces allowed O'Keeffe to bring native artists and traditional Irish culture onto the stage, interventions that were never politically insignificant. According to his own account, O'Keeffe persuaded the "famous Irish piper" Macdonnel to play some of Carolan's tunes in one of the early pieces he wrote for the Cork stage, and his description suggests that he arranged this performance to add dignity and importance to the piper and his music. "[T]he curtain went up," O"Keeffe wrote, "and discovered him [Macdonnel] sitting alone, in his own dress; he played, and charmed everyone." This respectful treatment would have had a particularly therapeutic social effect at this time, because, as O'Keeffe tells us, this famous piper had recently suffered public humiliation in the house of one of the local Protestant gentry (Macdonnel had been hired to play at a dinner party, but, finding that his chair had been put on a landing outside the dining room, he exited the house in a rage).[64] By showcasing the piper in his entertainment, O'Keeffe worked to heal this rift in the Cork community and restore dignity to Gaelic culture and the Gaelic artist. The Irish cultural elements that O'Keeffe wove through his wife's benefit performance at Crow Street in Dublin on April 15, 1777, were no less politically significant. The mainpiece on that occasion was Hugh Kelly's *False Delicacy,* a play that had recently proved a hit on the London stage. But it was followed by *Tony Lumpkin's Frolicks through Dublin, Written and to be spoken by Mr. O'Keeffe, With Humourous Accidents, Whimsical Adventures, and Comic Observations on Manners and Things,* and by O'Keeffe's new comedy, *The Shamroch; or St. Patrick's Day,* a piece, the author later noted, that included the "fine Irish airs of Carolan" as well as "Irish characters and customs, pipers, and fairies, foot-ball players, and gay hurlers."[65] As is evident from the description of the pageant that rounded out the evening, such inclusions could work to subvert dominant paradigms of British hegemony while gesturing simultaneously at alternate, more egalitarian modes of social and political being:

> After the farce will be exhibited a grand emblematical, Festive, Choral, Procession and Pageant: Consisting of Kings of Leinster, Munster and Connaught; Strongbow, Earl of Pembroke; De Courcy, Baron of Kinsale; Sitric, King of the Danes; Hibernia, in a Triumphal Carr; each attended with their respective Arms, Achievements, Ensigns and Appendages; Druids, Bards, Games, Banshees, Leporehauns, Hibernians in their original and present State, Peace, Fame, Hospitality, Industry, Etc. Etc. Etc.
>
> To conclude with a song by Carolan, the ancient Irish Bard, and Grand Chorus by all the Characters. Carolan Mr. Owenson.[66]

By placing native Irish kings, Anglo-Normans, Danes, and "Hibernians" (the name Irish Protestant patriots often used for themselves) on an equal footing, this "grand emblematical . . . Pageant" created an image of a society that was inclusive and intercultural, and its final musical number would have worked to reinforce this image. The new imagined community of Ireland, the "Grand Chorus by all the Characters" would have suggested, is a polyvocal one, where people of all backgrounds have a voice. As Mary Helen Thuente points out, there are interesting parallels between this theatrical spectacle and the "Grand Procession" that occurred during the Belfast Harp Festival of 1792; during that celebration, hundreds of United Irishmen and Volunteers paraded behind a banner of Hibernia in a triumphal car, creating a similar spectacle of a new "united Irish" nation.[67]

The "Mr. Owenson" who played "Carolan" in the above pageant similarly expanded cultural boundaries through his Irish-inflected reworking of the debased stage Irishman role. In 1802 *The Thespian Dictionary* reported that Owenson "chiefly supported the Irish characters, in which he was a favourite, particularly with the galleries," but it also added that "his representation of them [the Irish characters] was "*high-coloured*, and would therefore have been too *coarse* for an English audience."[68] On occasion, Owenson's performances could also be too "high-coloured" for

Anglophile Irish theatergoers as is clear from the remarks the critic for the *Freeman's Journal* made on Owenson's first performance on the Irish stage in 1776. While praising the actor's "spirit," his "fine figure," and his "brogue"—he was playing the role of Major O'Flaherty in Richard Cumberland's *The West Indian*—the critic found fault with Owenson for abruptly introducing a song from an opera by a local Dublin author (McDermott's *The Milesian*) into the play and for lacing his dialogue with phrases from his native Irish: "The Gentleman will forgive me, if I hint, that although it is perfectly natural in a man when his mind is strongly agitated, to express his overflowing in his own *native* language, even when talking to people in an acquired one, yet his uttering phrases in *Irish* so *very* frequently, seemed rather a local compliment, than a judicious use of them; and might by some be construed into a clap-trap. Let him ask himself, would he use so many, if performing the same character in England? The answer will justify this remark."[69] The mixed reaction to Owenson's Major O'Flaherty—while this newspaper critic obviously does not like it, O'Keeffe reports that it was "a great favorite"[70]—may also have been owing to a Jacobite subtext in Owenson's performance of this role. W. A. Donaldson, writing some thirty years after the actor's death, remarks that Owenson's O'Flaherty was "a rich specimen of the Irish officer of the old school—witty, bold, and chivalrous," and he reveals that the actor often sang "the ancient pathetic melody of 'Drimindhua Deelish'" in this role.[71] As noted in chapter 3, "Drimindhua Deelish" ("Drimin Duh") was an allegorical Jacobite song, and this song, coupled with the Irish officer's Gaelic interpolations and his history of foreign service, would have associated O'Flaherty with the "wild geese," the Irish exiles in service overseas whose longed-for triumphant return was so frequently the subject of Jacobite poetry.[72] It is also clear that this Jacobite subtext continued to be legible to Dublin theatergoers; as W. J. Fitzpatrick reports, when the audience became "strongly anti-Irish and Orange in their feelings" in the last decade of the century, Owenson was hissed off the Dublin stage for singing this song.[73]

For the most part, however, Owenson succeeded in pleasing Irish theatergoers with his improvisations and Irish interpolations during the 1770s and 1780s, and this success can be attributed to his familiarity with both the top and the bottom of Irish society. In his everyday life Owenson retained his connection with the political and cultural subculture of his native Connaught, keeping an open house for pipers, storytellers, and the large stream of poor relatives and friends who came to Dublin looking for jobs.[74] But he was also a guest in the homes of the rich and powerful, and by all accounts, he had the accomplishments to fit equally into that company; the obituary that appeared in the *Freeman's Journal* of May 28, 1812, reported that "Owenson's liberal education, polished manners, and exquisite humour rendered him a welcome guest at the first tables."[75] This ability to bridge worlds was also apparent in his dramatic art, judging from the description of how he played Philim O'Flaherty in George Colman's prelude *New Brooms* (another one of his acclaimed roles).[76] If played according to script, the role of Philim O'Flaherty would have worked, like the prototypical Teague, to justify the existing unequal distribution of power between native Irish and English subject. When Philim is asked, for example, whether he has "a voice" that would enable him to go on the English stage (this is Philim's expressed ambition), the Irishman replies confidently that he has. But his linguistic and cultural incompetence are clearly meant to demonstrate the foolishness of his desire to enter the theatrical or, by implication, any public arena. Philim says, "Voice! oh, by my sowle, voice enough to be heard across the channel, from the Gate or the Hid, to ould Dublin:— and then I can sing, *Arrah my Judy, Arrah my Judy!* and the Irish howl!— *Hubbub-o-boo!* (*howling*)—oh, it would do your heart good to hear it."[77] When Owenson played the role of Philim at Crow Street for the first time on May 2, 1777, he undermined this debased stereotype by again giving a masterful performance of an Irish song, and this time he drew on an Irish Protestant patriot tradition as well as the native Irish literary and musical tradition. In place of *Arrah my Judy* and "howling," Fitzpatrick reports that he sang "some favourite Italian and Irish songs, particularly Carolan's 'Receipt for Drinking' in Irish, and 'Ple Raca na Ruarka' in English and Irish, the Irish by Carolan, the translation by Dean Swift."[78] Like the newsboy Paddy in Whyte's poem, it could be argued, Owenson gave a performance that mediated between Irish national traditions and that served to "announce" (as Paddy did) a new intercultural mode of political being.

❖❖❖

By the time Volunteer associations first sprang up all around Ireland in fall 1778, then, the Dublin stage was ripe for a revolutionary "aggregate" drama, and the Volunteers themselves provided the immediate script for such a drama through their political theater inside and outside the playhouse. The Volunteer movement, at first view, might seem a very unlikely breeding ground for revolution. The ostensible purpose of the Volunteers was to defend Ireland from domestic and foreign enemies in the wake of the withdrawal of the regular militia during the American war, and the commanders of Volunteer corps were drawn mainly from the Protestant landowning class that formed the backbone of the existing political establishment.[79] In limited numbers, however, Catholics and men from a lower socioeconomic class began participating in these associations, and as contemporary observers noted, this encounter between Irishmen from different class and religious backgrounds began to generate a new kind of political consciousness. Sir Jonah Barrington, for example, writes that "the familiar association of all ranks, which the nature of their new military connections necessarily occasioned, every day lessened that wide distinction, which had hitherto separated the higher and lower orders of society," and he adds that by 1782 "[p]olitical subjects [had become] topics of regular organized discussion in every district in Ireland and amongst every class and description of its population. They paraded as soldiers and they debated as citizens."[80] A Volunteer marching song from 1782 makes the same point. The beating drum of the Volunteers and a shared history of economic and political oppression under England's rule, this song suggests, was bringing "a whole nation" together:

> Was she not a fool
> When she took off our wool,
> To leave us so much of the
>   Leather, the leather
> It ne'er entered her pate,
> That a sheepskin well beat
> Would draw a whole nation
>   Together, together.[81]

When Catholics and the "lower orders of society" paraded as Volunteers, they also created a visual image of this wider "nation," since, as Nancy Curtin points out, citizenship in the eighteenth century was in part defined by the right to bear arms.[82] By allowing these marginalized groups to carry arms in their military parades, the Volunteers implicitly redefined the boundaries of the political nation.

In more direct ways, too, Volunteer street theater often challenged the existing power structure. On November 4, 1779, for example, while the issue of free trade was being debated in Parliament, the Volunteer corps from the city and county of Dublin gathered in large numbers on

College Green and discharged their guns around the statue of King William, which had been decorated on that occasion by signs that read "Relief to Ireland," "The Volunteers of Ireland: Motto—Quinquaginta mille juncti, parati pro patria mori," "A short Money Bill—A Free-Trade—or else!!!" and "The Glorious Revolution" (fig. 6).[83] The Volunteers thereby disengaged the constitutional nationalist subtext that, I have argued, was always implicit in Irish Williamite celebrations, transforming this ritual into an overt assertion of Irish social and economic liberty. The *Freemen's Journal* also stressed the difference in the military overtones of this Williamite celebration. At previous parades, the paper notes, the military on the scene had been "mercenaries," who were "ill-calculated to convey to . . . enthusiasts of liberty a pleasing recollection of the constitutional blessings of the *glorious Revolution*." On this occasion, however, "the scene was changed—a body of a thousand citizens, men of various professions, ranks and fortunes, appeared under arms, perfectly disciplined, and appointed in all respects," and when James Fitzgerald, the duke of Leinster and commander of the Dublin corps, threw up his hat and shouted huzza, "there was not a covered head in the multitude; the cheers, resounded from street to street, through the whole city, gathering strength in progress." If we are to credit this account, the Catholic population also joined in the celebration: "In the evening, a thing never done on the 4th of November, the whole city was illuminated; and it was observable that all distinctions of religion and prejudice were suspended. The ancient Jacobite, who found hithertofore in William's partiality towards England with regard to this country, a patriotic mask for his political antipathy, was content to yield on this occasion, comforting himself that the King, upon this day, was made to recant. In short, there was never such harmony and delight."[84] Even as it stresses domestic harmony, however, this paper reveals that the people showed "rude disapprobation" of the garrison they met after the parade, a signal of the public's growing animosity toward government and its forces. And in the next four years, this animosity was articulated in the increasingly revolutionary placards on the Williamite monument. On November 4, 1782, the inscriptions around the statue read, "The Volunteers of Ireland by persevering will overthrow the Fencible Scheme, procure an unequivocal Bill of Rights, and effectually establish the Freedom of their Country," and on November 4, 1783, the placards stated starkly, "The Volunteers of Ireland, having overturned the cadaverous simple Repeal, must now effectuate an equal Representation of the People."[85]

Figure 6. *The Dublin Volunteers in College Green*. Painted by Francis Wheatley. Reproduction courtesy of the National Gallery of Ireland.

The Volunteer drama that occurred in Dublin playhouses (Smock Alley, Crow Street, Fishamble Street, Capel Street) between 1779 and 1784 was an extension of this street theater. At the benefit performance for the "Sick Poor of the Manufacturing Parishes of the City of Dublin" at Crow Street on December 10, 1779, for example, the performance was *King Lear*, but all the supporting roles were played by "Gentlemen Volunteers" and the highlight of the evening's entertainment was clearly the preplay show staged by the Dublin corps of Volunteers to honor their commander, the duke of Leinster. The *Dublin Evening Post* reported on this show as follows:

> To pay that tribute of respect to their Noble Commander, he so eminently deserves, the grenadier company of the Dublin Volunteers assembled in the area before Leinster-house, and attended with their martial music, escorted the gallant Duke, and amiable Duchess, in their chairs, to Crow-street Theatre. The Duchess was received by the corps under arms, and escorted to the side box, elegantly fitted up for the occasion. Soon as she appeared, the music struck up, "Health and joy to the Duchess, etc." The Duke soon after appeared in the box, when the music immediately changed to the Volunteers march. Two grenadiers took their stations, as yeomen of the guard, near the box, while the Noble Fair received the loudest applause and acclamations of one of the most crowded, polite, and fashionable audiences, that ever graced a theatre.[86]

The show of Volunteer support for the duke of Leinster was also politically motivated, if we are to believe the commentary of government supporters. Describing this spectacle in a letter, John Beresford noted that the playhouse drama occurred the day after the duke of Leinster gave a forceful speech in Parliament denouncing the viceroy, Lord Buckinghamshire (free trade was still being debated), and Beresford implies that this spectacle at the playhouse was a continuation of this defiance. The FitzGeralds, he wrote with evident disgust, came into the theater "as king and queen," and they "seemed perfectly happy with their new dignity."[87]

The Volunteer prologues, epilogues, interludes, masques, operas, songs, and dances (there was even a "Hibernian Minuet and Volunteer Gavotte")[88] that were delivered on the stage itself were no less subversive, if we are to judge from *The Contract*, a full-length comic opera "of Irish manufacture" that played at both Smock Alley and Crow Street theaters in 1782 and 1783.[89] On the surface this is a loyalist production. In the song that the Volunteer hero of this opera, Charles Ingot, sings in the third act, for example, the Irish Volunteers are represented as faithful allies of England who are happy to unite with her in a struggle against a common foe:

> As heav'n born freedom's sacred fire,
> 　O'er Europe beam'd her charms,
> Ierne's sons attun'd their lyre,
> 　And nobly flew to arms;
> Let once the sister kingdoms join,
> 　In friendship and in love,
> A host of foes may all combine,
> 　But we'll victorious prove.[90]

But the first song that this character sings sounds a note of Irish exceptionalism more in keeping with an Irish nationalist discourse than with the discourse of a loyal "sister kingdom," and according to the *Dublin Evening Post*, this song, "set to the favourite air the Volunteer's March," was "exceedingly well received and encored":[91]

> In what hist'ry can you find,
> Of all the soldiers of mankind,
> A host of heroes, Sir, d'ye mind,
> 　To match our Volunteers?
> In antient or in modern days,
> Did poets ever tune their lays
> To patriots crown'd with so much bays,
> 　As Irish Volunteers?
> 　　　II
> What bright days throughout the year,
> At our reviews the nation cheer,
> When crowds immense haste far and near,
> 　T'admire our Volunteers!
> The brave alone deserve the fair,
> The ladies, Sir, who judges are,
> Assert no soldiers can compare
> 　With Irish Volunteers. (5)

It was undoubtedly because it conjured up this image of a "nation" united behind an Irish fighting force that this song was later reproduced in *Paddy's Resource* (1795), one of the songbooks of the United Irishmen.[92]

It is also clear from the songs of the working-class character, Humphrey Search, that unlike the existing political structure, the "nation" that stands united behind the Volunteers counts the unpropertied as well as property owners among its members. The part of Humphrey in this opera was undoubtedly intended to provide some of the broader comic relief traditionally associated with servant characters; indeed, the *Dublin Evening Post* notes that John Cornelys's rendering of the following "*Dublin News-boys song*" in the character of Humphrey was "too humorous . . . not to meet an encore":[93]

> When I have clean'd my master's shoes,
>   And in the morning early,
> To hear the hawkers cry the news,
>   O how my heart goes cheerily!
>   Freeman's Journal.
>   Faulkner's Journal—
>   Bloody news—bloody news—
> The shoes I black—then read, good lack!
>   The charming—charming news.
>   II
> When master's dined, and I likewise,
>   And evening fast approaches,
> Again the news-boys hail the skies,
>   And drown the very coaches;
>   Dublin Evening Post—
>   Gen'ral Evening Post—
>   Bloody news—bloody news—
> I wipe my glasses—read what passes—
>   O charming—charming news. (9–10)

But what the song also evoked when it described this Dublin servant's love of newspapers was a new kind of Irish public sphere in which the working class as well as the men of property could participate, and this new, more comprehensive political sphere would have been given further definition when Cornelys, who at one time was apprenticed to a Dublin stay maker,[94] sang the following patriotic song:

Hibernia is a noble land,
> True glory she has won,
She'll henceforth give her own command,
> For firm is every son:
To time's last end, we'll e'er defend,
> Our country and our king,
And with delight, morn, noon and night,
> The song of freedom sing.
> II
Our commerce soon from ev'ry port,
> To ev'ry port shall steer,
And all the world with pride resort,
> To trade with freedom here.

As Jean Howard points out in another context, the ideological import of a theatrical production is determined as much by the *material* practices a production embodies as by the dramatic fable it tells, and in this case the physical presence of this player would have added a further subversive class dimension to the already politically charged words of the song.[95] The spectacle of a working-class Dubliner like Cornelys articulating the above words would have suggested that the new Hibernia emerging from the political and economic struggles of the late 1770s and 1780s—the Hibernia that would "henceforth give her own command"—was both more egalitarian and more independent, a nation where poor men as well as rich men could have a voice.

When players like John O'Keeffe and Robert Owenson played the role of the Volunteer in these kinds of Volunteer performances, the entertainments would have acquired yet another level of political complexity, gesturing at a Hibernia that was united across ethnic and cultural as well as class lines. O'Keeffe's daughter, Adelaide, later related that when her father was young, he studied "fortification and drawing" to help him with a future career in "foreign military service,"[96] a biographical detail that suggests the young O'Keeffe was originally being groomed for military duty in the Jacobite army overseas. By the late 1770s, however, Adelaide recounted that her father "gloried in being marshalled a Dublin Volunteer, his own little son being in the Light Infantry Corps, and his brother a lieutenant in the same,"[97] a shift that suggests O'Keeffe and his family now saw the Volunteers as the best hope for themselves and for others like them who had lost their lands and social status after the 1688–91 wars. This hope is also apparent in the "Song in Honour of the Hibernian Military Associations," which O'Keeffe wrote and sang on the stage of Crow Street in 1780. O'Keeffe's "Song" begins:

Let the shrill Trumpet sound
    To the Nations around,
While HIBERNIA gives Breath to the Strain;
    'Tis her Genius that sings,
    And on Vict'ry's Wings,
Her loud Fame shall spread wide o'er the Main.
    Her Sons greatly fir'd,
    By Freedom inspir'd,
Independent of venal Regard;
    When his Country's the Word,
    See each Youth grasps a Sword,
And bright Glory's the wished-for Reward.[98]

Under a loyalist cover—in the second verse France is named the "Soup-maegre Foe" against which Ireland arms itself—this dispossessed native Irishman could effect an imaginative reappropriation of "his Country" in this kind of Volunteer discourse while simultaneously creating a visual image for the spectator of a Hibernia in which "each Youth"—there are no qualifiers on the basis of ethnicity or religion here—could play his part. When he sang the above words, O'Keeffe would have worn the uniform and carried the martial arms of the Dublin Volunteer, material signifiers of Irish citizenship.

Owenson's performances in the role of Volunteer would have worked to similar ideological effect. Two weeks after O'Keeffe sang the above song, for example, Owenson sang a "Song in the Character of a Volunteer" against the backdrop of a "Grand Emblematical Transparency . . . representing *Britannia, Hibernia, and America,* on *the Subject of the Free Trade of Ireland,*"[99] and at his own benefit performance in February 1783, he interspersed commemorations of Volunteer events with traditional Irish songs, local humor, and topical political commentary. The *Hibernian Journal* announced that his benefit on that occasion would include "A Prelude called *The New Register Office or, Paddy O'Carrol in high life.* Mr. Patrick O'Carrol, by Mr. Owenson, in which Character will be introduced several new Songs and Planxties, with Thady Mollowny's Description of the Spaniards attacking Gibraltar, or a new Way of crying French, Dutch, and Spanish News; likewise, Murrogh O'Driscol's Journey to Dublin, with his Description of the Humours of Patrick's Day, the Town, Taverns, the Volunteers marching from the Royal exchange to be reviewed in Phoenix-Park."[100] At a purely structural level, too, this kind of performance would have created a powerful prototype for the syncretic political subject that was configured a decade later in the writings of the United Irishmen. The "We" later enunciated in the *Declaration* of the United Irishmen is a collective entity that foregrounds its own internal differences even in the act of asserting its unity: on the one hand, it speaks authoritatively on behalf of a stable and apparently timeless entity variously referred to as "Ireland," the people," "our country" "the nation"; on the other, it admits its own composite and heterogeneous nature when it points to "the intestine divisions among Irishmen" or when it acknowledges that it "require[s] a cordial union among ALL THE PEOPLE OF IRE-LAND" to accomplish its political objectives.[101] The entertainment described above created a discursive model for this new kind of composite collective subject. English-style comedy (*The New Register Office* was a take-off of Joseph Reed's *The Register Office*), traditional Irish songs, commentary from the European military front, Volunteer commemorations, and descriptions of local Dublin scenes are all seamlessly interwoven into a single dramatic text here, a mingling of discourses and cultural traditions that gestures at an imagined community in which "All the people of Ireland" could exist in a "cordial union."

It was this kind of composite collective subject, too, that was articulated in the improvised performance that took place at Smock Alley on July 10, 1784, an event that took place (as the *Gentleman's Magazine* noted) against a larger citywide "theater of riot." During 1784, as Smyth points out, Dublin witnessed "a near-continuous sequence of street disorders": attacks on foreign importers intensified after a downturn in the economy left many artisans out of work; hostility to government grew over a paving bill that seemed to undermine municipal and local rights and liberties; and the increased presence of soldiers (recently disbanded from the American war) on Dublin streets exacerbated existing tensions between the local people and the military.[102] Newspaper reports from that year suggest that this climate of grievances had begun affecting the playhouse before the July event. On May 22, 1784, for example, the *Dublin Evening Post* reported that to prevent the viceroy from being hissed when he attended Smock Alley, "the Upper Gallery, which was the place principally dreaded," would be filled with "soldiers, his Grace's footmen, and a mob hired to clap and to huzza," and on June 10 the same paper reported that people were being issued tickets on the promise that they would clap for the viceroy in an attempt "to extort a semblance of respect to their principal from the inhabitants of Dublin, whose charters he has infringed."[103] A complaint supposedly coming from a gentleman in the pit, which the *Hibernian Journal* printed on June 21, suggests that the issue of Irish "stuff" was again surfacing in the playhouse. "Of what use is a non-importation agreement among a few hundreds of men in this metropolis, who perhaps purchase annually eight or ten pounds value of Irish woollen cloth, while the women of each of their families think little of having from fifty to one hundred pounds on them at a time of foreign manufactures?" this gentleman writes, and he complains that in the boxes at the playhouse a few nights previously "upwards of 10,000£ of foreign manufacture appeared on the persons of our fair country-women."[104]

The viceroy's disdainful treatment of the "aggregate" body's petition, then, brought these tensions to a head. Early in 1784 freeholders of the county and city of Dublin under the leadership of Napper Tandy, John Keogh (a Catholic), and Joseph Pollock—all future United Irishmen—began to hold what came to be known as "aggregate meetings" to agitate for parliamentary and other kinds of reform. At a city hall meeting on June 21, 1784, a committee that included Tandy and Keogh drew up a petition listing the citizens' grievances, which they intended to submit to the king via the viceroy. "Aristocratic Influence . . . has rendered the Representation of the People merely nominal," this petition stated, and it went on to condemn the government for the following "most wanton and reiterated Acts of Oppression": its refusal to protect manufacturing; its infringement on the chartered rights of the city; its violation of the rights of the subject by illegal imprisonment; its introduction of a press bill and a stamp act; and its maintenance of a standing army in peace time. Like the Dungannon Volunteer meeting of 1782, too, this petition linked parliamentary reform with the idea of religious tolerance for the majority population; the petition explicitly asked the English king's permission to "condemn that remnant of the penal code of laws, which still oppress our roman catholic fellow-subjects."[105] When a correspondent for the *Freeman's Journal* later argued that "the signal . . . to begin the horrid work and throw down the gauntlet of defiance at all government" was given "when . . . the aggregate meeting published their unintelligible jargon of Protestant and Papist government,"[106] he was also acknowledging the radical nature of this petition; by speaking a new language of inclusion, the "aggregate" body was indeed throwing down "the gauntlet of defiance" at a discriminatory sociopolitical order.

This defiant kind of "jargon" also began to be heard in the press and playhouse as the viceroy refused to receive this petition from the aggregate body. On July 5 the *Hibernian Journal* angrily denounced the viceroy for the "contemptuous and insolent manner" in which he kept this body of citizens waiting, and that same night the Smock Alley audience showed what it thought of this behavior at a command performance. The duke of Rutland came to the playhouse to see Sarah Siddons give one of her celebrated performances in the role of Isabella, but what he got instead, the *Hibernian Journal* reports, was a "new species of entertainment," courtesy of the audience:

> Last Monday evening, his Grace the Duke of Rutland, and his suite, were surprised with a new species of entertainment, at the Theatre in Smock-Alley, divided into acts, but similar to no kind of Drama that we ever heard of; it has not yet received any particular name, but may be called a sentimental medley of dry toasts, which being well sprinkled with true attic salt, was highly relishing to every son of genius not of English breed. The rod and the wreath were most judiciously applied, in a stile perfectly laconic, and worthy the antient Spartan freedom, as may appear from the following interludes dispersed between the acts of the Manager's play:
> Before the first Act,
> Duke of Rutland—a groan.
> General Lord Charlemont, and the Volunteers March—a clap.
> General George Washington—a clap.
> Thirteen United States of America—13 cheers.
> Independence to Ireland—3 cheers and 3 claps.
> Increase to the Volunteers of Ireland—3 cheers and 3 claps.
> 2nd Act
> The Memory of the Marquis of Granby—a clap.
> His Son, the Duke of Rutland—a groan.
> Lord Temple—a clap
> Duke of Rutland—a groan.
> Lady Temple—a clap.
> Duchess of Rutland's Beauty—a clap.
> 3rd Act
> Louis the XVIth, the Assertor of the Rights of Mankind—3 cheers.
> Bishop of Derry—a clap.

Captain Napper Tandy, Chairman of the Dublin Committee—a clap.
Col. Sir Edward Newenham—a clap.
Col. Flood—a clap.
Col. Brownlow—a mixture.

4th Act

Gallows Paul's Fate to the Enemies of Ireland—a clap.
Tarring and Feathering—a clap.
The Castle Hacks—a loud groan.
Aids du Camp behind the chair—a loud groan
Dissolution to the present P[arliamen]t—a clap.[107]

The carnivaleque drama that occurred on July 10, then, was a continuation of this "new species of entertainment," and again the opposition press was implicated in this event. As noted at the beginning of this chapter, the viceroy eventually met with the leaders of the aggregate body on July 6, but he publicly expressed his "entire disapprobation" of this body's petition. After commenting on "the impertinent answer given by our wretched Governor to the High Sheriffs, so insulting to the people," the *Hibernian Journal* of July 9 noted that the viceroy was to honor the Theatre Royal again "with his august presence on Saturday night," and it urged its readers to go there to express their feelings for this ruler: "[L]et us then with glowing hearts and ready hands Tomorrow evening to the Theatre repair, to testify our love, and with reiterated plaudits greet this best of Viceroys and this best of men."[108] What this paper was calling for, of course, was a show of the very opposite kind of political sentiment, and the irony clearly was not lost on Dublin theatergoers. As the *Volunteers Journal* reported the following Monday, "the clamour of a justly incensed people" filled the playhouse from the moment the viceroy entered until his departure, and the efforts of Dublin Castle officials to arrest the ringleaders, who were positioned in different parts of the house, only intensified the audience's anger. After venting their rage on the castle officials, the paper reports, "the people again directed their fury against the hated object in the stage-box, and pursued him even out of the house, to the gates of the castle, with their groans and hisses—'till the horse-guards rushing out, protected him from the further reproaches of a justly irritated people."[109]

In using the term "the people" to describe the force that mounted this assault on the Dublin Castle administration, however, this newspaper suggests that this event also had a significance beyond local Dublin politics, and this suggestion is borne out by a closer analysis of the riotous crowd. In the audience that assembled in the theater that evening, it is possible to see the outline of that "united" nation embodied in the Volunteer drama described above. Significantly, all those who played leading roles in the evening's activities were themselves members of local Volunteer corps, and like the Volunteers in the scripted drama, they came from different social, religious, and ethnic backgrounds. Handy Pemberton, the man who was ejected from the box next to the viceregal box for reputedly whipping the crowd in the upper gallery into a frenzy before the castle party arrived, [110] for example, was a lawyer, a member of the Lawyers corps of Volunteers, and a member of the established church. But he came originally from a Quaker background, and in his frequent letters to the opposition press in the year before the "riot," he had asserted his identification with the majority population by signing himself the "Trueborn Irishman" and by defending the rights of Catholics.[111] The artisan class was represented by a man identified in the press reports as "E———t," a slator and a member of the Builders corps, and by a man named Smyth, a journeyman goldsmith and a member of the Goldsmiths Volunteer corps; the former supposedly gave the signal for the outcry by pelting potatoes from the upper gallery, while the latter was arrested and put in the castle guardhouse for reportedly rapping the panels of the gallery with his stick.[112] The Catholic presence in this crowd, as usual, is harder to detect, but it is registered in a fictitious account in the government press that purports to describe the rioters plotting this disturbance. According to the *Freeman's Journal,* the chair of the organizational meeting of the "Sons of Faction, Riot, and Disorder" that took place in Tenter Fields in the Liberties was a "Mr. Teague Blarney."[113]

The discourse that emanated from the disturbance itself also resembled the discourse in the Volunteer performances described above in that it was a syncretic amalgamation of material from different cultural and political traditions. As soon as the viceroy entered the theater, the audience called for "The Volunteers March" in place of "God Save the King," and in effecting this musical displacement, it could be argued, these theatergoers were acting out defiance of the government that was implicit in most Volunteer patriotic rhetoric. This was certainly how the government press interpreted this symbolic act. "[B]y loudly reprobating that odious song *God Save the King,*" the *Freeman's Journal* wrote with heavy sarcasm, the frequenters of the upper gallery showed their "sincere detestation of monarchy" and their "spirit of republicanism."[114] This spirit of republicanism, it could be argued, ultimately had its roots in an English commonwealth ideology. But when audience members followed "The

Volunteers March" with a rousing rendition of "Charley over the water"—
that song was sung, we are told, "by a band, at the theatre, at least equal
in number to that at the late commemoration of Handel"[115]—they were
also drawing on a native Irish and Jacobite tradition to express their political dissatisfaction, and it was this other tradition that was also implicitly
valorized by this transgressive musical act. Undoubtedly, some audience
members sang this song merely to insult "Charlie Bad-Manners" (as the
opposition press nicknamed the viceroy) by identifying him with the autocratic Stuarts. But as the government press noted when it condemned this
Jacobite song, it also revived "the reprobated pretension of the House of
Stuart"[116] and by extension the reprobated political aspiration of a dispossessed Gaelic people.

The opposition press was no less eclectic when it came to finding discursive frames to interpret this event. When the *Volunteers Journal*, for example, prefaced its account of the theater disturbance with a picture of a
man on the executioner's block and the caption "Thus fell a Strafford
[*sic*],"[117] it was framing the overthrow of the viceroy at the theater in an
English commonwealth tradition of resistance and implicitly threatening
the viceroy with the same fate (execution) as Wentworth, Earl of Stafford,
one of the most imperialist of Ireland's viceroys. That Stafford had established the first Theatre Royal in Ireland also added an additional cultural
valence to this threat. The era of castle dominance over the Irish stage, the
image suggests, is over. This seventeenth-century dissenting and leveling
tradition was invoked, too, when the same paper recounted the theatrical
event in mock-biblical verses, some of which I cite here:

> 12. But behold the people were sore angered at the unjust usage they
> received.
> 13. And they murmured and said, we have not deserved thus of these
> rulers, their insults neither have we merited.
> 14. And when the governor went to the house of amusement, some of
> the people followed him thither.
> 15. And they expressed their resentment in loud murmurs and hissing,
> and they did offend the ruler with scoffing and abuse, for verily he had
> aggrieved them sore.
> 16. At the wheels of his chariot did they pursue him with dreadful
> hissing—yea, even to his palace walls.
> 17. And he betook him from their sight like a timid hare, in the bottom
> of his palace hid he his head.[118]

As in the English radical dissenting tradition, the theatrical rising is here retold in Old Testament language, and the Dublin public is cast (however jokingly) as the chosen people who throw off the yoke of the Pharaoh in the form of an English governor. The correspondent for the *Dublin Evening Post* who signed himself "Finn Mac Comhall," however, clearly sees the event as the embodiment of a native Irish rather than an English dissenting spirit, and it is the long tradition of Gaelic opposition to English rule that is also subtly invoked when this correspondent reminds the viceroy of "the spirit of Irishmen." "Let your treatment at the Theatre, last Saturday se'en-night, sink deep into your mind, as a specimen of the temper of the people, and as a warning not to exasperate them too far," Finn Mac Comhall writes, and he goes on to ask, "Think you, that the spirit of Irishmen will quietly submit to see their liberties artfully undermined in the Senate, and openly violated in the resort of public amusement?"[119] The "people" that displayed its "temper" in the theater event of July 10, 1784, this bardlike voice suggests, had its roots not only in an Anglo but also a Gaelic past.

Containing a "National Theater"

The Stage Act of 1786

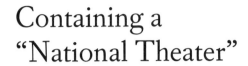

In 1899 when Lady Gregory was in the process of setting up the new Irish Literary Theatre at the Abbey, she came across an unexpected obstacle in the shape of a stage bill that forbade the licensing of any theater in Dublin without government permission. "We found there was an old Act in existence, passed just before the Union," she wrote, "putting a fine of £300 upon any one who should give a performance for money in any unlicensed building."[1] This "old Act" was the Act for Regulating the Stage in the City and County of Dublin (26 George III, 1786), and its provisions gave the government the exclusive right to grant theatrical patents and enormous latitude in determining the nature of these patents. On the premise that "a well regulated theatre in the city of Dublin, being the residence of the chief governor or governors of Ireland," would be "productive of publick advantage, and tend to improve the morals of the people," the act proclaimed that His Majesty and his heirs had the right to licence a theater (or theaters) for terms not exceeding twenty-one years "under such restrictions, conditions, and limitations as to him or them shall seem meet," and it explicitly forbade entertainment at any site other than the patented playhouse (or playhouses) after June 1, 1786. After that date, it stated, "no person or persons shall, for hire, gain, or any kind of reward whatsoever or howsoever, act, represent, or perform, or cause to be acted, represented, or performed, any interlude, tragedy, comedy, prelude, opera, burletta, play,

farce, pantomime, or any part or parts therein, on any stage or in any theatre, house, booth, tent, or other place within the said city of Dublin, or
the liberties or suburbs, or county thereof, or within the county of Dublin
under any colour or pretence whatsoever, save and except in such theatre
or play-house as shall be so established or kept by letters patent as afore-
said." This ban was also extended to "any house or place where wine, ale,
beer, or other liquors shall be sold or goods of any kind retailed," the only
exemption being for "the exhibition of any feats of horsemanship, puppet-
shew, or such like species of entertainment."[2]

Roach's New and Complete History of the Stage from its origin to its present state (1796) suggested that the Stage Act—the first piece of legislation
regulating the theater in Ireland—was the result of skillful political maneuvering on the part of the manager of Smock Alley, Richard Daly, in the
wake of the 1784 disturbance at Smock Alley. "A riot in Dublin in 1785 [sic]
when the Lord-Lieutenant went to the theatre," this history relates, "gave
Mr. Daly an opportunity (not withstanding his protestation on the stage
that he would obey the public, whose servant alone he was) of obtaining an
exclusive patent, by favoring the ministerial side."[3] Six years later The
Thespian Dictionary offered a similar account of this bill. Under the entry
for Richard Daly, it reads: "During the administration of the late Duke
of Rutland, a riot took place at the theatre (the lord lieutenant having
been there), occasioned by a political party; when Mr. Daly, by his conduct, so ingratiated himself with government, that a bill was passed for de-
priving the lord mayor of the power of licensing theatres, by which means
Mr. Daly put to defiance all future opposition. He then became sole theatrical monarch; and, in such situation, naturally incurred the ill-will of
many."[4] To the extent that these accounts read the Stage Act as a response
to recent political disturbances in the theater, they are correct; however, I
suggest that they also underestimate the government's role in pushing this
piece of legislation, and they overlook another determining factor by failing to mention Robert Owenson's "national theater" at Fishamble Street.

The government's involvement becomes more apparent if we follow
the money trail leading to this bill. In 1789 John Magee, the proprietor of
the vehemently antigovernment Dublin Evening Post, claimed that Daly
accomplished his design in getting an exclusive patent with the aid of Francis Higgins, editor of the Freeman's Journal, and he suggested that Higgins,
in effect, was a secret co-sharer in the patent. "Pray, might it be asked,"
Magee wrote, "how this same mouthing mummer—this half faced Country 'Squire,' Richard Daly, Esq—tricked poor Tom Ryder out of the

Patent? It has been alleged that it was by a maneuver of the Sham 'Squire' [Higgins] and that the Justice [Higgins] actually has half the patent."[5] There is also a paper trail to support Magee's allegations concerning Higgins's involvement. In 1798, after Daly was forced to flee the country to avoid creditors in the wake of his enforced retirement from Crow Street, he petitioned Edward Cooke, the undersecretary of state for the Camden administration, for financial help and reminded Cooke that most of his debts had been "creat'd by the Securities enter'd into for the satisfying the Private Property that interfered with the Stage Bill for regulating Theatre."[6] As W. H. Lawrence notes, the mortgage documents that survived under Higgins's name in the Registry of Deeds office reveal that Higgins was one of Daly's principal creditors and thus in effect part owner of the patent.[7] At the time he was bankrolling Daly's patent, however, Higgins himself was secretly on the payroll of the government (in the next decade he would be a key informer on the United Irishman), a link that strongly suggests that the Stage Bill must be seen in the context of the authorities' larger effort to contain and manage the unrest of 1784.

The government and its supporters in Parliament adopted a number of different strategies—some directly repressive, others indirectly so— to deal with the perceived "Dublin problem" of that year. In 1786 a version of the highly controversial London police bill was introduced and debated in the Irish Parliament; in 1787 the Act to prevent tumultuous Risings and Assemblies, and for the more effectual Punishment of Persons guilty of Outrage, Riot, and illegal Combination, and of administering and taking unlawful Oaths was passed; and around the same time, a limited rustification scheme, designed to disperse and resettle the volatile weaving community, was pursued.[8] As Brian Inglis points out in *The Freedom of the Press in Ireland, 1784–1841*, the opposition press also came under fire from the government in the wake of the unrest of 1784. During the 1784–85 period, the House of Commons repeatedly brought lawsuits against the *Volunteers Journal*, the *Dublin Evening Post*, and the *Hibernian Journal* for publishing seditious or libelous material (in one case, for example, prosecuting the *Volunteers Journal* for publishing a seditious letter from Handy Pemberton, the hero of the 1784 theatrical "riot"); and a number of these newspapers' publishers or printers, including John Magee, were thrown in prison or had their offices ransacked. In June 1784, too, the House of Parliament passed the Press Bill (the first of its kind), which made it easier to identify and prosecute newspaper printers, proprietors, and publishers, and by increasing stamp and advertisement duties the same year, they made it harder for opposition newspapers to function economically. Last but not least, the government and its supporters attempted to buy off the opposition press, and as the case of Francis Higgins indicated, they were sometimes successful. The *Freeman's Journal,* which was founded in the 1760s by Charles Lucas, had been one of the best known of the Irish opposition papers, and like the *Volunteers Journal* and the *Hibernian Journal,* it had been charged with publishing libelous material in April 1784. By June 2, 1784, however, the *Freeman's Journal* was making loud professions of its "impartiality," which as Inglis points out, were an "unmistakable sign of government sympathies."[9]

From comments in the *Freeman's Journal* in the aftermath of the 1784 "riot," it is clear that the playhouse was also seen as contributing to the "Dublin problem." In its first issue after this disturbance, this paper warned that the "rabble . . . who daring to shew disrespect to the representative of majesty . . . will become if we allow them, not only comptrollers of our recreative amusements, but our lords in matters in the state, if we suffer their *levelling principle* to intimidate and rule us." And by March 1785 it was reporting plans for curbing this "rabble" who were creating nightly disturbances at Smock Alley: "To such a heighth are the noisy and illiberal excesses carried, night after night, in the upper gallery at the Theatre-Royal, that the Magistrates, we hear, have already had one meeting to devise some effectual plan to suppress them. And we hear also, that several families of consequence propose to enter into subscriptions, for the purpose of prosecuting with every rigour the law will admit, all offenders who shall be apprehended in the act of disturbing or insulting any part of the audience."[10] Comments in this and other newspapers during the same season also throw light on why some "families of consequence" were anxious to enter into such subscriptions. A "Card" in the same March 5–8 issue of the *Freeman's Journal* revealed that "a set of ill behaved people" in the theater galleries were insulting "with groans and hisses, any persons in the boxes, lattices or pit, whom they shall think proper to name or point out,"[11] and a report that appeared in the *Volunteers Journal* in June 1785 indicates that Smock Alley audiences were again voicing their negative opinion of the government through the medium of the drama itself. Commenting on reaction to a speech about "senators" who "Cheat the deluded people with a shew / Of Liberty, which yet them ne'er must taste of" in a recent revival of Otway's *Venice Preserv'd,* the latter reported that "the *spirit* of an ABUSED PEOPLE could not resist its [this speech's] force—which breaking out in the most extravagant plaudits—plaudits which from their *long* continuance seemed to convince *many*, whose *confusion* betrayed how severely they felt the effects of the *satire*—that these incomparable lines were not as *pointless* as they may be generally imagined."[12]

The Fishamble Street theater, which Robert Owenson had opened after he split from Daly's company in 1784, was a similar site of political dissent. In her *Memoirs* Lady Morgan reported that her father's venture as a theatrical manager sprang from his belief that the time was finally ripe for creating a national theater. Owenson had always believed that theaters should be erected "like Martello towers, at regular intervals over the land for the protection and instruction of the national mind,"[13] she writes, and the political developments of the 1780s encouraged him to try to realize this dream: "At a moment when Irish nationality was rising above the level of unavailing complaint; when Irishmen hawked their grievances as beggars hawk their sores; when the glorious body of Irish volunteers became the Praetorian bands of the land, not to impose, but to break her chains; my father snatched the epithet, and gave his theatre the name of 'National'" (66). Lady Morgan also states that her father was "backed by some of the best men of the time; patriots, in the best sense of the word" (66), and she suggests that the opening performance reflected the nationalist sentiment of the Fishamble Street performers and these patriotic supporters:

> The first performance was to be altogether national, that is Irish and very Irish it was. The play chosen was *The Carmelite*, by Captain Jephson, with an interlude from Macklin's farce of *The Brave Irishman*, and a farce of O'Keeffe's *The Poor Soldier*. The overture consisted of Irish airs ending with the Volunteer's March, which was chorused by the gallery to the accompaniment of drums and fifes. . . .
>
> My father wrote and spoke the prologue in his own character of an "Irish Volunteer." The audience was as national as the performance; and the pit was filled with red coats of the corps to which my father belonged; and the boxes exhibited a show of beauty and fashion, such as Ireland above all other countries can produce. (22–23)

Lady Morgan also blames "the Government" and its intervention in granting Daly the exclusive patent for this theater's demise, and she implies that this action was politically motivated:

> The National Theatre flourished. Everyone took boxes, but few paid for them. Orders were given in profusion, when, lo! in the midst of

the apparent success of this rival to the great Royalties, Government granted an exclusive patent for the performance of the legitimate drama to—Mr. Daly! with the additional honour of creating him deputy Master of the Revels, a distinction which had nearly fallen into abeyance. In a capital so dramatic as Dublin, the event made a great sensation, which, however, soon subsided, but not before my father's friends devised legal grounds to sue for remuneration for his losses. Mr. Daly agreed to an arbitration; Lord Donoughmore and Denis Bowes, M. P., were arbitrators and became guarantees to my father for an income of three hundred a year for ten years on the promise that no paid actor should appear on the boards of the National Theatre. My father also accepted, provisionally, the deputy managership of the Theatre Royal; and everyone appeared contented, except the creditors for debts incurred in getting up this phantom theatre. (24–25)

This explanation of why the theater was shut down, I suggest, is credible despite the many factual inaccuracies that have led some historians to doubt its veracity. Advertisements in contemporary newspapers reveal that the Fishamble Street theater did not open with the plays described above but rather with Hugh Kelly's *The School for Wives,* a comedy that had played in Dublin for some eleven years; and the afterpiece on that occasion (December 20, 1785) was *The Waterman,* with Owenson playing the role of Tom Tugg.[14] These and other inaccuracies lead Lawrence, for one, to question just how much of Lady Morgan's account should be believed: "all is fish," he writes dryly, "that comes to her net."[15] A closer look at the newspaper advertisements for that season, however, indicates that Lady Morgan is compressing and conflating different performances in her account rather than inventing them out of whole cloth. *The Carmelite,* for example, did premiere on January 17, 1785, at Fishamble Street (though it was written by the Englishman Richard Cumberland, not by the Irishman Jephson); and a week after the theater opened, Owenson appeared as Captain O'Blunder in Sheridan's (not Macklin's) *The Brave Irishman.*[16] During this December 27 performance, too, the manager played a leading role in a new prelude that incorporated "Irish airs" and Volunteers' tunes, and although there is no record of whether he performed in Volunteer uniform or whether he was "chorused by the gallery to the accompaniment of drums and fifes," it is quite possible that these events occurred. The advertisement for this prelude reveals that there was an Irish and a Volunteer emphasis throughout this entertainment:

A new Prelude called
The Manager, and the Irish Actor
Manager, Mr. Brennan; Paddy Aughy (the Irish Actor) Mr. Owenson, in which Character will be introduced several New Songs and Planxties, particularly, a celebrated Medley, adapted to the most favourite Irish Lilts, called
The Humours of Patrick's Day; or
Thady Mullowny's Journey to Dublin
Giving a Description of the City, the Taverns, Etc. and of the Volunteers marching from the Royal Exchange, to be reviewed in the Phoenix Park; and a new Harmonious Song, called
Paddy Aughy's Description of his Sweet Heart Bridget
After which will be performed
The Wonder with the Farce *The Brave Irishman*.[17]

On January 10, 1785, the *Volunteers Journal* announced that "a number of officers intend to perform the Comedy of the West Indian at the New Theatre, in Fishamble Street for the benefit of a public charity,"[18] and it seems very likely, given Owenson's Volunteer connections, that these "officers" were members of one of the Dublin Volunteer corps.

Lady Morgan's implication that the government closed down the theater because it was too "national" is also credible, though the "nationalism" that Owenson's theater supported had more in common with the cross-cultural, interdenominational nationalism of the United Irishman than with the later Celtic and Catholic-identified nationalism of Yeats and Lady Gregory. By 1785–86 there was a pronounced political split in the Volunteer movement; while some corps helped the authorities to police the unruly city, others, most notably Napper Tandy's Liberty corps, still recruited and drilled Catholics and lower-class Protestants.[19] As Smyth notes, there was also continuity between Tandy's increasingly radical corps of Volunteers and the revolutionaries of the 1790s; when a United Irishman club sprang up in Dublin for the first time in 1791; significantly, it was described as "chiefly composed of the Tandean party of the city."[20] The support that Owenson's theater received from the uncompromisingly antigovernment and Catholic-run *Volunteers Journal*[21] and the attacks it was subjected to from the reactionary *Freeman's Journal* suggest it was associated with this more radical wing of the Volunteers. As soon as the playhouse opened in December 1784, the *Freeman's Journal* tried to discourage prospective theatergoers by reminding them of the collapse of the Grove Room at Fishamble Street a number of years previously, and it also worked to depress attendance by casting doubts on Owenson's managerial and acting abilities. After a performance of *The West Indian* at the end of December, for instance, it attacked the company in a language that subtly reminded readers of Owenson's humble native Irish origins: "Such personas and such actors are only suited to the meridian of a market town, or country barn, but in the metropolis of Ireland must become an insult on the public taste and judgement."[22] The *Volunteers Journal*, meanwhile, regularly carried advertisements for Fishamble Street and puffed its plays and players, using every possible opportunity to rebut the *Freeman's Journal*'s attacks. It dismissed the latter's first attack, for example, as "impertinent prejudice" stemming from "a dread of the success of the new Theater," and it reported approvingly when Owenson responded on the stage to this criticism in the December 27 performance mentioned above. *"The Prelude, called the Manager and the Irish actor* was much admired, and some temporary strokes, which he [Owenson] introduced, and which appeared to have been wrung from him by very illiberal abuse, added to the applause he received," the *Volunteers Journal* wrote, " . . . for after all the scurrility that may be thrown on any side, it cannot mislead the general sense of the town."[23]

The benefit performance that Owenson staged on April 16 for William Bingley confirmed his and this theater's alliance with the radical wing of the Volunteer movement and the "Tandean party." Bingley, an Englishman and friend of the English radical reformer John Wilkes, was one of the printers of the *Volunteers Journal,* and along with Matthew Carey (the Catholic manager of the paper), he had been arrested in April 1784 for publishing an issue that among other things demanded Ireland's complete political severance from England. Bingley was released from prison on that occasion because the House of Commons could not prove he was the proprietor of the press, but when he filed an action against the deputy sergeant for wrongful arrest in February 1785, he was again thrown in prison. Even from that location, however, he continued to write his stridently antigovernment paper *The Reformist.*[24] At the end of March 1785 advertisements for an April 16 benefit performance for Mr. Bingley at Fishamble Street began appearing in the *Volunteers Journal,* with a note of thanks from Bingley and his family to Owenson and the amateur performer who had agreed to perform that night ("A Gentleman of the City having kindly undertaken to do a capital part in Tragedy, for which Mr. Bingley and his Family return their unfeigned thanks, as also to Mr. Owenson and his Company who are pleased to bestow him a free benefit"). And if there was any remaining doubt about Owenson's connections with the city's radicals, it was dispelled by the announcement that tickets for this benefit could be purchased (among other locations) "at the home of James Napper Tandy at 108 Abbey-Street."[25]

The Stage Act, then, put an end to this kind of radical theater, and its timing as well as the nature of the opposition to it suggest that it was designed with precisely such an aim in mind. Lawrence disputes Lady Morgan's claim that the new patent was the reason for the theater's closure on the grounds that Fishamble Street had closed its doors in June 1785 more than a year *before* Daly received his exclusive patent and his appointment as deputy master of the revels (the Stage Act came into effect in June 1786, and the latter appointment was made in November 1786).[26] But the Stage Act was given its first reading in the Irish House of Commons on June 13, 1785,[27] and an item in the *Freeman's Journal* suggests that Daly came to a financial settlement with Owenson around this time, just as the controversy over the proposed bill was heating up. In its June 25–28, 1785, issue the *Freeman's Journal* devoted most of the front page to an article entitled "Observations on, and a Review of the Dublin Stage," in which it defended the proposed legislation and touted the evils of theatrical competition, and after listing all the unsuccessful competitors to the patented theater, it mentioned "Mr Owenson who experimented with shares" and who, having lost money, "has wisely come into terms with Mr. Daly."[28] W. J. Fitzpatrick, Lady Morgan's biographer, puts the matter slightly differently but perhaps more accurately when he writes, "Daly, whose exclusive patent was then pending, made ample advances to a reconciliation with Owenson, and apprehensive lest he should make interest against the coveted licence, Daly offered him a re-engagement on advantageous terms, with the situation of acting manager."[29]

The Tandean party's active opposition to this intended Daly monopoly also suggests that it read the exclusive patent as a government mechanism for silencing the voice of the radicalized element in the Dublin public. On June 27, 1785, at a specially convened "Post-Assembly" meeting of the Dublin Corporation, seven members of the common council carried a petition against the impending Stage Act, and as was revealed during the second reading of the bill in the House of Commons on July 20, two of the names on the petition were James Napper Tandy and John Binns, among the leaders of the "aggregate meetings" of the previous year.[30] This petition, like earlier ones against theatrical monopoly bills, was made on behalf of the lord mayor's right to license plays, but the discussion that reportedly took place at this city hall meeting reveals that other more populist rights were also at stake. During this meeting, according to Richard Hely Hutchinson, some of the "city gentlemen" who opposed the Stage Act had been heard to say, "*What-shall our lips be sealed in the Theatre—no groaning any tyrant Viceroy—no hisses—no clapping of hands for the Volunteers and Lord Charlemont?*" Hely Hutchinson, the member who had introduced the stage legislation into Parliament, reported this statement to the House of Commons as part of an effort to show why the Tandean party's petition should be discounted by all right-minded politicians. But in repeating these remarks, he also inadvertently records for history the voice of the Irish radical crowd who had made the theater a revolutionary site in the last quarter of the eighteenth century.

The Tandean party's failure to defeat the Stage Act and win this theatrical revolution, like the larger failure of the United Irishman's revolution, then laid the ground for that forgetting discussed in the introduction of this book. Commenting on Walter Benjamin's famous sixth thesis on the philosophy of history in which he expresses the idea that "*even the dead* will not be safe from the enemy if he wins," Slavoj Zizek writes, "The risk of the defeat of the actual revolution endangers the past itself because the actual revolutionary conjunction functions as a condensation of past missed revolutionary chances repeating themselves in the actual revolution."[31] The passage of the Stage Act of 1786, which effectively brought a halt to the revolution in the Irish theater, similarly endangered the theatrical past, making it harder for subsequent generations to see not only the disruptive political theater of that moment but also a whole history of disruptive political performances extending back to the beginning of the eighteenth century.

Notes

Introduction

1. Thomas Sheridan, *An Humble Appeal to the Publick, Together with some Considerations on the Present critical and dangerous State of the Stage in Ireland* (Dublin, 1758), 13. Subsequent references appear in the text.

2. Thomas Sheridan, *Mr. Sheridan's Speech Addressed to a Number of Gentlemen Assembled with a View of considering The Best Means to establish one good Theatre in this City* (Dublin, 1772), 15–16.

3. Robert Hitchcock, *An Historical View of the Irish Stage*, 2 vols. (Dublin, 1788–94), 2:116. Subsequent references appear in the text.

4. See, for example, Hitchcock's remarks on the disgraceful state of the stage when only "the lowest of the people" attended and its more "rational" state when the nobleman and the "grave citizen" were present (*An Historical View*, 1:122, 162–63).

5. Esther K. Sheldon, *Thomas Sheridan of Smock-Alley* (Princeton: Princeton University Press, 1967), 61. Subsequent references appear in the text.

6. In his letter to Richard Shackleton of February 21, 1747, for example, Edmund Burke says that Kelly had "a great party who call'd their cause the Gentlemans quarrel" (*The Correspondence of Edmund Burke*, ed. T. W. Copeland [Cambridge and Chicago: Cambridge University Press and University of Chicago Press, 1958–71], 83).

7. David Lloyd, *Ireland after History* (Notre Dame, Ind.: Notre Dame University Press, 1999), 19–36.

8. See Charles Lucas [A. Freeman, Barber and Citizen, pseud.], *A Second Letter to the Free Citizens of Dublin* (Dublin, 1747), 10; and his *Letter to the Free-Citizens of Dublin* (Dublin, 1747), 5. For the "Connaught Counts" identification, see *The Down-Fall of the Counts: A New Ballad to the Tune of Derry Down, Etc.* (Dublin, 1747).

9. Daniel Corkery, *The Hidden Ireland* (Dublin: Gill and Macmillan, 1924; rpt. 1967), 17–41.

10. La Tourette Stockwell, *Dublin Theatres and Theatre Customs, 1637–1820* (Kingsport, Tenn.: Kingsport Press, 1938), 174, 175–76. Subsequent references appear in the text.

11. Joseph Roach, "Theater History and Historiography: Introduction," in *Critical Theory and Performance*, ed. Janelle G. Reinelt and Joseph R. Roach (Ann Arbor: University of Michigan Press, 1992), 294.

12. Richard Schechner, *Performance Theory* (New York: Routledge, 1977; rpt. 1994), 73.

13. See D. E. S. Maxwell, "Irish Drama 1899–1929: The Abbey Theatre," in *The Field Day Anthology of Irish Writing*, ed. Seamus Deane (Derry, Northern Ireland: Field Day Publications, 1991), 2:562; and Loren Kruger, *The National Stage: Theatre and Cultural Legitimation in England, France, and America* (Chicago: University of Chicago Press, 1992).

14. Christopher Murray, "Drama 1690–1800," in *The Field Day Anthology of Irish Writing*, 1:500, 501.

15. J. C. Beckett, "Literature in English 1691–1800," in *A New History of Ireland*, ed. T. W. Moody and W. E. Vaughan (Oxford: Clarendon Press, 1986), 4:428.

16. Lloyd, *Ireland after History*, 26.

17. Ernesto Laclau and Chantal Mouffe, *Hegemony and Socialist Strategy* (London: Verso, 1985), 131.

18. Thomas Bartlett, *The Fall and Rise of the Irish Nation: The Catholic Question, 1690–1830* (Dublin: Gill and Macmillan, 1992), 30–44, 38. For other studies on "colonial nationalism" or "Irish Protestant nationalism," see J. G. Simms, *Colonial Nationalism, 1698–1776* (Cork: Mercier Press, 1976); J. L. McCracken, "Protestant Ascendancy and the Rise of Colonial Nationalism, 1714–60," in *A New History of Ireland*, 4:105–22; and Patrick Kelly, "William Molyneux and the Spirit of Liberty in Eighteenth-Century Ireland," *Eighteenth-Century Ireland* 3 (1988): 133–48.

For the view that the Irish Protestant tradition of agitation constitutes a "patriotism" that is *not* a nationalism, see Joep Th. Leerssen's "Anglo-Irish Patriotism and Its European Context: Notes Towards a Reassessment," *Eighteenth-Century Ireland* 3 (1988): 7–24.

19. See Sean Connolly, *Religion, Law and Power: The Making of Protestant Ireland, 1660–1760* (Oxford: Clarendon Press, 1992), 41–59; Bartlett, *The Fall and Rise of the Irish Nation*, 47.

20. See Bartlett, *The Fall and Rise of the Irish Nation*, 47–48; Kevin Whelan, "The Catholic Community in Eighteenth-Century County Wexford," in *Endurance and Emergence: Catholics in Ireland in the Eighteenth Century*, ed. T. P. Power and Kevin Whelan (Dublin: Irish Academic Press, 1990), 129–70; Thomas P. Power, "Converts," in *Endurance and Emergence*, 101–27; and Kevin Whelan, "An Underground Gentry? Catholic Middlemen in Eighteenth-Century Ireland," *Eighteenth-Century Ireland* 10 (1995): 7–77.

21. *The True Life of Betty IRELAND. With her Birth, Education, and Adventurers. Together with Some Account of her elder sister BLANCH of BRITAIN* (London and Dublin, 1753), 22. This pamphlet has been attributed to Sir Richard Cox.

22. Cited in Maureen Wall, "The Rise of a Catholic Middle Class in Eighteenth-Century Ireland, " in Wall, *Catholic Ireland in the Eighteenth Century: Collected Essays of Maureen Wall*, ed. Gerard O'Brien (Dublin: Geography Publications, 1989), 76. See also Bartlett, *The Fall and Rise of the Irish Nation*, 46–47; and David J. Dickson, "Catholics and Trade in Eighteenth-Century Ireland: An Old Debate Revisited," in *Endurance and Emergence*, 85–100.

23. For Catholic political activism in the first three quarters of the century, see Maureen Wall, *Catholic Ireland in the Eighteenth Century*, 73–170; and Bartlett, *The Fall and Rise of the Irish Nation*, 45–65. For Catholic involvement in the United Irishmen, see Marianne Elliott, *Wolfe Tone: Prophet of Irish Independence* (New Haven: Yale University Press, 1989), 121–33, 151–71.

24. Louis Cullen, "Catholics under the Penal Laws," *Eighteenth-Century Ireland* 1 (1986): 27.

25. Jim Smyth, *The Men of No Property: Irish Radicals and Popular Politics in the Late Eighteenth Century* (New York: St. Martin's Press, 1992), 121–56, 142. The figures for the population of Dublin are given in Patrick Fagan, "The Population of Dublin in the Eighteenth Century with Particular Reference to the Proportions of Protestants and Catholics," *Eighteenth-Century Ireland* 6 (1991): 149.

26. Richard Schechner, *Between Theater and Anthropology* (Philadelphia: University of Pennsylvania Press, 1985), 35–116.

27. Joseph Roach, "Kinship, Intelligence, and Memory as Improvisation," in *Performance and Cultural Politics*, ed. Elin Diamond (London: Routledge, 1996), 218.

28. Connolly, *Religion, Law and Power*, 135, 133–39.

29. T. C. Barnard, "The Uses of 23 October 1641 and Irish Protestant Celebrations," *English Historical Review* 106 (1991), 889–920. The citation from the sermons is on p. 900.

30. Bartlett, *The Fall and Rise of the Irish Nation*, 13–14.

31. Joep Th. Leerssen, *Mere Irish and Fíor-Ghael* (Amsterdam: John Benjamins, 1986), 115.

32. *The Works of George Farquhar*, ed. Shirley Strum Kenny (Oxford: Clarendon Press, 1988), 4.1.348. All subsequent references are to this edition.

33. [Henry Brooke], *The Farmer's Letter to the Protestants of Ireland* (Dublin, 1745), 1:7.

34. Between 1722 and 1758 alone, for example, *The Beaux Stratagem* was performed at least fifty-eight times on the Dublin stage (John C. Greene and Gladys L. H. Clark, *The Dublin Stage, 1720–1745* [London: Associated University Presses, 1993], 425; and Sheldon, *Thomas Sheridan of Smock-Alley,* 463–64). For the continued popularity of this play in the later part of the century, see William J. Lawrence's unpublished "Notebooks on the History of the Dublin Stage" (University of Cincinnati Library), vols. 18–53.

35. Paul Abbott, "Authority," *Screen* 20 (1979): 15–16.

36. Frantz Fanon, *The Wretched of the Earth*, trans. Constance Farrington (New York: Grove Press, 1963), 51; Homi K. Bhabha, "The Other Question," *Screen* 24 (1983): 29.

37. Connolly, *Religion, Law and Power,* 124. Connolly argues that the positive interaction between the upper and lower echelons of Irish society at official and unofficial public gatherings and festivities proves that Ireland is better described as a relatively stable, and unified, ancien régime rather than as a conflicted, colonial society. "In Ireland, as elsewhere in early modern Europe," he argues, "the authority of some and the subordination of others existed within a framework of shared expectations and a degree of mutual accommodation" (128).

38. Elin Diamond, introduction to *Performances and Cultural Politics,* ed. Elin Diamond (London: Routledge, 1996), 2.

39. Bhabha, "The Other Question," 29.

40. Laclau and Mouffe, *Hegemony and Socialist Strategy,* 136.

Chapter 1.   "A mind to turn Play'r"

1. *A New Song on the Whiggs Behaviour at the Play House on the 4th of this Instant, November 12, at a Play call'd TAMERLAIN*, in *Lloyd's News-Letter*, November 8, 1712; as cited in William Smith Clark, *The Early Irish Stage: The Beginnings to 1720* (Oxford: Clarendon Press, 1955), 131.

2. *Lloyd's News-Letter*, November 8, 1712, and November 18, 1712, in Lawrence, "Notebooks on . . . the Dublin Stage," 45–49, 55. For Phipps's speech, see *The Resolutions of the House of Commons in Ireland, Relating to the Lord-Chancellor Phips [sic], Examined; with Remarks on the Chancellor's Speech. By a Member of the House of Commons in Ireland* (London, 1714), 4–7.

3. *Dickson's Dublin Intelligence*, February 10, 1713, in Lawrence, "Notebooks on . . . the Dublin Stage," 64–65; David Hayton, "The Crisis in Ireland and the Disintegration of Queen Anne's Last Ministry," *Irish Historical Studies* 22 (1981): 197.

4. *The Resolutions of the House of Commons in Ireland,* 2–3. See also Hayton, "The Crisis in Ireland," 205–6.

5. Ireland, *A Collection of the Protests of the Lords of Ireland, From 1634 to 1770* (London, 1771), 38, 38–39.

6. See Clark, *The Early Irish Stage*, 128–13; and Hayton, "The Crisis in Ireland," 193–213.

7. *The Conduct of the Purse of Ireland in a Letter to a Member of the Late Oxford Convocation, Occasioned By their having conferr'd the Degree of Doctor upon Sir C—— P——* (London, 1714), 11–12. Subsequent references are cited in the text.

8. *The Resolutions of the House of Commons in Ireland*, iii, ii, 14, 16.

9. *Ireland's Lamentation: Being a Short, but Perfect, Full and True Account of the Situation, Nature, Constitution and Product of Ireland. Written by an English Protestant that lately narrowly escaped with his Life from thence* (London, 1689), 26. Subsequent references are cited in the text.

10. *A true and perfect journal of the affairs in Ireland since his majesty's arrival* (London, 1690), in J. G. Simms, *Jacobite Ireland, 1685–91* (London: Routledge and Kegan Paul, 1969), 157.

11. *London Gazette*, July 14, 1690, in Simms, *Jacobite Ireland*, 156.

12. J. T. Gilbert, *A History of the City of Dublin* (Dublin: McGlashan and Gill, 1859), 3:21.

13. Ibid., 3:19–20, 22.

14. J. G. Simms, *William Molyneux of Dublin* (Dublin: Irish Academic Press, 1982), 91.

15. Francis Godwin James, *Ireland in the Empire, 1688–1770* (Cambridge, Mass.: Harvard University Press, 1973), 32.

16. Cited in Connolly, *Religion, Law and Power*, 75.

17. Cited in James, *Ireland in the Empire, 1688–1770*, 32.

18. William Molyneux, *The Case of Ireland Stated*, ed. J. G. Simms (1698; rpt. Dublin: Cadenus, 1977), 17. Subsequent references are cited in the text.

19. Cited in Simms, *Colonial Nationalism, 1698–1776*, 39.

20. Ibid., 43.

21. Jacqueline Hill, *From Patriots to Unionists: Dublin Civic Politics and Irish Protestant Patriotism, 1660–1840* (Oxford: Clarendon Press, 1997), 68. Hill notes, however, that these laws were not rigorously enforced; some Catholics remained in the Corporation.

22. Gilbert, *A History of the City of Dublin*, 3:40–41.

23. Hill, *From Patriots to Unionists*, 68, 69.

24. Gilbert, *A History of the City of Dublin*, 3:42.

25. For Brodrick's anti-Catholicism and his role in the 1692 and 1703–4 Parliaments, see Connolly, *Religion, Law and Power*, 75–76, 78, 127, 281–82. For the resolutions of the Irish Commons in 1703, see James, *Ireland in the Empire, 1688–1770*, 59. For Molesworth as a commonwealthman, see Caroline Robbins, *The Eighteenth-Century Commonwealthman* (Cambridge, Mass.: Harvard University Press, 1959), 88–133.

26. Hill, *From Patriots to Unionists*, 71.

27. For the queen's reply, see James Anthony Froude, *The English in Ireland in the Eighteenth Century* (New York: Scribner, 1897), 1:305. The comment to Brodrick is cited in Connolly, *Religion, Law and Power*, 92.

28. Joseph Roach, *The Cities of the Dead* (New York: Columbia University Press, 1996), 36, 36–39.

29. William Rufus Chetwood, *A General History of the Stage* (London, 1749), 53.

30. *Freeman's Journal*, in Clark, *The Early Irish Stage*, 100.

31. See Clark, *The Early Irish Stage*, 78, 84, 108–9.

32. Cited in Lawrence, "Notebooks on . . . the Dublin Stage," 3:22.

33. Clark, *The Early Irish Stage*, 121, 123, 196, 201.

34. Ibid., 120.

35. Ibid., 83.

36. John Dunton, *The Dublin Scuffle* (Dublin, 1669), 339, in Stockwell, *Dublin Theatres*, 41. Emphasis added.

37. Cited in Stockwell, *Dublin Theatres*, 39.

38. Clark, *The Early Irish Stage*, 103, 119.

39. See "The Sharers' Reply to Mr. Thurmond," in Clark, *The Early Irish Stage*, 201.

40. Clark, *The Early Irish Stage*, 57, 72.

41. Ibid., 112, 200. Other Irish-born actors who were achieving prominence at this time were Robert Wilks and William Bowen.

42. See Christopher Murray, introduction to William Philips, *St. Stephen's Green, or, The Generous Lovers*, ed. Christopher Murray (Mountrath, Portlaoise: Dolmen Press, 1980), 8.

43. Eileen MacCarvill, "Jonathan Swift, Aodh Buí Mac Cruitín, and Contemporary Thomond Scholars," *North Munster Antiquarian Journal* 11 (1968): 38. See also Moody and Vaughan, *A New History of Ireland*, 4:lxi, 55, 402.

44. Philips, *St. Stephen's Green, or, The Generous Lovers*, ed. Christopher Murray (Mountrath, Portlaoise: Dolmen Press, 1980), 57. All subsequent references are to this edition.

45. Benedict Anderson, *Imagined Communities* (London: Verso, 1983), 63, 62.

46. See Murray, introduction to Philips, *St. Stephen's Green*, 44–45.

47. See Leerssen, *Mere Irish and Fíor-Ghael*, 33–66.

48. Clark, *The Early Irish Stage*, 204.

49. Nicholas Rowe, *Tamerlane, A Tragedy*, ed. Landon C. Burns Jr. (Philadelphia: University of Pennsylvania Press, 1966), 18. All other references to *Tamerlane* are to this edition. For contemporary political allusions, see Willard Thorp, "A Key to Rowe's *Tamerlane*," *Journal of English and Germanic Philology* 39 (1940): 124–27; and Donald B. Clark, "The Source and Characterization of Nicholas Rowe's *Tamerlane*," *Modern Language Notes* 65 (1950): 145–52.

50. See Burns, introduction to *Tamerlane*, 6–7.

51. For English anxiety about the buildup of the post-1688 fiscal-military state, see John Brewer, *The Sinews of Power: War, Money and the English State, 1688–1783* (London: Unwin Hyman, 1989), xix.

52. Lawrence suggests that *Tamerlane* was regularly performed in Dublin from 1703 on, a date that seems plausible given that the play was available in print in 1702 ("Notebooks on . . . the Dublin Stage," 36).

53. Linda Colley, *Britons: Forging the Nation, 1707–1837* (New Haven: Yale University Press, 1992), 5.

54. Cited in Barnard, "The Uses of 23 October 1641," 894.

55. William King, *The State of the Protestants of Ireland under the late King James's Government* (London, 1691), 224.

56. Ibid., 227, 228.

57. John Loftis, *The Politics of Drama in Augustan England* (Oxford: Clarendon Press, 1963), 31, 32, 31–34.

58. Anderson, *Imagined Communities*, 7.

59. Ibid., 87, 83–111.

60. Hayton, "The Crisis in Ireland," 194–96.

61. Ibid., 197.

62. Ibid., 197–98; Molesworth's comment is cited in Moody and Vaughan, *A New History of Ireland*, 4:29.

63. *Her Majesty's Prerogative in Ireland; The Authority of the government and Privy-Council There: and the Rights, Laws, and Liberties of the City of Dublin Asserted and Maintain'd in Answer to a Paper Falsely Intituled The Case of the City of Dublin, in relation to the Election of a Lord-Mayor and Sheriffs of the said City* (London, 1712), 4–5.

64. King to Jonathan Swift, in *The Correspondence of Jonathan Swift, D.D.,* ed. F. Elrington Ball (London: Bell and Sons, 1912), 2:281–82.

65. James, *Ireland in the Empire*, 73–75; Froude, *The English in Ireland in the Eighteenth Century*, 347–48.

66. Barnard, "The Uses of 23 October 1641," 916; *The Resolutions of the House of Commons in Ireland*, 5

67. Robert Munter, *The History of the Irish Newspaper, 1685–1760* (Cambridge: Cambridge University Press, 1967), 127; Gilbert, *History of the City of Dublin*, 3:42.

68. *Lloyd's News-Letter*, November 8, 1712, in Lawrence, "Notebooks on . . . the Dublin Stage," 45–49.

69. Ibid., 47.

70. Garth's prologue is cited in Clark, *The Early Irish Stage*, 130–31.

71. Clark, *The Early Irish Stage*, 130.

72. *A New Song on the Whiggs Behaviour*, in Clark, *The Early Irish Stage*, 131.

73. *Lloyd's News-Letter*, November 8, 1712, in Lawrence, "Notebooks on . . . the Dublin Stage," 47–48.

74. "To the Reader," in *A Defence of the Constitution: or, An Answer to an Argument in the Case of Mr. Moor; Lately publish'd by One of her Majesty's Council* (Dublin, 1714).

75. Hayton, "The Crisis in Ireland," 199–206, 206.

76. *The Speaker. A Poem inscribed to Alan Brodrick, Esq. Speaker to the Honourable House of Commons Met at Dublin, November 25, 1713* (Dublin, 1713), 2.

77. Ibid., 2–3.

78. Clark, *The Early Irish Stage*, 133.

79. Homi K. Bhabha, "Dissemination: Time, Narrative, and the Margins of the Modern Nation," in *Nation and Narration*, ed. Homi K. Bhabha (London: Routledge, 1990), 300.

Chapter 2. Disrupting the "Government Play"

1. According to Dyche and Pardon's *A new general English Dictionary* (1735), as cited in *The Compact Edition of the Oxford English Dictionary* (Oxford: Oxford University Press, 1971), "Stuff, in Weaving, is any Sort of Commodity made of Woollen Thread, etc., but in a particular Manner those thin light ones that Women make or line their Gowns of or with" (3109).

2. Sheridan's prologue and Swift's epilogue were published in Matthew Concanen's *Miscellaneous Poems, Original and Translated by Several Hands* (London, 1724), 205–10. All citations are from this edition and are cited in the text.

3. Cited in Swift, *The Correspondence of Jonathan Swift, D.D.*, 3:75.

4. *Hibernian Journal*, July 19, 1784.

5. Greene and Clark, *The Dublin Stage*, 171–72.

6. Mairead Dunlevy, *Dress in Ireland* (New York: Holmes and Meier, 1989), 175.

7. Cited in Robbins, *The Eighteenth-Century Commonwealthman*, 146.

8. Cited in James, *Ireland in the Empire, 1688–1770*, 59.

9. Oliver W. Ferguson, *Jonathan Swift and Ireland* (Urbana: University of Illinois Press, 1962), 51–52.

10. Cited in James, *Ireland in the Empire, 1688–1770*, 74.

11. James Kelly, "Jonathan Swift and the Irish Economy in the 1720s," *Eighteenth-Century Ireland* 6 (1991): 8–9.

12. Cited in Irvin Ehrenpreis, *Swift: The Man, His Works, and the Age* (Cambridge, Mass.: Harvard University Press, 1983), 3:117, 157.

13. See Isolde Victory, "The Making of the 1720 Declaratory Act," in *Parliament, Politics and People*, ed. Gerard O'Brien (Dublin: Irish Academic Press, 1989), 9–29.

14. Cited in J. L. McCracken, "Protestant Ascendancy and the Rise of Colonial Nationalism, 1714–60," in *A New History of Ireland*, 4:110–11.

15. Cited in Victory, "The Making of the 1720 Declaratory Act," 21. There is no contemporary evidence to show that Molyneux's book was burned by the English House of Commons, though it was widely believed in Ireland that it was.

16. Cited in *The Field Day Anthology of Irish Writing*, 1:882.

17. Cited in Ehrenpreis, *Swift: The Man, His Works, and the Age*, 3:122.

18. Jonathan Swift, *A Proposal for the Universal Use of Irish Manufacture*, in *The Prose Works of Jonathan Swift*, ed. Herbert Davis (Oxford: Basil Blackwell, 1939–68), 9:16. Subsequent references are to this edition.

19. Jonathan Swift, *The Story of the Injured Lady*, in *The Prose Works of Jonathan Swift*, 9:9, 5. Subsequent references are to this edition.

20. Carole Fabricant, *Swift's Landscape* (Notre Dame, Ind.: University of Notre Dame Press [1982], 1995), 210–68.

21. Ferguson, *Jonathan Swift and Ireland*, 54–55.

22. *A Defence of English Commodities Being an Answer to the Proposal For the Universal Use of Irish Manufactures*, in *The Prose Works of Jonathan Swift*, 9:271.

23. Hitchcock, *An Historical View of the Irish Stage*, 1:84.

24. Clark, *The Early Irish Stage*, 137.

25. See James Kelly, "'The Glorious and Immortal Memory': Commemoration and Protestant Identity in Ireland, 1660–1800," *Proceedings of the Royal Irish Academy* 94C (1994): 35–36.

26. Mary Louise Pratt, *Imperial Eyes: Travel Writing and Transculturation* (London: Routledge, 1992), 81. For the legitimation crisis in European colonialism, see 72–75.

27. "A Defence of English Commodities," in *The Prose Works of Jonathan Swift*, 9:274.

28. See Tighearnan Mooney and Fiona White, "The Gentry's Winter Season," in *The Gorgeous Mask*, ed. David Dickson (Dublin: Trinity History Workshop, 1987), 1–16.

29. *St. James's Evening Post*, October 18–20, 1733, cited in Lawrence, "Notebooks on . . . the Dublin Stage," 6:27–28.

30. *St. James's Evening Post*, November 13, 1733, cited in Lawrence, "Notebooks on . . . the Dublin Stage," 6:29–30.

31. Mary Delany, *Letters from Georgian Ireland: Correspondence of Mary Delany, 1731–68*, ed. Angelique Day (Belfast: Friar's Bush Press, 1991), 32.

32. Cited in *Cibber and Sheridan: or, the Dublin Miscellany. Containing All the Advertisements, Letters, Addresses, Replys, Apologys, Verses, etc, etc, etc. Lately publish'd on Account of the Theatric Squabble* (Dublin, 1743), 74.

33. John C. Greene, introduction to Greene and Clark, *The Dublin Stage*, 45.

34. Hitchcock, *An Historical View of the Irish Stage*, 2:227. Emphasis added.

35. See "A Second Song, Sung at the Club at Mr. Taplin's the Sign of the Drapier's Head in Truck-Street," in *The Field Day Anthology of Irish Writing*, 1:482–83.

36. See Shadwell's advertisement in *The Dublin Intelligence,* December 19, 1713.

37. *A Letter of Advice to a Young Poet* is published in *The Prose Works of Jonathan Swift,* 9:337, 343–44. This tract has been attributed to Swift, but as Herbert Davis points out, there is little support for this (xxiv–xxvii).

38. Charles Shadwell, *Irish Hospitality; or Virtue Rewarded,* in *Five New Plays* (London, 1720), 319–20. All subsequent references are to this edition.

39. Both remarks are cited in Ehrenpreis, *Swift: The Man, His Works, and the Age,* 3:157, 158.

40. Charles Shadwell, *Rotherick O'Connor, King of Connaught: or the Distress'd Princess,* in *Five New Plays* (London, 1720), [213]. All subsequent references are to this edition

41. Wheatley, *"Beneath Ierne's Banners,"* 30–45.

42. Bishop Evans of Meath made this last remark (Victory, "The Making of the 1720 Declaratory Act," 21).

43. For a reading of this ending as more ambivalent and more conciliatory toward the Irish Protestant patriot position, see Wheatley, *"Beneath Ierne's Banners,"* 39–45.

44. Cited in Ann Rosalind Jones and Peter Stallybrass, "Dismantling Irena: The Sexualizing of Ireland in Early Modern England," in *Nationalisms and Sexualities,* ed. Andrew Parker, Mary Russo, Doris Somuer, and Patricia Yeager (New York: Routledge, 1992), 157–58.

45. Cited in Jones and Stallybrass, "Dismantling Irena," 167. This article provides an excellent analysis of the politics of dress in sixteenth-century colonial Ireland.

46. Dunlevy, *Dress in Ireland,* 92–96, 135–38.

47. *St. James's Evening Post,* October 29–31, 1723, cited in Lawrence, "Notebooks on . . . the Dublin Stage," 4:101.

48. See James, *Ireland in the Empire,* 115.

49. Kelly, "Jonathan Swift and the Irish Economy in the 1720s," 36; Delany, *Letters from Georgian Ireland,* 240.

50. Jonathan Swift, *The Drapier's Letters to the People of Ireland,* ed. Herbert Davis (Oxford: Clarendon Press, 1935), 102–3.

51. Concanen, *Miscellaneous Poems,* 211–12.

52. Ibid., 213.

53. In his collected works, Sterling states the prologue was "spoken on the King's Birthday, 1731, by Mrs. Sterling, when a Bill was brought into the House of Commons by Marcus Anthony Morgan, Esq. for prohibiting the wearing of Gold and Silver Lace, Embroidery, etc" (*The Poetical Works of Rev. James Sterling* [Dublin, 1734], 28). All subsequent citations from Sterling are to this collection and are included in the text.

54. See Greene and Clark, *The Dublin Stage,* 113.

55. Cited in Kelly, "Jonathan Swift and the Irish Economy in the 1720s," 25.

56. Ibid., 31; Greene and Clark, *The Dublin Stage*, 123.

57. Delany, *Letters from Georgian Ireland*, 239. Subsequent references are included in the text.

58. "Ierne's Answer to Albion," in *To the Ladies A Poem. To which is added, Ierne's Answer to Albion. By a Lady* (Dublin, 1745), 6.

59. Ibid., 6–7.

Chapter 3.   "But *Drimin duh* is still in favour . . ."

1. Greene gives March 1722 as the date of this play's first performance, and he records another performance in April 1722–23 (Greene and Clark, *The Dublin Stage*, 97, 442).

2. James Sterling, *The Rival Generals* (London, 1722), x. All subsequent references are to this edition.

3. There is no extant record of a Dublin performance of this play, but Greene has informed me that William Clark lists March 31, 1722, as the date of a Smock Alley performance of *Hibernia Freed* in his unpublished notecards. Greene also noted that the play was published in Dublin, as evidenced by an advertisement in Harding's *Impartial Newsletter* in August 1722. I thank John Greene for this information.

The play premiered in London at the Lincoln's Inn Field Theater on February 13, 1722, and it was performed seven times at that location (see Emmett Avery, ed., *The London Stage, 1660–1800; Part Two, 1700–1729* (Carbondale: Southern Illinois Press, 1960), 2:665–69.

4. Murray, introduction to Philips, *St. Stephen's Green, or, the Generous Lovers*, 17. See also Wheatley's excellent discussion of the play in "*Beneath Ierne's Banners,*" 49–62.

5. William Philips, *Hibernia Freed. A Tragedy* (London, 1722), 3. All subsequent references are to this edition.

6. Matthew Pilkington, "The Progress of Music in *Ireland*. To Mira," in *The Field Day Anthology of Irish Writing*, 1:410, 411.

7. Oliver Goldsmith, "The History of Carolan: The Last Irish Bard," in *The Field Day Anthology of Irish Writing*, 1:667–68.

8. Joseph Cooper Walker, *Historical Memoirs of the Irish Bards* (Dublin, 1786; rpt. New York: Garland, 1971), 156. All subsequent references are to this edition.

9. Harry White, *The Keeper's Recital: Music and Cultural History in Ireland, 1770–1970* (Notre Dame, Ind.: University of Notre Dame Press, 1998), 14–15. For a similar argument about the musical divide in eighteenth-century Dublin, see also Brian Boydell, introduction to *A Dublin Musical Calendar, 1700–1760* (Dublin: Irish Academic Press, 1988), 11–12.

10. See Boydell, *A Dublin Musical Calendar*, 16, 18.

11. The Irish poet Dáibhí Ó Bruadair used this image to convey his utter sense of despair after the Jacobite defeat in his poem "An Longbriseadh" (The Shipwreck) (1698).

12. Lawrence Whyte, "An Historical Poem, On the Rise and Progress of the Charitable and Musical Society, now assembling at the Bull's-Head in Fishamble-street, Dublin," in *Poems on various subjects, serious and diverting, never before published* (Dublin, 1740), 218. All subsequent citations from this poem are to this edition. For a description of the location of this tavern, see Gilbert, *A History of the City of Dublin*, 1:142–43. For a succinct account of the makeup and movement of this musical society, see also Nicolas Carolan, introduction to *A Collection of the Most Celebrated Irish Tunes* (Dublin: Folk Music Society of Ireland, 1986), xiii–xx.

13. "The Broken Jug," in *Poems on various subjects*, 127–28.

14. For Whyte's background and Dublin connections, see Patrick Fagan's introduction to Whyte's poetry in *A Georgian Celebration: Irish Poets of the Eighteenth Century* (Dublin: Branar Press, 1989), 32–35.

15. Lawrence Whyte, "The Character of an Honest Jolly Companion," in *Original Poems on Various Subjects, Serious Moral, and Diverting*, 2d ed. (Dublin, 1742), 37. The English translation is Whyte's.

16. Whyte, *Poems on various subjects*, vii–viii.

17. Fagan, *A Georgian Celebration*, 32–35.

18. Gilbert, *A History of the City of Dublin*, 1:68.

19. Tadgh Ó Neachtain mentions John Fergus (Eoin Ó Fearghusa) in a poem that lists the Irish scholars in his father's circle who were living in Dublin in the 1720s (T. F. O'Rahilly, "Irish Scholars in Dublin in the Early Eighteenth Century," *Gadelica* 1 [1912–13], 161–62).

20. Lawrence Whyte, "An Elegy on the much lamented Death of Patt. Beaghan, late Governor of the Club at the George in Fishamble-street, Dublin, who resigned his Government in this World, on Tuesday the 16th Day of April, 1723 in the 57th year of his Age," in *Poems on various subjects*, 162.

21. Whyte, "An Historical Poem," in *Poems on various subjects*, 220.

22. O'Conor to Daniel O'Conor, March 3, 1756, in *Letters of Charles O'Conor of Belanagare*, ed. Robert E. Ward, John F. Wrynn, and Catherine Coogan Ward (Washington, D. C.: Catholic University of America, 1988), 10.

23. See Robert E. Ward, John F. Wrynn, and Catherine Coogan Ward, introduction to *Letters of Charles O'Conor*, xxi–xxxiv.

24. O'Conor to Bryan O'Conor, [1754], in *Letters of Charles O'Conor*, 7.

25. O'Conor to Denis O'Conor, [November 17, 1751], in *Letters of Charles O'Conor*, 6–7.

26. O'Conor to Daniel O'Conor, March 3, 1756, in *Letters of Charles O'Conor*, 10.

27. O'Conor to Dr. John Curry, March 15, 1760, in *Letters of Charles O'Conor*, 84.

28. Whyte, "An Historical Poem," in *Poems on various subjects*, 220.

29. Carolan, introduction to *A Collection of the Most Celebrated Irish Tunes*, xxvi–xxvii.

30. Whyte, "The Parting Cup, or the Humours of Deoch an Doruis," in *Poems on various subjects*, 80–81.

31. Bill Rolston, "Music and Politics in Ireland: The Case of Loyalism," in *Politics and Performance in Contemporary Northern Ireland*, ed. John P. Harrington and Elizabeth J. Mitchell (Amherst: University of Massachusetts Press, 1999), 40.

32. See Boydell, *A Dublin Musical Calendar*, 41.

33. Donal O'Sullivan, *Carolan, the Life, Times and Music of an Irish Harper* (London: Routledge and Kegan Paul, 1958), 53–64, 121–22. Carolan's harp is today in the collection of O'Conor memorabilia in Clonalis House, Castlerea, County Roscommon (*Letters of Charles O'Conor of Belanagare*, xxiii).

34. Cited in O'Sullivan, *Carolan*, 122.

35. Ibid., 122.

36. See Andrew Carpenter and Alan Harrison, "Swift's 'O'Rouke's Feast' and Sheridan's 'Letter': Early Transcripts by Anthony Raymond," in *Proceedings of the First Munster Symposium on Jonathan Swift*, ed. H. J. Real and H. J. Vienken (Munich: Wilhelm Fink 1985), 27–46; C. G. Ó Háinle, "Neighbors in Eighteenth-Century Dublin: Jonathan Swift and Sean Ó Neachtain," *Eire* 21 (1986): 106–21; Andrew Carpenter, "Irish and Anglo-Irish Scholars in the Time of Swift: The Case of Anthony Raymond," in *Literary Interrelations: Ireland, England, and the World*, ed. Wolfgang Zach and Heinz Kosok (Tübingen: Gunter Narr, 1987), 11–19; and Alan Harrison, *Ag cruinniú meala: Anthony Raymond (1675–1726), ministéir Protastúnach agus léann na Gaeilge i mBaile Átha Cliath* (Baile Átha Cliath: Clóchomhar Tta, 1988).

37. This is a translation from the Irish by Alan Harrison, as cited in Andrew Carpenter, "Irish and Anglo-Irish Scholars in the Time of Swift," 15.

38. Leerssen, *Mere Irish and Fíor-Ghael*, 287–89, 288.

39. Jonathan Swift, "The Description of an *Irish-Feast*, Translated Almost Literally Out of the Original *Irish*," in *The Field Day Anthology of Irish Writing*, 1:400.

40. See D. J. O'Donoghue, *The Poets of Ireland* (Dublin: Hodges Figgis, 1912; rpt. New York: Johnson Reprint Corporation, 1970), 72; *Dictionary of National Biography*, s.v. "Coffey, Charles."

41. Edward MacLysaght, *Irish Families, Their Names, Arms and Origins* (Dublin: Hodges Figgis, 1957), 82; O'Rahilly, "Irish Scholars in Dublin in the Early Eighteenth Century," 162.

42. In addition to the two dramatic works listed below, Coffey wrote prologues for the Dublin stage (see his *Poems and Songs* [Dublin, 1724]), and he is also reputed to have acted Aesop at Smock Alley (he is addressed in one contemporary pamphlet as the "Hibernian Aesop"; see note 59 below). Vanbrugh's *Aesop*

was performed at Smock Alley during the 1723–24 and 1725–26 seasons (Greene and Clark, *The Dublin Stage,* 102, 109–10).

43. *Wife or No Wife,* in Charles Coffey, *Poems and Songs* (Dublin, 1724), 15. All subsequent references are to this edition.

44. Swift, "The Description of an *Irish-Feast,*" in *The Field Day Anthology of Irish Writing,* 1:399.

45. Charles Coffey, *The Female Parson or Beau in the Sudds* (London, 1730), 15.

46. See MacCarvill, "Jonathan Swift, Aodh Buí Mac Cruitín, and Contemporary Thomond Scholars," 36–37, 40.

47. John Bender, *Imagining the Penitentiary: Fiction and the Architecture of Mind in Eighteenth-Century England* (Chicago: University of Chicago Press, 1987), 13, 15.

48. Charles Coffey, *The Beggar's Wedding. A New Opera as it is acted in Dublin, with great applause* (Dublin, 1729), ii, v, viii. Subsequent references are to *The Beggar's Wedding. A New Opera as it is acted in Dublin, with great applause and at the Theatre in the Hay-Market* (London, 1729; rpt. In *Irish Ballad Operas and Burlesques I,* in vol. 22 of *The Ballad opera: a collection of 171 original texts of musical plays printed in photo-facsimile,* selected and arranged by Walter H. Rubsamen [New York: Garland, 1974]).

49. Joseph O'Carroll, "Contemporary Attitudes towards the Homeless Poor, 1725–1775," in *The Gorgeous Mask,* ed. David Dickson (Dublin: Trinity History Workshop, 1987), 64–85.

50. Cited in O'Carroll, "Contemporary Attitudes towards the Homeless Poor," 68.

51. Frank Llewelyn Harrison, "Music, Poetry and Polity in the Age of Swift," *Eighteenth-Century Ireland* 1 (1986): 60, 51–56.

52. *Sources of Irish Traditional Music c. 1600–1855,* ed. by Aloys Fleischmann and Micheál Ó Súilleabháin (New York: Garland, 1998), 1:109–11.

53. Whyte, "The Parting Cup," in *Poems on various subjects,* 91.

54. Micheál Ó Súilleabháin, preface to *Sources of Irish Traditional Music,* 1:xxi–xxii. I am very grateful to Professor Ó Súilleabháin for bringing this information on "The Black Joke" to my attention.

55. See Máirín Nic Eoin, "Secrets and Disguises? Caitlín Ní Uallacháin and Other Female Personages in Eighteenth-Century Irish Political Poetry," *Eighteenth-Century Ireland* 11 (1996): 7–45.

56. Coffey, preface to *The Beggar's Wedding* (Dublin, 1729), ii–iii.

57. See Greene and Clark, *The Dublin Stage,* 119.

58. *Doctor Anthony's Advice to the Hibernian Aesop: or An Epistle to the Author of the B——gs W——g* (Dublin, 1729).

59. Lawrence, "Notebooks on . . . the Dublin Stage," 5:142: Greene and Clark, *The Dublin Stage,* 120.

60. Boydell, *A Dublin Musical Calendar,* 72, 108, 109.

61. *A New Opera-Epilogue to the Tragedy of Richard the Third* (Dublin, 1731); Lawrence, Notebooks on . . . the Dublin Stage," 5:52.

62. Cited in Andrew Carpenter, *Verse in English from Eighteenth-Century Ireland* (Cork: Cork University Press, 1998), 44–45.

63. *The Upper Gallery. A Poem* (Dublin, 1731), 5. All subsequent references are included in the text. Lawrence speculates that the author of this poem was John Lawson (1712–59) ("Notebooks on . . . the Dublin Stage," 6:61).

64. *A Dissertation on Italian and Irish Musick, with some Panegryrick on Carrallan our late Irish Orpheus* was published in Whyte's *Poems on various subjects* (154–59). All references here, however, are to the edition of the poem that appears in *The Field Day Anthology of Irish Writing*, 1:412–15.

65. T. J. Walsh, *Opera in Dublin, 1705–1797: The Social Scene* (Dublin: Allen Figgis, 1973), 48; Greene and Clark, *The Dublin Stage*, 168.

66. Walsh, *Opera in Dublin*, 48–50.

67. "Lilibulero" was composed to satirize Catholic hopes during the 1688–91 wars, and as Carpenter notes, it became "the standard protestant triumphalist anthem" in eighteenth-century Ireland" (*Verse in English*, 37).

68. See J. O. Bartley, *Teague, Shenkin and Sawney* (Cork: Cork University Press, 1954), 129. Bartley suggests that "my dear" may be a garbled version of the Irish exclamatory phrase *mo Dia* (my God), and "honey" may be a corruption of the Irish vocative, *a dhuine* (oh person).

69. See notes 17 and 18 to *A Dissertation*, in *The Field Day Anthology of Irish Writing*, 1:413

70. Cited in *Old Dublin Songs*, ed. Hugh Shields (Dublin: Folk Music Society of Ireland, 1988), 22.

71. Greene and Clark, *The Dublin Stage*, 189, 191,197. See *Poems on various subjects* (229) for Whyte's prologue.

72. "Droimeann Donn Dilis," in *An Duanaire, 1600–1690: Poems of the Dispossessed*, ed. Sean Ó Tuama and Thomas Kinsella (Mountrath, Portlaoise: Dolmen Press, 1981), 310–11.

73. Nic Eoin, "Secrets and Disguises," 44.

Chapter 4.   The Gentlemen's Quarrel and the Politics of the '45

1. Sheldon, *Thomas Sheridan of Smock-Alley*, 84–10, 103. All subsequent citations appear in the text.

2. Lucas, *A Letter to the Free-Citizens of Dublin*, 5. All subsequent references are cited in the text.

3. Wall, *Catholic Ireland in the Eighteenth Century*, 116, 57; F. J. McLynn, "'Good Behaviour'": Irish Catholics and the Jacobite Rising of 1745," *Eire-Ireland* 16 (1981): 52–53.

4. McLynn, "'Good Behaviour,'" 43.

5. Cited in Wall, *Catholic Ireland,* 57.

6. Cited in Wall, *Catholic Ireland,* 116.

7. Cited in W. Ernst, *Lord Chesterfield* (London: Grolier Society, n.d.), 1:307.

8. Ibid., 286.

9. Ibid.

10. Ibid., 285–86.

11. Ibid., 297–98.

12. Cited in Wall, *Catholic Ireland,* 57.

13. See Jonathan Clark, *English Society, 1660–1832* (Cambridge: Cambridge University Press, 2000), 114–15; and Donald Greene, *The Politics of Samuel Johnson* (New Haven: Yale University Press, 1960), 99–100.

14. Helen Margaret Scurr, *Henry Brooke* (Minneapolis: University of Minnesota Press, 1927), 64.

15. Greene and Clark, *The Dublin Stage,* 387.

16. Cited in Greene and Clark, *The Dublin Stage,* 387.

17. *The Farmer's Letter to the Protestants of Ireland* (Dublin, 1745), 1:3. This Dublin edition contains all six of the Farmer's Letters. All subsequent references appear in the text.

18. Benjamin Victor, *The History of the Theatres of London and Dublin* (London, 1761), 1:139.

19. See the introduction.

20. The paper is attributed to the Reverend John Jones in Walter Harris's *Fiction Unmasked: or an Answer to a Dialogue lately published by a Popish Physician, and pretended to have passed between a Dissenter, and a Member of the Church of Ireland . . .* (Dublin, 1752). This pamphlet attacks both *The Impartial Examiner* and John Curry's *Brief Account* (see note 23, below).

21. *The Impartial Examiner, or the Faithful Representer of the Various and Manifold Misrepresentations imposed on the Roman Catholics of Ireland, in the Several Charges laid at their Doors by the Scribblers of the Farmer's, Merchant's, and Drapier's Letters, and Charitable and Seasonable Advices, the Editors of the Magazines, and the Printers of the Journals, Courants, Occurrences, News-Letters, Gazettes, Pamphlets, and other modern Public Papers, Etc, which are daily printed in Dublin* (Dublin, 1746). All subsequent references appear in the text.

22. For a discussion of some of these pamphlets, however, see McLynn, "'Good Behaviour,'" 53–56.

23. John Curry, *A Brief Account from the Most Authentic Protestant Writers of the Causes, Motives, and Mischiefs, of the Irish Rebellion on the 23rd Day of October 1641, Deliver'd in a Dialogue Between a Dissenter and a Member of the Church of Ireland, as by Law Established* (London, 1747), 1.

24. John Curry, *Historical Memoirs of the Irish Rebellion* (London, 1758).

25. Edmund Burke, from *Letter to a Peer of Ireland* (1782), in *The Field Day Anthology*, 1: 820–21.

26. Sheldon, *Thomas Sheridan of Smock-Alley*, 313.

27. Thomas Davies, *Memoirs of the Life of David Garrick, Esq.* (London, 1780), 1:86.

28. Cited in Sheldon, *Thomas Sheridan of Smock-Alley*, 316, 318.

29. Cited in Alexander Chalmers, *The Works of the English Poets, from Chaucer to Cowper* (London, 1810), 17:427.

30. Sheldon, *Thomas Sheridan of Smock-Alley*, 317, 68.

31. Ibid., 318.

32. *A Serious Enquiry into the Cause of the Present Disorders of this City* (Dublin, 1747), 9. All subsequent references are cited in the text.

33. Leo Hughes, *The Drama's Patrons: A Study of the Eighteenth-Century London Audience* (Austin: University of Texas Press, 1971), 23–25.

34. Kristina Straub, *Sexual Suspects: Eighteenth-Century Players and Sexual Ideology* (Princeton: Princeton University Press, 1992), 153–61, 168–73.

35. Hughes, *The Drama's Patrons*, 9–14; the citation is from *A Dialogue in the Green-room upon a Disturbance in the Pit* (1763), as given in *The Drama's Patrons*, 12.

36. *The Conduct of the Purse in Ireland*, 14–15.

37. For the view that Sheridan was a descendant of Donnchadh Ó Sioradain, see Fintan O'Toole, *A Traitor's Kiss: The Life of Richard Brinsley Sheridan* (London: Granta Publications, 1997), 3–7. For the view that Sheridan's grandfather was, instead, a Gaelic-speaking farmer named Patrick, see Vivian Mercier, *The Irish Comic Tradition* (Oxford: Clarendon Press, 1962), 93.

38. O'Toole, *A Traitor's Kiss*, 12–16.

39. *An Enquiry into the Plan and Pretensions of Mr. Sheridan*, 30–31.

40. Sheridan identifies Kelly as a Trinity graduate who "had left it [Trinity] but a few months" in his pamphlet, *A Full Vindication of the Conduct of the Manager of the Theatre-Royal* (Dublin, 1747), 10. This suggests that the E. Kelly in question was Edmund Kelly who entered Trinity as a pensioner on July 10, 1744 (see *Alumni Dublinenses*, ed. G. D. Burtchaell and T. U. Sadleir [Dublin: Thom and Co., 1935]).

41. Arch Elias, ed. *Memoirs of Laetitia Pilkington* (Athens: University of Georgia Press, 1997), 2:714.

42. Burke, *The Correspondence of Edmund Burke*, 84.

43. Cullen, "Catholics under the Penal Laws," 29.

44. Thomas P. Power, "Converts," in *Endurance and Emergence*, 122–23.

45. James Kelly, *"That Damn'd Thing Called Honour": Duelling in Ireland, 1570–1860* (Cork: Cork University Press, 1995), 55–56; Bartlett, *The Fall and Rise of the Irish Nation*, 48.

46. Kelly, *"That Damn'd Thing Called Honour,"* 57–59.

47. Cited in Davis's edition of Swift, *The Drapier's Letters to the People of Ireland*, 227–28.

48. Charles Lucas, *A Description of the Cave of Kilcorny, in the Barony of Bur-ren in Ireland, wrote by Mr. Charles Lucas, Apothecary, in the Year 1740*, in *Esdall's News-Letter*, April 16, 1750.

49. Kevin Whelan, *The Tree of Liberty: Radicalism, Catholicism and the Con-struction of Irish Identity, 1760–1830* (Notre Dame, Ind.: Notre Dame University Press, 1996), 3–56.

50. Alan Gailey, *Irish Folk Drama* (Cork: Mercier Press, 1969), 68–69, 94–96.

51. Cited in Gailey, *Irish Folk Drama*, 95–96.

52. Alan Harrison, *The Irish Trickster* (Sheffield: Sheffield Academic Press, ca. 1989).

53. See Gilbert, *History of the City of Dublin*, 3:42–43.

54. George Anne Bellamy, *An Apology for the Life of George Anne Bellamy* (London, 1785), 1:159–60.

55. Mr. Francis Liberty (pseud.), *A Letter of Thanks to the Barber, for the In-defatigable Pains to Suppress the Horrid and Unnatural Rebellion, Lately broke out in this City, But by His Means, now happily Extinguished* (Dublin, 1747), 6. All sub-sequent references are in the text.

56. Charles Lucas [A. Freeman, Barber and Citizen, pseud.], *A Second Letter to the Free-Citizens of Dublin* (Dublin, 1747), 15. All subsequent references appear in the text.

57. *A New Ballad on a Late Drubbing* ([Dublin], n.d).

58. Mercier, *The Irish Comic Tradition*, 155–71.

59. Leerssen, *Mere Irish and Fíor-Ghael*, 287–88.

60. *The Farmer's Yard. A New Fable for Aesop* ([Dublin], 1747), 3, 4, 5. All subsequent references are cited in the text.

61. Leerssen, *Mere Irish and Fíor-Ghael*, 240.

62. Jack Pilkington, *The Real Story of John Carteret Pilkington* (London, 1760), 171, 172.

63. See chapter 3.

64. Bartlett, *The Fall and Rise of the Irish Nation*, 50–55.

65. John Browne, *The Gentlemen's Apology to the Ladies, for their being dis-appointed at the Play-House, on Wednesday the 11th of February, 1746–7*, in *Dublin in an Uproar: or, the Ladies robb'd of their Pleasure* (Dublin, 1747), 6. All subse-quent references appear in the text. In *The Tradesmen's Answer to a False Scurrilous Paper, intituled, The Gentlemen's Apology to the Ladies, etc.* (Dublin, 1747), Lucas identifies the writer of this pamphlet as "H..lp..y" or Halfpenny Browne (John Browne of the Neale). In the third Barber's *Letter*, Lucas acknowledges that he is the author of *The Tradesmen's Answer* (4).

66. *Dublin Journal*, March 3–7, 1747.

67. Charles Lucas [A. Freeman, Barber and Citizen, pseud.], *A Third Letter to the Free-Citizens of Dublin* (Dublin, 1747), 4.

1. William Dennis to Richard Shackleton, January 14, 1747 (O. S.), in James Prior, *The Life of Oliver Goldsmith, M. B., from a variety of original sources* (Philadelphia: E. L. Cary and A. Hart, 1837), 315. All subsequent references are included in the text.

2. See, for example, Robert M. Krapp, "Class Analysis of a Literary Controversy: Wit and Sense in Seventeenth-Century English Literature," *Science and Society* 10 (1946): 80–92; and Peter Stallybrass and Allon White, *The Politics and Poetics of Transgression* (Ithaca: Cornell University Press, 1986), 110.

3. These remarks are reported in the anti-Sheridan pamphlet *A Letter to the Admirers of Mr. Sh——N* (Dublin, 1748).

4. *European Magazine* 35 (February 1794): 110.

5. *The Tickler* (Dublin, 1748). This collection contains issues 1 through 7 of *The Tickler*. All subsequent references to these first seven issues are to this edition and are cited in the text.

6. See chapter 4.

7. *European Magazine* 35 (February 1794): 110; *Dictionary of National Biography*, s.v. "Hiffernan, Paul."

8. *A Narrative of the Barbarous and Bloody Murder of P..l H..ff..n, M. D. Committed by Himself on Monday, the 17th Day of October, Inst Being a LETTER from Mr. R..d D..ck..n of S..l..r C..t Castle-Street Dublin, to J..n B..ne Esq; at the Hague* (Dublin, 1748), 6.

9. Ibid., 2.

10. See chapter 4.

11. Burke to Richard Shackleton, February 21, 1747, in *The Correspondence of Edmund Burke*, 1:83, 84.

12. [William Dennis,] *Brutus's Letter to the Town* (Dublin, 1747), 3, 4. All subsequent references are cited in the text.

13. Burke to Richard Shackleton, March 12, 1747, in *The Correspondence of Edmund Burke*, 1:88.

14. J. G. A. Pocock, "Burke and the Ancient Constitution," in *Politics, Language and Time: Essays on Political Thought and History* (New York: Atheneum, 1971), 202–32.

15. Conor Cruise O'Brien, *The Great Melody: A Thematic Biography and Commented Anthology of Edmund Burke* (Chicago: University of Chicago Press, 1992), 22.

16. Seamus Deane, "Edmund Burke," in *The Field Day Anthology of Irish Writing*, 1:807–9.

17. Burke to Richard Shackleton, April 26, 1745, in *The Correspondence of Edmund Burke*, 1:63.

18. Dennis to Richard Shackleton, May 28, 1747, in *The Correspondence of Edmund Burke*, 1:93.

19. Burke to Charles O'Hara, July 3, 1761, in *Edmund Burke, New York Agent with his letters to the New York Assembly and intimate correspondence with Charles O'Hara, 1761–1776* (Philadelphia: American Philosophical Society, 1956), 277.

20. See chapter 4, penultimate paragraph.

21. Burke to Charles O'Hara, July 10, 1761, in *Edmund Burke, New York Agent*, 278–79.

22. See Sean Murphy, "Charles Lucas, Catholicism and Nationalism," *Eighteenth-Century Ireland* 8 (1993): 83–102; and "Charles Lucas and the Dublin Election of 1748–1749," *Parliamentary History*, (New York: St. Martin's Press, 1983), 2:93–111.

23. Murphy, "Charles Lucas, Catholicism and Nationalism," 87, 88.

24. Ibid., 86.

25. Murphy, "Charles Lucas and the Dublin Election," 93–94.

26. *An Apology for the Conduct and Writings of Mr. C——s L——s, Apothecary; wherein The seeming Oddity of his setting up and recommending himself to the Freemen and Citizens of D–BL–N, as the only fit Person to represent them in Parliament, is clearly accounted for in A letter to a Friend* (Dublin, 1749), 8.

27. Victor, *The History of the Theatres of London and Dublin*, 1:113.

28. Lucas [A. Freeman, Barber and Citizen, pseud.], *A Letter to the Free-Citizens of Dublin*, 7.

29. Victor, *The History of the Theatres of London and Dublin*, 1:114.

30. Ibid., 1:115.

31. Smyth, *The Men of No Property*, 4.

32. Sheldon, *Thomas Sheridan of Smock-Alley*, 69, 70.

33. Ibid., 80.

34. Cited in Sheridan, *An Humble Appeal to the Publick*, 11.

35. *A Serious Enquiry into the Cause of the Present Disorders of this City*, 8.

36. Bryan Coleborne, "The Dublin Grub Street: The Documentary Evidence in the Case of John Browne," *Swift Studies* 2 (1987): 15.

37. Lucas [A. Freeman, Barber and Citizen, pseud.], *A Third Letter to the Free-Citizens of Dublin*, 4.

38. Cited in A. P. I. Samuels, *The Early Life, Correspondence and Writing of the Rt. Hon. Edmund Burke LL. D.* (Cambridge: Cambridge University Press, 1923), 187.

39. Charles Lucas, *The Complaints of Dublin: Humbly offered to his Excellency William Earl of Harrington . . . By Charles Lucas, a Free Citizen* (Dublin, 1749), 24–25.

40. *The Tickler* 26 (July 19, 1749): 1.

41. Cited in Sheldon, *Thomas Sheridan of Smock-Alley*, 329.

42. *Mr. Nobody's Anti-Ticklerian Address to Mr. Lucas* (Dublin, 1748), 14.

43. Ibid., 15.

44. Michael McKeon, "Cultural Crisis and Dialectical Method: Destabilizing Augustan Literature," in *The Profession of Eighteenth-Century Literature*, ed. Leo Damrosch (Madison: University of Wisconsin Press, 1992), 54–55.

45. *The Tickler* 35 (October 20, 1749).

46. Alardyce Nicoll, *The World of Harlequin: A Critical Study of the Commedia dell'Arte* (Cambridge: Cambridge University Press, 1963), 87.

47. The prologue to *Punch turn'd School-Master* was published in Matthew Concanen's *Miscellaneous Poems* (London, 1724), 338–40. Mrs. Sterling's critique was delivered in *A New Opera-Epilogue to the Tragedy of Richard the Third* (Dublin, 1731).

48. Jonathan Swift, "Mad Mullinex and Timothy," in *The Poems of Jonathan Swift*, ed. Harold Williams, 3:776–77. All subsequent references appear in the text.

49. Ehrenpreis, *Swift: The Man, His Works, and the Age*, 3:580.

50. See the notes on this poem in *The Poems of Jonathan Swift*, 3:1108–9. This poem was formerly attributed to Swift, but Williams speculates it was Dr. Sheridan's.

51. *Punch's Petition to the Ladies*, in *The Poems of Jonathan Swift*, ed. William Ernst Browning (London: G. Bell and Sons, 1910), 2:294. All subsequent references appear in the text.

52. See Swift's "Billet to the Company of Players," in *The Poems of Jonathan Swift*, 1:306–9; and "Epilogue. To Mr. Hoppy's Benefit-Night, at Smock-Alley," in *The Poems of Jonathan Swift*, ed. Browning 1:130–31. In his fourth *Drapier's Letter*, Swift also sarcastically alludes to a *"Favourite Secretary"* who had "descend[ed] to be *Master of the Revels*, which by his *Credit and Extortion* he hath made *Pretty Considerable"* (cited in *The Poems of Jonathan Swift*, 1:306).

53. [Edmund Burke,] *Punch's Petition to Mr. Sh———n, to be admitted into The Theatre Royal* (Dublin, 1748).

54. Scott Shershow, *Puppets and "Popular" Culture* (Ithaca: Cornell University Press, 1995), 121.

55. *The Reformer* 1 (January 28, 1748), 1. All subsequent references to this issue appear in the text.

56. The poor quality of the entertainments is discussed in the first and second issues (January 28 and February 4, 1748); the poor quality of his players and the barbarism of his audience are the focus of the third issue (February 11, 1748).

57. For the most part, Samuels reproduces only the essays from *The Reformer* in *The Early Life, Correspondence and Writing of . . . Edmund Burke*, 296–329.

58. Patrick Fagan, *Dublin's Turbulent Priest: Cornelius Nary, 1658–1738* (Dublin: Royal Irish Academy, 1991), 198.

59. I am grateful to Joanna Finegan of the National Library of Ireland for her helpful remarks on this print and for the information she provided on William Jones and Andrew Miller. I would also like to acknowledge Neil York's help in locating this print.

60. Lucas published a pamphlet entitled *Develina Libera: An Apology for the Civil Rights and Liberties of the Commons and Citizens of Dublin* in 1744.

61. Hiffernan alluded to this "Curious Frontispiece" in the advertisement for the collected edition of *The Tickler* that appeared in *The Tickler* 10 (September 14, 1748).

62. This seventh issue was subtitled *Being an Answer to Asper against Buffone*, and in it Hiffernan responded to a recent anti-Ticklerian pamphlet, *Asper Against Buffone. Or a Warning to the Tickler*, which threatened (among other things) to expose Hiffernan's identity if he continued his attacks on Lucas. To show his contempt for such threats, Hiffernan provides a pen picture of himself in a short poem in this issue; he describes himself as having "Black frowning brows" over "hollow eyes," a "medical grimace," a body "somewhat gross," a humor that is "Various . . . fiery, morose"; in sum, he is a "Good-natur'd, peevish, gay, phantastic thing" (52–53). The heavy-browed, grimacing clown of this "Curious Frontispiece" matches this description, and the single word that appears on the pamphlet Lucas holds in his hand—*Asper*—further signals this discursive context.

63. *The Reformer Reform'd, being an Address from Thomas Telltruth, Esq; To the Reformer. With a Defence of the Manager of the Theatre-Royal, from groundless Assertions* (Dublin, 1748), 8. This pamphlet, which was internally dated January 28, 1748, was very likely the pamphlet that Burke sent Shackleton in his letter of February 2, 1748 (Burke writes, "[Y]ou see by the enclosed that the scribblers do us the honour to take notice of us"). It was clearly *not* a copy of *The Tickler* as Samuels suggests (*The Early Life, Correspondence and Writing of . . . Edmund Burke*, 163). The first issue of *The Tickler* did not appear until February 18, and in any case the Trinity trio were in an alliance with Hiffernan.

64. Dennis to Richard Shackleton, February 4, 1748, in Prior, *The Life of Oliver Goldsmith*, 318–19.

65. *The Reformer* 5 (February 25, 1748), 1. All subsequent references to this issue are cited in the text.

66. Thomas O. McLoughlin, "The Context of Edmund Burke's *The Reformer*," *Eighteenth-Century Ireland* 2 (1987): 43.

67. *The Reformer* 4 (February 18, 1748), 1–3.

68. *The Reformer* 7 (March 10, 1748), 1–4.

69. *The Reformer* 9 (March 24, 1748), 2, 1–3.

70. Thomas O'McLoughlin, "The Context of Edmund Burke's *The Reformer*," 51–55.

71. *The Reformer* 6 (March 3, 1748), 1.

72. For the identification of Asper as Hiffernan, see also Samuels, *The Early Life, Correspondence and Writing of . . . Edmund Burke*, 172.

73. See chapter 6.

Chapter 6. "A company . . . zealous for their Country's Honour"

1. William Rufus Chetwood, *A General History of the Stage: From Its Origin in Greece Down to the Present Time* (London, 1749), 75.

2. Lawrence, "Notebooks on . . . the Dublin Stage," 12:87–88.

3. Cited in Sheldon, *Thomas Sheridan of Smock-Alley*, 126.

4. McLoughlin, "The Context of Edmund Burke's *The Reformer*," 41.

5. Ibid.

6. *The Reformer* 8 (March 17, 1748), 1, 2. All subsequent references to this issue are cited in the text.

7. Foote had played earlier at Capel Street with the original breakaway group who had built the theater in 1745 (Greene and Clark, *The Dublin Stage*, 36).

8. Simon Trefman, *Sam. Foote, Comedian, 1720–1777* (New York: New York University Press, 1971), 23–30. This "Chocolate" pretext was necessary to avoid prosecution under the English Licensing Act.

9. See Sheldon, *Thomas Sheridan of Smock-Alley*, 126, 328.

10. *Dublin Journal*, April 2–5, 1748.

11. In its sixth issue on March 3, for example, *The Reformer* advertised that this English player would soon treat the "Nobility and Gentry" to his "Chocolate" in the Capel Street theater (4). Subsequent references to this issue are cited in the text.

12. Laetitia Pilkington, *Memoirs of Laetitia Pilkington*, ed. Arch Elias (Athens: University of Georgia Press, 1997), 1:328. All subsequent references appear in the text.

13. Lawrence, "Notebooks on . . . the Dublin Stage," 12:98–99; Sheldon, *Thomas Sheridan of Smock-Alley*, 126.

14. Pilkington, *Memoirs of Laetitia Pilkington*, 2:666–67, 713–15.

15. Jack Pilkington, *The Real Story of John Carteret Pilkington*, 12. All subsequent references appear in the text.

16. Pilkington, *Memoirs of Laetitia Pilkington*, 2:355.

17. For this correspondence and its accounts of Laetitia's visits to Browne, see Pilkington, *The Real Story of John Carteret Pilkington*, 241–57.

18. *The Stage or Coronation of King Tom. A Satyr . . . By B——t B——n.* (Dublin, 1753), in Lawrence, "Notebooks on . . . the Dublin Stage," 15:30–31.

19. Burke to Richard Shackleton, March 12, 1747, in *The Correspondence of Edmund Burke*, 1:88. Burke states in this letter that Brenan "has lately published a Thing calld Fleckno's Ghost." As the twentieth-century editor of Burke's correspondence notes, this lost poem is most likely a version of *The Stage or Coronation of King Tom*, a poem that is closely modeled on Dryden's *Macflecknoe*. In a letter to Colley Cibber, dated November 17, 1748, Victor also mentions buying a poem titled *A Satire on the Theatrical King Tom* on a Dublin street, and from the description

he gives, it is clear that this is Brenan's satire (*The History of the Theatres of London and Dublin*, 2:211).

20. See Arch Elias, "Male Hormones and Women's Wit: The Sex Appeal of Mary Goddard and Laetitia Pilkington," *Swift Studies* 9 (1994): 14.

21. Pilkington, *Memoirs of Laetitia Pilkington*, 2:260, 647.

22. Ibid., 599, 663.

23. *Dublin Journal*, March 19–22, 1748. See also Pilkington, *Memoirs of Laetitia Pilkington*, 2:565.

24. See chapter 4.

25. See Elias, "Male Hormones and Women's Wit."

26. *Dublin Journal*, April 19–23, 1748.

27. *Dublin Journal*, March 22–26, 1748.

28. *The Reformer* 11 (April 7, 1748), 4; and 12 (April 14, 1748), 4.

29. See Sheldon, *Thomas Sheridan of Smock-Alley*, 320.

30. *Pue's Occurrences*, April 30–May 3, 1748.

31. *The Self-Enamour'd; or the Ladies Doctor . . . by P. H. M. D.* (Dublin, 1750). All subsequent references are cited in the text.

32. *The Tickler* (September 8, 1748).

33. Cited in Hill, *From Patriots to Unionists*, 106–8.

34. [Brooke], *An Occasional Letter from the Farmer, to the Free-Men of Dublin* (Dublin, 1749), as cited in Hill, *From Patriots to Unionists*, 106–7.

35. *Dublin Courant*, March 25–28, 1749.

36. See chapter 5.

37. *Little John and the Giants*, in *Irish Ballad Operas and Burlesques II*, selected and arranged by Walter H. Rubsamen, in *The Ballad Opera: A Collection of 171 Original Texts of Musical Plays Printed in Photo-Facsimile* (New York: Garland, 1974), 23:24. All subsequent references are to this facsimile edition of the first published version of the ballad opera that appeared in Henry Brooke's *A Collection of Plays and Poems*, vol. 4 (London, 1778). The songs without the libretto were printed shortly after the first production in *The Songs in Jack the Giant-Queller. An Antique History. By Henry Brooke, Esq* (Dublin, 1749).

38. Luke Gibbons, *Transformation in Irish Culture* (Notre Dame, Ind.: University of Notre Dame Press and Field Day Publications, 1996), 141.

39. See chapter 3.

40. *The Songs in Jack the Giant-Queller*, 12.

41. Nic Eoin, "Secrets and Disguises?" 33–45.

42. W. H. Grattan Flood, *A History of Irish Music* ([1905] rpt. Shannon: Irish University Press, ca. 1970), 256.

43. These last two tunes are included in *The Songs in Jack the Giant-Queller* (29, 32) but are not in *Little John and the Giants*.

44. Victor, *The History of the Theatres of London and Dublin*, 1:140; Flood, *A History of Irish Music*, 256.

45. *A Letter to the Admirers of Mr. Sh———n* (Dublin, 1748). This pamphlet carries an advertisement for the collected edition of *The Tickler*, and it was published by Hiffernan's publisher, Halhed Garland.

46. *A Letter to Mr. W–dw–rd Comedian* (n.p., n.d). For Laetitia Pilkington's likely authorship of this pamphlet, see Pilkington, *Memoirs of Laetitia Pilkington*, 2:652–53.

47. *Dublin Courant*, February 28–March 4, 1749. See also Sheldon, *Thomas Sheridan of Smock-Alley*, 136.

48. *Dublin Courant*, April 29–May 2, 1749; May 10–23, 1749.

49. *The Election. A Comedy of Three Acts. As it is now acting in London with great Applause* (London, 1749). All subsequent references appear in the text.

50. Shershow, *Puppets and "Popular" Culture*, 4.

51. Burke's eighteenth-century biographer, Robert Bisset, claimed that Burke had written several essays in 1749 ridiculing Lucas's arguments and style (*The Life of Edmund Burke* [London, 1798], 19). This claim has since been disputed, most notably by Samuels who argued that Burke wrote *for* not against Lucas (*Early Life*, 180–202, 389–95). For a summary of this dispute to date, see Sean Murphy, "Burke and Lucas: An Authorship Problem Re-Examined," *Eighteenth-Century Ireland* 1 (1986): 143–56.

52. McKeon, *The Origins of the English Novel*, 185.

53. See chapter 5.

54. See *Mr. No-Body's Anti-Ticklerian Address to Mr. Lucas* (Dublin, 1748), 13. For Paul Farrell, see Patrick Fagan, "The Dublin Catholic Mob (1700–1750)," *Eighteenth-Century Ireland* 4 (1989): 138.

55. See Wall, *Catholic Ireland in the Eighteenth Century*, 61–84.

Chapter 7.   Staging the Nation

1. Victor, *The History of the Theatres of London and Dublin*, 1:153–60. All subsequent references appear in the text.

2. Sheridan, *An Humble Appeal*, 34, 22.

3. Thomas Sheridan, *A Vindication of the Conduct of the late Manager of the Theatre-Royal Publick. Humbly address'd to the Publick* (1754), rpt. in *An Humble Appeal*, 31, 27.

4. Ibid., 24.

5. Sheridan, *An Humble Appeal*, 34.

6. Smyth, *The Men of No Property*, 126.

7. Murphy, "Charles Lucas and the Dublin Election of 1748–1749," 97–98.

8. Ibid., 103–4, 108.

9. Ibid., 105–6.

10. Cited in Murphy, "Charles Lucas, Catholicism and Nationalism," 90.

11. [Charles O'Conor], *A Counter-Appeal to the People of Ireland* (Dublin, 1749), 9, 11–12.

12. Michael Reilly to Charles O'Conor, October 12, 1749, in *Letters of Charles O'Conor of Belanagare*, 4.

13. *Dublin Journal*, September 12–16, 1749, in Lawrence, "Notebooks on . . . the Dublin Stage," 12:147–48.

14. For these records, see Lawrence, "Notebooks on . . . the Dublin Stage," 13:47–51.

15. For the beginning of this anti-Sheridan campaign at Capel Street, see chapter 6.

16. *The Play-House Journal*, no. 1 (January 18, 1750). The connection with Hiffernan derives from the fact that this paper carries an advertisement for a Capel Street production of *The Inamorato; or the Ladies Doctor*, Hiffernan's farce.

17. See *A Letter to Mr. W–dw–rd*, cited in chapter 5 above.

18. *Dublin Journal*, September 12–16, 1749.

19. Sheldon does not seem to realize that Harrington is a figure for the viceroy. She reads the pamphlet literally and concludes that "it suggests the power of the prompter in the eighteenth-century theater" (*Thomas Sheridan of Smock-Alley*, 144).

20. *A Full and True Account of the Woefull and Wonderfull Apparition of Hurloe Harrington, Late Prompter to the Theatre-Royal in Dublin . . . in a Letter from the Reverend Parson Fitz-Henery to his G——e the A. B. of C——y* (London, 1750), 12, 17. Subsequent references are cited in the text.

21. Cited in Sheldon, *Thomas Sheridan of Smock-Alley*, 149.

22. Ibid., 149–50.

23. See chapter 3.

24. Sheldon, *Thomas Sheridan of Smock-Alley*, 130.

25. *Dublin Journal*, November 29–December 3, 1748.

26. *The Censor, or, the Citizen's Journal*, June 3, 1749.

27. *The Political Manager: or the Invasion of the Music-Hall, set Forth* (Dublin, 1749).

28. *Dublin Journal*, September 26–30, 1749, and October 10–15, 1749.

29. *Dublin Journal*, October 3–7, 1749. This letter is cited in full in Boydell, *A Dublin Musical Calendar*, 130.

30. James Digges La Touche, *A short but true history of the rise, progress, and happy suppression, of several late insurrections commonly called rebellions in Ireland* (Dublin, 1760), 16–17.

31. Sheldon, *Thomas Sheridan of Smock-Alley*, 145–48.

32. Ibid., 148.

33. C. Litton Falkiner, "Archbishop Stone," in *Essays Relating to Ireland* (New York: Kennikat Press, 1909), 94–108; J. L. McCracken, "The Conflict between the Irish Administration and Parliament, 1753–6," *Irish Historical Studies* 3

(1942–43): 159–66. McCracken, however, disputes Falkiner's contention that this was a struggle between the castle and Parliament; he argues rather that it was merely a struggle between rival parliamentary parties.

34. Declan O'Donovan, "The Money Bill Dispute of 1753," in *Penal Era and Golden Age,* ed. Thomas Bartlett and D. W. Hayton (Belfast: Ulster Historical Foundation, 1979), 74–77.

35. Cited in O'Donovan, "The Money Bill Dispute of 1753," 77.

36. Gilbert, *A History of the City of Dublin,* 3:101; O'Donovan, "The Money Bill Dispute of 1753," 64.

37. Falkiner, "Archbishop Stone," 109; McCracken, "The Conflict between the Irish Administration and Parliament, 1753–6," 170.

38. Falkiner, "Archbishop Stone," 102–4.

39. *The True Life of Betty IRELAND with her Birth, Education, and Adventures* has been attributed to one of the most important spokesmen for the "Patriots," Sir Richard Cox.

40. *Hibernia Pacata: or, A Narrative of the Affairs of Ireland from the Famous Battle of Clontarf, where Brian Boirom defeated the Norwegians, till the Settlement under Henry II. Written Originally in Irish, And now first Translated by Father Neri of Tuam, and Adorned with Notes by several Hands* (Dublin, 1753), 5–6. "Father Neri" is possibly an allusion to the Dublin priest Father Cornelius Nary (1658–1738), one of the first Catholics to speak out publicly against the penal laws.

41. Ibid., 8.

42. [Beaumont Brenan], *Patriots. A Poem By B——t B——n——* (Dublin, 1754), 7, 9. Brenan also uses the term "Erin" in a later part of the poem (see p. 11).

43. Sheldon, *Thomas Sheridan of Smock-Alley,* 170, 337, 356.

44. Alicia Lefanu, *Memoirs of the Life and Writings of Mrs. Francis Sheridan* (London, 1824), 68–70.

45. Sheldon, *Thomas Sheridan of Smock-Alley,* 170.

46. These lines are cited in *The Nettle,* October 24, 1751, a satirical paper. The tone and the close reading style of this satire is reminiscent of Paul Hiffernan.

47. Benjamin Victor, *Original Letters, Dramatic Pieces, and Poems* (London, 1776).

48. Sheldon, *Thomas Sheridan of Smock-Alley,* 172.

49. Ibid., 195.

50. *Mr. Sh——n's Apology to the Town; with the Reasons which unfortunately induced him to his late Misconduct* (Dublin, 2754 [1754]), 5.

51. Lefanu, *Memoirs of the Life and Writings of Mrs. Francis Sheridan,* 36–38; Victor to Charles Lucas, April 1753, in *Original Letters, Dramatic Pieces, and Poems,* 1:199.

52. J. Fitzgerald, *The Romance of the Irish Stage* (London, 1897), 2:5.

53. Victor, *The History of the Theatres of London and Dublin,* 1:158–59.

54. John Watkins, *Memoirs of the Public and Private Life of the Right Honorable R. B. Sheridan* (London, 1817), 72.

55. "The Groans of the Barracks" allusion and the promise that "*Places, Pensions and Promises*" would be available from "Caiphas" (the high priest who betrayed Christ in the biblical story) also suggest that this satirist's specific focus was the anticipated renewed clash between Primate Stone and the Boyle party over the behavior of Arthur Nevil Jones, the surveyor-general. Jones, who was a protégé of Stone's, had been the subject of an investigation by the Boyle party during the 1751–52 season for allegedly mismanaging the funds for a barracks building project, and it was widely expected (correctly, as it turned out) that the Jones affair would be an issue of contention again in the 1753–54 session (see McCracken, "The Conflict between the Irish Administration and Parliament, 1753–6," 164–65, 168).

56. This mock-playbill is included with a set of Irish political and theatrical tracts in the British Library (B. M. 1890. e. 5).

57. Sheldon, *Thomas Sheridan of Smock-Alley*, 444; Lawrence, "Notebooks on . . . the Dublin Stage," 13:127.

58. *Political Fire-Eating. Ergo sum Solo* (Dublin, 1753).

59. See Ireland, *By the Lord Lieutenant and Council of Ireland, a proclamation* (Dublin, 1754).

60. *A Proclamation by his Grace Hack-ball, King of State Mendicants in the Kingdom of EUTOPIA*, in *An address from the independent electors of the antient, loyal, and ever memorable town of Inniskillen. To the right Hon. the E. of Kildare, the Right Hon. Henry Boyle, Sir Richard Cox. . . . To which are added, Sir Tady F———s recantation, or a tragic-burlescal poem . . . addressed to the Right Hon. The Earl of Kildare. My Lord Chief Joker's proclamation against libels. Haekball's ditto. And 40 original patriot Inniskillen toasts* (Belfast, 1754), 13.

61. Ibid., 13.

62. *The Stage or Coronation of King Tom*, in Lawrence, "Notebooks on . . . the Dublin Stage," 15:19. Subsequent references are included in the text.

63. See chapter 1.

64. *The Secret History of the two last Memorable S...ss...ons of Parliament* (Dublin, 1754), 67–68.

65. Ibid., 68.

66. *Universal Advertiser*, March 13, 1753.

67. *Bucks Have at Ye All*, in James Love, *Cricket, an Heroic Poem: Illustrated with the critical observations of Scriblerus Maximus. To which is added an Epilogue, call'd Bucks Have at Ye All. Spoken by Mr. King at the Theatre Royal in Dublin in the character of Ranger in the Suspicious Husband* (London, 1770), 30.

68. Ibid., 30.

69. Sheldon, *Thomas Sheridan of Smock-Alley*, 199.

70. O'Donovan, "The Money Bill Dispute of 1753," 66.

71. *Mahomet the Imposter. A Tragedy* (London, 1744), 2. All subsequent citations are included in the text.

72. *Dublin Spy,* February 8, 1754, in *The Orrery Papers,* ed. the Countess of Cork and Orrery (London, 1903) 2:123.

73. *The Dublin Journal,* February 2–5, 1754.

74. Harold Lawton Bruce, *Voltaire on the English Stage* (Berkeley: University of California Publications in Modern Philology, 1918), 57.

75. Cited in Arthur H. Scouten, ed., *The London Stage, Part 3, 1729–1747,* 2 vols. (Carbondale: Southern Illinois University Press, 1961), 2:1104.

76. For the popularity of this play, see Bruce, *Voltaire on the English Stage,* 69–70.

77. *The Curtain Lecture: or, The Manager Run Mad. A Dialogue between a Stage-Director and his Wife* (London, 1758), in Lawrence, "Notebooks on . . . the Dublin Stage," 15:3–4.

78. *Universal Advertiser,* March 5, 1754, in Lawrence, "Notebooks on . . . the Dublin Stage," 14:136.

79. Both letters are cited in the appendix to *Remarks on Two Letters signed Theatricus and Hibernicus* (Dublin 1754). The citations are from pp. 10, 11, 13, 14.

80. *A grand debate between court and country. At the Theatre-Royal, in Smock-Alley. Lately in a letter to the c———t party, with Mr. Sh———n's aplogy to the c———ry party* (n.p., n.d.), 7, 8.

81. *Remarks on Two Letters signed Theatricus and Hibernicus,* 4. Subsequent references are cited in the text.

82. *The Sighs and Groans of Mr. Sh———n, with A full Account of a Comical Farce that was acted last Saturday Night at the Theatre in Smock-Alley, and the Occasion thereof. Also, An account of the Manager's rude Behavior to the Audience at the Play of MAHOMET* (Dublin, 1754). Subsequent references appear in the text. Sheldon does not include this pamphlet in her account of the "riot."

83. *A Vindication of the Conduct of the late Manager of the Theatre-Royal Publick. Humbly address'd to the Publick* (1754), in *An Humble Appeal,* 19, 23.

84. *An Epistle from Th———S Sh———n Esq; to the Universal Advertiser* (Dublin, 1754), 5–6.

85. Victor, *The History of the Theatres of London and Dublin,* 1:166–67.

86. *Mr. Sh———n's Apology to the Town,* 4. Subsequent references appear in the text.

87. *The Play-House prorogued: or, a Vindication of the Conduct of the Manager. Addressed to the Town* (Dublin, 1754), 5.

88. *The Stage or Coronation of King Tom,* in Lawrence, "Notebooks on . . . the Dublin Stage," 32.

89. *An Epistle from Th———s Sh———n Esq to the Universal Advertiser,* 4.

Chapter 8.   Rehearsing Revolution

1. *Gentleman's Magazine* 54 (1784): 550.

2. Ibid., 632.

3. Smyth, *The Men of No Property*, 138.

4. The *Gentleman's Magazine* mistakes the date; the "riot" occurred on Saturday, July 10, 1784.

5. Antonio Gramsci, *Selections from the Prison Notebooks of Antonio Gramsci*, ed. and trans. Quintin Hoare and Geoffrey Newell Smith (New York: International Publishers, 1971), 349.

6. Victor to Sackville Bale, March 1755, in Victor, *Original Letters*, 1:236–39.

7. James Fitzgerald to Emily Fitzgerald, May 10, 1755, in *Correspondence of Emily, Duchess of Leinster (1731–1814)*, ed. Brian Fitzgerald (Dublin: Stationery Office, 1949), 1:15.

8. Emily Fitzgerald to James Fitzgerald, May 15, 1755, in *Correspondence of Emily, Duchess of Leinster*, 1:17.

9. *A Letter to Messieurs Victor and Sowdon, Managers of the Theatre-Royal* (Dublin, 1755), 9.

10. Stockwell, *Dublin Theatres and Theatre Customs*, 120–22.

11. Sheldon, *Thomas Sheridan of Smock-Alley*, 239–43.

12. Sheridan to Samuel Richardson, March 16, 1758, in *The Correspondence of Samuel Richardson*, ed. Anna Laetitia Barbauld (London, 1804), 4:172.

13. *The Case of the Stage in Ireland* (Dublin, 1758), 47–48.

14. George Stayley, *The Rival Theatres: or, a Play house to be let. A Farce to which is added The Chocolate-Makers: or Mimicry Exposed. An Interlude with a Preface and Notes commentary and explanatory by Mr. George Stayley, Comedian* (Dublin, 1759).

15. *Mr. Sheridan's Speech Addressed to a Number of Gentlemen Assembled with a View of considering The Best Means to establish one good Theatre in this City* (Dublin, 1772), 15–16, 21.

16. *Hibernian Journal*, February 26–28, 1772; *Dublin Journal*, March 5–7 and 7–10, 1772.

17. *Hibernian Journal*, November 20, 1779.

18. *Freeman's Journal*, January 4–6, 1780.

19. Thomas Bartlett, "The Townshend Viceroyalty, 1767–72," in *Penal Era and Golden Age: Essays in Irish History, 1690–1800*, ed. Thomas Bartlett and D. W. Hayton (Belfast: Ulster Historical Foundation, 1979), 93–97, 112.

20. See *Baratariana. A Select Collection of . . . Political Pieces Published during the Administration of Lord Townshend in Ireland* (Dublin, 1777).

21. *Hibernian Journal*, January 31–February 3, 1772.

22. *Roach's New and Complete History of the Stage, from its origin to its present state* (London, 1796), 79.

23. Wheatley, *"Beneath Ierne's Banners,"* 101–21, 120.

24. Hitchcock, *An Historical View of the Irish Stage,* 1:85.

25. Cited in Stockwell, *Dublin Theatres and Theatre Customs,* 182.

26. Ibid., 188–90.

27. *Freeman's Journal,* February 11–14, 1777.

28. *Hibernian Journal,* July 6, 1774.

29. *Freeman's Journal,* March 12–13, 1778.

30. *Hibernian Journal,* March 1, 1782, in Lawrence, "Notebooks on . . . the Dublin Stage," 36:54–55.

31. In the preliminary advertisement to his *Poems on Various Subjects,* 3d ed. (Dublin, 1795), Samuel Whyte says *The Theatre* circulated in manuscript form during a private performance of *Jane Shore* in 1779 and was first printed when the play was revived in 1790 (ix–xi).

32. *The Theatre, a Didactic Essay, In the Course of which are pointed out the Rocks and Shoals to which Deluded Adventurers are Inevitably exposed,* in Samuel Whyte, *Poems on Various Subjects,* 6–7.

33. See William Cooke, *Memoirs of Charles Macklin* (London, 1804), 2:11–12.

34. *Dublin Magazine* (June 1762): 377.

35. For the stage Irishman and the "brogue," see, for example, G. C. Duggan, *The Stage Irishman: A History of the Irish Plays and Stage Characters from the Earliest Times* (Dublin: Talbot Press, 1937); J. O. Bartley, *Teague, Shenkin and Sawney* (Cork: Cork University Press, 1954); and Leerssen, *Mere Irish and Fíor-Ghael,* 85–168.

36. James Thomas Kirkman, *Memoirs of the Life of Charles Macklin* (London, 1799), 1:61–64, 64.

37. David Hayton, "From Barbarian to Burlesque: English Images of the Irish c. 1660–1750," *Irish Economic and Social History* 15 (1988): 21–25, 21.

38. Thomas Sheridan, *A Course of Lectures on Elocution: Together with Two Dissertations on Language* (London, 1762), 68.

39. *An Essay on the Antient and Modern State of Ireland* (Dublin, 1760), 54. This pamphlet is possibly a response to Sheridan's *Oration, Pronounced before a Numerous Body of the Nobility and Gentry in Fishamble-street* (Dublin, 1757), in which the manager proposed linking the theater to a new educational academy that would stress oratory and the English language.

40. *An Essay on the Antient and Modern State of Ireland,* 29.

41. *Hibernia Curiosa. A Letter from a Gentleman in Dublin, to his Friend at Dover in Kent* (Dublin, 1764), 43–44, 45.

42. Cited in Lawrence, "Notebooks on . . . the Dublin Stage," 19:4, 20:18.

43. Cooke, *Memoirs of Charles Macklin,* 235–36.

44. R. B. McDowell, "Colonial Nationalism, 1760–82," in *A New History of Ireland,* 4:198.

45. Charles Macklin, *The True-born Irishman or the Irish Fine Lady*, in *Four Comedies by Charles Macklin*, ed. J. O. Bartley (London: Archon Books, 1968), 85. All subsequent references are cited in the text.

46. Sean Murphy, "Municipal Politics and Popular Disturbances: 1660–1800," in *Dublin through the Ages*, ed. Art Cosgrove (Dublin: College Press, 1988), 87.

47. Bartley, *The True-born Irishman*, note 2, 84.

48. Lucas [A. Freeman, Barber and Citizen, pseud.], *A Letter to the Free-Citizens of Dublin*, 5.

49. Macklin's name was originally MacLoughlin and Owenson's was originally MacOwen. O'Keeffe went by the name "Keeffe" in the 1760s and 1770s.

50. Sidney Owenson, *Lady Morgan's Memoirs: Autobiography, Diaries and Correspondence* (London, 1862), 67.

51. Kirkman, *Memoirs of the Life of Charles Macklin*, 1:161, 165–66.

52. John O'Keeffe, *Recollections of the Life of John O'Keeffe*, 2 vols. (London, 1826), 1:89–91.

53. Leerssen, *Mere Irish and Fíor-Ghael*, 255–56.

54. Cited in Mercier, *The Irish Comic Tradition*, 165. The translation is also Mercier's (166).

55. Cited in Lawrence, "Notebooks on . . . the Dublin Stage," 19:51–52.

56. O'Keeffe, *Recollections*, 1:62.

57. Kirkman, *Memoirs of the Life of Charles Macklin*, 2:2–3.

58. "An Account of the Life and Genius of Mr. Charles Macklin, Comedian," in *An Apology for the Conduct of Mr. Charles Macklin, Comedian* (London, 1773), 37.

59. For O'Keeffe's native Irish Catholic background, see his *Recollections*, 1:7–9. On December 7, 1770, O'Keeffe played Pat Fitzmongrel to Macklin's O'Dogherty in *The True-born Irishman* at the Capel Street theater (Lawrence, "Notebooks on . . . the Dublin Stage," 25:65).

60. See Lawrence, "Notebooks on . . . the Dublin Stage," 25:63–75, for an account of these performances.

61. O'Keeffe, *Recollections*, 1:44, 146–47.

62. *Hibernian Magazine* (April 1782): 204.

63. Lawrence, "Notebooks on . . . the Dublin Stage," 25:68; *Freeman's Journal*, March 15–17, 1777.

64. O'Keeffe, *Recollections*, 1:246–47.

65. *Freeman's Journal*, April 10–12, 1777; O'Keeffe, *Recollections*, 2:70, 49.

66. *Freeman's Journal*, April 10–12, 1777.

67. Mary Helen Thuente, *The Harp Re-strung* (Syracuse, N.Y.: Syracuse University Press, 1994), 51.

68. *The Thespian Dictionary* (London, 1802), s.v. "Owenson, Mr."

69. *Freeman's Journal*, October 26–29, 1776.

70. O'Keeffe, *Recollections*, 1:354.

71. W. A. Donaldson, *Fifty Years of an Actor's Life; Or, Thespian Gleanings* (London, 1858), 41.

72. See J. G. Simms, "The Irish on the Continent, 1691–1800," in *A New History of Ireland*, 4:637.

73. William John Fitzpatrick, *Lady Morgan: Her Career, Literary and Personal* (London 1860), 61.

74. Owenson, *Lady Morgan's Memoirs*, 72–76.

75. *Freeman's Journal*, May 28, 1812.

76. Fitzpatrick, *Lady Morgan*, 23.

77. George Colman, *New Brooms*, in *The Plays of George Colman the Elder*, ed. Kalman A. Burnim (New York: Garland, 1983), 4:20.

78. Fitzpatrick, *Lady Morgan*, 23.

79. Maurice R. O'Connell, *Irish Politics and Social Conflict in the Age of the American Revolution* (Philadelphia: University of Pennsylvania Press, 1965), 68–102.

80. Cited in O'Connell, *Irish Politics and Social Conflict*, 97–98. For Catholic and working-class involvement in this organization, see also Smyth, *The Men of No Property*, 137–38.

81. Cited in Georges-Denis Zimmermann, *Irish Political Street Ballads and Rebel Songs, 1780–1900* (Geneva: La Sirene, 1966), 122.

82. Nancy Curtain, *The United Irishmen: Popular Politics in Ulster and Dublin, 1791–98* (Oxford: Clarendon Press, 1994), 29–32.

83. Gilbert, *A History of the City of Dublin*, 3:47.

84. *Freeman's Journal*, November 4–6, 1779.

85. Gilbert, *A History of the City of Dublin*, 3:50.

86. *Dublin Evening Post*, December 9, 1784; December 11, 1784.

87. John Beresford to Robinson, December 13, 1779, in Lawrence, "Notebooks on . . . the Dublin Stage," 34:73–74.

88. *Freeman's Journal*, March 29–31, 1781.

89. This opera, which Lawrence attributes to Robert Houlton ("Notebooks on . . . the Dublin Stage," 36:68), was first performed at Smock Alley on May 14, 1782. It opened at Crow Street on February 7 the following year, and it played at least five times during that season. The songs but not the libretto for this opera were published (see note 88). The phrase "of Irish manufacture" is taken from the enthusiastic review that appeared in the *Dublin Evening Post*, February 8, 1783.

90. *The Songs, Duets, Trio's Choruses, and Finales in the New Comic Opera of the Contract: As Performed at the Theatre-Royal, Smock-Alley* (Dublin, 1783), 24. All subsequent references to the songs are cited in the text.

91. *Dublin Evening Post*, February 8, 1783. The newspaper printed the song in its review.

92. Zimmermann, *Irish Political Street Ballads and Rebel Songs,* 122. For the role of songbooks in the dissemination of United Irishmen ideology, see Thuente, *The Harp Re-strung,* 125–69.

93. *Dublin Evening Post,* February 8, 1783.

94. See P. H. Highfill et al., *A Biographical Dictionary of Actors, Actresses, Musicians, Dancers, Managers and Other Stage Personnel in London, 1660–1800* (Carbondale: Southern Illinois University Press, 1973), 3:500–501.

95. Jean E. Howard, *The Stage and Social Struggle in Early Modern England* (London: Routledge, 1994), 83.

96. Adelaide O'Keeffe, *O'Keeffe's Legacy to His Daughter* (London, 1834), xxii.

97. Ibid., xxii–xxiii.

98. This song was printed in the *Hibernian Journal,* November 1, 1779. O'Keeffe sang it at a benefit performance on March 13, 1780 (Lawrence, "Notebooks on . . . the Dublin Stage," 34:123).

99. *Freeman's Journal,* March 21–23, 1780. This transparency, according to an advertisement in the *Journal* on February 12–15, was based on a drawing by Francis Wheatley.

100. *Hibernian Journal* February 19–21, 1783.

101. "Declaration and Resolutions of the Society of United Irishmen" cited in Marianne Elliott, *Wolfe Tone: Prophet of Irish Independence* (New Haven: Yale University Press, 1989), 139–41.

102. Smyth, *The Men of No Property,* 135–36.

103. *Dublin Evening Post,* May 22, 1784; June 10, 1784.

104. *Hibernian Journal,* June 21, 1784.

105. For the "Humble Petition of the Freemen, Freeholders, and Inhabitants of the City of Dublin," see the *Hibernian Journal,* June 23, 1784, and the *Volunteers Journal,* July 7, 1784. For a more detailed account of the aggregate meetings, see Hill, *From Patriots to Unionists,* 176–79.

106. *Freeman's Journal,* July 10–13, 1784.

107. *Hibernian Journal,* July 7, 1784.

108. *Hibernian Journal,* July 9, 1784.

109. *Volunteers Journal,* July 12, 1784.

110. *Freeman's Journal,* July 10–13, 1784.

111. See Pemberton's letters to the *Dublin Evening Post,* January 25, 1783; March 27, 1783; and April 10, 1783.

112. *Volunteer Evening Post,* July 10–13, 1784.

113. *Freeman's Journal,* July 10–13, 1784.

114. *Freeman's Journal,* July 20–22, 1784.

115. *Volunteers Journal,* July 12, 1784.

116. *Volunteer Evening Post,* July 10–13, 1784.

117. *Volunteers Journal*, July 12, 1784.

118. *Volunteers Journal*, July 16, 1784.

119. *Dublin Evening Post*, July 21, 1784.

Epilogue

1. Augusta Gregory, *Our Irish Theatre* (London: Putnam, 1913), 17.

2. "An Act for Regulating the Stage in the City and County of Dublin," in *The Irish Statutes: Revised Edition. 3 Edward II to the Union*, ed. W. F. Cullinan (London, 1885), 632–33.

3. *Roach's New and Complete History of the Stage*, 78.

4. *The Thespian Dictionary*, s.v. "Daly, Richard."

5. *Dublin Evening Post*, July 30, 1789.

6. Cited in Lawrence, "Notebooks on . . . the Dublin Stage," 49:92.

7. Ibid., 94–95.

8. See Smyth, *The Men of No Property*, 138–39; and *The Irish Statutes*, 633–37.

9. Brian Inglis, *The Freedom of the Press in Ireland, 1784–1841* (London: Faber and Faber, 1954), 19–45, 36.

10. *Freeman's Journal*, July 10–13, 1784; March 5–8, 1784.

11. *Freeman's Journal*, March 5–8, 1784.

12. *Volunteers Journal*, June 17, 1785.

13. Owenson, *Lady Morgan's Memoirs*, 65. All subsequent references are included in the text.

14. *Volunteers Journal*, December 22, 1784; John Greene, "Robert Nugent Owenson and the Myth of the First National Theatre," paper given at the American Society for Eighteenth-Century Studies, 1998. I am grateful to Professor Greene for sharing this paper with me.

15. Lawrence, "Notebooks on . . . the Dublin Stage," 39:142, 141–43.

16. *Volunteers Journal*, January 17, 1785; *Saunder's News-Letter*, December 24, 1784.

17. *Saunder's News-Letter*, December 27, 1784.

18. *Volunteers Journal*, January 10, 1785

19. Hill, *From Patriots to Unionists*, 177.

20. Smyth, *The Men of No Property*, 141.

21. The *Volunteers Journal* was under the control of Mathew Carey, a Catholic (see Hill, *From Patriots to Unionists*, 173).

22. See *Volunteers Journal*, December 22, 1784, for an account and a rebuttal of the *Freeman's Journal*'s first critique. For the *Freeman's Journal*'s attack on *The West Indian*, see Lawrence, "Notebooks on . . . the Dublin Stage," 39:146.

23. *Volunteers Journal*, December 22 and 29, 1784.

24. Inglis, *The Freedom of the Press*, 25, 40. See also Bingley's letters to the *Volunteers Journal* on March 18, 1785, and March 21, 1785, and his account of his arrest in *The Reformist*, February 21, 1785.

25. *Volunteers Journal*, March 30, 1785.

26. Lawrence, "Notebooks on . . . the Dublin Stage," 39:142.

27. Ibid., 39:112.

28. *Freeman's Journal*, June 25–28, 1785.

29. Fitzpatrick, *Lady Morgan*, 37.

30. For an account of the Post-Assembly meeting, see *Freeman's Journal*, July 2–5, 1785. For an account of the House of Commons debate during the second reading, see *Freeman's Journal*, July 21–23, 1785.

31. Slavoj Zizek, *The Sublime Object of Ideology* (London: Verso, 1989), 139.

Works Cited

Abbott, Paul. "Authority." *Screen* 20 (1979): 11–64.

"An Account of the Life and Genius of Mr. Charles Macklin, Comedian." In *An Apology for the Conduct of Mr. Charles Macklin, Comedian.* London, 1773.

Alumni Dublinenses. Edited by G. D. Burtchaell and T. U. Sadleir. Dublin: Thom and Co., 1935.

Anderson, Benedict. *Imagined Communities.* London: Verso, 1983.

An Duanaire 1600–1690: Poems of the Dispossessed. Edited by Seán Ó Tuama and translated by Thomas Kinsella. Mountrath, Portlaoise: Dolmen Press, 1981.

An Apology for the Conduct and Writings of Mr. C——s L——s, Apothecary; wherein The seeming Oddity of his setting up and recommending himself to the Freemen and Citizens of D–BL–N, as the only fit Person to represent them in Parliament, is clearly accounted for in A letter to a Friend. Dublin, 1749.

Asper Against Buffone. Or a Warning to the Tickler. Dublin, 1748.

Avery, Emmett L., ed. *The London Stage, 1660–1880. Part 2, 1700–1729.* 2 vols. Carbondale: Southern Illinois University Press, 1960.

Baratariana. A Select Collection of . . . Political Pieces Published during the Administration of Lord Townshend in Ireland. Dublin, 1777.

Barnard, T. C. "The Uses of 23 October 1641 and Irish Protestant Celebrations." *English Historical Review* 106 (1991): 889–920.

Bartlett, Thomas. *The Fall and Rise of the Irish Nation: The Catholic Question, 1690–1830.* Dublin: Gill and Macmillan, 1992.

———. "The Townshend Viceroyalty, 1767–72." In *Penal Era and Golden Age: Essays in Irish History, 1690–1800,* edited by Thomas Bartlett and D. W. Hayton. Belfast: Ulster Historical Foundation, 1979.

Bartley, J. O. *Teague, Shenkin and Sawney.* Cork: Cork University Press, 1954.

Beckett, J. C. "Literature in English 1691–1800." In *A New History of Ireland,* vol. 4, *Eighteenth-Century Ireland, 1691–1800,* edited by T. W. Moody and W. E. Vaughan. Oxford: Clarendon Press, 1986.

Bellamy, George Anne. *An Apology for the Life of George Anne Bellamy.* Vol. 1. London, 1785.

Bender, John. *Imagining the Penitentiary: Fiction and the Architecture of Mind in Eighteenth-Century England.* Chicago: University of Chicago Press, 1987.

Bhabha, Homi K. "Dissemination: Time, Narrative, and the Margins of the Modern Nation." In *Nation and Narration,* edited by Homi K. Bhabha. London: Routledge, 1990.

———. "The Other Question." *Screen* 24 (1983): 18–36.

Bisset, Robert. *The Life of Edmund Burke.* London, 1798.

Boydell, Brian. *A Dublin Musical Calendar, 1700–1760.* Dublin: Irish Academic Press, 1988.

[Brenan, Beaumont]. *Patriots. A Poem By B———t B———n———.* Dublin, 1754.

———. *The Stage or Coronation of King Tom. A Satyr . . . By B———t B———n.* Dublin, 1753.

Brewer, John. *The Sinews of Power: War, Money and the English State, 1688–1783.* London: Unwin Hyman, 1989.

[Brooke, Henry]. *The Farmer's Letter to the Protestants of Ireland.* Dublin, 1745.

———. *Little John and the Giants.* In *Irish Ballad Operas and Burlesques II.* Selected and arranged by Walter H. Rubsamen. Vol. 23 of *The Ballad opera: A collection of 171 original texts of musical plays printed in photo-facsimile.* New York: Garland, 1974.

———. *An Occasional Letter from the Farmer, to the Free-Men of Dublin.* Dublin, 1749.

———. *The Songs in Jack the Giant-Queller. An Antique History. By Henry Brooke, Esq.* Dublin, 1749.

[Browne, John]. *The Gentlemen's Apology to the Ladies, for their being disappointed at the Play-House, on Wednesday the 11th of February, 1746–7.* In *Dublin in an Uproar: or, the Ladies robb'd of their Pleasure.* Dublin, 1747.

Bruce, Harold Lawton. *Voltaire on the English Stage.* Berkeley: University of California Publications in Modern Philology, 1918.

Bucks Have at Ye All. In James Love, *Cricket, an Heroic Poem: Illustrated with the critical observations of Scriblerus Maximus. To which is added an Epilogue, call'd Bucks Have at Ye All. Spoken by Mr. King at the Theatre Royal in Dublin in the character of Ranger in the Suspicious Husband.* London, 1770.

Burke, Edmund. *The Correspondence of Edmund Burke.* Edited by T. W. Copeland. Cambridge and Chicago: Cambridge University Press and University of Chicago Press, 1958–71.

———. Correspondence with Charles O'Hara. In *Edmund Burke, New York Agent with his letters to the New York Assembly and intimate correspondence with Charles O'Hara, 1761–1776*. Philadelphia: American Philosophical Society, 1956.

———. From *Letter to a Peer of Ireland* (1782). In *The Field Day Anthology of Irish Writing*, vol. 1, edited by Seamus Deane. Derry, Northern Ireland: Field Day Publications, 1991.

[Burke, Edmund]. *Punch's Petition to Mr. Sh———n, to be admitted into the Theatre Royal*. Dublin, 1748.

[Burke, Edmund, et al.] *The Reformer*. Dublin, 1748.

Carolan, Nicholas. *A Collection of the Most Celebrated Irish Tunes*. Dublin: Folk Music Society of Ireland, 1986.

Carpenter, Andrew. "Irish and Anglo-Irish Scholars in the Time of Swift: The Case of Anthony Raymond." In *Literary Interrelations: Ireland, England, and the World*, edited by Wolfgang Zach and Heinz Kosok. Tübingen: Gunter Narr, 1987.

———. *Verse in English from Eighteenth-Century Ireland*. Cork: Cork University Press, 1998.

Carpenter, Andrew, and Alan Harrison. "Swift's 'O'Rouke's Feast' and Sheridan's 'Letter': Early Transcripts by Anthony Raymond." In *Proceedings of the First Munster Symposium on Jonathan Swift*, edited by H. J. Real and H. J. Vienken. Munich: Wilhelm Fink, 1985.

The Case of the Stage in Ireland. Dublin, 1758.

The Censor, or, the Citizen's Journal.

Chalmers, Alexander. *The Works of the English Poets, from Chaucer to Cowper*. Vol. 17. London, 1810.

Chetwood, William Rufus. *A General History of the Stage: From Its Origin in Greece Down to the Present Time*. London, 1749.

Cibber and Sheridan: or, the Dublin Miscellany. Containing All the Advertisements, Letters, Addresses, Replys, Apologys, Verses, etc, etc, etc. Lately publish'd on Account of the Theatric Squabble. Dublin, 1743.

Clark, Donald B. "The Source and Characterization of Nicholas Rowe's *Tamerlane*." *Modern Language Notes* 65 (1950): 145–52.

Clark, Jonathan. *English Society, 1660–1832*. Cambridge: Cambridge University Press, 2000.

Clark, William Smith. *The Early Irish Stage: The Beginnings to 1720*. Oxford: Clarendon Press, 1955.

Coffey, Charles. *The Beggar's Wedding. A New Opera as it is acted in Dublin, with great applause*. Dublin, 1729.

———. *The Beggar's Wedding. A New Opera as it is acted in Dublin, with great applause and at the Theatre in the Hay-Market*. London, 1729. In *Irish Ballad Operas and Burlesques I*. Vol. 23 of *The Ballad opera: A collection of 171 original texts of musical plays printed in photo-facsimile.* Selected and arranged by Walter H. Rubsamen. New York: Garland, 1974.

————. *The Female Parson or Beau in the Sudds.* London, 1730.

————. *Wife or No Wife.* In *Poems and Songs . . . Love Letters and a Novel nam'd Loviso.* Dublin, 1724.

Coleborne, Bryan. "The Dublin Grub Street: The Documentary Evidence in the Case of John Browne." *Swift Studies* 2 (1987): 12–24.

Colley, Linda. *Britons: Forging the Nation, 1707–1837.* New Haven: Yale University Press, 1992.

Colman, George. *New Brooms.* In *The Plays of George Colman the Elder,* vol. 4, edited by Kalman A. Burnim. New York: Garland, 1983.

Concanen, Matthew. *Miscellaneous Poems, Original and Translated by Several Hands.* London, 1724.

The Conduct of the Purse of Ireland in a Letter to a Member of the Late Oxford Convocation, Occasioned By their having conferr'd the Degree of Doctor upon Sir C—— P——. London, 1714.

Connolly, Sean. *Religion, Law and Power: The Making of Protestant Ireland, 1660–1760.* Oxford: Clarendon Press, 1992.

Cooke, William. *Memoirs of Charles Macklin.* Vol. 2. London, 1804.

Corkery, Daniel. *The Hidden Ireland.* Dublin: Gill and Macmillan, 1924; rpt. 1967.

Cullen, Louis. "Catholics under the Penal Laws." *Eighteenth-Century Ireland* 1 (1986): 23–36.

Curry, John. *A Brief Account from the Most Authentic Protestant Writers of the Causes, Motives, and Mischiefs, of the Irish Rebellion on the 23rd Day of October 1641, Deliver'd in a Dialogue Between a Dissenter and a Member of the Church of Ireland, as by Law Established.* London, 1747.

————. *Historical Memoirs of the Irish Rebellion.* London, 1758.

The Curtain Lecture: or, The Manager Run Mad. A Dialogue between a Stage-Director and His Wife. London, 1758.

Curtain, Nancy. *The United Irishmen: Popular Politics in Ulster and Dublin, 1791–98.* Oxford: Clarendon Press, 1994.

Davies, Thomas. *Memoirs of the Life of David Garrick, Esq.* Vol. 1. London, 1780.

Deane, Seamus. "Edmund Burke." In *The Field Day Anthology of Irish Writing,* vol 1, edited by Seamus Deane. Derry, Northern Ireland: Field Day Publications, 1991.

"Declaration and Resolutions of the Society of United Irishmen." In Marianne Elliott, *Wolfe Tone: Prophet of Irish Independence.* New Haven: Yale University Press, 1989.

A Defence of English Commodities Being an Answer to the Proposal For the Universal Use of Irish Manufactures. In *The Prose Works of Jonathan Swift,* vol. 9, edited by Herbert Davis. Oxford: Basil Blackwell, 1939–68.

A Defence of the Constitution: or, An Answer to an Argument in the Case of Mr. Moor; Lately publish'd by One of her Majesty's Council. Dublin, 1714.

Delany, Mary. *Letters from Georgian Ireland: Correspondence of Mary Delany, 1731–68.* Edited by Angelique Day. Belfast: Friar's Bush Press, 1991.

[Dennis, William]. *Brutus's Letter to the Town.* Dublin, 1747.

Dennis, William. Correspondence to Richard Shackleton. In James Prior, *The Life of Oliver Goldsmith, M. B., from a variety of original sources.* Philadelphia: E. L. Cary and A. Hart, 1837.

Diamond, Elin, ed. *Performances and Cultural Politics.* London: Routledge, 1996.

Dickson, David J. "Catholics and Trade in Eighteenth-Century Ireland: An Old Debate Revisited." In *Endurance and Emergence: Catholics in Ireland in the Eighteenth Century,* edited by T. P. Power and Kevin Whelan. Dublin: Irish Academic Press, 1990.

Dickson's Dublin Intelligence.

Doctor Anthony's Advice to the Hibernian Aesop: or An Epistle to the Author of the B——gs W——g. Dublin, 1729.

Donaldson, W. A. *Fifty Years of an Actor's Life; Or, Thespian Gleanings.* London, 1858.

The Down-Fall of the Counts: A New Ballad to the Tune of Derry Down, Etc. Dublin, 1747.

Dublin Courant.

Dublin Evening Post.

Dublin Journal.

Dublin Magazine.

Dublin Spy. In *The Orrery Papers,* edited by the Countess of Cork and Orrery. London, 1903.

Duggan, G. C. *The Stage Irishman: A History of the Irish Play and Stage Characters from the Earliest Times.* Dublin: Talbot Press, 1937.

Dunlevy, Mairead. *Dress in Ireland.* New York: Holmes and Meier, 1989.

Dunton, John. *The Dublin Scuffle.* Dublin, 1669.

Ehrenpreis, Irvin. *Swift: The Man, His Works, and the Age.* Vol. 3. Cambridge, Mass.: Harvard University Press, 1983.

Elias, Arch. "Male Hormones and Women's Wit: The Sex Appeal of Mary Goddard and Laetitia Pilkington." *Swift Studies* 9 (1994): 5–16.

———, ed. *Memoirs of Laetitia Pilkington.* Vol. 2. Athens: University of Georgia Press, 1997.

Elliott, Marianne. *Wolfe Tone: Prophet of Irish Independence.* New Haven: Yale University Press, 1989.

"Epilogue. To Mr. Hoppy's Benefit-Night, at Smock-Alley." In *The Poems of Jonathan Swift,* vol. 1, edited by William Ernst Browning. London: G. Bell and Sons, 1910.

An Epistle from Th——— S Sh———n Esq; to the Universal Advertiser. [Dublin, 1754].

Ernst, W. *Lord Chesterfield.* London: Grolier Society, n.d.

An Essay on the Antient and Modern State of Ireland. Dublin, 1760.

European Magazine.

Fabricant, Carole. *Swift's Landscape.* Baltimore: Johns Hopkins University Press, 1982; rpt. Notre Dame, Ind.: University of Notre Dame Press, [1982] 1995.

Fagan, Patrick. "The Dublin Catholic Mob (1700–1750)." *Eighteenth-Century Ireland* 4 (1989): 133–42.

———. *Dublin's Turbulent Priest: Cornelius Nary, 1658–1738.* Dublin: Royal Irish Academy, 1991.

———. *A Georgian Celebration: Irish Poets of the Eighteenth Century.* Dublin: Branar Press, 1989.

———. "The Population of Dublin in the Eighteenth Century with Particular Reference to the Proportions of Protestants and Catholics." *Eighteenth-Century Ireland* 6 (1991): 121–56.

———. *The Second City: Portrait of Dublin 1700–1760.* Dublin: Branar Press, 1986.

Falkiner, C. Litton. "Archbishop Stone." In *Essays Relating to Ireland.* New York: Kennikat Press, 1909.

Fanon, Frantz. *The Wretched of the Earth.* Translated by Constance Farrington. New York: Grove Press, 1963.

Farquhar, George. *The Beaux Stratagem.* In *The Works of George Farquhar*, vol. 4, edited by Shirley Strum Kenny. Oxford: Clarendon Press, 1988.

The Farmer's Yard. A New Fable for Aesop. [Dublin,] 1747.

Ferguson, Oliver W. *Jonathan Swift and Ireland.* Urbana: University of Illinois Press, 1962.

Fitzgerald, Emily and James. Correspondence. In *The Correspondence of Emily, Duchess of Leinster (1731–1814).* Vol. 1. Edited by Brian Fitzgerald. Dublin: Stationery Office, 1949.

Fitzgerald, J. *The Romance of the Irish Stage.* 2 vols. London, 1897.

Fitzpatrick, William John. *Lady Morgan: Her Career, Literary and Personal.* London, 1860.

Flood, W. H. Grattan. *A History of Irish Music.* 1905; rpt. Shannon: Irish University Press, ca. 1970.

Freeman's Journal.

Froude, James Anthony. *The English in Ireland in the Eighteenth Century.* Vol. 1. New York: Scribner, 1897.

A Full and True Account of the Woefull and Wonderfull Apparition of Hurloe Harrington, Late Prompter to the Theatre-Royal in Dublin . . . in a Letter from the Reverend Parson Fitz-Henery to his G——— e the A. B. of C———y. London, 1750.

Gailey, Alan. *Irish Folk Drama.* Cork: Mercier Press, 1969.

Gentleman's Magazine.

Gibbons, Luke. *Transformation in Irish Culture.* Notre Dame, Ind.: University of Notre Dame Press and Field Day Publications, 1996.

Gilbert, J. T. *A History of the City of Dublin.* 3 vols. Dublin: McGlashan and Gill, 1859.

Goldsmith, Oliver. "The History of Carolan: The Last Irish Bard." In *The Field Day Anthology of Irish Writing,* vol. 1, edited by Seamus Deane. Derry, Northern Ireland: Field Day Publications, 1991.

Gramsci, Antonio. *Selections from the Prison Notebooks of Antonio Gramsci.* Edited and translated by Quintin Hoare and Geoffrey Nowell Smith. New York: International Publishers, 1971.

A grand debate between court and country. At the Theatre-Royal, in Smock-Alley. Lately in a letter to the c——t party, with Mr. Sh——n's aplogy to the c——ry party [Dublin, 1754].

Greene, Donald. *The Politics of Samuel Johnson.* New Haven: Yale University Press, 1960.

Greene, John C. "Robert Nugent Owenson and the Myth of the First National Theatre." Paper presented at the American Society for Eighteenth-Century Studies, 1978.

Greene, John C., and Gladys L. H. Clark. *The Dublin Stage, 1720–1745.* London and Toronto: Associated University Presses, 1993.

Gregory, Augusta. *Our Irish Theatre.* London: Putnam, 1913.

Harris, Walter. *Fiction Unmasked: or an Answer to a Dialogue lately published by a Popish Physician, and pretended to have passed between a Dissenter, and a Member of the Church of Ireland . . .* Dublin, 1752.

Harrison, Alan. *Ag cruinniú meala: Anthony Raymond (1675–1726), ministéir Protastúnach agus léann na Gaeilge i mBaile Átha Cliath.* Baile Átha Cliath: Clóchomhar Tta, 1988.

———. *The Irish Trickster.* Sheffield: Sheffield Academic Press, 1989.

Harrison, Frank Llewelyn. "Music, Poetry and Polity in the Age of Swift." *Eighteenth-Century Ireland* 1 (1986): 37–63.

Hayton, David. "The Crisis in Ireland and the Disintegration of Queen Anne's Last Ministry." *Irish Historical Studies* 22 (1981): 193–213.

———. "From Barbarian to Burlesque: English Images of the Irish c. 1660–1750." *Irish Economic and Social History* 15 (1988): 5–31.

Her Majesty's Prerogative in Ireland; The Authority of the government and Privy-Council There: and the Rights, Laws, and Liberties of the City of Dublin Asserted and Maintain'd in Answer to a Paper Falsely Intituled The Case of the City of Dublin, in relation to the Election of a Lord-Mayor and Sheriffs of the said City. London, 1712.

Hibernia Curiosa. A Letter from a Gentleman in Dublin, to his Friend at Dover in Kent. Dublin, 1764.

Hibernia Pacata: or, A Narrative of the Affairs of Ireland from the Famous Battle of
    Clontarf, where Brian Boirom defeated the Norwegians, till the Settlement under
    Henry II. Written Originally in Irish, And now first Translated by Father Neri of
    Tuam, and Adorned with Notes by several Hands. Dublin, 1753.
Hibernian Journal.
[Hiffernan, Paul]. *The Election. A Comedy of Three Acts. As it is now acting in Lon-*
    don with great Applause. London, 1749.
————. *The Self-Enamour'd; or the Ladies Doctor . . . by P. H. M. D.* Dublin, 1750.
————. *The Tickler.* Dublin, 1748–49.
Highfill, P. H., et al. *A Biographical Dictionary of Actors, Actresses, Musicians,*
    Dancers, Managers and Other Stage Personnel in London, 1660–1800. Vol. 3.
    Carbondale: Southern Illinois University Press, 1973.
Hill, Jacqueline. *From Patriots to Unionists: Dublin Civic Politics and Irish Protes-*
    tant Patriotism, 1660–1840. Oxford: Clarendon Press, 1997.
Hitchcock, Robert. *An Historical View of the Irish Stage.* 2 vols. Dublin, 1788–94.
Howard, Jean E. *The Stage and Social Struggle in Early Modern England.* London:
    Routledge, 1994.
Hughes, Leo. *The Drama's Patrons: A Study of the Eighteenth-Century London Au-*
    dience. Austin: University of Texas Press, 1971.
"Ierne's Answer to Albion." In *To the Ladies A Poem. To which is added, Ierne's*
    Answer to Albion. By a Lady. Dublin, 1745.
The Impartial Examiner, or the Faithful Representer of the Various and Manifold Mis-
    representations imposed on the Roman Catholics of Ireland, in the Several Charges
    laid at their Doors by the Scribblers of the Farmer's, Merchant's, and Drapier's
    Letters, and Charitable and Seasonable Advices, the Editors of the Magazines, and
    the Printers of the Journals, Courants, Occurrences, News-Letters, Gazettes, Pam-
    phlets, and other modern Public Papers, Etc, which are daily printed in Dublin.
    Dublin, 1746.
Inglis, Brian. *The Freedom of the Press in Ireland, 1784–1841.* London: Faber and
    Faber, 1954.
Ireland. "An Act for Regulating the Stage in the City and County of Dublin."
    In *The Irish Statutes: Revised Edition. 3 Edward II to the Union.* Edited by
    W. F. Cullinan. London, 1885.
————. *By the Lord Lieutenant and Council of Ireland, a proclamation.* Dublin,
    1754.
————. *A Collection of the Protests of the Lords of Ireland, from 1634 to 1770.* Lon-
    don, 1771.
Ireland's Lamentation: Being a Short, but Perfect, Full and True Account of the Situ-
    ation, Nature, Constitution and Product of Ireland. Written by an English
    Protestant that lately narrowly escaped with his Life from thence. London, 1689.
The Irish Statutes: Revised Edition. 3 Edward II to the Union. Edited by W. F. Cul-
    linan. London, 1885.

James, Francis Godwin. *Ireland in the Empire, 1688–1770.* Cambridge, Mass.: Harvard University Press, 1973.

Jones, Ann Rosalind, and Peter Stallybrass. "Dismantling Irena: The Sexualizing of Ireland in Early Modern England." In *Nationalisms and Sexualities,* edited by Andrew Parker, Mary Russo, Doris Sommer, and Patricia Yaeger. New York: Routledge, 1992.

Kelly, James. "Jonathan Swift and the Irish Economy in the 1720s." *Eighteenth-Century Ireland* 6 (1991): 7–36.

———. *"That Damn'd Thing Called Honour": Duelling in Ireland, 1570–1860.* Cork: Cork University Press, 1995.

———. "'The Glorious and Immortal Memory': Commemoration and Protestant Identity in Ireland, 1660–1800." *Proceedings of the Royal Irish Academy* 94C (1994): 25–52.

Kelly, Patrick. "William Molyneux and the Spirit of Liberty in Eighteenth-Century Ireland." *Eighteenth-Century Ireland* 3 (1988): 133–48.

King, William. Letter to Jonathan Swift. 1711. In *The Correspondence of Jonathan Swift,* vol. 2, edited by F. Elrington Ball. London: Bell and Sons, 1912.

———. *The State of the Protestants of Ireland under the late King James's Government.* London, 1691.

Kirkman, James Thomas. *Memoirs of the Life of Charles Macklin.* Vol. 1. London, 1799.

Krapp, Robert M. "Class Analysis of a Literary Controversy: Wit and Sense in Seventeenth-Century English Literature." *Science and Society* 10 (1946): 80–92.

Kruger, Loren. *The National Stage: Theatre and Cultural Legitimation in England, France, and America.* Chicago: University of Chicago Press, 1992.

Laclau, Ernesto, and Chantal Mouffe. *Hegemony and Socialist Strategy.* London: Verso, 1985.

LaTouche, James Digges. *A short but true history of the rise, progress, and happy suppression, of several late insurrections commonly called rebellions in Ireland.* Dublin, 1760.

Lawrence, William J. "Notebooks on the History of the Dublin Stage." University of Cincinnati Library.

Leerssen, Joep Th. "Anglo-Irish Patriotism and Its European Context: Notes towards a Reassessment." *Eighteenth-Century Ireland* 3 (1988): 7–24.

———. *Mere Irish and Fíor-Ghael.* Amsterdam: John Benjamins, 1986.

Lefanu, Alicia. *Memoirs of the Life and Writings of Mrs. Francis Sheridan.* London, 1824.

A Letter of Advice to a Young Poet. In *The Prose Works of Jonathan Swift,* vol. 9, edited by Herbert Davis. Oxford: Basil Blackwell, 1939–68.

A Letter to Messieurs Victor and Sowdon, Managers of the Theatre-Royal. Dublin, 1755.

A Letter to Mr. W——dw——rd Comedian. [Dublin, 1748].

A Letter to the Admirers of Mr. S——N. Dublin, 1748.

Libertus. *Remarks on Two Letters signed Theatricus and Hibernicus.* Dublin, 1754.

Liberty, Mr. Francis. *A Letter of Thanks to the Barber, for the Indefatigable Pains to Suppress the Horrid and Unnatural Rebellion, Lately broke out in this City, But by His Means, now happily Extinguished.* Dublin, 1747.

Lloyd, David. *Ireland after History.* Notre Dame, Ind.: University of Notre Dame Press, 1999.

Lloyd's News-Letter.

Loftis, John. *The Politics of Drama in Augustan England.* Oxford: Clarendon Press, 1963.

London Gazette.

Lucas, Charles. *The Complaints of Dublin: Humbly offered to his Excellency William Earl of Harrington . . . By Charles Lucas, a Free Citizen.* Dublin, 1749.

———. *A Description of the Cave of Kilcorny, in the Barony of Burren in Ireland, wrote by Mr. Charles Lucas, Apothecary, in the Year 1740.* In *Esdall's News-Letter,* April 16, 1750.

———. *Develina Libera: An Apology for the Civil Rights and Liberties of the Commons and Citizens of Dublin.* Dublin, 1744.

———. [A. Freeman, Barber and Citizen, pseud.]. *A Letter to the Free-Citizens of Dublin.* Dublin, 1747.

———. [A. Freeman, Barber and Citizen, pseud.]. *A Second Letter to the Free-Citizens of Dublin.* Dublin, 1747.

———. [A. Freeman, Barber and Citizen, pseud.]. *A Third Letter to the Free-Citizens of Dublin,* 1747.

[Lucas, Charles]. *The Tradesmen's Answer to a False Scurrilous Paper, intituled, The Gentlemen's Apology to the Ladies, etc.* Dublin, 1747.

MacCarvill, Eileen. "Jonathan Swift, Aodh Buí Mac Cruitín, and Contemporary Thomond Scholars." *North Munster Antiquarian Journal* 11 (1968): 36–46.

Macklin, Charles. *The True-born Irishman or the Irish Fine Lady.* In *Four Comedies by Charles Macklin,* edited by J. O. Bartley. London: Archon Books, 1968.

MacLysaght, Edward. *Irish Families, Their Names, Arms and Origins.* Dublin: Hodges Figgis, 1957.

Maxwell, D. E. S. "Irish Drama 1899–1929: The Abbey Theatre." In *The Field Day Anthology of Irish Writing,* vol. 2, edited by Seamus Deane. Derry, Northern Ireland: Field Day Publications, 1991.

McCracken, J. L. "The Conflict between the Irish Administration and Parliament, 1753–6." *Irish Historical Studies* 3 (1942–43): 159–79.

———. "Protestant Ascendancy and the Rise of Colonial Nationalism, 1714–60." In *A New History of Ireland,* vol. 4, *Eighteenth-Century Ireland, 1691–1800,* edited by T. W. Moody and W. E. Vaughan. Oxford: Clarendon Press, 1986.

McDowell, R. B. "Colonial Nationalism, 1760–82." In *A New History of Ireland*, vol. 4, *Eighteenth-Century Ireland, 1691–1800*, edited by T. W. Moody and W. E. Vaughan. Oxford: Claredon Press, 1986.

McKeon, Michael. "Cultural Crisis and Dialectical Method: Destabilizing Augustan Literature." In *The Profession of Eighteenth-Century Literature*, edited by Leo Damrosch. Madison: University of Wisconsin Press, 1992.

———. *The Origins of the English Novel, 1600–1740*. Baltimore: Johns Hopkins University Press, 1987.

McLoughlin, Thomas O. "The Context of Edmund Burke's *The Reformer*." *Eighteenth-Century Ireland* 2 (1987): 37–55.

McLynn, F. J. "'Good Behaviour': Irish Catholics and the Jacobite Rising of 1745." *Eire-Ireland* 16 (1981): 43–58.

Mercier, Vivian. *The Irish Comic Tradition*. Oxford: Clarendon Press, 1962.

Miller, James, and John Hoadly. *Mahomet the Imposter. A Tragedy.* London, 1744.

Molyneux, William. *The Case of Ireland Stated*. 1698. Ed. J. G. Simms. Rpt. Dublin: Cadenus, 1977.

Moody, T. W., and W. E. Vaughan, eds. *A New History of Ireland*, vol. 4, *Eighteenth-Century Ireland, 1691–1800*. Oxford: Clarendon Press, 1986.

Mooney, Tighearnan, and Fiona White. "The Gentry's Winter Season." In *The Gorgeous Mask*, edited by David Dickson. Dublin: Trinity History Workshop, 1987.

Mr. Nobody's Anti-Ticklerian Address to Mr. Lucas. Dublin, 1748.

Mr. Sh———n's Apology to the Town; with the Reasons which unfortunately induced him to his late Misconduct. Dublin, 2754 [1754].

Munter, Robert. *The History of the Irish Newspaper, 1685–1760*. Cambridge: Cambridge University Press, 1967.

Murphy, Sean. "Burke and Lucas: An Authorship Problem Re-Examined." *Eighteenth-Century Ireland* 1 (1986): 143–56.

———. "Charles Lucas and the Dublin Election of 1748–1749." In *Parliamentary History*, vol. 2. New York: St. Martin's Press, 1983.

———. "Charles Lucas, Catholicism and Nationalism." *Eighteenth-Century Ireland* 8 (1993): 83–102.

———. "Municipal Politics and Popular Disturbances: 1660–1800." In *Dublin through the Ages*, edited by Art Cosgrove. Dublin: College Press, 1988.

Murray, Christopher. "Drama 1690–1800." In *The Field Day Anthology of Irish Writing*, vol. 1, edited by Seamus Deane. Derry, Northern Ireland: Field Day Publications, 1991.

———. Introduction to William Philips, *St. Stephen's Green, or, The Generous Lovers*. Mountrath, Portlaoise: Dolmen Press, 1980.

A Narrative of the Barbarous and Bloody Murder of P...l H...ff...n, M. D. Committed by Himself on Monday, the 17th Day of October, Inst Being a LETTER from

Mr. R...d D...ck...n of S...l...r C...t Castle-Street Dublin, to J...n B...ne Esq; at the Hague. Dublin, 1748.

The Nettle. Dublin, 1751.

A New Ballad on a Late Drubbing. [Dublin], n.d.

A New Opera-Epilogue to the Tragedy of Richard the Third. Dublin, 1731.

A New Song on the Whiggs Behaviour at the Play House on the 4th of this Instant, November 12, at a Play call'd TAMERLAIN. Dublin, 1712.

Nic Eoin, Máirín. "Secrets and Disguises? Caitlín Ní Uallacháin and Other Female Personages in Eighteenth-Century Irish Political Poetry." *Eighteenth-Century Ireland* 11 (1996): 7–45.

Nicoll, Allardyce. *The World of Harlequin: A Critical Study of the Commedia dell'Arte.* Cambridge: Cambridge University Press, 1963.

O'Brien, Conor Cruise. *The Great Melody: A Thematic Biography and Commented Anthology of Edmund Burke.* Chicago: University of Chicago Press, 1992.

O'Carroll, Joseph. "Contemporary Attitudes towards the Homeless Poor, 1725–1775." In *The Gorgeous Mask,* edited by David Dickson. Dublin: Trinity History Workshop, 1987.

O'Connell, Maurice R. *Irish Politics and Social Conflict in the Age of the American Revolution.* Philadelphia: University of Pennsylvania Press, 1965.

[O'Conor, Charles]. *A Counter-Appeal to the People of Ireland.* Dublin, 1749.

O'Conor, Charles. *Letters of Charles O'Conor of Belanagare.* Edited by Robert E. Ward, John F. Wrynn, and Catherine Coogan Ward. Washington, D. C.: Catholic University of America Press, 1988.

O'Donoghue, D. J. *The Poets of Ireland.* Dublin: Hodges Figgis, 1912; rpt. New York: Johnson Reprint Corporation, 1970.

O'Donovan, Declan. "The Money Bill Dispute of 1753." In *Penal Era and Golden Age,* edited by Thomas Bartlett and D. W. Hayton. Belfast: Ulster Historical Foundation, 1979.

Ó'Háinle, C. G. "Neighbors in Eighteenth-Century Dublin: Jonathan Swift and Seán Ó Neachtain." *Eire* 21 (1986): 106–21.

O'Keeffe, Adelaide. *O'Keeffe's Legacy to His Daughter.* London, 1834.

O'Keeffe, John. *Recollections of the Life of John O'Keeffe.* 2 vols. London, 1826.

Old Dublin Songs. Edited by Hugh Shields. Dublin: Folk Music Society of Ireland, 1988.

O'Rahilly, T. F. "Irish Scholars in Dublin in the Early Eighteenth Century." *Gadelica* 1 (1912–13): 156–62.

O'Sullivan, Donal. *Carolan, the Life, Times and Music of an Irish Harper.* London: Routledge and Kegan Paul, 1958.

O'Toole, Fintan. *A Traitor's Kiss: The Life of Richard Brinsley Sheridan.* London: Granta Publications, 1997.

Owenson, Sidney. *Lady Morgan's Memoirs: Autobiography, Diaries and Correspondence.* London, 1862.

Philips, William. *Hibernia Freed. A Tragedy*. London, 1722.

―――. *St. Stephen's Green, or, The Generous Lovers*. Edited by Christopher Murray. Mountrath, Portlaoise: Dolmen Press, 1980.

Pilkington, Jack. *The Real Story of John Carteret Pilkington*. London, 1760.

Pilkington, Laetitia. *Memoirs of Laetitia Pilkington*. Edited by Arch Elias. Athens: University of Georgia Press, 1997.

Pilkington, Matthew. "The Progress of Music in *Ireland*. To Mira." In *The Field Day Anthology of Irish Writing*, vol. 1, edited by Seamus Deane. Derry, Northern Ireland: Field Day Publications, 1991.

The Play-House Journal. Dublin, 1750.

The Play-House prorogued: or, a Vindication of the Conduct of the Manager. Addressed to the Town. Dublin, 1754.

Pocock, J. G. A. *Politics, Language and Time: Essays on Political Thought and History*. New York: Atheneum, 1971.

Political Fire-Eating. Ergo sum Solo. Dublin, 1753.

The Political Manager: or the Invasion of the Music-Hall, set Forth. Dublin, 1749.

Power, Thomas P. "Converts." In *Endurance and Emergence: Catholics in Ireland in the Eighteenth Century*, edited by T. P. Power and Kevin Whelan. Dublin: Irish Academic Press, 1990.

Pratt, Mary Louise. *Imperial Eyes: Travel Writing and Transculturation*. London: Routledge, 1992.

Prior, James. *The Life of Oliver Goldsmith, M. B., from a variety of original sources*. Philadelphia: E. L. Cary and A. Hart, 1837.

A Proclamation by his Grace Hack-ball, King of State Mendicants in the Kingdom of EUTOPIA. In An address from the independent electors of the antient, loyal, and ever memorable town of Inniskillen. To the right Hon. The E. of Kildare, the Right Hon. Henry Boyle, Sir Richard Cox. . . . To which are added, Sir Tady F――s recantation, or a tragic-burlescal poem . . . addressed to the Right Hon. The Earl of Kildare. My Lord Chief Joker's proclamation against libels. Haekball's [sic] ditto. And 40 original patriot Inniskillen toasts. Belfast, 1754.

Pue's Occurrences.

Punch's Petition to the Ladies. In *The Poems of Jonathan Swift*, vol. 2, edited by William Ernst Browning. London: G. Bell and Sons, 1910.

The Reformer Reform'd, being an Address from Thomas Telltruth, Esq; To the Reformer. With a Defence of the Manager of the Theatre-Royal, from groundless Assertions. Dublin, 1748.

The Resolutions of the House of Commons in Ireland, Relating to the Lord-Chancellor Phips [sic], Examined; with Remarks on the Chancellor's Speech. By a Member of the House of Commons in Ireland. London, 1714.

Roach, Joseph. *The Cities of the Dead*. New York: Columbia University Press, 1996.

———. "Kinship, Intelligence, and Memory as Improvisation." In *Performance and Cultural Politics*, edited by Elin Diamond. London: Routledge, 1996.

———. "Theater History and Historiography: Introduction." In *Critical Theory and Performance*, edited by Janelle G. Reinelt and Joseph R. Roach. Ann Arbor: University of Michigan Press, 1992.

Roach's New and Complete History of the Stage, from its origin to its present state. London, 1796.

Robbins, Caroline. *The Eighteenth-Century Commonwealthman.* Cambridge, Mass.: Harvard University Press, 1959.

Rolston, Bill. "Music and Politics in Ireland: The Case of Loyalism." In *Politics and Performance in Contemporary Northern Ireland*, edited by John P. Harrington and Elizabeth J. Mitchell. Amherst: University of Massachusetts Press, 1999.

Rowe, Nicholas. *Tamerlane. A Tragedy.* Edited by Landon C. Burns Jr. Philadelphia: University of Pennsylvania Press, 1966.

Samuels, A. P. I. *The Early Life, Correspondence and Writing of the Rt. Hon. Edmund Burke LL. D.* Cambridge: Cambridge University Press, 1923.

Saunder's News-Letter.

Schechner, Richard. *Between Theater and Anthropology.* Philadelphia: University of Pennsylvania Press, 1985.

———. *Performance Theory.* New York: Routledge, 1977; rpt. 1994.

Scouten, Arthur H., ed. *The London Stage. Part 3, 1729–1747.* 2 vols. Carbondale: Southern Illinois University Press, 1961.

Scurr, Helen Margaret. *Henry Brooke.* Minneapolis: University of Minnesota Press, 1927.

The Secret History of the two last Memorable S...ss...ons of Parliament. Dublin, 1754.

A Serious Enquiry into the Cause of the Present Disorders of this City. Dublin, 1747.

Shadwell, Charles. *Irish Hospitality; or Virtue Rewarded.* In *Five New Plays.* London, 1720.

———. *Rotherick O'Connor, King of Connaught: or the Distress'd Princess.* In *Five New Plays.* London, 1720.

———. "A Second Song, Sung at the Club at Mr. Taplin's the Sign of the Drapier's Head in Truck-Street." In *The Field Day Anthology of Irish Writing*, vol. 1, edited by Seamus Deane. Derry, Northern Ireland: Field Day Publications, 1991.

Sheldon, Esther K. *Thomas Sheridan of Smock-Alley.* Princeton: Princeton University Press, 1967.

Sheridan, Thomas. Correspondence to Samuel Richardson. In *The Correspondence of Samuel Richardson.* Vol. 4. Edited by Anna Laetitia Barbauld. London, 1804.

———. *A Course of Lectures on Elocution: Together with Two Dissertations on Language.* London, 1762.

———. *A Full Vindication of the Conduct of the Manager of the Theatre-Royal.* Dublin, 1747.

————. *An Humble Appeal to the Publick, Together with some Considerations on the Present critical and dangerous State of the Stage in Ireland.* Dublin, 1758.

————. *Mr. Sheridan's Speech Addressed to a Number of Gentlemen Assembled with a View of considering The Best Means to establish one good Theatre in this City.* Dublin, 1772.

————. *An Oration, Pronounced before a Numerous Body of the Nobility and Gentry in Fishamble-street.* Dublin, 1757.

————. *A Vindication of the Conduct of the late Manager of the Theatre-Royal Publick. Humbly address'd to the Publick.* Dublin, 1754.

Shershow, Scott. *Puppets and "Popular" Culture.* Ithaca: Cornell University Press, 1995.

The Sighs and Groans of Mr. Sh———n, with A full Account of a Comical Farce that was acted last Saturday Night at the Theatre in Smock-Alley, and the Occasion thereof. Also, An account of the Manager's rude Behavior to the Audience at the Play of MAHOMET. Dublin, 1754.

Simms, J. G. *Colonial Nationalism, 1698–1776.* Cork: Mercier Press, 1976.

————. "The Irish on the Continent, 1691–1800." In *A New History of Ireland,* vol. 4, *Eighteenth-Century Ireland, 1691–1800,* edited by T. W. Moody and W. E. Vaughan. Oxford: Carendon Press, 1986.

————. *Jacobite Ireland, 1685–91.* London: Routledge and Kegan Paul, 1969.

————. *William Molyneux of Dublin.* Dublin: Irish Academic Press, 1982.

Smyth, Jim. *The Men of No Property: Irish Radicals and Popular Politics in the Late Eighteenth Century.* New York: St. Martin's Press, 1992.

The Songs, Duets, Trio's Choruses, and Finales in the New Comic Opera of the Contract: As Performed at the Theatre-Royal, Smock-Alley. Dublin, 1783.

Sources of Irish Traditional Music, c. 1600–1855. Edited by Aloys Fleischmann and Micheál Ó Súilleabháin. New York: Garland, 1998.

The Speaker. A Poem inscribed to Alan Brodrick, Esq. Speaker to the Honourable House of Commons Met at Dublin, November 25, 1713. Dublin, 1713.

Stallybrass, Peter, and Allon White. *The Politics and Poetics of Transgression.* Ithaca: Cornell University Press, 1986.

Stayley, George. *The Rival Theatres: or, a Play house to be let. A Farce to which is added The Chocolate-Makers: or Mimicry Exposed. An Interlude with a Preface and Notes commentary and explanatory by Mr. George Stayley, Comedian.* Dublin, 1759.

St. James's Evening Post.

Sterling, James. *The Poetical Works of Rev. James Sterling.* Dublin, 1734.

————. *The Rival Generals.* London, 1722.

Stockwell, La Tourette. *Dublin Theatres and Theatre Customs, 1637–1820.* Kingsport, Tenn.: Kingsport Press, 1938.

Straub, Kristina. *Sexual Suspects: Eighteenth-Century Players and Sexual Ideology.* Princeton: Princeton University Press, 1992.

Swift, Jonathan. *The Correspondence of Jonathan Swift, D.D.* Vol. 1. Edited by F. Elrington Ball. London: G. Bell and Sons, 1910.

———. "The Description of an *Irish-Feast*, Translated Almost Literally Out of the Original Irish." In *The Field Day Anthology of Irish Writing*, vol. 1, edited by Seamus Deane. Derry, Northern Ireland: Field Day Publications, 1991.

———. *The Drapier's Letters to the People of Ireland*. Edited by Herbert Davis. Oxford: Clarendon Press, 1935.

———. *The Poems of Jonathan Swift*. 3 vols. Edited by Harold Williams. Oxford: Clarendon Press, 1937.

———. *A Proposal for the Universal Use of Irish Manufacture*. In *The Prose Works of Jonathan Swift*, vol. 9, edited by Herbert Davis. Oxford: Basil Blackwell, 1939–68.

———. *The Story of the Injured Lady*. In *The Prose Works of Jonathan Swift*, vol. 9, edited by Herbert Davis. Oxford: Basil Blackwell, 1939–68.

The Thespian Dictionary. London, 1802.

Thorp, Willard. "A Key to Rowe's *Tamerlane*." *Journal of English and Germanic Philology* 39 (1940): 124–27.

Trefman, Simon. *Sam. Foote, Comedian, 1720–1777*. New York: New York University Press, 1971.

A true and perfect journal of the affairs in Ireland since his majesty's arrival. London, 1690.

The True Life of Betty IRELAND. With her Birth, Education, and Adventurers. Together with Some Account of her elder sister BLANCH of BRITAIN. London and Dublin, 1753.

Universal Advertiser.

The Upper Gallery. A Poem. Dublin, 1731.

Thuente, Mary Helen. *The Harp Re-strung*. Syracuse, N.Y.: Syracuse University Press, 1994.

Victor, Benjamin. *The History of the Theatres of London and Dublin*. Vol. 1. London, 1761.

———. *Original Letters, Dramatic Pieces, and Poems*. 3 vols. London, 1776.

Victory, Isolde. "The Making of the 1720 Declaratory Act." In *Parliament, Politics and People*, edited by Gerard O'Brien. Dublin: Irish Academic Press, 1989.

Volunteer Evening Post.

Volunteers Journal.

Walker, Joseph Cooper. *Historical Memoirs of the Irish Bards*. Dublin, 1786; rpt. New York: Garland, 1971.

Wall, Maureen. *Catholic Ireland in the Eighteenth Century: Collected Essays of Maureen Wall*. Edited by Gerard O'Brien. Dublin: Geography Publications, 1989.

Walsh, T. J. *Opera in Dublin, 1705–1797: The Social Scene*. Dublin: Allen Figgis, 1973.

Watkins, John. *Memoirs of the Public and Private Life of the Right Honorable R. B. Sheridan*. London, 1817.

Wheatley, Christopher. *"Beneath Ierne's Banners": Irish Protestant Drama of the Restoration and Eighteenth Century*. Notre Dame, Ind.: University of Notre Dame Press, 2000.

Whelan, Kevin. "The Catholic Community in Eighteenth-Century County Wexford." In *Endurance and Emergence: Catholics in Ireland in the Eighteenth Century,* edited by T. P. Power and Kevin Whelan. Dublin: Irish Academic Press, 1990.

————. *The Tree of Liberty: Radicalism, Catholicism and the Construction of Irish Identity, 1760–1830*. Notre Dame, Ind.: University of Notre Dame Press, 1996.

————. "An Underground Gentry? Catholic Middlemen in Eighteenth-Century Ireland." *Eighteenth-Century Ireland* 10 (1995): 7–77.

White, Harry. *The Keeper's Recital: Music and Cultural History in Ireland, 1770–1970*. Notre Dame, Ind.: University of Notre Dame Press, 1998.

Whyte, Lawrence. *Original Poems on Various Subjects, Serious Moral, and Diverting*. 2d ed. Dublin, 1742.

————. *Poems on various subjects, serious and diverting, never before Published*. Dublin, 1740.

Whyte, Samuel. *Poems on Various Subjects*. 3d ed. Dublin, 1795.

York, Neil. *Neither Kingdom nor Nation: The Irish Quest for Constitutional Rights, 1698–1800*. Washington, D. C.: Catholic University Press, 1994.

Zimmermann, Georges-Denis. *Irish Political Street Ballads and Rebel Songs, 1780–1900*. Geneva: La Sirene, 1966.

Zizek, Slavoj. *The Sublime Object of Ideology*. London: Verso, 1989.

Index

Abbey Theatre, 281. *See also* Irish Literary
 Theatre
Abbott, Paul, 14
accent, Irish: defense of, 252–54; English
 bias against, 14, 252–54
actors: Irish-born, 33–34; in Irish "stuff,"
 54–55, 62; rights and status of, 1–2,
 117, 129–31, 143, 235–38; and
 viceregal court, 32, 224
"aggregate" meetings and petitions, 16,
 241, 243, 275–77, 289
Anderson, Benedict, 35, 42–43
anti-importation movement, 220, 241,
 243, 275. *See also* Irish manufacture;
 Irish "stuff"
*Apology for the Conduct and Writings of
 Mr. C———s L———s, Apothecary,
 An,* 160
*Approved Receipt to make an English
 Tragedy . . . , An,* 230–32, 234
Ashbury, Joseph, 34
audience: Catholic presence in, 111–16,
 238–39, 250–51, 278; disruptive
 behavior of, 1–2, 209–10, 228–30,
 238–40, 276–78; diversity of, 33–34,
 109–10, 115–16, 249–51, 277–78;

English orientation of, 6–7;
 intrusion behind the scenes of, 2, 117;
 "Ladies" in, 33–34, 45, 47, 53, 63,
 65–67, 78, 80; Orange presence in,
 264; patriot presence in, 45, 48, 55,
 110–11, 209–11, 217–18, 229–31,
 237–40, 242, 244–45, 248–50,
 260–61, 269, 276–80; upper gallery
 in, 2, 109–11, 162–63, 216–19,
 228–29, 230–31, 238–40, 242,
 244–45, 250, 274–75, 284–85.
 See also command performances;
 "government play"
Aungier Street theater, 111, 183, 216,
 222, 245

Browne, John, 118, 132–34, 139, 155, 156,
 164, 187–89, 238; *The Gentlemen's
 Apology to the Ladies,* 144–45
Bruce, Harold Lawton, 319n74
Buckinghamshire, Lord, 269
Bucks Have at Ye All, 228–29
Bull's-Head Tavern, 89, 100–101, 218, 233
Bunkle, John, 112
Burke, Edmund: and the Capel Street
 opposition, 184–87, 192, 201; on

About the Author

HELEN M. BURKE is associate professor of English at Florida State University.